VOICES OF THE NHL

A COLLECTION OF BIOS & STORIES FROM BROADCASTERS ACROSS THE NATIONAL HOCKEY LEAGUE

BY: MATTHEW BLITTNER

ISBN: 978-0-578-95040-2
ISBN-13: 978-0-578-95040-2

DEDICATION

In this world, it's not enough to merely believe in yourself. Rather, you need others to believe in you as well.

To that end, this book would not have been completed without the support of my family and friends.

Specifically, I'd like to dedicate this book to my parents -- Mandi and Seth -- and sister Tara for their constant support even during the toughest times. And to my friends -- Arianna Rappy, Stef Hicks, Leanna Gryak, Maggie Wince, Walt Bonné, Daniel Greene, Jared Fertig, Jason Russo, Peter Koutros and Robert DeVita -- who were always there for me when I needed them and I thank them for that.

CONTENTS

INTRODUCTION

"He shoots, he scores!" -- Foster Hewitt.

Known as "The Dean of Hockey Broadcasting," Foster Hewitt was one of the most influential broadcasters in NHL history and the first to coin the phrase, *"He shoots, he scores!"* It was his work on Maple Leafs broadcasts, as well as on the iconic *Hockey Night in Canada* broadcasts, which led to Hewitt being inducted into the Hockey Hall of Fame in 1965 as a Builder. But his legacy didn't end there as Hewitt also helped to cultivate the next generation of broadcasters, which included his own son, Bill. And as a means of honoring the elder Hewitt, The Hall of Fame created the "Foster Hewitt Memorial Award," in 1984, which is presented yearly to one outstanding hockey broadcaster, as voted on by the NHL Broadcasters' Association.

Hewitt passed away in 1985, however, his dedication to the art of broadcasting is still felt to this day thanks to the current (as of the 2020-2021 NHL season) group of NHL broadcasters, many of whom grew up listening to his broadcasts and were thus inspired to follow in his footsteps.

Now, Hewitt was not the only influential hockey broadcaster, as the likes of: Bob Cole; Dan Kelly and Danny Gallivan are also cited by many current NHL broadcasters as the voices of their formative years. And it is thanks to these four and others that the modern day NHL broadcasters are in the positions they are in.

The art of broadcasting a Hockey game has steadily evolved over the years. First, from just being on local radio stations, to then expanding the range of the radio. And eventually they even made their way to television. Today you can even tune in to games on just about any smart device (i.e. cell phones, computers, tablets, etc.)

Back in the Original Six Era (1942-1967) there were limited opportunities for fans of the game to hear or watch a live NHL broadcast. There were only six teams (Boston Bruins, Chicago Blackhawks, Detroit Red Wings, Montreal Canadiens, New York Rangers and Toronto Maple Leafs) and not every game was broadcast live on the favored medium of the day. Not to mention, the technology then was lightyears behind where it is now; so even when the games were broadcast, the reach wasn't anywhere near what it is today when fans can watch or listen to practically any game they want regardless of where they live. All you need is a television, a radio, a smartphone or even a computer and barring occasional blackout restrictions, you can tune in anytime, anywhere.

Even after the Original Six Era came to an end thanks to expansion, it was still no easy task to tune in to an NHL broadcast. For example, in Canada, there were generally two to three nationally broadcast games thanks to the famous, "Hockey Night in Canada" program -- one on Wednesday nights and one or two on Saturday nights. That's it. Beyond that, good luck. And the situation in the United States wasn't much better.

Oh sure, a St. Louis Blues fan, living in St. Louis could tune in -- at least on radio -- to most of their team's broadcasts and hear the legendary Dan Kelly call a game as only he could. But if you rooted for the Blues and lived several hours away, your chances of catching the game live were far lower. Although, on a clear night, with the right transistor radio, you could actually succeed in getting a game that wasn't remotely close to you geographically. However, that was only under ideal circumstances.

Of course, that meant fans, especially young kids who were told by their parents that games started too late for them to attend in-person because they had school the next day had to then get creative if they wanted to support their team. In fact, many of today's NHL broadcasters grew up having "gone to bed" only to sneak a transistor radio under their pillow so they could listen to the voice of their favorite team and that wound up inflaming their passion for the sport of hockey even more.

If you were in New York, long after the Americans had folded and long before the Islanders came to town, you still had the Rangers to root for. Blueshirts fans of a certain age -- long before Sam Rosen and Joe Micheletti, or even Rosen and John Davidson -- will fondly recall (or maybe unfondly, depending on the outcome of the game) the WHN 1050 radio team of Bert Lee (Sr.) on play-by-play and Ward Wilson doing the color commentary. And without a doubt, if the home team was trailing Lee (Sr.) would turn to Wilson and exclaim, *"Time enough for one-goal, Ward? Time enough for 20!"*

If you were a fan in Philadelphia, in the early years for the expansion team Flyers, you almost always had Gene Hart on the call in some capacity; be it either on television or radio. And across the state in Pittsburgh, Pennsylvania, the Penguins have had "The Master of Catchphrases" himself, Mike Lange on their radio and/or television calls since the 1974-75 season.

Of course, as The NHL continued to spread across the continent as the years went on, more teams joined the league and therefore more broadcasters did too. Some, like Matt McConnell -- currently the television voice in Arizona for the Coyotes -- were fortunate enough to have the opportunity to be the voice of several different teams throughout the course of their careers. Meanwhile, others like Tom Reid -- currently the radio analyst for the Minnesota Wild -- went from playing the game on the ice, to breaking it down inside the booth. And let's not forget the rare few who called a singular team home for their whole careers -- at least as of the 2020-21 season -- like, Nick Nickson, who joined the LA Kings in 1981 and is still there as the voice of Kings' radio broadcasts.

Along the way some networks and stations decided to expand the role of "Hosts" by making specific broadcasters the host of the team's pre-game, intermission and post-game shows. The role had already existed in some shape and form for years as people such as Ron MacLean with Hockey Night In Canada had made iconic careers out of hosting. But the expansion of hosting duties led to people like Jason Myrtetus and Josh Getzoff getting the opportunity to bring an added dimension to their team's broadcasts.

Furthermore, after the NHL came back from the season-long lockout that cost the league the 2004-05 campaign, networks across the NHL -- both regionally and nationally -- decided to shake up the traditional broadcast system of a play-by-play announcer paired with a color analyst.

Starting in the mid-2000s, networks and stations took it to another level by placing a broadcaster either between the benches during games, or in the case of arenas that didn't have that space available, positioned them just off the ice near the zamboni entrance.

The purpose was to provide an additional, previously untapped element to broadcasts, by having somebody at ice-level who could analyze the action of the game that was being missed by the booths up above. And it also allowed for unique soundbytes that had previously been uncaptured. So, all in all, it was a win-win-win for broadcasters, networks and the league.

In fact, one of the biggest named broadcasters to hold down this position has been NBC's Pierre McGuire, who has been right on top of some very memorable exchanges over the years. However, these broadcasters need to have more than just excellent reporting skills. They also need to have on-the-mark reflexes as pucks consistently fly their way at high velocities. Thankfully, more often than not, the pucks miss these broadcasters; although that's not always the case. (For those curious about the rare hits, you can YouTube them; with one of the most well known ones happening to MSG Network's John Giannone).

All in all, there are many different broadcasting roles and styles that populate the NHL. And one of the purposes of this book is to shine a light on the tremendous job that these broadcasters do. Another purpose is to hopefully get fans to tune in to broadcasts beyond just those of their favorite team in an effort to grow the game of hockey.

I'm not trying to compare apples to oranges, but the NFL, for years, has grown its game to the point where each network's NFL announcers will get the chance at some point during the season to call games for nearly every team in the league, thus giving fans in various different markets a taste of their abilities. For example, CBS, who at one time did actually carry NHL games, on NFL Sundays will almost always have the esteemed Jim Nantz on the call for their "A-game" of the week. But that means Nantz won't remain with any one team, thus giving fans around the league a chance to become fans of him as well as get to know his style and mannerisms.

While that system works for the NFL and its partner networks, it isn't a system that would necessarily work in the NHL, nor is it one I would advocate for, as many teams have broadcasters who have been with them for decades and are viewed as a sort of gatekeeper to the franchise's history; even acting as the soundtrack for multiple generations.

So, the question then becomes, how do the highly regionalized broadcasters -- with the exception of the national ones -- in the NHL manage to show their talents to fans outside their team's market? Well, the advent of the "Hockey Package" offered by many cable networks, as well as the ability to stream games online has allowed fans to tune in to most any game they want. But fans still need a reason to *want* to tune in to a game that doesn't feature their favorite team or player. And one way to interest the fans in these announcers is to connect with them on a more personal level. If fans feel like they can relate to the stories of the lives of the broadcasters, perhaps they may be more inclined to tune in to the broadcasts featuring those announcers, thus giving them a chance to expand their hockey fandom.

For the purposes of this book, I spoke with *at least* one broadcaster from each of the 31 teams who played during the 2020-21 season and I also made sure to focus on those announcers who are currently calling games this season. And just to make sure I gave you the most possible broadcasters to read about, I also included those who work for NBC, The NHL Network, Sportsnet and Hockey Night In Canada.

The following broadcasters gave their time to this project and opened up about their early lives, how they fell in love with the sport of hockey, why they chose to pursue the careers they did and some off-ice and on-ice stories from their time with their current teams: Rick Ball, John Bartlett, Brendan Batchelor, Josh Bogorad, Andy Brickley, Jamison Coyle, Ken Daniels, Willy Daunic, Dan Dunleavy, Dan D'Uva, John Forslund, Jim Fox, Josh Getzoff, Steven Goldstein, Dave Goucher, Bob Heethuis, Shane Hnidy, E.J. Hradek, Jim Jackson, Chris Kerber, Don La Greca, Matt Loughlin, Ron MacLean, Matt McConnell, Bob McElligott, Conor McGahey, Pierre McGuire, Steve Mears, Jack Michaels, Gord Miller, David Mishkin, Randy Moller, Brian Munz, Jason Myrtetus, Tyson Nash, Nick Nickson, Darren Pang, Greg Picker, Daryl Reaugh, Tom Reid, Francisco X. Rivera, Dan Robertson, Dan Rusanowsky, Tim Saunders, Judd Sirott, Nicolas St-Pierre, Tripp Tracy, John Walton, Pete Weber, John Wiedeman, Dan Wood and Paul Woods.

With that being said, it's time to drop the puck and I'm going to throw it up to the booth so we can get this game underway.

ANAHEIM DUCKS

DAN WOOD
RADIO: COLOR ANALYST

First Season on Ducks Radio: 2009-10
Seasons on Ducks Radio (including 2020-21): 12

Birthday: June 17, 1958 Hometown: Livermore, CA

College/University: San Jose State

BIOGRAPHY

Sometimes life throws a curveball, or rather, a hip-check your way. How you react to it will determine if you came through successfully or failed. You can sit back, watch and let the situation control you, or you can take charge and go after it proactively.

For Dan Wood, the dream was to be a professional baseball player. Don't laugh. Millions of kids have the same dream. His first life curveball situation resulted in him pivoting to pursue a career as a Sports Writer. Then, years later, a hip-check came his way and he took the proactive approach to become a broadcaster; which he still is to this day. So, how did each of those situations unfold? Dan, take it away.

WOOD: "When I was a kid, I loved sports and my dad loved sports and pretty much all I thought about was sports. However, my dad was not a hockey fan. He liked other sports. But I had a neighbor, a friend of mine whose dad was a big hockey fan. They had moved to

California from Iowa and his dad got me into hockey because he used to take his son and myself to (Golden) Seals games when the Seals were in the NHL in the late-60's. And that was my first exposure to the game.

"I didn't have the opportunity to play hockey when I was a kid, but I did play roller hockey in our driveways. His dad made sticks for us. He made pucks for us and we played on old time roller skates, not roller blades, but the old time roller skates. And so that's where my love of hockey began. Growing up though, when I was in High School, I decided that I wanted to be a Sports Writer and that's what I pursued.

"I went to San Jose State and majored in Journalism, with a concentration in reporting and editing because I wanted to be a Sports Writer for a newspaper. And really what I wanted to do was cover baseball; ultimately, baseball was kind of my first love. That was my goal, but the way things worked out, I was working for a chain of newspapers in Northern California when the Sharks came about and our paper needed someone to cover the Sharks.

"I was one of only two people on our staff who had any knowledge of hockey whatsoever. So, they asked me to do it and I did and began covering the Sharks in their first season in 1991-92. And just as fate would have it, I've been around hockey ever since, because I covered the Sharks for nine-years. Then, I got a job at the Orange County Register, covering the Ducks in 2000. And then in 2009, I made the transition from newspaper to radio."

Hey, Dan, you're a Radio Color Analyst, so let's use some analysis to peel back the onion further and go deeper into your journey.

WOOD: "I was born and grew up wanting to be a Major League Baseball player. I played baseball throughout my childhood and into High School. And if I do say so myself, I was a pretty decent High School baseball player.

"But midway through High School, I came to the realization that I was not good enough, that I was never going to get the chance to follow my dream and play baseball professionally. It was about that same time, somewhere along, maybe my sophomore or junior year of High School, I was taking (a) journalism (class) and was on the High School newspaper staff. And I realized that I had an ability to write. And my love of sports and my ability to write just kind of went together; sports and writing, sports writer.

"So it was at that point that I made the decision that I wanted to pursue a journalism degree and try to be a sports writer. And I never really wavered. I mean, I've always considered myself very fortunate, because unlike a lot of people, I had a passion, I knew what it was. I did everything I could do. I've always felt bad for people who don't really have a passion and don't really know what they want to do. I was lucky because I did.

"I was the type who, when I was in High School, I would go to school early so I could go to the library and read all of the Bay Area sports sections before school. There weren't really any particular writers who I followed. I was a San Francisco Giants fan and an Oakland Raiders fan. And so those were the teams I followed most closely and whoever was covering those teams for the respective papers; that was my primary focus.

"Broadcasters though, it's kind of ironic that I wound up in broadcasting because (the way) I grew up listening to games was kind of the standard story of laying in bed with a transistor radio, even when you were supposed to be asleep, listening to games.

"It was more baseball than it was hockey, because initially, there was no hockey in the Bay Area. And then when the Seals came about, I don't even really recall whether their games were on the radio. I was listening to baseball and football on the radio. And as far as favorite broadcasters, the San Francisco Giants have had just an endless number of great broadcasters from: Russ Hodges, who began in New York with the Giants and his partner Lon Simmons in the early days. And then going forward with people like Al Michaels and then Lindsey Nelson and Hank Greenwald, to today with Duane Kuiper and Mike Krukow on TV. I think Giants fans were really spoiled because there were so many great broadcasters in football and even basketball, because there was a man named Bill King, who also did the San Francisco Warriors before they were Golden State.

"He was an absolutely legendary broadcaster in California. He did the Warriors, the Raiders, he even did the Raiders when they moved to LA. He was a fantastic Play-by-Play guy. Those were my local people and of course, National people too. I mean, I remember Curt Gowdy and people like that, doing football and baseball. Joe Garagiola (Sr.). Howard Cosell on Monday Night Football with Don Meredith and Frank Gifford.

And I always really did follow and like broadcasting. I never anticipated doing that because I thought I would be a sports writer my entire career. But things change and things happen. It's interesting how it all worked out."

Okay, now we're getting somewhere, but we can still go deeper. Dan, the same way that you've helped young writers and broadcasters by giving them guidance, who were the writers and broadcasters who helped you during your career?

WOOD: "I guess the first one was when I was in college, between my junior and senior year of college, which was 1979, one of the requirements in our major was we had to do an internship at a newspaper.

"I think it was 12-weeks and most people did those internships at very small community type papers. But the San Jose Mercury News, which in those days was really a good newspaper, along with the San Francisco Chronicle, one of the two biggest in the Bay Area, were soliciting for interns and they had never had one in sports. Their interns had always been on the news side. I applied, never anticipating that I would get it, but I did and I wound up working at The Mercury News in the summer of 1979. And there was a gentleman named Rick Vacek among others.

"He was the primary one who I felt really took interest in me and helped build my confidence and taught me some things. I've always looked back on that summer and Rick Vacek as someone who gave me an awful lot of encouragement and helped me. And just as a real quick aside I remember being at The Mercury News that summer when we learned of the plane crash that killed Thurman Munson. That's my other overriding memory of that summer was just how stunning and horrible that was.

"One other person who I would mention is a guy who was a Sports Editor of mine in the '90s at a newspaper called the Contra Costa Times. His name is Danny DeFreitas. He was just one of those people who, I mean, if you were a coach, it would be that he was someone you want to run through a wall for.
He was just a great motivator. Our paper in those days was really, really good and it was largely because of Danny and I think he had a big impact on me in terms of just motivation.

"Actually, let me mention two other people as well, because they were important. One is a guy named Bob Goll. He hired me in 1985 to be the Sports Editor of a community paper called the Valley Times in Pleasanton, California. He really showed a lot of faith in me and gave me a lot of opportunities. And I've always felt like I owe him a lot for that.

"The other person who comes to mind was a co-worker in the early-80's and his name was Frank Garland. In terms of work ethic, that's what I learned from him. He was the type of guy who, when something needs to be done, he doesn't wait around for someone else to do it. He just jumps in and does it. And through working with him and watching him, I learned a lot about the importance of that. To this day, he's a very close friend of mine. He probably wouldn't like me saying it, but I learned an awful lot from him and I'm very appreciative of him for that.

"(And) there's one other person I'd like to mention who I shouldn't overlook actually, maybe two. First and foremost, Jim Kelley, the late-great Sports Writer at the Buffalo News, who went into broadcasting in his later years. He was the President of the Professional Hockey Writers Association for a number of years. He was a guy who, when I tried to transfer into broadcasting and I had known him for a long time, he was kind of a mentor to a lot of those of us who were younger than Jim.

"I solicited his input and his advice on how I could make the transition from newspapers to radio, because he had kind of done it. He gave me a world of great advice and support. So, if we're going to mention people, I don't want to overlook Jim Kelley because he was a terrific guy and I know he did that for an awful lot of people, including myself. So, he needs to be mentioned.

"The other one is Sherry Ross, who formerly was the Devils Radio Color Analyst. She had a long career in newspapers before getting the job as the Devils Radio Color Analyst. I kind of felt like she was a real trailblazer, because not only is she a woman, but she went from being a Sports Writer to doing radio for an NHL team. I feel like she kind of paved the way for someone like myself. So I want to throw her in there too."

We're almost there. Now that we know how Wood made it through his years as a writer, let's find out about the hip-check that saw him transform from a writer to a broadcaster.

WOOD: "I think it's important to emphasize that I loved being a Sports Writer. I absolutely loved doing what I was doing. However, in the late-2000 decade, newspapers were not the healthiest financially and I saw an awful lot of my friends and co-workers lose their jobs. And while I never felt like I was in imminent danger of losing my job, I figured at some point I might very well, especially getting up in years and making pretty good money, relatively speaking. I figured at some point, my time would come and I was not comfortable that I would have a job as long as I needed to have a job.

"So, in about 2008, the entire 2008-09 season, which was my last at The Register covering the Ducks, I was trying to figure out another way I could make a living, because I didn't think I was going to be able to do it in newspapers forever.

"I spent that whole season, as I traveled around covering the Ducks, trying to talk to everyone I knew; just kind of throwing the lines in the water, trying to get advice, trying to figure out another avenue that I could pursue.

"I did not anticipate it would be broadcasting. I don't know what I thought it would be, but I certainly didn't have that at the top of the list. The one thing I really thought I could do was work for an NHL team, not as a scout, but as a person who would research draft prospects, as far as their character and what type of people they are; because you always hear teams talk about that.

"I know the Sharks were really good at doing that when I was covering them. I actually talked to Bob Murray, who had just become the Ducks' General Manager not too long before that and I pitched him the idea of hiring me to be someone who could research and use my reporting skills and investigative skills to find out about draft prospects.

"In other words, you give me a list of names of guys you're thinking about drafting and let me go talk to their third grade teacher and find out about them as people, because I'm not a scout. I could never be a scout. But I could get information of that sort. I felt like and I still feel like that would be really valuable to the people doing the drafting. So I pitched that to Bob Murray. He said he was interested and intrigued, but he also said he didn't have the money in the budget to hire someone for a position like that. So I struck out there, but I talked to as many people as I could about as many possibilities as I could think of.

"Almost off-handedly, one night at a game; I had known Steve Carroll since I began covering the Ducks, because he and I actually started with the Ducks (at the same time). He started as a broadcaster. I started covering them as a Sports Writer. It was the same season, although he was at the beginning of that season and I was near the end. Anyway, I'd known him for a long time and I was talking to him one night.

"I knew the Radio Color Analyst, a former NHL player named Brent Severyn, was in a tough spot because his family lived in Dallas. He was working for the Ducks. He was commuting to the job and it was really a difficult situation for him, family-wise. So I knew there was a chance that he might not continue in that role. So, I told Steve one night, I just said, 'Hey, you know, if that job ever opens up, let me know, because if it does, I'd like to throw my hat in the ring.'

"Well, I didn't think a whole lot about it. I figured it was just another thing I was talking to somebody about. It would never amount to anything. But when that season ended, Steve called me and he said, 'Brent's leaving. The job is going to be open. So if you're interested, now's the time.' So I jumped on it and I called the Ducks Broadcasting Chief and told him I was interested. Initially, I don't think they took me seriously because I had no radio experience. I wasn't a former player, which most Color Analysts are former players. The only thing I had going for me was the fact that I knew the team. I knew the organization and they knew me. I think I had the respect of the organization as a fair reporter with decent character.

"So, basically, I drove them crazy. I called them left and right. I called in favors from everybody I knew; former players, people in the broadcasting industry, everyone who I could think of asking them to either make a phone call or write a letter or an email on my behalf. And a lot of them did. Eventually, I got really lucky too, because I think they had their eye on someone who they thought they were going to hire and that didn't work out.

"All this time, as the summer was progressing and they were getting nearer and nearer to the regular-season, they needed someone. So, they wound up having me and one other person go in and basically audition; calling a period of a game off of a monitor, with Steve doing the Play-by-Play. I was on the color, to the best of my very limited ability. I remember after that audition, the guy who was going to make the hire, his name was Aaron. As he was walking me out after I did that audition, he told me, 'call off the dogs. We don't need to hear from anybody else on your behalf.'

"I was trying to space it out so they wouldn't hear from somebody everyday. I had a couple other people who I was going to have make calls on my behalf. And I told them, 'don't. Just stop.' So, sort of to my surprise, going from having felt like they didn't take me seriously in the beginning, they offered me the job and I owe an eternal kind of gratitude to Aaron, because he really thought outside the box and he took a chance on someone. I know Aaron had to answer the same question a lot of times from people saying, 'why did you hire him?' It made no sense.

"He took a chance on me and the one thing I promised Aaron, I said, 'look, if I fail at this, it will not be because I did not work hard enough.' I said, 'I'm going to give you everything I have.' That's the one thing I think I can really hang my hat on, because I'm not a former player.

"Brent Severyn, he was a tough guy. Anytime there was a fight, he could talk first-hand about what it's like to be in a fight. I can't do that. I don't know what it's like to do that. I don't know what it's like to score a goal or make a great back-check to save a goal. But what I do know is I can work hard. I can research things. I can get information. I can outwork anybody else. And that's what I promised Aaron I would do. And here we are 11-years later, so I guess it worked out okay."

FAVORITE TEAM(S)/PLAYER(S) GROWING UP

WOOD: "Honestly, when I was a kid, I wasn't so much a (California) Golden Seals fan, even though I did go to games. In those days, if I remember correctly, in the late-60's, there was a Game of the Week, an NHL Game of the Week on CBS. I would watch those games on TV and really the teams that I gravitated toward were the Bruins and the Blackhawks. I liked them both and (it was) Bobby Orr and Bobby Hull, etc. So those were probably my favorite teams as a kid."

HOCKEY AFTER DARK -- TALES AWAY FROM THE RINK

WOOD: "The one that comes to mind immediately is kind of a funny story. I don't remember exactly when it was, it must've been around, I'm guessing 2013, somewhere in that range. We were on the plane, on the Ducks charter and in those days, Steve (Carroll) and I sat kind of in the middle of the plane, at I guess, a bulkhead aisle, where when we would take off landing we put our bags under the sheet in front of us. But you couldn't reach it if you were sitting down. You had to get up to go access your bag.

"I believe it was before takeoff, I had put my bag under the seat and then I needed something out of it. So, I got up out of my seat and I was bending over to access my bag. All of a sudden, from behind, unbeknownst to me, I felt someone tickling me on the side, the ribs and I was, of course, completely taken aback. I had no idea what was going on. I turned around and there was a player running away back toward the back of the plane where the players sat.

"Well, it turned out it was Nick Bonino, who was a young Ducks player at that point, who really hadn't made his way into the league yet. I came to find out that the veterans on the team had put him up to doing this as a practical joke or as a little, not hazing, but just a little thing you might make a rookie do. So, before I knew it, I sat back down and here comes George Parros, who was a Stanley Cup champion, a veteran leader on the team and he's got something in his hand that he's pretending is a microphone.

"He's acting like he's going to interview me about this experience. So the whole thing was a practical joke that they pulled on Bonino and I was kind of an unwitting participant. It was a little embarrassing, but no big deal.

"But anyway, I talked to Nick about it later and it actually kind of, I always felt like Nick Bonino and I had sort of a bond that a broadcaster and a player typically don't have, just because of that incident. And I asked Nick about it later and I said, 'you know, what the hell was going on there?' And he said, 'well, they told me that I had to go tickle a broadcaster and you just happened to be in the position. You were an easy target. So you're the one that I got.' So, it was funny. And like I said, it kind of created a bond, I think between Nick and I, that has endured over the years. It was kind of cool."

WOOD'S FAVORITE DUCKS MOMENT AS A BROADCASTER

The sheer nature of sports is that, beyond the excitement of the plays, at its core, sports are a form of entertainment. Entertainment comes in many forms and causes many different reactions and emotions. One minute you're cheering your lungs out and the next you're bawling like a baby. You never know when, where or how the more impactful moments are going to come about and what type of emotions they're going to generate.

It's like a Broadway play, just without a script. And for Dan Wood, a seemingly innocent retirement tradition became something much, much more.

WOOD: "Teemu Selanne's final regular season game, which was in 2014. He had announced his retirement. It was April 13, 2014. The Ducks were playing Colorado at home and they wound up winning the game in overtime on a goal by Nick Bonino. But that's irrelevant. What matters here is Jean-Sebastien Giguere, the former Ducks goaltender, all-time fan-favorite in Anaheim, along with Teemu Selanne, was playing goal for Colorado that night. And he had lost the game in overtime.

"Well, after the game, Selanne was going to go for a skate as a lot of retiring players do and he literally pulled Giguere off the Avalanche bench after the game and forced Giguere to skate with him. This was a moment that was supposed to be all about celebrating Selanne and his career. But Teemu, being the guy who he is, wanted to include Giguere in that, because he knew how much Giguere meant to the fans in Anaheim as well.

"Giguere didn't want to do it, but Teemu made him come off the bench and skate with him that night after the game. There was not a dry eye in the house. Honest to God, I was fighting back tears in the broadcast booth. It was the single greatest moment I had ever seen in a sports context. It was just so Teemu, the man that he is and Giguere equally so.

"Those two are the two most beloved players in Ducks history. (Them) skating together, I mean it was impossible not to have tears in your eyes.

"The next day at practice, I pulled Teemu aside and I said, 'Teemu, that was the greatest moment I've seen in 30-years covering sports.' And now it will be closer to 40. I said it was the greatest moment I've ever seen in sports. And he looked at me and he goes, 'pretty cool, huh?' I was like, 'yeah, Teemu, it was pretty cool.' Honestly, I've seen a lot of things in sports. From Little League to Stanley Cup Finals, World Series, Super Bowls; there has never been a moment, ever, that even came close to having that impact on me and everybody else who was in that building."

MESSAGE TO DUCKS FANS

As is a common theme amongst members of the sports media, it is a well known fact that without the fans our jobs would either A) not exist or B) they'd have a lot less meaning. So, each of the broadcasters in this book took a couple of minutes to address you, the fans, directly.

WOOD: "I think Ducks fans have been very fortunate over the years because the team won a Stanley Cup and then the more recent version, while it did not win the Stanley Cup, the Ducks won five consecutive division championships. They were a Stanley Cup contender for several years in a row and I don't want to use the term spoiled, but I think in a sense, Ducks fans were because they were accustomed to success. And so, now that you kind of have to pay the Piper for that, like all good teams do, I mean, look at the Kings, the Blackhawks, the Red Wings; some Ducks fans have a hard time with that because maybe they haven't been Ducks fans long enough to understand that it doesn't always work out that way.

"You don't always get to be one of the top half dozen teams in the league. So, I would just say, maintain the faith and hang in there because the cycle will come around to where they are a contender again.

And I think it's important, especially in Southern California, if you don't win, there's so many other things to do here that people lose interest pretty quick. And it's just a fact of life. But I would say hang in there because there are going to be good times ahead for the franchise again."

ARIZONA COYOTES

BOB HEETHUIS
RADIO: PLAY-BY-PLAY

First Season on Coyotes Radio: 2005-06
Seasons on Coyotes Radio (including 2020-21): 16

Birthday: January 3, 1961 Hometown: Muskegon, MI

College/University: Michigan State

BIOGRAPHY

There are certain colleges and universities that are known for having exceptional broadcasting programs. Syracuse, Ithaca, Fordham and others all come to mind when you think about the top broadcast programs; but so does Michigan State, which has produced more than its fair share of sports broadcasters.

In fact, Bob Heethuis is one of their prominent alumni. But did you know, he initially went to Michigan State seeking to play on their baseball team?

HEETHUIS: "Where I grew up in Muskegon was actually on the opposite side of the state of Detroit. We're a little town right on Lake Michigan and actually right up the coast from Chicago. So it's almost equal distance from Chicago and Detroit, but I was always a Detroit fan for all the sports. I was an only child, very fortunate to have wonderful, loving and supportive parents.

"My dad was a huge sports fan and so, from an early age, I was indoctrinated into sports, pretty much all of them. Hockey was a big favorite of my dad's as well. So we were Red Wings fans from the get-go and also, our hometown team I should say, was called the Muskegon Mohawks. We had a pro team in our town that played in the old IHL.

"My dad had season tickets to those games. I would go from an early age and really loved watching hockey and was a student of the game. And ironically, hockey was the only sport that I never played growing up.

"I played baseball, basketball, football, organized, but not any organized play for me in hockey except countless hours of playing on roads and icy ponds. But I just loved the game. When I was old enough to go to college, it was Michigan State at that time. I did want to get into broadcasting, but I also thought that maybe I could play baseball there. I was a really big baseball fan as well and had some moderate success in High School.

"So, when I was a senior (in High School), they wrote me a letter saying, 'you're welcome to come and walk on our team.' I had attended a Michigan State baseball camp, so my intention was to go there. Every teenager has stars in his eyes and he thinks he's going to be the next Detroit Tiger or whatever. So I went to State to hopefully play baseball and also obviously to get into communications, because I had always loved doing that.

"As an only child I would sit in front of the TV sometime and you have a lot of extra time on your hands. So you fill time by doing different things. I would turn down the sound on television and announce the games and play a board game called stratomatic baseball and announce those games also; just into my tape recorder or whatever. So I really focused on broadcasting at a very young age, but I was always intent on trying to pursue a career in baseball.

"Well, I got to Michigan State and tried out for the freshman team. There were about a hundred other guys there and by the end of the fall practice my baseball career was over. I didn't make the team. I knew I had to fall back on my other love and that was broadcasting, so I was very fortunate to be a part of Michigan State's student radio network and got involved doing all kinds of things. And then, when you got some experience, they would allow you to actually call games on the student station. So we were able to do basketball, hockey and baseball. They didn't let students do football back then. I really loved announcing the hockey games.

"When I graduated from college in December of 1983, with a degree in telecommunications, I wasn't really zeroing in on hockey. As most college graduates do, you send your resume and your tape all around the country to different radio and TV stations and different teams. Then the weirdest of all luck for me, after so many different rejection letters, lo and behold, my hometown team was changing ownership and the new owner came in and wanted to not only change the name and the entire franchise, but also change broadcasters.

"I had just graduated from college in December and by June I was hired to be the new Muskegon Lumberjacks broadcaster and Public Relations Director. I think the ownership wanted someone local to kind of relate to the fans a little bit and also to help sell advertising to local businesses. And so that's how I got my start in the summer of 1984."

In case you're wondering how Heethuis developed his love for broadcasting while still attempting to be an athlete, look no further than the likes of Jim Gordon, Dan Kelly, Mike Lange, Ernie Harwell and Bruce Martyn; all of whom Heethuis loved to watch/listen to whenever he got the chance. Those were the voices of his youth and he carried over what he learned from them into his own broadcasting career; all while crafting his own style.

Of course, he had plenty of time to develop his own style as he spent quite a few years after college working in the minor leagues before eventually making his way to the NHL.

HEETHUIS: "I was with my hometown team (the Muskegon Mohawks) for eight-years. It was great because I was in my hometown and got to be around friends and family. Our team was very successful. We were the primary affiliate of the Pittsburgh Penguins back when the Pens were in the first part of their first dynasty. So we had really good teams and we were able to supplant the Pittsburgh Penguins with tremendous minor league prospects. We were able to go to The Finals of the IHL called the Turner Cup Finals six times in eight-years; winning two championships.

"After eight-years the IHL started to get bigger and grow into bigger markets so our ownership decided to move the team to Cleveland,

Ohio. I remember the conversation distinctly. Our owner said, 'Bob, thanks for all you've done, but you're not coming to Cleveland.' For the first time I was looking for work; I was without a job. As it just so happened the Phoenix Roadrunners found out I wasn't going to Cleveland and they had an opening in their Broadcast/PR department.

"So I got a call that summer of 1992 and they offered me an opportunity to come to Phoenix to work for the Roadrunners, do some broadcasting and also public relations. It was a real career benefit for me. I worked for the Phoenix Roadrunners for five-seasons from '92 through '97.

"Then after five-years with the Roadrunners, the Coyotes came to town and the Roadrunners decided that they couldn't compete, obviously. So they went under and for the second time I was looking for work.

"So I wound up as the host of the pre-game show, the intermissions and the post-game show on radio for the Coyotes; which included a call-in show. It was a great experience for me because it was something that I hadn't done before. I hadn't hosted a call-in show and dealt with fans like that; especially after tough losses and things like that.

"It was a real learning experience. It was my indoctrination into the NHL and I was so thrilled just to be part of an NHL broadcast. I did that for seven-years. Then, after the '03-'04 season they decided they were going to split the broadcast (back into traditional radio and television) again and they were kind enough to give me the job as the radio play-by-play announcer; with one caveat though. It was the summer of 2004 and the huge lockout was looming.

"So I was hired with the knowledge that my job as Play-by-Play announcer wouldn't start until the season started. I waited another year in limbo. Finally, in 2005, I was able to start my NHL Play-by-Play broadcasting career."

FAVORITE PLAYER(S) GROWING UP

HEETHUIS: "Well back when I was growing up in the '70s, the Red Wings were going through a really tough time. It was a situation where they didn't have a lot of stars. Gordie Howe's era had just ended.

"Although, when I was really young, I certainly remember Gordie and everyone loved him. I remember that defenseman Reed Larson in the 1970s was known for his great shot. John Ogrodnick, players like that. I was also a big New York Islanders fan because my hometown team was, at that time, a secondary affiliate of the New York Islanders. And so, some of the future Islanders came through our town and played, like Chico Resch.

"I saw him as a rookie. He was a rookie goaltender for the Muskegon Mohawks and a defenseman named Bob Lorimer. Hector Marini. There's a few others probably that I'm leaving out, but they got their starts with the old Muskegon Mohawks. And so, as a youth, I went to every game and really idolized those guys.

"I liked the Red Wings and actually really followed the New York Islanders throughout the '70s and then obviously into their dynasty when those players had grown into being NHLers; especially Chico Resch and Bob Lorimer. So, I loved the Islanders as well.

"At times during that period, I think I'm maybe even related more to the Isles than the Red Wings, because of the fact that the Red Wings just didn't have that much success in the 1970s. But I loved their announcer, Bruce Martyn. From an early age, I really knew that I wanted to get into broadcasting if the baseball thing didn't work out, which obviously there was a very small chance of that.

"And so I loved the Red Wings announcer Bruce Martyn, who was just tremendous. Of course, my all-time favorite announcer was the Tigers,' late great Ernie Harwell. So those are the guys who I really followed."

HOCKEY AFTER DARK -- TALES AWAY FROM THE RINK

Just when you think you've seen and heard it all, something new comes out of left field. NHL Players have been hung out of windows by teammates. There have been players threatened by mobsters. Media members have been detained at the border because of the team they cover. The list goes on and on.

But when you bring a Great Dane dog to the Four Seasons hotel during the NHL playoffs, now that's just something else.

HEETHUIS: "It involves our team playing in the 2012 Western Conference Quarter-Final series against Chicago and the Coyotes were the underdogs against the Blackhawks. We had a three-games-to-two series lead. I think every game in the first five of that series had gone into overtime and we had won two overtime games at United Center to go up three-games-to-one and then Chicago made it three-games-to-two with an overtime victory in our arena.

"So we went back to Chicago for Game Six and it was in April of 2012. So, anyway, at that time, my wife and I owned a rental property back in Michigan, because the town that we're from is kind of a little resort town on Lake Michigan. A lot of tourists come in the summer. So we had a cottage that we rented out to summer visitors.

"Every spring my wife would leave early from Arizona and go back to Michigan to get this cottage ready for the rental season. So when we were playing Chicago in the playoffs, my wife was already in Michigan. Our town is just about 180 miles from Chicago.

"So we get to Game Six with an opportunity for us to clinch. So, mid-afternoon one of my best friends back home calls and says, 'is there any way that you can get me a ticket to the game? I want to drive down there and see you and see if the Coyotes can win.' I checked it out and I said, 'yeah, I think so.' And then I said, 'let me call my wife and see if Melissa wants to go as well.' Those two knew each other very well also. So I called her and lo and behold, she wants to come, cause we hadn't seen each other for about a month. So she wants to come as well. So my friend and my wife drove down from Muskegon, Michigan.

"There was one catch though. My wife and I owned a 160-pound Great Dane dog. At that time, there was such a quick decision made to come to this game that my wife couldn't find anyone to watch the dog. So the dog came along. So I was able to procure two tickets to the game. My wife and my friend drove down and they made it in time and when they got to the arena I was able to arrange for them to park in a special lot.

"I was inside obviously getting ready for the game, but apparently the first thing was, my wife walked this big, 160-pound, Great Dane throughout the parking lot at United Center and then they left him in the car, cause it was cool back then; it was in April.

"It was cold enough where he could be left in the car with the window open. The parking lot attendants vowed they would watch him and make sure that he was okay and nobody was going to mess with him. So they came into the game. The dog stayed in the car. The Coyotes won 4-0. They clinched the series. It was the first ever playoff series victory for the Coyotes since they had moved from Winnipeg in 1996 and this was 2012. It was a really momentous occasion.

"Obviously everyone was really, really happy and a great time for me to be able to broadcast that game. So then, after the game, everyone is celebrating and everyone's happy and it's late into the evening and it's about a three-and-a-half hour drive back to our hometown from Chicago.

"So my wife said to me, 'I don't want to drive back. Is there any way that we can stay with you in the hotel?' So I said, 'well, obviously there's one thing that has to be dealt with first and that's whether the dog can stay or not.' So we went to the hotel, a beautiful hotel. I think it was the Four Seasons in Chicago. Long story short, we went in first and asked for the Manager and asked if we could bring a dog. And he said, 'yes, we allow dogs in our hotel.' And I said, 'well, what about a 160-pound Great Dane?' He knew we were with the Coyotes and worked for the Coyotes and were part of the Coyotes traveling party. So I'll never know whether a Great Dane is actually allowed there or if he made a special acceptance just for us because we were with the Coyotes.

"Everyone was in a great mood. And they said the dog could come in. So all of a sudden here I come with my wife and my friend, marching a Great Dane through the lobby of the Four Seasons in Chicago. We got on the elevator and went up to the 22nd floor. The dog's name was Jack. Unfortunately, Jack is no longer with us. But Jack stayed the night at the Four Seasons.

"He woke up the next morning and looked out the window. We were 22 stories up and he took a step back. He couldn't believe looking out and seeing all the buildings below. That was a unique night."

HEETHUIS'S FAVORITE COYOTES GAME HE'S CALLED

The Coyotes haven't had much to celebrate since moving to Arizona over two decades ago. Oh sure, they've had some terrific players and some exciting singular moments. However, sustained success has eluded the dessert franchise. So, that's what makes the team's 2011-12 playoff run all the more special, because it was the one time that the team actually went on a nice run. And it all started with a series against the Blackhawks.

HEETHUIS: "It was April 23rd, 2012, in Chicago. We had gone to overtime the previous five games against Chicago and they had been the better team in that series. Mike Smith was unbelievable. We had scored timely goals. We were the heavy underdog and had no business winning that series at that time.

"Then in Game Six, Chicago comes out and outshoots the Coyotes 11 to 1 or, something like that, in the first nine-minutes and then 16 to 2 in the first period. And we come out of it scoreless. I mean, I've never seen a goaltending display like Mike Smith put on in the first period in Game Six of that Western Conference Quarter-Final in 2012 at United Center. It was unbelievable. And then Oliver Ekman-Larsson scores in the second to give the Coyotes a 1-0 lead.

"And then they score three more times in the third. I think for the game we were outshot 39-20, or something like that. But we won the game 4-0 and Mike Smith had the 39-save shutout and the Coyotes won their first ever playoff series since moving to Arizona. That would probably be the game that is most memorable that sticks out."

MESSAGE TO COYOTES FANS

As is a common theme amongst members of the sports media, it is a well known fact that without the fans our jobs would either A) not exist or B) they'd have a lot less meaning. So, each of the broadcasters in this book took a couple of minutes to address you, the fans, directly.

HEETHUIS: “Well, it's elementary, just in capital letters: THANK YOU. Thank you for your support. Thank you for your passion. Thank you for your patience. Thank you for your resiliency, throughout all of the ups and downs of Coyotes hockey since 1996. I mean, this is my 15th year as the play-by-play radio guy and I believe we're on our sixth ownership group, including being owned by the NHL for five-years. So, there's been a lot of change in the ownership group. There's been a lot of rumors, of course, that this franchise would be moving to another destination and other locations. Obviously there has not been a significant amount of playoff success outside of 2012, when the team went to the Western Conference Final.

“We've been into the playoffs several times, lost in the first-round several times. This year, we won the qualifying round. But through it all, the Coyotes fans have really been supportive. It's certainly not the largest fan base in the NHL. I mean, it's not like Leafs Nation or you could give a myriad of other long time, established, very successful NHL franchises that have waiting lists for season tickets and things like that. But the Coyotes fan base sometimes gets a really bad rep in the media and I think it's unwarranted. We've got a real legion of loyal fans here and people who stuck by the team, like I mentioned, through all the ups and downs and a real solid base. They're passionate. They love the Coyotes. They love their hockey.

“Minor hockey has grown in the state of Arizona. I don't know if it's maybe as high as almost 200 or 400% since the Coyotes came here and among the leaders in growth in terms of minor hockey in the entire United States over the last several years. And that's just one example of the interest and the passion in the game of hockey that is here in the state of Arizona and in the Valley and in the Phoenix area.

“Right now, we're under the second year of another ownership group and I believe, in the end, it will be our strongest. Mr. Alex Meruelo and his family own the team. The team is very stable now. We have a brand new president, who has just had a tremendous career in business in Xavier Gutierrez. And a new General Manager, Bill Armstrong, who helped to build that St Louis team as their Head Scout, their Director of Amateur Scouting and most recently as their Assistant General Manager. Now he's going to lead our team. Rick Tocchet, in my opinion, is a really good coach. So, we've got a strong foundation behind the scenes. I really believe that under this ownership group, the Coyotes will be a successful franchise, not only on the ice, but off of the ice going forward. And I'm fully confident of that.

"The fans have been great. Obviously they're going to have to hang in there a little bit longer, but, just to start out. But by just saying a huge thank you for everything they have weathered, if you will, here in Arizona with the Coyotes over the years. And they still are very faithful and they still are very loyal and they're still a pretty solid base.

"And then, on a personal (note), thanks for all the interactions I've had with the fans, who've always been very supportive of me, very complimentary of me. Whenever I see them at different events surrounding the team, or after games or whatever different Coyotes promotions. Whenever we interact with the fans, they're always just so kind and again, so complimentary and so a big personal thank you from my interaction with them and a huge thank you just for their support and their patience and loyalty hanging in with our franchise."

MATTHEW MCCONNELL
TV: PLAY-BY-PLAY

First Season on Coyotes TV: 2011-12
Seasons on Coyotes TV (including 2020-21): 10

Birthday: March 9, 1963 Hometown: Gary, IN

College/University: Michigan State

BIOGRAPHY

A chance encounter and a heart-to-heart. Sometimes, that's all it takes. Nobody ever said you have to have your entire life planned from the moment you learn to speak. After all, there's so much for you to learn, to experience and to do. Most people probably change their life plans a million times over before settling on what they want for themselves.

As it so happens, Matthew McConnell knows exactly how that goes. He happened to stumble upon watching a hockey game with his dad. He went to college for finance and ended up flunking. He switched to broadcasting after a heart-to-heart conversation with his uncle and now, several decades after his journey first began, he is firmly entrenched as the television voice of the Arizona Coyotes.

I know there's a lot there to digest and a lot of things that happened between Step A and Step Z, so I'll let McConnell regale the tale for you.

MCCONNELL: "My dad, when I was little, was watching the Chicago Blackhawks game in the basement on WGN TV. We were living in Gary, Indiana, which was only about 35 miles Southeast of Chicago. So we got all the Chicago television stations. WGN carried all the Blackhawks games and I was real little and I went downstairs and he had the Blackhawks game on.

"I said, 'Dad, what are you watching?' He said, 'well, I'm watching the Blackhawks game.' I knew nothing about hockey. I knew nothing about the Blackhawks, but I kind of sat down and I watched the game and I was very intrigued. I was probably five-years-old at the time.

"I was very intrigued with the game and the speed as a little kid. The actions, the movement, the excitement. I just found that mesmerizing as a little guy. After that I watched a few more games and then that led to my dad taking me to my first Blackhawks game and from there it just kind of grew. I was a Blackhawks fan because I listened to the games on the radio with Lloyd Pettit. At that point, I was also actually a St. Louis Blues fan a little bit because I listened to Dan Kelly on KMOX. So one year for Christmas, my family got me a Blues Jersey. They got me a pair of skates and I learned how to skate when I was probably in First Grade or Kindergarten.

"I learned to skate on the swamps because we didn't live too far from Lake Michigan. The swamps would fill up with water in the winter time when we'd go skating. There were no hockey rinks or anything like that. I actually had learned how to skate on my sister's white figure skates. And then, I got the Blues Jersey and I got hockey skates and I thought I had just hit the lottery. I always had an interest in Play-by-Play, but I never really thought that it was practical because there are so few jobs available. But I always enjoyed listening to the broadcasters and I thought it was something that maybe I could do someday.

"I used to throw on my roller skates in my driveway and I'd reenact the Stanley Cup Final. I'd put an outline of tape up against the garage door and fire tennis balls off it with a hockey stick and I do the Play-by-Play to myself. That's kind of how it all began for me.

"But when I got to Michigan State, I thought I was going to be a finance major. After my first term I failed two of my three classes. One of them was a math class, which was a requirement and the other one was a science class. I ended up getting a B in English and I had a 0.75 grade point average. So I was thinking, 'man, I don't know if I'm going to be able to get by this math. I don't know if finance is really going to work for me. I don't know if I can do this.'

"So I went home at Christmas and the report card had already come and it showed the 0.75 grade point average. My mom and dad weren't too happy with that because they were paying the tuition and my sports writer uncle came over for Christmas and I had a heart to heart with him.

"I said, 'Uncle John, I don't know if I'm cut out for a finance degree because I don't think I can get by the math and one of the things I've always thought about doing is getting into sports broadcasting or sports journalism; maybe something like you do. Maybe I'll become a broadcaster and do Play-by-Play.' I'll never forget, he was sitting in the chair and he had a glass of scotch. He raised the scotch, it had a couple of big ice cubes and he took a big old sip. And he goes, 'all I can tell you is this. You don't want to get 20-years down the road and look back and say what if?'

"That was a life changing moment for me. I said, 'you know what? He's telling me to go pursue my dream.' My real dream was to do sports Play-by-Play. So I said, 'that's it I've made my decision.' I went back to Michigan State. I changed my degree from finance to telecommunication. Telecommunication did not have a math requirement. So I was in the clear and I didn't have to worry about math anymore. I got through the science portion that was required and I was on my way."

Of course, McConnell may have been on his way, but he still needed to develop his skills as a broadcaster. He did grow up loving to listen to Lloyd Pettit and Dan Kelly, both of whom were major sources of inspiration for him. But it was a chance encounter with Pettit that really sealed the deal.

While working for the IHL's Flint Generals, McConnell happened upon Pettit sitting in the front row of the stands prior to a game in Milwaukee against the Admirals. McConnell, while starry-eyed, had the gumption to introduce himself to Pettit and even asked Pettit to listen to a demo tape of his. The broadcasting icon agreed and eventually told McConnell that he thought he had a future in the business. Well, looks like he was right.

After calling games for the Generals, McConnell eventually made his way to the NHL, first with the Anaheim Ducks in 1993 as their radio broadcaster, before moving onto Pittsburgh, Atlanta, Minnesota, back to Atlanta and then finally to Arizona, where he's been since the 2011-12 season. And it'll bring a smile to the faces of Coyotes fans everywhere to know that McConnell doesn't plan on leaving anytime soon.

FAVORITE PLAYER(S) GROWING UP

MCCONNELL: "I was Bobby Hull on my driveway every single day. I was Bobby Hull with a tennis ball on the blade of my stick firing a shot for the Stanley Cup winner, if you will. I loved Bobby Hull.

"My dad took me to a Blackhawks game early one night at the old Chicago Stadium. They had a gate that was called Gate Three-and-a-half. It was all kind of like where the VIP's would go in and the players. I don't know if the media went in at Gate Three-and-a-half or not, but my dad said, 'this is where all the players come in. Why don't we stand here and see if we can catch Bobby Hull?' So, we stood there and I remember it was a Stanley Cup playoff game because the Blackhawks program had a Stanley Cup on it.

"Sure enough, I'm standing there and my dad gave me his real nice gold cross pen and I'm standing there and here comes Bobby Hull and he looks at me and he says, 'Hey, how are you doing?' And I very politely said, 'Mr. Hull, I'm a huge fan. May I please have your autograph?' And he signed it. His signature was just beautiful.

"He signed right across the Stanley Cup that was on the cover of the program. He was a huge idol of mine. I just thought the world of him and he was probably the first.

"When we went on to Pittsburgh, I was a pretty big Penguins fan during my High School years. They used to practice at the Mount Lebanon Ice Rink, which was right down the hill from Mount Lebanon High School, which I attended.

"On my way home from school, at two in the afternoon, a lot of times they would be practicing in the afternoon and I'd stop in and see guys. That was George Ferguson, Randy Carlyle, Greg Millen, Denis Herron, all those guys at the time. Ross Lonsberry, Orest Kindrachuk. That was a big thing. But in terms of my favorite player growing up, it'd have to be Bobby Hull."

HOCKEY AFTER DARK -- TALES AWAY FROM THE RINK

The crazy things that broadcasters put up with can be as funny as anything that happens during a skit of SNL. Even when things are kind of serious, a well timed interaction or comment can turn the situation into a comedy.

Well, it turns out that Matt McConnell has the timing part down as he was able to take the fairly serious situation that his broadcast partner Tyson Nash was going through and turned it into an entire section of laughing fans.

MCCONNELL: "It was earlier in that series (Coyotes-Blackhawks 2011-12 Opening-Round), when Marian Hossa was hit by Raffi Torres. I was there when the hit happened. Right after the hit happened, we went to a replay sequence and my broadcast partner, Tyson Nash called it a clean hit. Now keep in mind, you're getting one video and in defense of Tyson, he's having to make a split-second decision on whether or not the hit was clean or not. And he called it a clean hit.

"Well, Tyson got death threats. He had voicemails left at his hotel room. He was, next to Raffi, probably Public Enemy Number One around that series.

"So on the off day between Game Three and Game Four, Tyson found one of those dollar stores in Chicago and he bought one of those disguises. The fake glasses with the fake mustache and everything. He ended up wearing it during our open for Game Four, like he was incognito.

"He didn't want anybody to see that it was really him. It was just such a hoot. We were laughing. The funny thing is, there was this beer vendor and the beer vendor was carrying his tray of beers. He was looking up at the press box and he's screaming at Tyson.

"Tyson didn't hear him. So I said, 'Tyson, there's somebody trying to get your attention.' So Tyson took off his headset and he was like to the vendor,' yeah, what do you want?' The beer vendor was probably 40-feet from him and he was holding his tray of beers.

"The beer vendor said 'clean hit my ass. clean hit my ass.' And Tyson looked at him and said, 'Oh yeah, mix in a salad.' Because the guy was a big guy. He was huge. The whole section below us started laughing and cracking up. They started applauding Tyson up in the booth and the beer vendor, after he said that, just kind of froze."

MCCONNELL'S FAVORITE COYOTES GAME HE'S CALLED

Everybody loves when a team goes on a bit of a Cinderella type run. You never know when it's going to happen, but when it does, you sit back and enjoy it; even if you wouldn't normally root for that team. The only exception is if the team you actually root for is going up against the Cinderella team, in which case you hope your team ends the fairytale.

Well, the 2011-12 Coyotes were one of those Cinderella teams and in the Opening Round of the playoffs, they went up against the mighty Chicago Blackhawks, who had won the Stanley Cup two years prior. So, when the Coyotes had a chance to close out the series in Game Six, in Chicago no less, it was a memorable night for all involved, including the broadcasters.

MCCONNELL: "I would have to say the biggest highlight since I've been here was the playoff run they had in 2011-12, when they made it to the Western Conference Final. Maybe the most memorable game of that run was Game Six in the Opening Round in Chicago.

"To this day, I think Mike Smith's performance in Game Six of that series against the Blackhawks was the best goaltending performance I have ever seen live, bar none. At one point the shots were 23 to 2, I think, in favor of the Blackhawks and the Coyotes ended up winning the game 4-0. There was a Shane Doan strip of Johnny Oduya during a carry out of the defensive zone. He went in and scored. We had Kyle Chipchura get a goal.

"But that performance by Mike Smith is the single best. I remember after the game, we got back to the hotel and a few of us went down to a little bar called Dublin's, which is down right off of Rush Street. We went down and we went in there to celebrate, to have a few beers and later on that night, who came walking in, it was Mike Smith and he was there with Marty Turco.

"It turns out Marty Turco was one of Smitty's mentors. They're good, close personal friends. They went in to have a couple of pops and

Marty was at the game. He sat in the stands. He was there to support Mike. They were just so excited and so happy. Marty was so proud of what Mike was able to accomplish that night."

MESSAGE TO COYOTES FANS

As is a common theme amongst members of the sports media, it is a well known fact that without the fans our jobs would either A) not exist or B) they'd have a lot less meaning. So, each of the broadcasters in this book took a couple of minutes to address you, the fans, directly.

MCCONNELL: "Keep the faith and trust the process. I think there's a lot of excitement here right now with Bill Armstrong coming in as the new General Manager. We've got a good young group, a good young hockey core; some real good young kids to build around. And I do think the franchise is headed in the right direction. We've got world-class goaltending with Darcy Kuemper and Antti Raanta. So, keep the faith and let the process play out."

TYSON NASH
TV: COLOR ANALYST

First Season on Coyotes TV: 2009-10
Seasons on Coyotes TV (including 2020-21): 12

Birthday: March 11, 1975 Hometown: Edmonton, AB

College/University: N/A

BIOGRAPHY

Going from a career as a professional hockey player to a career as a sports broadcaster is not as easy as some may think. Yes, plenty of former players make the transition from the ice to the booth, but it's not like they can just adapt their skills from playing to broadcasting. They have to learn a new set of skills entirely, all while keeping what they knew from playing, because that's what allows them to have keen insights as a broadcaster.

Tyson Nash hasn't had an easy life. Not as a child. Not as a player and depending on your view of certain stories, probably not as a broadcaster either. But he has excelled at everything he's done and he's to be commended for his perseverance. So, with that being said, let's journey together through Nash's life; with him as the tour guide of course.

NASH: "I think, initially, you fall in love with the game and that's how it was for me. When you experienced it for the first time as a young kid, you're on the outdoor rink, you feel the freedom, the wind in your face, the cold. You drink hot chocolate after. It's just the whole event leading up to it. You're playing with your buddies. It's just unexplainable. For me, it started as a getaway. I don't think any kid at five, six, seven, eight-years-old is even dreaming of a plan to play in the NHL. I didn't have a great childhood, so for me, hockey was my getaway. I was able to get away from all the troubles at home and the sadness of stuff growing up. It was an outlet for me. And that's kind of how hockey started for me."

You never want to hear about struggles in a person's home life, especially as a kid. Children should be able to enjoy life. So, for the sake of our tour guide, let's get to the part where hockey became a profession. Nash worked his way up through the minors and eventually found himself in the press box at Madison Square Garden as one of the Vancouver Canucks' Black Aces during the 1994 Stanley Cup Final.

Nash didn't get to play in any of those games as he had to wait until the 1998-99 season to make his NHL debut. And by that time, he was no longer with the Canucks. Rather, he was with the St. Louis Blues.

After appearing in two-games during the '98-'99 season, Nash went on to carve out a semi-regular spot in the Blues' lineup for the next four-seasons before going to Phoenix for the final two-seasons of his career (2003-04 and 2005-06).

NASH: "I was no dummy. You think you're going to play forever. I knew the writing was on the wall my last couple of years. Then you start poking around. You start looking and I unfortunately never made enough money to retire. I knew I had to do something after hockey and I always loved broadcasting. I love the camera. I love talking to people. I think I had a personality for it. Most importantly, you kind of think about those things and I was lucky enough that a job became available, because they don't become available very often.

"Our President at the time, Doug Moss, came to me. I had a job and I was going to Tampa Bay to play and be a part of their organization. He came to me and said, 'listen, you can go play in Tampa, probably end up in their farm system. Or you can take this job and do this for the next 15-20 years.' And I said, 'yeah, absolutely. I'm doing this.' I didn't want to uproot my family. I didn't want to go to the minors again after playing in the NHL for so long. I wanted to stay in the NHL. I wanted to keep my family together.

"Maybe I have to take a hit on the chin. Maybe this isn't the job right now that I want, cause I still want to play hockey. But sometimes you have to do what's right for the family. I had a great career for a guy who played like I played and I'm very proud of it. But it was the right time. It was the best decision I honestly ever made, because there's not a day that I get into that press box and I put that headset on. I am just so blessed and so grateful because those jobs, like I said, don't come around very often."

So, when Nash decided to hang up his skates and traded them in for a microphone or headset, he needed to learn the nuances of broadcasting and he had some terrific broadcasters who helped him out along the way.

NASH: “When you're playing, you think you know everything. You look at the broadcasters, you're like, 'Aw, man, that's going to be easy. You're just talking about hockey. How hard can it be?'

“Well, I'll tell you what, you get that microphone on and when you have to talk for two-and-a-half, three-hours about a game and about players, there's so much more that goes into it. You gotta be clean in your sentences and how you speak and in your thought processes. You can't have a lot of the 'ums,' all the crutch words we use to get through our conversations, sometimes that we don't even know about.

“Obviously working with Bob Heethuis, he's like the Godfather in Arizona. He's been around forever. The hardest worker in hockey when it comes to notes and preparation. And then, Dave Strader, a Hall of Fame broadcaster, God rest his soul. He was obviously a best buddy of mine. The stories he would tell, how I would look forward to going out for dinners with him. And sometimes how he pulled me aside and would be like, 'Hey, I know you're nervous. Last night when we did this broadcast. Start thinking about that. Start looking at that.' So there's a lot of different ways he helped me to expand and be a better broadcaster. He helped me evolve into what I am today.

“And then, Matt McConnell, I've worked with him for a number of years and they all bring something different to the table and they all help you at different moments in your career because you evolve and you get better every year.

“It's all about reps. You get better with anything, with everything, when you do it over and over again. And that's kind of how it's been for me with broadcasting. Matt McConnell, he just lets me go. He lets me be me. And that's what I love about him. We have great banter and great chemistry back and forth. I love what I do.

“It's the best job in hockey. I don't get beat up anymore and I get to travel the world and see old friends, see old teammates and the rinks and Scouts up in the press box. That press box is a special, special place for guys who have played the game and the friendships that you had and that you can still maintain because of it.”

FAVORITE PLAYER(S) GROWING UP

NASH: "Growing up in Edmonton, it's colder than ever outside. And there's not a whole lot to do other than belly up on the couch and watch hockey. And I grew up in Sherwood Park, which is just outside of Edmonton. So I watched the Edmonton Oilers back in the heyday when they were winning Stanley Cups.

"You're watching the best player in the world and to ever play the game in Wayne Gretzky and Jari Kurri and Mark Messier and Paul Coffey. No matter what position you played or you liked, they had the best player in the world, at that time, playing it with the Edmonton Oilers. And when they're winning Cups and you're a young kid, it's something special.

"I had Wayne Gretzky wallpaper. Wayne Gretzky bedsheets. But, as a hockey player, everyone wants to score the goals and be Wayne Gretzky. But not many can. And you have to be realistic. As I got a little bit older, 10, 11, 12, it was Esa Tikkanen. This guy was worth the price of admission. You would watch this guy, he was so entertaining. He was always in somebody's face chirping and chopping and slashing somebody.

"That's who I watched, because I was like, 'that's a guy maybe I could emulate.' And ultimately that's kind of what my career turned into and that's the player who I kind of turned into. But he was so much fun to watch. And I'll obviously always remember him and the tough guys too. We had Dave Semenko, Kelly Buchberger, Kevin McClelland, Marty McSorley, they were tough as they came. And so you were always entertained. You never left the Northlands Coliseum, that's what they called at the time, disappointed or unentertained."

HOCKEY AFTER DARK -- TALES AWAY FROM THE RINK

Being involved with professional sports can oftentimes seem like a fairytale come true. There's the fame and fortune associated with players, the stories that would make your hair curl regardless of whether you're a player, writer or broadcaster and the constant travel that makes even the most welltodo people jealous.

Tyson Nash has experienced and seen it all, but even he could not have predicted the craziness that befell him during the Coyotes' 2011-12 playoff run.

NASH: "Broadcasting is obviously the second best job in the world, playing is the best. But this is as close as you get to the action. As a former player you kind of call it like you see it. Sometimes you get caught without a filter. It happens so quickly.

"We were playing against Chicago in the playoffs, Raffi Torres was on the Coyotes and Marian Hossa was in Chicago and Hossa got the puck, came up through the neutral zone, cut across the red line and Raffi Torres caught him in the train tracks. I think everybody knows probably what I'm talking about with this hit, because it was shown all across the world.

"When I saw it in real time and again, I played back in the time when those were the types of hits you were looking for. You were looking to knock a guy out of a game, as barbaric as sometimes that sounds. It just is what it is.

"You're playing for all the marbles when it comes to playoff hockey. I mean, you never like to see anyone get hurt, but unfortunately Raffi, when I looked at it the first time, I thought it was clean. It happened so fast and you're looking at it from way up high in Chicago Stadium and then we're, at the time, looking at a replay on just a 13-inch monitor. So that's where I saw the replay and I was like, 'that's a clean hit. That's as clean a hit as you're gonna see. Marian Hossa basically needs to keep his head up.'

"So that was the road I went down with that call and obviously the passionate fans in Chicago didn't like it. They let their voices be heard. In fact, we were staying at, I believe it was the Ritz Carlton at the time. And I think I had 50 voice messages by the time I got back to my hotel room. How they knew we were staying there is beyond me. But I had a number of death threats. People telling me they were gonna find me on Michigan Avenue or run me over. It gets worse. It gets real nasty from there. I appreciate the passion and the love for the game as far as Chicago fans go. But, I don't know about the death threats.

"We had a couple of days off, or at least a day off in between games and I'm like, 'this is crazy. This is unbelievable. The death threats. The full-time security I had just walking around town.' They were telling me, 'just please stay in your hotel room. Just don't go anywhere until the next game.' Well, I went out and I bought a costume, a pair of glasses that came with a little mustache and I ended up wearing them on the broadcast because we were in the booth. So, we're in the booth and we had this big giant Fox Sports Arizona banner behind us. And I'm like, 'Oh, this is great. This'll be real hard to find me in a stadium full of 21,000 screaming fans.'

"So we took down the banner and I'll never forget I had the glasses and the mustache on. I ended up taking them off during the game. But at one of the breaks, I see this guy walking towards me and it's the beer vendor and he's got this big, huge tray of beers and he's got it strapped around his neck. And he's a big dude and he's walking all the way up to the top of the stadium and I can see his mouth flapping. He's raising his arms and pointing at me.

"So I take my headset off and he's yelling at me. He's like, 'Nash, you bum, you don't know...' I just gave it right back to him. I'm the wrong guy probably to go after as far as chirps go. I laid into him. He was a big guy. I think I told him to mix in a water and a salad. All I remember is that people all around us were just laughing their butts off at the conversation going back and forth there. They enjoyed it."

NASH'S FAVORITE COYOTES GAME HE'S CALLED

Many would say the ultimate honor for a hockey player is to be enshrined in the Hockey Hall of Fame. Some would it's having your name engraved on the Stanley Cup in recognition of being a champion. And others still would insist that it's when a player gets his jersey sent to the rafters at his old home arena.

For Tyson Nash, he was able to be part of the jersey ceremony for a longtime friend and teammate of his in Shane Doan. And at that time, Nash was already a broadcaster with the Coyotes, so it was quite the experience for him; especially since he was asked to give a speech.

NASH: "The biggest moment for me as a broadcaster was a couple of years back when we put Shane Doan's jersey up into the rafters. I was honored to be able to give one of the speeches for Shane Doan, a guy who's been a huge part of the Arizona Coyotes from day one. He's one of my best friends. We lived together in Junior. I was traded to the Arizona Coyotes from the St. Louis Blues. We played together in the National Hockey League and he's one of the best humans and best players I've ever been around. So, I had the opportunity to give a speech in front of all our fans in Arizona to honor Shane and it was something special, just because what he's meant to the team, to the city and to the people in that city was just such an honor for me to get a chance to do."

MESSAGE TO COYOTES FANS

As is a common theme amongst members of the sports media, it is a well known fact that without the fans our jobs would either A) not exist or B) they'd have a lot less meaning. So, each of the broadcasters in this book took a couple of minutes to address you, the fans, directly.

NASH: "Just hang on. I think we're doing really great things, with the new hiring of our General Manager this year. Bill Armstrong comes in, he's a champion, he's a winner. He knows what it takes to win. He knows the players that it takes to win. He won a cup with the St. Louis Blues. He's won at every level that he's been a part of. This is who you want running your franchise. And you look at Rick Tocchet, again, it's the leadership and that's where it starts; at the top. And we have some of the best of it. We're building the players to make that happen and sometimes as a fan, it's hard to see, it's hard to hang on because you lose year-after-year and you want to win a Cup so badly. But just hang on, believe in the process, because it's going to happen. But it does take time. Unfortunately, you gotta have the right players and that doesn't happen overnight."

BOSTON BRUINS

ANDY BRICKLEY
TV: COLOR ANALYST

First Season on Bruins TV: 1997-98
Seasons on Bruins TV (including 2020-21): 24

Birthday: August 9, 1961 Hometown: Melrose, MA

College/University: University of New Hampshire

BIOGRAPHY

If there's any broadcasting role that's made for former professional athletes, it's that of Color Commentary. I mean, think about it. The Color Analyst needs to be able to break down what just happened in the action and be able to speak intelligently and insightfully about why whatever happened actually happened and whether or not it was avoidable or necessary. Well, who better to do that than a former player who has lived through it?

Andy Brickley never had any intentions of becoming a broadcaster. Even when the NHL was done with him as a player, he still continued to play the game at a professional level in the IHL (International Hockey League). If it was strictly up to Brickley, I'm 99.99% certain he'd still be playing to this day -- almost 30-years after he last suited up in an NHL game.

However, life and injuries get in the way of what you want and you have to adjust your plans. So, for Brickley, that meant an unexpected second career as a Color Analyst for the Boston Bruins; first on radio and then, for the last 24-years and counting, on television. So, let's go back in time, with Brickley as our tour guide and find out how he got from Point A to Point B (as in Bruins).

BRICKLEY: "I come from a very long line of athletes; a very athletic family. We played every sport, depending on what season it was. I had four brothers. There were seven children in my family. But what made me want to be an NHL player was, when I was eight and 10, the Bruins won The Cup in '70 and '72.

"Those teams were just everything that you wanted to be when you grew up to be a hockey player. They were swashbuckling. They had unbelievable skill and talent. They were accessible to the fan base. When you're at that impressionable age, eight, nine, 10, 11, 12, that's what you dream about. I'm one of the fortunate few who not only dreamed about it, but made it to the NHL and played for my hometown team.

"And now I'm so lucky to have the job of covering them on a daily basis, doing the games on television. That's pretty rare in our business, to be from your hometown, play for your hometown team and then cover them on television. So, I know how blessed I am. So, that was the real reason that you wanted to be (a hockey player) and I'm speaking for everybody who was my age at that time. If you didn't play hockey, we didn't consider you an athlete, because the Bruins were so immensely popular. That was the driving force that made you want to be a hockey player."

The popularity of the Bruins may have been what made Brickley want to be an NHLer, but what made him appreciate broadcasting was the voice and style of Bob Wilson.

BRICKLEY: "For the games I listened to on radio, I listened to Bob Wilson and his awesome voice. They generally carried the late West Coast games. I'd have practice that following morning where I had to be up at four o'clock to get to the rink, but I wanted to hear that game from Vancouver; so I would stay up.

"I'd be in bed, but I would stay awake and listen to Bob Wilson calling the games from the West Coast. I had such an appreciation for his ability to paint a picture for me, because the game was on radio and I couldn't see the action. It was appointment viewing.

"The Bruins were must see television. This was before NESN came along and it was TV38. The whole rabbit ears on top of the TV in order to get the reception. You planned your entire day to build up to that seven o'clock puck drop or whatever time the puck drop was that particular night.

"I know that in between periods, we would talk hockey, would actually set up a little rink on the sun porch or wherever we were watching the game. We'd play a little hockey ourselves in between periods, but still watched the in between periods coverage. Of course, when I first started, I probably didn't have an appreciation for Play-by-Play or Color, because you're too young and you're more involved with the players.

"Don Earle was the first guy who I heard call games before Fred Cusick took over. And then I basically grew up with Fred Cusick. Then, when Derek Sanderson retired and moved into the color seat and replaced Johnny Peirson, Johnny was very analytical in his ability to analyze the game. So I learned a lot from both of those guys.

"Derek was personality plus, but also knew the game real well. I think somewhere along the line, even though I had no intentions of getting into that business, some of the things stay with you. The ability to break down all the moving parts and in a very short amount of time, because hockey is such a fast sport. To be able to articulate, be insightful, maybe add a little humor, maybe draw on some of your experience that people would appreciate. I think I learned all that stuff just by watching the amount of games that I watched, watching the Bruins play while I was growing up."

Now, getting back to my early statement about how Brickley would still be playing if things were strictly up to him.

BRICKLEY: "Basically radio and television came to me. My NHL days were done in '93 and I kept playing. I played in the old IHL. I played in Denver and then I played in Salt Lake and it was fun. I was making a good living. I was enjoying hockey. I was making good money. I was playing with people who I liked.

"We won back-to-back championships and I would come home for the summer after the season. I lived by myself out there. My family was back in Boston. My wife worked, she had her own business. We had young kids. So I was kind of an absentee husband and father through the winter because I was committed to keep playing. And that's where I wanted to be.

"That's where the money was. That's where everything I wanted about hockey, non-NHL, was available to me. And they understood that. But, I had total reconstruction (surgery) on both knees. I had my back operated on. I had a life-threatening injury from this growth that had to be removed. So a lot of major things were happening to me.

"That was a not so subtle message, physically, to start thinking about what you're going to do when you retire. And I had a wife who strongly suggested I start thinking about it, because you're not as invincible as you think you are. I remember one day, I called Jack Edwards. Ironically. I knew him a little bit. He went to UNH where I went to school, even though we didn't overlap. He was Channel Seven Boston's Weekend Anchor. I asked him if I could go in and just kind of shadow him on a Saturday and see what he does. Which he was willing to do and happy to do it. I went in and watched him and it was like broadcast news.

"In those days, you got seven, eight minutes; not the two minutes that they get today. He wrote his own material. He had to organize. He had to prioritize all the different highlights they were going to show. It was really, really interesting, but I decided that was not what I wanted to do. It did not interest me. I just decided I was going to continue to play until my body fell apart. Then, when I was home, after my year in Salt Lake, I got a call from WBZ radio.

"The broadcaster who they had doing the Color, had a job description change with the financial company he worked for which prevented him from traveling. As much as he wanted to just do the home games, WBZ wasn't interested in that. They wanted somebody there for all 82-games.

"So they called me and said, 'would you please come in and audition?' So I said, 'sure, I'll come in and see what it's all about.' With no intention of doing the job. But I wanted to explore and see what was out there. I went in and auditioned and they offered me the job on the spot. I asked them, 'how did I end up on this short list?'

"They said, 'they went back through a lot of old videos. They wanted somebody who was a former Bruin. I had a leg up because I was from Boston. If I was on the air talking about the Bruins, the Bruins' history, I would be very believable, because I grew up and I lived it.' And they were looking for people who could handle being on camera and be concise. Those were the attributes that worked in my favor and that's how it all started. And then I had to decide whether I was ready to retire. After a long conversation with my wife, we decided this was a great opportunity to start a second career."

Brickley's first year doing Bruins games on radio was the 1996-97 season, one in which Boston finished in last-place in the Eastern Conference. However, it was a terrific learning experience for Brickley as it allowed him to learn how to handle such adversity and how to properly break it down for the listening audience without completely pummeling the team into oblivion.

The following year, 1997-98, Brickley moved over to doing Bruins games on television and he hasn't looked back. For a kid who just wanted to play hockey for the Boston Bruins, Brickley certainly has become as ingrained with the Bruins franchise as anybody ever has or ever will.

FAVORITE PLAYER(S) GROWING UP

BRICKLEY: "We all loved Bobby Orr. Derek Sanderson was such a huge personality. But the way I played the game, the way I was built and my skill set, probably John Bucyk was the guy who I idolized the most. I was kind of that wide body build when I was a young kid.

"I played left-wing. I scored a lot of goals and most of my goals came in, close around the net; scored a lot on the power-play. A lot of what John did as a player. He had a great number. Number Nine. Had a great nickname 'The Chief.' He was a gentlemanly player, but hit hard when he hit. So, I loved everything about his makeup as a player, as a teammate, as a leader and was on the best team in the league.

"So, that was the guy I gravitated towards the most. I loved every one of those guys. They all had an impact on me. I understood at an early age what team hockey was all about. It really wasn't necessarily about scoring goals and piling up points, like the top guys did. Everybody had a role. I mean, I was a huge fan of Ed Westfall and his ability to shadow players and kill penalties. I appreciated that at a young age and I think that made me slightly different than the average kid who I was playing with."

BRICKLEY'S FAVORITE BRUINS GAME HE'S CALLED

There are some broadcasters who, even though they long ago hung up their skates, still carry around the feelings of being an NHL player from time to time. What do I mean by that? I mean, there are some broadcasters, who even though their NHL playing careers are over, they still get those pangs of emotions that course through your body as a player during a big game.

As you might be able to tell from that introduction, Andy Brickley is one such broadcaster who still remembers those feelings he had as a player.

BRICKLEY: "Back in 2011, it'd been so long since the Bruins had won the Stanley Cup. I had gone to The Cup Final with the Bruins. I'd gone to the Conference Finals twice with the Bruins and we just couldn't get over the hump.

"I watched this team and what the city was like when they did win the Stanley Cup. And now, here I am broadcasting in 2011. Back in 2011, we got two rounds. NBC hadn't taken three rounds yet. So we actually had the first two rounds. And that first series with Montreal, your arch enemy, your historic rival and then you lose the first two at home.

"I thought Game Four of that series, after they had gone to Lake Placid in between games in order to prepare for this unbelievable, epic comeback series. I mean, those two Games: Three and Four, were incredibly memorable. Not just the Game Seven in that series. We broadcasted 2011 in Montreal and it reminded me of being a player.

"There was no better feeling than being sitting in that locker room in a puddle of sweat, maybe spitting a little blood, knowing you just beat those guys and probably their own fans in a playoff game.

"I know that feeling and I had that feeling as a broadcaster watching what that special Bruins team was doing."

MESSAGE TO BRUINS FANS

As is a common theme amongst members of the sports media, it is a well known fact that without the fans our jobs would either A) not exist or B) they'd have a lot less meaning. So, each of the broadcasters in this book took a couple of minutes to address you, the fans, directly.

BRICKLEY: "I would say, live in the moment. I think if you approach it that way; whether you're a player, a broadcaster, or a fan of the Boston Bruins, live in the moment. Play the game, it's right in front of you. Watch the game, that's right in front of you. You don't need to project. Don't try to predict what this team's going to be. Just enjoy the moment and really try to take in everything that you're watching. I think it's the greatest sport. And again, I played them all and I love them all. But I think hockey is the greatest sport. It's difficult to do on television. So yeah, pay attention and enjoy what you're watching and hopefully we do a good job to enhance that experience. But yeah, live in the moment."

JUDD SIROTT
RADIO: PLAY-BY-PLAY

First Season on Bruins Radio: 2017-18
Seasons on Bruins Radio (including 2020-21): 4

Birthday: January 6, 1969 Hometown: Chicago, IL

College/University: University of Michigan

BIOGRAPHY

When you know, you just know! What you may know can vary from person to person. But that feeling of being secure in knowing this is something you want, well, that's a whole other ballgame. When that feeling overtakes you, there's nothing that can or will deter you from following through. And for Judd Sirott, that feeling was knowing he wanted to be a professional Play-by-Play announcer. So, let's go back and find the source of this feeling and how Sirott went about acting on it.

SIROTT: "As a kid growing up in the suburbs of Chicago, I played every sport under the sun, except hockey. I played baseball, football, basketball, tennis, golf; I just loved sports. I used to devour the sports pages.

"I used to get the Sun-Times as a kid and would read that paper. I just loved sports and the Blackhawks weren't necessarily on my radar as a kid growing up, until about 1982. Hockey certainly has grown dramatically in the Chicago area in the past couple of decades with what Rocky Wirtz has done at the helm. What they have done for youth hockey is just taking it to a completely different level.

"But when I grew up, the closest public rink was probably 20- to 25-minutes away. I didn't really have that many friends who played the game. The only time that we really had a chance to play was in the winter when they would freeze up a parking lot or freeze up a park and then everybody would be out. They'd have a stick, a puck and they'd be playing. So that was my extent of hockey probably until about the age of 12 or 13.

"My best friend, who was living across the street, a guy named Jeff Sprenger, invited me over one day. He said, 'Hey, do you want to come over and watch the Blackhawks?' And I had never seen a game before. It was very hard to see the Blackhawks at the time, because they were not offered on free TV the way the Cubs and the White Sox and obviously the Bears and the Bulls were. Those were easily accessible to see. But hockey you couldn't see. They were offered on something called Sportsvision, and we did not have cable at the time. We did not have a paid TV package.

"He had it. He invited me over and he said, 'why don't you come over and watch the Blackhawks game?' So I'm like, 'sure.' And just as the game was about to start, he said, 'we're going to turn down the sound on TV and we're going to turn up the radio because you have to hear this guy who does the Blackhawks games on radio.'

"Kenny Wilson was doing the games on television, but Pat Foley was doing the games on radio. So we turned up Pat and watched the game. I saw Denis Savard for the first time and he was magnetic. He completely blew me away. The way that he was able to dangle with the puck, his artistry all over the ice, it was mesmerizing to watch. I think from that point forward, once I saw Savard and once I heard Pat and the excitement and the energy and just how much fun it sounded like he was having, something just clicked for me that this is what I want to do.

"From that point forward, I read and watched everything I possibly could about the game. And the more that I saw it, the more I fell in love with the game itself and the characters who played the game. Pat was fabulous. The way he was calling the goals, the way he would use his voice and just how much energy you could hear pouring out of his voice and the sound that was coming on, it was fantastic.

"As a kid growing up, the only way you could really get a sense of what the atmosphere and the flavor was like at Chicago Stadium was through Pat Foley. He was able to capture that and channel the energy from that legendary building.

"After (watching that game), I was hooked. I listened to absolutely every game that I possibly could. It didn't really matter to me that I couldn't see them at the time. It wasn't until many years later when the Blackhawks were offered for free and they had all the games on television. I think you have to really fast forward to the mid-2000s when

Rocky Wirtz took over. One of the first things that he did was that he put all of the games on television, home and away."

Once Sirott was able to get his fill of Blackhawks games, his passion for the sport was ignited, as was his passion for broadcasting. But it wasn't just Pat Foley who helped enable that spark inside Sirott.

SIROTT: "First two names come to mind and then I'll get to a third in the hockey world.

"I grew up with Harry Carey. Harry was actually first doing the White Sox when I was a kid and then later moved over to the Cubs in the early-80's. Harry's a legendary announcer. Harry was a must listen. It didn't matter if it was the beginning of the season or the end; whether it was the beginning of the game or the end. It didn't matter if the Cubs were winning or losing. What mattered was that you wanted to take some time and listen to Harry. Harry was a must listen all of the time.

"I think what gets lost with Harry was his ability to call the game. But beyond that, he was such a fun listen. He was such an engaging listen. He was such a great storyteller. And every day, it was something new. He was one of the guys who I absolutely adored as a kid growing up.

"We (Doc Emrick and I) joke about 'no menus,' because that was Harry's rule. After every night game, Harry would go out for a big Italian meal, but you were not allowed to see a menu until you had three martinis.

"I (also) loved Howard Cosell. Absolutely loved him. I loved Monday Night Football as a kid, because of the way Howard phrased things. The way he used his voice, used his inflection. He made Monday Night Football an event.

"I used to have to beg my mom as a kid, 'I'll go to bed after the halftime highlights.' I would watch Howard and listen to how he'd do those highlights.

"As far as hockey, Doc Emrick became a mentor because I had a chance to listen to Doc, to hear the way that he called games and his ability to spin his stories, weave them throughout the games and the excitement that he brought. It was different."

With his inspirations in place, now it was up to Sirott to follow through and take action. You don't just snap your fingers and become a broadcaster. There's a lot that happens in between.

SIROTT: "I was trying to watch and devour as much hockey as I could. I couldn't get enough of it. I wrote Pat Foley and Mike Emrick letters when I was in High School. My dad was all over me. He said, 'if this is something you really want to do, you ought to write these people letters.'

"So I did. I wrote Pat and he wrote me back. And I wrote Doc and Doc wrote me back. He said, 'you seem like you have a lot of questions and you're really interested in this profession. Here's my number. Why don't you give me a call and we'll talk.' I'll never forget running in from outside and Doc Emrick was on the phone. Who knows how long we chatted. I mean, we may have chatted for about 45-minutes and he's been a mentor and a friend ever since.

"To be able to have Doc as a sounding board, basically for almost 35-years, has just been invaluable.

"I knew that this is what I wanted to do since I was about 13-years-old. So, since that was the case, I had to choose a school that played hockey and a school that had a student radio station. So, Michigan certainly fit the bill. And in addition to that, it was a really good school. So when I was at University of Michigan, the hockey program wasn't what it is now. They're weren't a lot of people who were interested in doing hockey. Football and basketball however, were two nationally ranked programs. So everybody wanted to do those games. So when it came to hockey, I pretty much had free reign.

"I did as many games as I possibly could at U of M. I did just about all the home games for hockey. And I would occasionally travel to do some of the road games. I didn't have a car at the time. I went to Michigan State every now and then. Or I'd go to Joe Louis Arena when they played the GLI. (Great Lakes Invitational).

"I don't think I did any basketball games when I was at U of M and because of the long wait to do football, I got a chance to do one-game. It was my senior year, at home, against Iowa.

"I graduated from U of M in '91. The sports radio craze was just starting around the country. FAN had just started in New York. There was XTRA out in San Diego and Chicago was about to start the third all-sports station. It was The Score. So I began there on the ground floor. We went on the air in January of 1992 and I was the Executive Producer of the afternoon show. I was a Field Reporter, covered all the sports and then, ultimately, I was hosting every weekend by the time I left, which was in 1994.

"The last place that I thought a minor league team would pop up would be not only in an NHL city, but in an Original Six city. But the Chicago Wolves came into existence in 1994. I started with the Wolves from their inception in 1994 and spent 12 glorious years in the IHL. That's actually where I met my radio partner, Bob Beers, when he was still playing. Andy Brickley too. I met them both when they were playing. So I spent 12-years there doing the IHL and then, later, the IHL folded in with the American Hockey League in 2001-02. Then in 2006, there was a job that came open, the network at the time was called HDNet.

"It was owned by Mark Cuban. It was an all-high definition television network and they had an NHL package where they were televising games every Thursday and Saturday in the National Hockey League. I got a huge break, landed the job and did two-seasons there, which was phenomenal.

"So, I spent two-seasons there doing the national broadcasts every Thursday and Saturday, working mainly with Larry Murphy and John Vanbiesbrouck.

"(But then) Mark could not come to an arrangement with the NHL to extend his deal, so they ended those broadcasts in 2008 and as luck would have it, this was right around the time that not only had Rocky Wirtz taken over the Blackhawks, but the Blackhawks were moving their radio rights over to WGN Radio."

With the Blackhawks rights moving to WGN, so too did Sirott after reaching out to a contact of his. In fact, Sirott got the call about the Blackhawks job right after his second daughter had been born. He and his wife were still in the hospital when the station's Sports Director called and offered Sirott the job. By the way, he quickly accepted.

That began a 10-year run that saw Sirott call games for the Blackhawks, while also getting to do games for the Chicago Cubs.

However, after the Blackhawks 2016-17 season came to a close, Sirott and his family were on vacation when he heard through the grapevine that Dave Goucher, then of the Boston Bruins, was leaving his longtime post to become the first ever television voice of the new club on the block, the Vegas Golden Knights.

After making some calls, Sirott was able to land the job with the Bruins for the start of the 2017-18 campaign and he's been entrenched in Boston ever since.

FAVORITE PLAYER(S) GROWING UP

SIROTT: "Denis Savard is still my favorite player of all-time. I still tell him to this day that he's still my favorite player of all-time. I was a right-handed shot. I loved Al Secord, who was Savard's left-wing. But Al was a lefty. Al's ability to not only score goals, but to also intimidate. He was a guy who regularly racked up 200 or more penalty minutes during the heyday of his career. I mean, I loved Al, but because Savard was a righty and I was a righty, he was the guy I would try and be like if I were playing a pickup game."

HOCKEY AFTER DARK -- TALES AWAY FROM THE RINK

Oftentimes, it's the little things that make us happiest. We don't always need some grandiose event to make something be particularly memorable for us. And in Judd Sirott's case, it is a simple round-table sit-down, early in his career with the Blackhawks that is something he'll always cherish.

SIROTT: "I remember, sitting down, starting my career with the Blackhawks and I think we were outside getting ready for the Winter Classic at Wrigley Field. It was Stan Mikita, Bobby Hull, Tony Esposito, Pierre Pilote and I'm sitting as part of this group, getting a chance to shoot the breeze with these guys. It was surreal and it was special."

SIROTT'S FAVORITE BRUINS GAME HE'S CALLED

There's nothing quite like an age-old rivalry to get the blood flowing. And in the National Hockey League, there is no more storied rivalry than that of the one between the Boston Bruins and the Montreal Canadiens. There have been 750 all-time meetings between these two franchises (second most in NHL history behind the Canadiens and Maple Leafs (757)) and yet, this rivalry never gets old. Rather, a new, more exciting chapter is written each and every time the Bruins and Canadiens players stand across the ice from each other.

SIROTT: "Any game involving the Bruins and the Canadiens is always special, because of that rivalry; it's unmatched around the National Hockey League. Just off the top of my head, I remember the Bruins demolished The Habs 8-1 at the Bell Centre in November 2019. I remember Colby Cave, who tragically passed, getting his first career NHL goal in December of 2018 at the Bell Centre. So, again, any Bruins-Canadiens game is special."

MESSAGE TO BRUINS FANS

As is a common theme amongst members of the sports media, it is a well known fact that without the fans our jobs would either A) not exist or B) they'd have a lot less meaning. So, each of the broadcasters in this book took a couple of minutes to address you, the fans, directly.

SIROTT: "The passion for the Bruins is unrivaled around the National Hockey League. And in the booth, we can feel that energy and emotion and that makes The Garden a uniquely special place to call games. It never ceases to amaze me that wherever the Bruins travel, a sea of black and gold jerseys always goes with them.

"Beyond that, as an Original Six franchise, the Bruins are a treasure of hockey lore. Names like: (Eddie) Shore; (Lionel) Hitchman; (Dit) Clapper; (Milton) Schmidt; (Bobby) Orr; (Phil) Esposito; (Frank) Brimsek; (Rick) Middleton; (Cam) Neely; (Terry) O'Reilly; and (Ray) Bourque. And soon, two other names are going to join those retired numbers: (Zdeno) Chara and (Patrice) Bergeron. These are icons of the game and they authored some of the greatest moments in NHL history. It's a privilege to broadcast Bruins games and be a part of this amazing community."

BUFFALO SABRES

DAN DUNLEAVY
TV/RADIO (SIMULCAST): PLAY-BY-PLAY

First Season on Sabres TV/Radio (Simulcast): 2013-14
Seasons on Sabres TV/Radio (Simulcast) (including 2020-21): 8

Birthday: September 27, 1965 Hometown: Georgetown, ON

College/University: Niagara College

BIOGRAPHY

It's beyond stereotypical to state that Canadians have hockey in their blood from the moment they're born. But in the case of Dan Dunleavy, there's no way to tell his tale without acknowledging his Canadian upbringing.

DUNLEAVY: "Being born and raised in Canada and being a Toronto born kid, you pretty much, from day one, are exposed to hockey as soon as you're able to understand what's what. And when it comes to what you watch on television, what your parents watch on TV and what people do for seven-months out of the year, which is go to the hockey rink. That's what we do up there.

"So, the hockey love of the game came pretty quickly and growing up in an era of, for me Bobby Orr and Wayne Gretzky and then onto Mario Lemieux, until we get to the super modern era of the game where we're at now, it's pretty easy to fall in love with a game that had such an interesting and very classy and well representing the game players like Bobby and Wayne and even the Phil Esposito's who represented Canada, the '72 Team for Canada who won the Soviet series.

"That was a big deal North of The Border. The Canada Cup in '87 was another big deal. The Gretzky to Lemieux goal that was scored in Hamilton, Ontario, with Dale Hawerchuk, who took the face-off draw on that particular play. Dale who unfortunately just passed away. So there were a lot of reasons to fall in love with hockey."

Beyond just the players, Dunleavy also fell head-over-heels in love with the broadcasting side of the game. And he has several noteworthy predecessors to thanks for that.

DUNLEAVY: "The broadcasting love of things was, again, sitting on your couch and watching Hockey Night in Canada every weekend and plus a mid-week game that we had back in those days. I just knew it was something that if somebody could pay me to be at a hockey game and be that guy, that's something I would love to do.

"Without a doubt, I don't think you can avoid that in this business, when you're trying to take on this, call it a profession or an art form really, of calling a game and trying not to be an annoyance to anybody for three-hours or two-hours, who are listening to you. So for me, growing up, obviously you had your iconic voices who you just knew of, even if he didn't get to hear a lot of them, because you weren't born in that area, but you're Foster Hewitt. You're Bill Hewitt, of course, up there on Hockey Night in Canada with the Toronto Maple Leafs, really the first real big national name that had an effect on me, a guy by the name of Bob Cole, who was with Hockey Night in Canada for a number of years until recently.

"Dan Kelly is another voice I grew up listening to and admiring very much. And Danny Gallivan is probably, when you talk about guys who really invented their own flair and their own vocabulary for the game of hockey, Danny Gallivan is probably the number one guy who has really ever done that. I mean, even today, guys like myself or anyone else who does this job, try to fashion nicknames for players or names for moves, or what have you, but Danny Gallivan was doing that back before anybody ever did it. And he was probably one of the best at it. Dick Irvin was his Color Commentator at the time. And they did a lot of games on Hockey Night in Canada; did a lot of Montreal Canadiens games. I'd see a lot of Montreal-Boston games on TV and listened to Danny and Dick call games all the time.

"And I'd just really marvel at how much you couldn't stop listening and be interested in what Danny had to say next. For me, I try to pattern my game and my call a lot after the likes of Bob and Danny. And then as I mentioned, growing up in Southern Ontario, you had Toronto and you had Buffalo and really there's nobody who compares to Ted Darling and the way he called a game. For me, Ted was never a forced delivery. It was never something that was too corny or too fake. It was just something in the way that he was able to deliver his description of the game. There was a real freedom to his cadence. There was a real warm, but exciting, tone to his voice. And it was unique in his own way.

"So, Ted Darling, for me, was another massive influence and I quite happily carry over many of the ways that he would inflect in calling a hockey game into what I do now. It's really just a coincidence that I'm in Buffalo. Obviously, you don't plan for those things when you're 10-years-old or listening to hockey games, but it's pretty cool that you're with a team where, when you grew up listening to a guy like Ted Darling, you're actually calling a game for the same city.

"I think too, when you kind of grow up knowing this is something that you want to do, you become a fan of the broadcaster. And I know for a fact now, too, I'm sure you have your favorite broadcasters and I'm sure you have guys or gals that you just can't stand as broadcasters, because for whatever reason. It could be a tone of voice. It could be a delivery. Sometimes you can't explain it. You just might say, 'I don't like this person calling these games. I prefer so-and-so.' So you kind of grow up, for me, it's interesting, because, in the back of my mind, I often think to myself, 'I'm really trying to make a guy like Ted proud,' because he set such a high bar in Buffalo.

"And obviously, with RJ (Rick Jeanneret) doing his thing for the past now 50-years, the bar remains really high in this town. But to sit in a chair that Ted Darling sat in first, followed by Rick and then with me having that opportunity now; that's two pretty big standards have been set ahead of me, but you really want the team to win when they're done doing their thing, so you can kind of look back and say, 'Hey guys, all that work you put into this, a part of this is for you as well.' So, in the back of my mind, I always have it that one day, this team will win a Cup and one day I'll have the opportunity to be the guy to make that Stanley Cup winning call while I'm with the franchise. And I'll certainly be thinking about both guys who sat in the chair previously and didn't get a chance to say, 'the Buffalo Sabres are Stanley Cup champions.'"

While that passion for broadcasting was inflamed at an early age thanks to those who came before him, Dunleavy still needed to figure his way along the long and winding path that is present for those seeking to do this job for a living.

DUNLEAVY: "Now when you're young, you're not sure how you'd ever be able to do that, but as you start going through high school and find out that you can actually go to college for different broadcasting or journalism courses and find your way into the career that way, I immediately jumped at the opportunity when I had the chance to go to Niagara College and take a Radio and TV Broadcasting course.

"And while I was there, I had the chance to call a number of junior hockey games in and around the city of St. Catherines, Ontario; which for hockey fans, you can look up to the likes of Marcel Dionne, who knows and make St. Catherines a home and some really good players who came out of that area. So, for me, it was never really a question of what I wanted to do. I knew I wanted to do it. The question was, how do I get there? So just as you grow up and you find out how you need to go about things. So, once I went to college and graduated and did well there, I got into the business right away and radio, not television right away, but into radio. And then you just spend your years honing your career and then waiting for opportunities, which is exactly what I did."

While Niagara College was indeed where Dunleavy got his first taste of what it took to do the job he loves so much today, it was really in High School when he got a glimpse at what his future held.

DUNLEAVY: "I would go back to Grade 12 in high school. We walked into a television studio for the first time and I had a look at the equipment. I had a feel for the atmosphere and I knew right away that there was not another thing that I could think of coming out of school that I wanted to do other than be around that kind of atmosphere.

"I knew really early in my life, as far as teenage and going to work and finding jobs, I would not be a very good nine-to-five person. I needed something that had a little bit more adventure or its own unique personality, instead of waiting for breaks every four-hours for 15-minutes. That's not to put down that kind of work. It just wasn't for me. So after that point, getting into Niagara College and taking a broadcasting course, I mean, it was clear right away.

"When you find something you like to do and you excel at it, you invest your time in it and your energy. And I did that. So calling Junior B games when I was in college and having really no experience at doing that and just really having an idea for how things worked around the broadcast. Even when you do a small cable TV broadcast for the first time, you're really unaware of everything that goes into it. The different camera people. The people who work in the truck. The people who work sound. The people who work the lighting. The people who work the cameras. Your Producers. Your Directors. So you get a pretty early sense of, 'boy, there's more to this than meets the eye.' But the more you learn about it, the more you admire and kind of get excited about the opportunity to be part of a team like that."

After college was when things really started to fall into place for the young Dunleavy and it ended up being quite the whirlwind journey.

DUNLEAVY: "(After college) I went to work and I did seven-years or eight-years up in a radio station that did Sportscasting, but I was also a newscaster and a writer and a DJ. I did everything you could possibly do in this radio career until an opportunity in sports came up and it eventually did. About seven years into my career, I got a call from a Toronto station asking if I would come and work some weekends for them. And that was The FAN 590. It was The FAN 1430 back then.

"So I worked five-days a week at one station. Then I went and worked two-days on the weekend at the sports station, trying to make my way into that all sports atmosphere.

"Then, another station went on the air in Toronto and I got a call and I was offered a full-time sports position, just being a Sportscaster. And that was 680 News. They're still on the air in Toronto. And at that time, when I was offered that job, I went back to The FAN, which was the all sports station. 680 was a news station, looking for a sports guy. And I was already at The FAN, which was a sports station. And I was waiting for a good full-time job there. So when 680 offered me the job, I went back to The FAN and I said, 'look, I've got this job offer. What should I do? It's full-time. You've only given me a part-time job at that moment.' The guy running The FAN 590, his name was Alan Davis.

"He told me, 'you're not going anywhere. You're coming to work here full-time.' And that's where I started, really Year One of a 20-year career at The FAN in Toronto. While at The FAN in Toronto, I did: World championship Hockey; World Junior Hockey Championships for nine-years; Olympic Hockey and then one day I got a call from the Toronto Maple Leafs to come and be a Play-by-Play on radio for them. I did that for two-years before the Buffalo Sabres called and asked me to come to Buffalo."

If you're still hanging in there, just know, this is where the whirlwind truly begins.

DUNLEAVY: "When I worked at The FAN in Toronto, there was a guy by the name of Jack Armstrong, who worked with us and he was/still is a Toronto Raptors Television Analyst. He's also a former Head Basketball Coach at Niagara University, just outside of Buffalo, New York. Jack while working with me, had heard my calls in the World Junior Championships. We'd go coast-to-coast, across Canada with those. And they originated out of The FAN. He had heard my Ontario Hockey League calls. I did OHL games for a decade in Toronto.

"Jack had heard enough of my work. He came up to me one day and he said, 'you know, Rick Jeanneret's not going to last forever. They're going to need a replacement for him. And I know the President of the hockey team really well. You should apply for that job.' And I said, 'well, is there a job to apply for?' And he said, 'well, RJ is cutting back on his gigs. And I think you should take a shot at it.'

"I didn't have an agent or anything, so I just picked up a phone and I called the Sabres office. At the end of the day, I got down to having a meeting with Larry Quinn, who is the guy who Jack knew and still knows. Larry was President at the time and I brought him a demo tape and a resume. Mr. Quinn said to me at the time, 'look, I don't need to hear your demo. I don't need to see a resume. If Jack Armstrong recommended you, you're good enough for me. I want to give you a two-game audition.'

"So I went to Anaheim with Harry Neale one-night and we called the game. And after that, I didn't hear back from the Sabres at all. Then they called back and asked if I would do one more, a few weeks later. And I did a game in Ottawa. So, after those two-games, I got a phone call from the team and they had told me that they were going to give somebody else who was local in town the opportunity, who they felt had earned that chance. And that was a guy by the name of Kevin Sylvester. He was hosting the broadcast at the time, but he wanted to be the Play-by-Play guy.

"So they called up, they said, 'look, thanks for the two-games, but we're going to give Kevin the job.' I said, 'no worries, thanks for the opportunity.' Then, shortly after that, I got a call from the Toronto Maple Leafs and that's when they hired me to do their radio games.

"Fast forward about two-years and the Sabres called me. I was in Year Two of a three-year deal in Toronto and the Sabres called asking if I could get out of my Toronto contract and come work for them? Their exact words were, 'we should have hired you in the first place. We're wondering if you would join us now and work with us and replace Rick once he retires?' So that's how we got to where we're at now. I thought it was dead and gone. I thought it was over with as far as Buffalo goes. I was very happy of course, in Year Two of a three-year deal with the Maple Leafs.

"But it was quite flattering to be called and have someone say that maybe we missed on this one and we should have had you come in here a few years ago. Would you come here now? So I accepted the opportunity and that's where we're at now.

"I was cutting the grass in the backyard when they called. I thought Buffalo was dead and gone. I never, ever expected to work there. But I was out cutting the grass one summer and I got a phone call saying, 'yeah, we should have hired you a couple of years ago. Would you come now?' So it was pretty unique."

FAVORITE PLAYER(S) GROWING UP

DUNLEAVY: "First of all, I was never good enough, as far as skating goes, to emulate anyone. But when we did play on the pond, right outside the school that I went to from Kindergarten to Grade Five, at a school called Harrison Public School and they had an outdoor rink and they had floodlights out there.

"So, my buddy Ian and I would go out there every night and we would play. Back in those days, you were Bobby Orr. You were Phil Esposito. You were John Bucyk. You were Guy Lafleur. You were Ken Dryden, if you were in goal. You were Bernie Parent. You were Darryl Sittler, Lanny McDonald. Obviously, as time goes on, you can keep mentioning players who were impactful as far as people who you admired as players.

"But, certainly while I was growing up and obviously many of those years would have been the 1970s. You're looking at some really classic and iconic players who really helped build the game. So, those would be a few names I would throw out for you.

"I didn't spend a lot of time trying to be anybody else, to be honest, but certainly, I would think, growing up in the Toronto area, you certainly had your eye on the Maple Leafs and you were a fan of that team, even though the team wasn't doing that well. And they were very frustrating at the time. And then not far down the highway, of course, you had the Buffalo Sabres.

"When they came into the league and all of a sudden, in the 1970s, they did really well out of the gate for an expansion team and you have the French Connection line and you have some really iconic hockey players of that era, too. In Southern Ontario, where I grew up, you would see those games on a nightly basis with Ted Darling calling them on TV.

"So you were exposed to not only the Toronto Maple Leafs games but the Buffalo Sabres games as well."

HOCKEY AFTER DARK -- TALES AWAY FROM THE RINK

The job of a broadcaster is to bring you, the viewer/listener a clear and concise depiction of what is going on in the game. But that's not the only thing broadcasters need to do. They also need to develop quality chemistry with each other in order to allow their depictions of the games to flow smoothly. Now, you may be asking, "how do they develop the desired chemistry?"

Well, part of it is the sheer repetition of the job. However, the time spent away from the rink is also important as it allows the broadcasters to get to know each other on a more personal level and that deeper relationship often shows up in how they interact with each other when the lights and microphones are on.

So, for Dunleavy, it was and is important that he develop those strong bonds with his fellow Sabres broadcasters. And it's some of those experiences that he treasures most of all.

DUNLEAVY: "During my time with Buffalo, I think the most fun I've had has been when Brad May and Rob Ray were both part of our broadcast crew. I mean, there'd be many times we'd be on the road, if we found ourselves with an afternoon or a day off, for example, one story that comes to mind is in Denver, 'Razor,' 'Mayday' and myself, we went out to Red Rocks and we walked up and down the stairs in the amphitheater.

"Those two guys, being former teammates and really good friends to this day, kind of poking fun at one another as they try to get up and down the stairs. And then we took a drive to another little town that was just outside the city of Denver, and we had lunch. I mean, we didn't go on any major excursions because you didn't have a lot of time on the road to be honest, but just the time spent together with 'Razor' and 'Mayday' was probably the most fun I've ever had in working with this franchise.

"I do remember a time as I talk about it, we took a drive out to, we were in Vancouver, we took a drive up to Whistler. It was actually to visit a niece of mine who had taken a job out there. And on the way out 'Mayday' saw a sign about bungee jumping out in Whistler. And in true Brad May fashion, it was just something where we pulled off the Sea-to-Sky Highway and found the bridge where everybody was getting hooked up and to jump off this bridge and do a bungee jump.

"'Mayday' and 'Razor,' who was with us, and 'Razor's' kind of saying, 'you're not going to do it. You're not going to do it.' And that's all it took for Brad to get all hooked up. I remember Brad standing at the end of the platform and he was so afraid to make the jump, but he did it.

"We couldn't believe it as we watched him go over the edge. Little stories like that I think are really the ones that I'll forever hold in memory. It's really the camaraderie with those two guys, being on the road with them.

"It's a unique relationship between a couple of guys who really fought and bled for the Buffalo organization and then getting the opportunity to work together off-ice, I think it was a real highlight for those two as well. So it was great for me to be around those two. Brad, of course, is not working with us any longer. I wish he was. But he moved on and went on to work with Las Vegas for a little bit. And it's still a pleasure to work with 'Razor.'

"He and I spend a lot of close time away from the game when we're on the road; just talking about family and life and a little bit of hockey too. But mainly just about how you're coping with everything in life. And those are the parts of this game and being on the road that I enjoy."

As a quick aside to the bungee jumping story, Dunleavy made sure to later point out that only "Mayday" jumped.

DUNLEAVY: "'Mayday's' the only one who jumped. I looked at it and said, 'not a chance.'"

I can only imagine how faint of heart their Producer and Director were each feeling when the trio recounted the tale of their excursion to them later on.

DUNLEAVY'S FAVORITE SABRES GAME HE'S CALLED

There's nothing like overtime hockey. It's never expected and impossible to predict. And when you get beyond regulation, that's when memorable things occur. For Dunleavy, there was, at least on the surface, a rather innocent matchup between the San Jose Sharks and his Buffalo Sabres on February 7, 2017, that would soon become anything but.

San Jose was making its annual one-and-done trip to Buffalo to take on a Sabres team who was in the midst of its fourth consecutive sub-.500 season and hardly seemed like a worthy adversary for the playoff-bound Sharks. And yet, there they were dropping the puck for the opening face-off inside the KeyBank Center.

The Sabres' own Matt Moulson opened the scoring at the 7:24 mark of the first period with a power-play goal to give Buffalo a rather early 1-0 lead. Too bad it didn't last.

For much of the next 40 or so minutes, it was an all Sharks affair as San Jose scored four unanswered goals to take a 4-1 lead and only had just over half of the third period left to play in the game. Stick a fork in the Sabres, they were done. Or so we thought.

A power-play goal from Ryan O'Reilly cut the Sabres deficit to 4-2 and had the Buffalo fans hoping, praying for more. Then, in quick succession, Evander Kane (remember the name) and Kyle Okposo tallied goals of their own to bring the Sabres Faithful to their feet, in awe of what they just witnessed. Buffalo trailed no more! This was a brand new game with the score knotted at 4-4.

Neither team could score the go-ahead goal in regulation so they went to overtime, each hoping to secure the all-important second point. The fans in attendance, as well as the players on the ice and the broadcasters in the booth, didn't have to wait long to find out who came out victorious.

DUNLEAVY: "For me, there's just certain rinks where you can't help but immerse yourself in the atmosphere and enjoy the call of the game.

"I do remember a game, the Sabres were playing San Jose. Buffalo fell behind in the game and then found a way to muster up a rally and come back and win it.

"There was a play up ice that really cemented the victory. It was Jack Eichel along with Evander Kane, who as you can imagine, with Jack being such a fast skater, it's tough to find somebody who's able to keep up with his stride and speed up ice. And at this point in time, when Evander Kane was on the team, he was the one player who could fashion an odd-man rush in a hurry. And they did that.

"Jack carried the puck up the ice and he found Evander Kane over on his left and Evander buried it to really cement the comeback. The place was going crazy. I remember that call and I got a lot of messages from people who work in the industry, saying how much they enjoyed the call. It's nothing that you can ever think of. It just happens in the moment. It was a simple 'Eichel carries, Kane buries,' but it was just the energy and the tone and the pace and how the play developed that all of a sudden I had some co-workers throughout the industry saying, 'Hey, great call.'

"If I remember correctly, I think even RJ sent me a note saying, 'great job on the winning call.' That will always stand out for me."

MESSAGE TO SABRES FANS

As is a common theme amongst members of the sports media, it is a well known fact that without the fans our jobs would either A) not exist or B) they'd have a lot less meaning. So, each of the broadcasters in this book took a couple of minutes to address you, the fans, directly.

DUNLEAVY: "To Buffalo Sabres fans, thanks for being who you are. I mean, if you ever come to Buffalo and whether it's a Sabres fan or a Bills fan, you know what you get right out of the gate. There is absolutely nothing phony. They're very educated. They're very passionate. And certainly, since I came on board, I would say, because you're never going to have 100% when you've got Hall of Famers, like Rick Jeanneret ahead of you and Ted Darling, who preceded even RJ as the voice of the team, it can at times be a hard nut to crack because you're never going to be that guy.

"You're never going to be Sam Rosen. You're never going to be Doc Emrick. As good as John Forslund is, Doc set a real high bar for a guy like John, who I think will match it. But I would say to the people of Buffalo, I would say, thanks for welcoming the kid from Southern Ontario into a pretty lofty chair.

"People here made me feel very welcome. I understand that at times, there'll be nights where they wish it was RJ's voice of the call and it turns out it's mine. And over the years, we've kind of grown together. I thank people for letting me kinda have those years to grow into the role and understand and get to learn more about the people of Western New York and the fans of the Buffalo Sabres.

"Like I said, they're not phony; you know what you get right out of the gate. They're passionate. They love their teams. And they've had a lot of years of frustration in this city. I have said to our owner, Mr. Pegula, 'look, I'm here to call a Stanley Cup winner and it's going to happen.' And he just looked at me and he said, 'I'm going to hold you to that one.' So, one day that's going to come true. I can't put a date on it, but it's going to happen."

CALGARY FLAMES

RICK BALL
TV: PLAY-BY-PLAY

First Season on Flames TV: 2014-15
Seasons on Flames TV (including 2020-21): 7

Birthday: June 23, 1966 Hometown: Kelowna, BC

College/University: BC Institute of Technology

BIOGRAPHY

For those of you who want to become professional sports broadcasters, you need to know that there is no singular path to take. Oftentimes, the journey you embark on is a long, circular one that takes you through many different stops before you get to your preferred destination. And that usually takes years and years of hard work and patience. Not everybody has the intestinal fortitude to stick with it. But for those who do, the reward is often well worth it.

For Calgary's Rick Ball, the journey was a long arduous one, but one he enjoyed immensely and is still enjoying as the TV voice of the Flames broadcasts.

BALL: "I always loved hockey. It was hockey and football (American football). Those were my two favorite sports as a kid.

"In Canada we have the CFL, the Canadian Football League, which is basically American football with some weird rules specific to

Canada. I grew up as a big Vancouver Canucks fan and a big BC Lions fan. That was the football team in Vancouver.

"So those were my two loves in terms of being a sports fan. My dad was a sports fan as well. So, through him, I got interested in it and I started playing sports at a young age. I was not a good hockey player, oddly. It was just, hockey is an interesting sport. You really have a whole unique modality of getting around the playing surface that almost every other sport doesn't have. I mean, you learn to run five seconds after you learned to walk, but learning to skate is a whole other thing. And I was a terrible skater at a young age.

"I didn't take to hockey as a player really well. I gravitated more towards playing other sports because of that. So as I got older, I played football and basketball and really got into rugby at a later age; through High School. As much as I loved hockey, it wasn't my first love as a player, just because I was so bad at it.

"But I had a lot of appreciation for the game and what it took to play it at a high level. I still really, really enjoyed watching it though. So what wound up happening was, growing up in Kelowna, British Columbia, a smaller city, about four-hours sort of inland from Vancouver, kind of a resort town; they didn't have professional hockey.

"They had Junior Hockey there, which is the big feeder system into the NHL. So, I was a big fan of the local team and used to love listening to the games on the radio. And as I got a bit older, I realized that I wasn't going to be good enough to play sports at a high level beyond High School. But I always had an interest in broadcasting and it just so happened that the custodian in my High School was an old hockey coach and was the Analyst on the local Junior Hockey radio broadcasts. His name was Wayne Horning and Wayne kind of got wind that I was interested in broadcasting and just approached me one day.

"This was the custodian at the High School and said, 'I can introduce you to the Sports Director at the radio station, who also does the Play-by-Play.' I said, 'I'd love to meet him.' I just wanted to meet him. I mean, he was a local celebrity to me and just to see the inside of the radio station, I thought it would be pretty cool.

"So, he set up a meeting and the Sports Director's name was Brian Cooling and I was in 11th grade and Brian took a liking to me for whatever reason. I said to him at the end of that meeting, 'Hey, if you ever need anybody to fill in reports, like I played High School sports, from a basketball tournament or whatever, I'd be happy to call you and give you a report that you can use on the radio.' I assumed he would say no. But he said, 'yeah, sounds great.' So that's what I started doing. In High School, I started calling in reports, oftentimes from events that I played in, for the radio station.

"I loved doing it. I thought it was pretty cool. And back then, it's different now,I mean, radio is not what it used to be, but at the time it was big time. Even in a small city like Kelowna, being on the radio was pretty cool. So, I started doing that and that led to doing more. He'd sort of send me out to cover stuff and basically gave me gas money. I did it for free, but I just loved the whole idea of it.

"That kind of got my foot in the door; it really got me interested in the business. And through that experience, after I finished High School, I got into the broadcast journalism program at BCIT, which was, especially at that time, really tough to get into. They had a ton of applicants and only accepted a few.

"So the fact that I had a little bit of practical experience and some good words from people who worked at the radio station, got me in the door there. And when I graduated, I got hired back full-time as an employee, as opposed to a stringer at that same station. So that's how I got started.

"I don't want to say I sort of fell into it, but it kind of happened by fluke. I never thought of it as a career, ever, until an opportunity was presented to me and it's kind of funny how certain things nudge you onto a path and I got that and really enjoyed it."

Even with his small amount of experience, Ball proved he could handle the work. And he was able to use what he learned to shape his broadcasting style. Of course, he was also able to draw on those broadcasters who had inspired him in the first place.

BALL: "When I was growing up and even when I started working in the business, early on in my career, every game wasn't on television back then. People forget this. But I mean, you might get like in Vancouver, you'd get a Wednesday night game on one of the local stations and then you'd get the Hockey Night in Canada game on Saturday, and that'd be it. I mean, you might get 25-games a year on TV.

"So what wound up happening for fans of the Vancouver Canucks and probably almost every other sports team, because TV wasn't as prevalent as it is now, is the radio became the game.

"A guy who I got to know through the course of my career and is just a wonderful man, his name is Jim Robson. He's in the Hockey Hall of Fame in the Broadcaster Wing and deservedly so. I got to listen to him from as early as I can remember on the radio. And that was the vast majority of games that you had to experience because most of them were not on television.

"So Jim Robinson was the Vancouver Canucks to me. It was lucky for me to have a guy of that caliber calling those games that I listened to. I remember as a kid laying in bed, I had my little clock radio and would put the hockey game on to fall asleep. That would be Jim Robson calling the Canucks games. He was just a great broadcaster and a terrific person on top of all that.

"So my two influences early on were him and then the gentleman I mentioned earlier, who was the local Play-by-Play guy for the Junior team in Kelowna, named Brian Cooling. They were my sort of two main guys. And then in terms of a National guy, I was a huge Bob Cole fan and still am to this day. He was the main voice on Hockey Night in Canada for decades. When I was growing up, he was the guy who was calling all the big games. He called the Stanley Cup Finals, all the big international games. He was the voice of every major game that you watched on a national level. Those were the three main guys, but less so Bob, because I didn't hear him as much.

"Jim Robson was the guy who influenced me the most. Jim was a very sort of detail oriented guy. He wasn't over the top. He wasn't flashy in any way, but he was just right on top of the play, very descriptive. His word economy was excellent and he knew his stuff. He had a really good sort of way to reflect what was going on on the ice with the inflection of his voice and yet not be over the top. And I think when you hear a lot of guys who've come out of Vancouver as Play-by-Play guys, there's been a lot of guys who've gone on to have national broadcasts.

"I've done a bunch of Hockey Night in Canada games. Jim Hughson is a BC guy, who's the main Hockey Night in Canada guy now. John Shorthouse, the Canucks Play-by-Play guy is a really good broadcaster. And we all sort of, we're not exactly like Jim Robson, but you can hear the influence in all of us in that we're not over the top guys; whereas you go to other cities where the Play-by-Play guy is much more energetic. And they were influenced by the guys they heard.

"So there's no doubt in my mind that the lineage of BC Play-by-Play, hockey guys in particular, doing hockey the way they do it, is a direct connection to the way Jim Robson called games, because we all listened to him and we're influenced by what we heard."

Now it's time to find out about the long circular journey I mentioned earlier. Ball's career has taken him all over and through multiple different roles and sports. The passion he displayed and still displays for broadcasting is what kept him going and hopefully Flames fans take notice of that.

BALL: "So, I was in Kelowna and then I actually went to a place called Prince George, which is in central BC, for a year because it was also a TV station; I wanted to get some TV experience. So, I was in Prince George for a year; that would have been in '87-'88 out of school. I worked in Kelowna full-time for a year and went to Prince George for a year.

"I thought I'd get a taste of doing some television as well as radio; it was a combination up there. And then I wound up going back to Kelowna after that and spent the next, I want to say eight-years or so in Kelowna; maybe nine. So, after that year in Prince George, I wound up going back to Kelowna and it actually wound up being a really good move because what happened when I went back to Kelowna, after a little while, the Western Hockey League came to town. The Western Hockey League is the top tier of Junior Hockey.

"There's three leagues in Canada that are at the top. They call it Major Junior. That's where most of your NHL talent comes from. They got a team in Kelowna called the Rockets, in 1995 and I was able to do the Play-by-Play.

"For a couple seasons before that I was doing Play-by-Play for a lower tier team. We did the playoffs and that was my first taste of it. But once the Rockets came to town I applied for that job. I was already working at the station that got the rights and I wound up getting it. It really turned my career in a whole different direction because that's when I got a taste of Play-by-Play; that's what I really wanted to pursue.

"So, when the Rockets came to town, we did every game on the radio. They had a 70-game season plus playoffs. So that was a ton of experience. I wound up doing that and rode the buses across Western Canada and the Northwest U.S. They have teams in Portland, Seattle, in Spokane and from as far away as Portland, Oregon; all the way across the border of Manitoba, which a bus between those two is about a 20-hour bus ride. And that's how they traveled.

"As a Play-by-Play guy, you climb onto that iron lung and you rumble across the frozen Tundra of the Canadian Prairie's for seven-months out of the year, calling Junior Hockey games out of medium-sized towns across the country and down into The States.

"I loved every minute of it. I mean, the bus travel drove me crazy after a while, but doing the games, I would not trade it for the world. And you're doing Play-by-Play 70-80 times a year. That's the only way to get better at it. I have young broadcasters all the time, send me demo tapes and ask me for advice. The one thing I say is 'just do as many games as you can; even if it's just talking into your iPhone at some minor hockey rink calling a game.' You've got to practice. I went from a guy with very little Play-by-Play experience to a ton of it and went from probably being pretty awful to start to being half decent after five-years.

"So that's how I cut my teeth, doing hockey Play-by-Play in the Western Hockey League with the Kelowna Rockets. They were great to work with. The Hamilton family, Bruce Hamilton and Gavin Hamilton, ran the team. They still own it. It's become a cornerstone franchise in the Western Hockey League. They've been really successful there. It was just a great experience and really pushed my career along. So I did that from 1995 to 2000. And then, after I was doing that for a few years, I thought these (game recordings) aren't half bad. I'm not a big self-promoter.

"So I reached out to the Vancouver Canucks, just a cold call to their Director of Broadcasting at the time. His name was Chris Hebb. I got a hold of him and said, 'Hey, you don't know me probably, but my name is Rick Ball. I'm doing Play-by-Play in Kelowna and I'd love to come and say, hi, maybe drop off a demo one-day when I'm in Vancouver.' And he said, 'sure, let me know when you're in town.'

"I went to Vancouver the following summer on a trip to visit some friends and gave him a call. And he said, 'come on down.' We had a good meeting. At that time, you weren't sending MP3 files. You were still burning stuff on a CD. So I gave him a CD and he said, 'keep in touch.' I said, 'great.' I phoned him a few months later and he said, 'Hey, I really like your stuff.' I said, 'Oh great.' He said, 'just keep in touch.' So, every once or twice a year, I'd call and see how it's going.

"And then, that final year I was in Kelowna, he called me up and he said, 'would you be interested in doing some fill-in work on Canucks television Play-by-Play this next season?' And I said, 'yes, of course.' They had a situation 'cause Jim Hughson was calling the Canucks games -- the regional games -- but he was also doing national games at that time. And there were going to be the odd handful of games that next season where he would be either doing a national game or in transit getting from one place to another where he couldn't do the regional games and they needed somebody to fill-in. That's how I got my foot in the door.

"So, in 2000-01, I had actually left Kelowna and was working in Victoria. I had an opportunity to go there and work at another radio station. I was not doing Play-by-Play anymore. Oddly, I was just kind of the News and Sports Director. After five-years of riding the bus, as much as I loved that, I just couldn't do it anymore. So I got this opportunity to go to Victoria, which is on Vancouver Island. That's the same year that Chris Hebb called me up and said, 'Hey, we'd like you to do some games this year.' So I said, 'sure.' The station I was working at said, 'yeah, you can do them. We'll figure it out.' I think they wanted me to do 10, maybe 12 games that year on TV. But it was only for one-year. That conflict was only that year. So it wasn't like a long-term thing. It was just a short-term stop gap. They told me that going in. They said, 'listen, this is only going to be for this season. We're not going to have this issue next year.' I said, 'no problem. I'm going to do it anyway.'

"That was my first NHL experience, doing Canucks games on television in 2000 and 2001, while I was still doing a radio job in Victoria. So I was pretty busy. I'd do my regular gig, hop on the plane, fly to Vancouver or Chicago or New York or wherever they happened to be playing and hook up with the team there and come back. It was difficult then too, because it wasn't like now where you can get information and stay on top of everything.

"Again, not every game was televised and you didn't have the internet; at least not at the level that it's at now, where you can find out stuff as easily as you can. So it was a pretty good chore to try and stay sharp when you're not doing every game. But what wound up happening was, by doing those games at the same time, there was an all-sports radio station going on the air in Vancouver.

"So that got my name into the Vancouver market, which is the major city on the West coast in Canada. The radio station had gotten in touch with me and wanted to bring me over. And that's what wound up happening. So, from that experience, I was working in Victoria, doing Canucks games on television in Vancouver and across BC and then that brought me into the new all sports radio station in Vancouver; except they didn't have the Canucks rights yet. But what they did get as soon as I got there was the rights to the BC Lions football team in the Canadian Football League team.

"So in 2003, when I got hired at the radio station in Vancouver and now was working full-time in Vancouver for the first time; that next season they got the football. Even though I hadn't really done much football Play-by-Play, I grew up playing the sport, even coached it for a while; in minor football when I was still in Kelowna. So I got the job doing the BC Lions on the radio. So I called football for the next 10-years as well and did that in Vancouver as well.

"Then a few years after they got the football rights, they also wound up getting the Canucks rights. It might've been 2007, that the Canucks rights came over, maybe 2006. But they already had a very good Play-by-Play guy, he's still there, in John Shorthouse. So he came with them and kept doing the games on the radio. Now working at the same station I was on; until Jim Hughson left, who was doing regional television and went full-time to National TV in Canada. And then John took over the TV job in Vancouver and it left an opening with the radio.

"That was in 2008 and that's when I started doing Canucks on the radio as well. So I had that taste of the Canucks, filling in on those TV games in 2000-01 and I didn't do another NHL game until 2008. The way that it worked with John was that he kept doing the radio. The regional TV package was like 60 Canucks games.

"So he'd do the 20-games he wasn't doing on television, on the radio. I'd do the rest. They actually had another guy for a brief time as well, named Joey Kenward. But it wound up just being me and John. So I would do like 60-games on the radio when John was doing TV, plus I was still doing BC Lions football. And at the time I still was doing my own talk show, so I was really busy. But that became untenable. After a while I convinced the program director, it's impossible to do 60-hockey games, 20-football games and a full-time talk show. I just couldn't do it. So the next year I transitioned full-time to just doing Play-by-Play for football and hockey.

"I was doing Canucks and Lions on the radio and when the 2011 season came, the Canucks went to The Final and lost to Boston in seven that year. So, the hockey season was over and I was actually in Edmonton. The Canadian Football League starts in June and goes through November. So it was like late June, early July. And I was sitting in Edmonton to do a football game when I got an email from Joel Darling, who's one of the Executive Producers at Hockey Night in Canada. I'd never talked to him in my life.

"It just said, 'hi, it's Joel Darling with Hockey Night in Canada, please call me when you get a second.' I was like, 'okay.' So I called him back. What happened was the Atlanta Thrashers moved back to Winnipeg that summer.

"So all of a sudden, Hockey Night in Canada, which is like the Monday Night Football equivalent of hockey in Canada; they had an extra Canadian team they would have to cover and work into their schedule. So I spoke to Hockey Night in Canada and they were like, 'we're going to need somebody to do some games this year, because now we have one more Canadian team to do and there's going to be some games where we need to hire an extra crew. It won't be full-time but would you be interested in doing some work for Hockey Night in Canada?' I was like, 'yes.'

"That was the 2011-2012 season. I wound up doing six or seven Winnipeg Jets games that year, plus I was still doing the Lions and the Canucks on the radio.

"Then, the next year they had me actually stay out west and do the primary Western games. So it was basically: Vancouver, Edmonton and Calgary Hockey Night in Canada games. So 2011-12, 2012-13, 2013-14, those three seasons, I was doing Hockey Night in Canada on top of my other stuff. And it all was going pretty well. Hockey Night seemed very happy and it looked like it was going to transition into something even bigger and better."

Hold on to your hats Flames fans, we're almost up to you. You see, the "bigger and better" thing that Ball referenced, was the possibility of CBC getting football rights on top of hockey. But Rogers, a competing company, swooped in and landed the contracts that CBC wanted. And that left Ball in an interesting place.

BALL: "So, I was in Vancouver. I could have still kept doing the radio for the Canucks and for the Lions, but there would be no television component. So Rogers contacted me and they said, 'we'd love to bring you on board, but we already have John doing the Canucks games in Vancouver. So would you be interested in moving to Calgary?' And that's how that got started.

"We talked for a few months and since they controlled basically all of hockey television in the country, it seemed like a no brainer to me. I could've stayed in Vancouver and I would have loved that. But it seemed pretty clear to me that the move to make was to take the Rogers job, which is SportsNet and go to Calgary. So that's how I wound up in Calgary, which is another city I really like."

FAVORITE PLAYER(S) GROWING UP

BALL: "When I was a kid we had these player card collectible books that one of the gas station chains in Canada had. I remember I got all my different player cards of the Vancouver Canucks. The only one I was missing was Gary Smith, who was the goalie for the Canucks at the time. I was probably seven-years-old, maybe six at the time. I was so focused on getting the Gary Smith card that he became my favorite player at that time; just because of my pursuit of getting the Gary Smith card to finish off my collection of Canucks players. I really liked him.

"Then, when I got a little bit older when I probably knew a little bit more about the sport and followed the team in a more detailed way, guys like Stan Smyl, who was the captain of that Cinderella team in '82, that went to the Stanley Cup Final before they bowed out to the New York Islanders. Thomas Gradin was a really skilled European player. He played for the Vancouver Canucks; loved him. Harold Snepsts was a character guy back on the blue line.

"But my first memory of a Canucks player who I really enamored with was goalie Gary Smith. And it was for reasons that had nothing to do with how he played on the ice, but more to do with what seemed like an impossible pursuit of getting his player card."

HOCKEY AFTER DARK -- TALES AWAY FROM THE RINK

There are off the wall things that can happen to broadcasters and those experiences usually make for the best stories. Now, not all broadcasters are willing to share what happened and while others are. I'm happy to say that Rick Ball falls into the latter category. There are many ways I could try to describe his off-ice story, but I wouldn't do it justice, so, Rick, take it away.

BALL: "I've got a good story from Junior Hockey. You ride the bus everywhere when you're doing Junior Hockey. So, we were in Spokane, Washington, I was doing a Kelowna Rockets game. Bruce Hamilton, who owned the Rockets, was on the trip. And he said, 'Rick, there's a big snow storm blowing in tonight. We want to get the hell out of here as soon as this game's over. So you make your post-game show short as it can be, 'cause we gotta get outta here. I want to beat the storm.' I said, 'okay.' Game ends. Post-game show was like two-minutes. I was like, 'Rockets win 5-3, good-night everybody.' I packed up my stuff and rushed down to the bus. And then I realized, normally at the end of the game, I would tell the operator back at the radio station, 'Hey, roll tape. I'll give you a report that you can run tomorrow morning.

"But I forgot to do it because I was in a hurry. So the bus pulled out, snow was already starting to fall. They pulled into a Bobs Big Boy or something to get some hamburgers for the boys to eat on the bus, 'cause we want to get out of there. So, as the bus pulled into this parking lot, guys hopped off, I thought, 'Okay. So, perfect chance.' I had one of those old, big brick cell phones.

"So I hopped off the bus. I didn't want to do a report on the bus. I was standing in the parking lot and called the control room. I said, 'roll tape. I'll give you the report for the morning.' So, I was standing in the parking lot. By this point I'd changed into sweat pants and a t-shirt 'cause it's like a seven-hour bus ride. Standing in my running shoes. Snow was coming down and I'm like 'Rockets win 5-3, a couple of goals by Brett McLean. A nice game-clincher in the third period by Jason Deleurme.' And as I was talking, I had my back to the bus. I heard, behind me, the bus starting to pull away.

"Nobody realized I got off because they grabbed the burgers and got back on. I hopped off quietly. I was sitting there in the front. I looked and at that point the snow was up to my ankles. It was five below zero. I was in a t-shirt and sweatpants. My wallet, my money, it was all on the bus. All I saw was the tail lights going down the road, 'like, are you kidding me?'

"So I started running down the road. I caught up to the bus just as it was starting to gain speed. I was banging on the side of the bus with my cell phone. 'Hey, bleep, bleep, bleep, wait for me.' Anyway, thank God, one of the players noticed and said, 'stop.' They stopped the bus and I got on. Of course I was getting ridiculed. They were all laughing at me. What I didn't realize was I had not hung up the phone. So this entire episode was being recorded back at the radio station.

"The over-under on how many times that got played on the air over the next week is about 10,000, because you could hear it perfectly. You could hear the brakes let go in the background. You heard the bus pulling away, me screaming.

"So I learned a valuable lesson that day; never get caught with the bus leaving. Always be early and if you're going to step off, let somebody know you're heading out for a half a second. I might still be standing there in that parking lot at a Bobs Big Boy in Spokane in a block of ice all these years later, if things hadn't gone the other way."

BALL'S FAVORITE FLAMES GAME HE'S CALLED

Sometimes a game, rather than being defined or remembered for its entirety, is rather remembered for one or two individual moments. That doesn't mean the game has to be low-scoring or low on action. It just means that so much happened in the game that the one or two standout moments were just head and shoulders above everything else that happened.

For the Calgary Flames and Rick Ball that game was Halloween Night 2019, in the town of Nashville.

BALL: “It happened on October 31st 2019. It was the Calgary Flames and the Nashville Predators in Nashville. First of all, I love Nashville. It's just such a fun city. And it's a really great vibe in the arena. It's turned into a terrific hockey market. So the building was buzzing as it always is. And it was one of those wild back and forth games where the Flames wound up tying the game. Matthew Tkachuk scored in the final minute of regulation to tie it up. I think it was 5-5. It was a high scoring game.

“Then they went to overtime and in overtime, with time winding down, one last rush up the ice, Tkachuk came in over the blue line. I think he tried a shot but it got blocked. It came back to him and then he put the puck between his legs from the face-off dot; we're not talking in tight, like way out. He shot a wrist-shot, top corner for the game-winning goal with under a second ago in the game; in overtime.

“That's one of those games you dream of as a Play-by-Play guy. People always go, 'what do you like to see? What do you want?' I want a good game. That's the biggest thing to me. A good game makes my job easy. And that game was easy. Kelly (Hrudey) and I had so much fun. It took me a second to kind of process what had happened. I said to Kelly, 'did he put that between his legs?!' And Kelly was like, 'yes, he did!' I couldn't believe it. And that was just one of those games. It was just such a crazy game.”

FREQUENT PHRASE

Not every sports broadcaster has a catchphrase or saying that is unique to them. Some are actively against having such a phrase as part of their repertoire because they feel it’s disingenuous. However, you can still have something you’re known for saying without it being a catchphrase and that’s exactly the case with Rick Ball.

BALL: "Whenever there's some milling about or some pushing and shoving after a whistle and it winds up dissipating and they skate back to their bench, I'll often say 'cooler heads prevail.' It's a cliche, but I do use that one on a semi-regular basis. So, people like to associate 'cooler heads prevail' with me. I heard that phrase from Brian Cooling, who was the Sports Director who hired me for my first job, he used to say on the Junior Hockey broadcasts, 'cooler heads prevailed,' when I was growing up in Kelowna; all the time. And so, that is an homage to one of my first mentors in the business."

MESSAGE TO FLAMES FANS

As is a common theme amongst members of the sports media, it is a well known fact that without the fans our jobs would either A) not exist or B) they'd have a lot less meaning. So, each of the broadcasters in this book took a couple of minutes to address you, the fans, directly.

BALL: "I think there's been a lot of frustration because the team has had some good regular seasons and has not been able to translate that into playoff success. My message would be, don't panic. There are a lot of really good pieces on this team and I think they've got some good minds in charge of the organization. I think the future is bright. That doesn't mean it's perfect, or that there aren't issues that need to be addressed. No, but I like what they've got going on here on a lot of different levels and that would be my message to Calgary Flames fans: don't panic."

CAROLINA HURRICANES

TRIPP TRACY
TV/RADIO (SIMULCAST): COLOR ANALYST

First Season on Hurricanes TV/Radio (Simulcast): 1998-99
Seasons on Hurricanes TV/Radio (Simulcast) (including 2020-21): 23

Birthday: December 20, 1973 Hometown: Grosse Pointe Farms, MI

College/University: Harvard

BIOGRAPHY

There's no one way to become a professional sports broadcaster. In fact, in life, there's no one way to do just about anything. There's always a different path to take; you just have to keep an open mind and be honest with yourself.

Well, for those of you who don't know Tripp Tracy, that's exactly how his broadcasting career unfolded. You might even argue that's how his playing career came about as well.

TRACY: "When I was maybe five or six, somehow we went to a local rink and I don't know if my sister was figure skating or if I saw some hockey players in these cool helmets, but I said to my mom and dad, 'I really would like to play.' And they said, 'well, you're going to have to take a year of figure skating first,' which wasn't that appealing to me at the time. But I did.

"That was when I first fell in love with the sport. I bounced around at different positions before I ended up in goal. Then it was a very, very big decision in our family. I think when I was around nine or 10, because I made the travel hockey team and any parents would be able to tell you that if you commit to it, your holidays are different because you're going to hockey tournaments. For your siblings, if they're not playing, I had an older sister, their lives are different and we had a big vote as to whether or not I would be able to play on the travel team.

"My dad actually, who's since passed away, he voted no, but my mom voted yes. But then my dad totally fell in love with it."

There's actually a quick aside to this story.

TRACY: "The reason I tell you that story is because, when the Hurricanes won the Stanley Cup and I got the Stanley Cup for a day, my dad loved wine when he was alive. And I asked him what year that was, he didn't know why I was asking about when we voted about travel hockey. And he said, 'I think it was 1982 and 1982 was probably the favorite year of his favorite French wines. So he drank that 1982 out of the Stanley Cup."

Getting back to how Tracy's career path unfolded it's important to take note of his broadcast influences.

TRACY: "(My favorites were) Bob Cole, Harry Neale, Ron MacLean and Don Cherry, because where I am in Grosse Pointe, I can look over my shoulder, look over and see Windsor across the Lake. So, we got, aside from the American network, whoever it was at that point in time, we got CBC. We got Hockey Night in Canada. So, Bob and Harry and then obviously Ron and Don. Truthfully, that's why, (the game) when Carolina won (the Stanley Cup in 2006), they were playing Edmonton, Ron MacLean and Don Cherry asked me to come on after; that was with Ron and Kelly Hrudey.

"For me, that was an amazing thing, because I grew up with those guys. I've had very good relationships with all four. And that's what hockey gives you. Harry Neale specifically has been a mentor to me. Jim Rutherford, in the lockout of 2004-2005, encouraged me to get in touch with Harry Neale. I was a little intimidated to do so, even though I don't know why I was. Harry's such a wonderful guy. Keith Jackson, who called Michigan football games, would also be one who jumps out at me.

"I don't know if I learned anything because I'm a color guy, not a Play-by-Play guy, but I've always been a big golf fan, so Jim Nantz. Joe Morgan who just passed away, I remember watching him and how much I thoroughly enjoyed his analysis; very, very, very much so. Tim McCarver, maybe one other guy who, early in my broadcast career, I recognized.

"And then, at the NHL level, the person who really helped me right away and again, Jim Rutherford deserves a lot of credit, because he suggested that I talk to him. When I first started, for my first several years, John Davidson was doing color for the Rangers and those Rangers teams, pre-salary cap, for a couple of those years had the highest payroll in hockey and stunk.

"JD found a way with Sam, both who I'm very proud to call good friends. I love Sam Rosen and Kenny (Albert). You're talking about ultra great people, Joe Micheletti is right in that group too. But JD found a way with those bad Rangers teams to be able to point out and satisfy a Rangers fan as to why they weren't succeeding, without throwing a player and/or the organization under the bus. And he would simultaneously be able to sell the game and entertain.

"Later, that would probably be the single biggest piece of advice that I try to utilize in the 10-years that the Hurricanes didn't make the playoffs, between 2009 and 2019."

But how and why did Tracy go from playing to broadcasting in the first place?

TRACY: "I'd gotten drafted by the Flyers, who didn't sign me. I went into Hartford and I had a very good camp but Jean-Sebastien Giguere was a first-round pick, so I split time between the East Coast Hockey League and the American Hockey League both years. And really, I thought that to be able to feel like this was progressing correctly, I needed to graduate to being the call-up guy. So, the third guy in the organization and that didn't happen.

"I can admit this now, too. It's not hard for me to admit because it helps me and I don't have any regrets. But I was able to admit to myself that I stunk. But I was able to admit to myself that something happened when I was in college.

"I think it was somewhere in college, sophomore, junior year, that I went from expecting to win, to hoping to win. And wanting to make that big save and fearing giving up a tough goal when the game's on the line. As a goaltender, let alone any athlete, that's not a spot you want to be in. How it happened, I'm not sure. I did a couple of different things with my goaltending coach.

"I mean, my freshman year in Harvard, I was in the top leaderboard, right there in the top-five, maybe even top-three of goals-against and save percentage in the country. I did a couple of things different in the off-season. I don't know if that contributed. So, after the two-years, whether knowing or subconsciously, but knowing that I had been able to put on an NHL Jersey and have my parents in the stands and see that made it an easier decision.

"Once I saw I wasn't gonna be any higher on the Hurricanes depth chart, I started thinking about the next thing. Tim Thomas and I had some heated battles in college; they went both ways. When he was in Vermont, I was at Harvard and he's from Detroit here. We're very close friends. If I had dug in and did what he did and went to Europe, look, he was 28, 29, when he finally broke into the National Hockey League. Would I have been able to achieve the same journey? And I say, 'no,' because he was more talented than I was. Mentally he had that 'it factor' of what I'm saying somehow I lost.

"However people feel because broadcasting is a subjective business, no matter who you are. The best broadcasters, I mean, gosh, Vin Scully might even have some people who don't think he's any good. I doubt it. But I mean, it's a very subjective business. What I lost in a mental swagger, when I did that thing with Ron MacLean on Hockey Night in Canada after Game Seven, however many million people were watching, I was totally at ease totally and completely confident. However you feel about me, completely confident in my capabilities. And I said to myself as I was sitting down, 'this is what I lacked on the ice at the end.' So it was the right decision. Because of that, I've never had any regrets.

"When I decided to stop playing, I got a job essentially as an intern production assistant at CNNSI in Atlanta. I had no idea that within a month or six weeks, the Color Analyst for the Carolina Hurricanes, Bill Gardner would leave to go to Chicago and that Pete Karmanos Jr. who was the owner of the team, would take a chance on me with essentially zero experience. Really, essentially zero experience. So I was just trying to figure out how I was going to start to formulate my path in broadcasting and then that happened. So that's really essentially what went down."

It's now been over two-decades since Tracy joined the Hurricanes' broadcast booth and he's showing no signs of slowing down; which is music to the ears of Caniac fans everywhere.

FAVORITE PLAYER(S) GROWING UP

TRACY: "I would say, over the course of time, for my own position of goal, I loved watching Grant Fuhr; the way that he attacked the puck. Kevin Weekes and I always talk about those DNR Laser pads he wore. In the big scheme of things, two people, Steve Yzerman, based on everything he went through here in Detroit before he had success and he was living actually about a half-a-mile from my family. So I always was a huge Steve Yzerman fan. And a guy who played and had some very good years in the NHL and took me under his wing, Jimmy Carson, who scored 50-goals with the LA Kings.

"When he broke in with Luc Robitaille, Jimmy used to, actually there were a couple situations, where he was holding out and one in particular, before he came to the Red Wings from Edmonton. He used to, when he was trying to stay in shape, come out and shoot on me.

"I was 13 or 14, I want to say and here was a guy who scored 50 in the National Hockey League and he treated me like I was just one of the boys. He's from my hometown, went to the same high school. So Jimmy Carson would be a guy who definitely jumped out at me.

"I remember a neat story with Steve Yzerman. The year Detroit finally got over the hump and won their first Stanley Cup in 1997, I had been with Springfield in the American Hockey League and we got to the Calder Cup Semi-Finals where we lost to Hershey, the eventual Calder Cup champions.

"I came home and watched Steve and the Red Wings finally win The Cup against somebody who would become one of my dearest friends in hockey, Rod Brind'Amour; but I didn't know Rod at the time.

"So, I was playing golf the next week at a club here and Steve was taking a lesson. I ended up walking up to him at the driving range and he said to me, 'Tripp, I saw you got called up to the NHL. I just wanted to congratulate you.' I couldn't believe that because, when I was up, I backed up one game. I was only up for three-games against Dallas, Ottawa and the Rangers.

"He really would've had to be watching the transactions to know. It's not like it was headline material. So after he said the transaction occurred I said to him, 'you know, Steve, I got back from the American League and being able to watch you hoist the Stanley Cup was one of the great moments in my life.' He looked at me and in that world-class humor of his, he said, 'Tripp, I really hope your life gets better.'"

HOCKEY AFTER DARK -- TALES AWAY FROM THE RINK

Several decades ago, it was commonplace for professional athletes and sports media to develop friendships outside of the standard reporter-player relationship. You might go for a beer together after a game. You might even double-date.

However, thanks to the advent of social media and the rise of public relations executives, those days are firmly in the past.

But, every now and again, you do hear about a handful of players who managed to bond with one of the media people who cover them; usually it's a broadcaster for the team. And that's exactly what happened with the Carolina Hurricanes and Tripp Tracy.

TRACY: "I'm 46-years-old. I guess I would have been 45 at the time. The 'Canes hadn't made the playoffs in 10-years. And you know, as you get older, you get more seasoned so there's that natural separation between the broadcasters and the players, which is healthy, it becomes more and more. But I really enjoyed the group, these last couple of groups of Hurricanes.

"So, I screw around with them. I'm a young guy at heart. So, the team gets back in the playoffs, beats Washington, beats the Islanders and loses to Boston. A bunch of guys, Jordan Martinook, Petr Mrazek, Justin Faulk and Brock McGinn asked me to go down to Miami for one night together. And, I said, 'screw you guys, I'm your Color Analyst, I ain't going.' They said, 'we want you, will you come?' And I went.

"We took a plane down together and we had a great night. That was a lot of fun, because it's somewhat unique in Carolina. That's pretty special. I'm no spring chicken anymore. When I first got the job, I had friends who were on the team who I had played with in the American Hockey League and I was their age. I mean, most of the guys, when I first started, were older than me.

"I think I started at 23, 24, but now I'm an older guy. And for guys to connect like that, for us to connect, knowing that I have a job to do and they have a job to do, that doesn't get in the way. Maybe that means I'm doing it, to some degree correctly, like John Davidson did with regards to, when teams lose, pointing it out without throwing the player, the team or the organization under the bus."

And there's one other story that Tracy is fond of.

TRACY: "The team invited John Forslund and I into the dressing room after they won Game Seven, with just the boys and the Stanley Cup at the end of all of that. That was pretty neat. And as I mentioned, when I came back to that Detroit Red Wing victory in 1997 and Rod Brind'Amour was on the other side, I didn't know Rod at the time.

"The only thing I knew about Rod was that I played Junior Hockey with a great NHLer named Brian Rolston and when he went in the first-round in New Jersey, I remember him saying to me, 'Tripp, you're not going to get over this Rod Brind'Amour guy. He won't even put on the jersey until he makes the NHL.' That's the only thing I knew about him. And so, when he got traded, he ended up being my closest friend in the Hurricanes organization.

"We've had some very powerful moments over the years where I'd like to think we've proven the Frank Sinatra line of, 'a friend in need is a pest,' to be untrue; as much as I love Frank. Then, the big one is when Rod asked me to walk his mom down the aisle at his wedding."

TRACY'S FAVORITE HURRICANES GAMES HE'S CALLED

When you've been at the broadcast game as long as Tripp Tracy has, it's difficult to pick just one game that stands out as your most memorable, so he chose a handful.

TRACY: "In 2002, The 'Molson Miracle,' which was Carolina and Montreal in the second-round. Montreal was up two-one in the series. And I want to say they (the Canadiens) were up 3-0 after the second period. Ron Francis said (during the second intermission), 'Hey, we haven't thrown the kitchen sink at him yet.' The 'Canes came back and Niclas Wallin, who was just a super Hurricane, scored the winner in overtime."

For those of you unfamiliar with "The Molson Miracle," let me give you a little backstory.

It was the Spring of 2002 and the Hurricanes and Canadiens were squaring off in the second-round of the playoffs. The teams traded victories in the first two games before Montreal won "The Swing" game, Game Three to go up two-one in the series.

With momentum firmly on their side, Montreal headed into Game Four looking to push the Hurricanes to the brink of elimination and for the first 40-minutes of the game things went according to the Canadiens' plans. Armed with a 3-0 lead to start the third period, Montreal was 20-minutes away from taking a commanding 3-1 series lead.

That's when things got interesting.

Carolina scored three times in the third on goals from Sean Hill, Bates Battaglia and Erik Cole to tie the game at 3-3 and force overtime. (Cole's goal was scored with Carolina's net empty for the extra attacker).

Then, just 3:14 into overtime, Wallin scored to tie the series at two-games apiece and give Carolina the push it needed to eventually get past Montreal and head to the Conference Final.

Of course, that game also served as a precursor to Tracy's second memorable game; which took place four-years later (in 2006) and again featured a matchup between Montreal and Carolina.

TRACY: "Montreal has such a spectacular TV booth location with that gondola hanging over the ice, which probably made this next one even more memorable to be able to call in the first-round against Montreal. Montreal was really good that year. They won the first two games in Raleigh. Game Three, you've gone from Martin Gerber, who was an outstanding regular season goaltender and a huge reason the Hurricanes ended up winning The Cup, to Cam Ward who took over.

"You got a very good, underrated Montreal team, at home with a 2-0 lead. The place was going bonkers. I mean, Thank God. I would just try to get off the open of our broadcast so I could lose my microphone before I had to put on my headset and look and see, cause they would play U2's -- maybe my favorite band of all-time -- 'Where the Streets Have No Name' before the Canadiens hit the ice. And it was just unbelievable, with the light show on the ice. It's the best broadcast booth in the National Hockey League.

"So Game Three (Richard) Zednik scored in the second period. The Habs were up 1-0. Justin Williams high-sticked Saku Koivu unintentionally, but Koivu was knocked out for the rest of the series. Justin didn't even get a penalty. That was a break. So, in the third period, the 'Canes weren't generating much at all and they were about to go down 3-0 to a very good Montreal team. And a play that Bret Hedican and Rod Brind'Amour actually talked about between periods, right underneath, with that broadcast viewpoint and Roddy got a cross ice pass from Bret and just willed the puck into the net.

"And then Eric Staal ended up scoring on the power-play in overtime. The Hurricanes won four straight and won that series. I firmly believe, that was by far, the most significant victory of the 16 that you need to win the Stanley Cup. That it was your captain who just willed the puck home. A captain who had been to the Stanley Cup Final before and hadn't won. Another guy, Bret Hedican, who had been to two previous Stanley Cup Finals and had set it up, hadn't won. Being able to call that game, that moment, which I believe to be an iconic Hurricanes moment, is particularly memorable."

On to the next of Tracy's favorite games.

In the Spring of 2009, the Hurricanes were back in the playoffs for the first time since winning the Stanley Cup in 2006. Carolina survived a grueling seven-game series with the New Jersey Devils to set up a second-round date with the Boston Bruins.

Boston took Game One before Carolina took the next three. With a 3-1 series lead entering game Five, the Hurricanes appeared poised to move onto the Eastern Conference Final; but first, Boston had a little something to say.

The Bruins won Games Five and Six, but it was towards the end of Game Five when tempers flared and Carolina's Scott Walker punched Boston's Aaron Ward in the face and did significant damage to Ward. The Bruins were irate over the apparent sucker punch and were further incensed when the League rescinded its suspension of Walker, handing him just a $2,500.00 fine.

So, with the series tied at three-games apiece and in need of a Game Seven, plus with the subplots that go on in a series like this, who ended up being the hero for Carolina? That's right, it was Scott Walker.

With the score tied at two and the first overtime period nearly complete, Ray Whitney fired a shot from the right-wing boards towards Bruins netminder Tim Thomas, who could not absorb the puck. Walker flew down the slot and cashed in the loose puck for the series-clinching goal with 1:14 left in the overtime period.

TRACY: "Being with John Forslund and just seeing him call the Scott Walker overtime-winner and then finding out that Scott Walker's wife, Julia had been diagnosed with cancer during the course of that series. It was pretty neat to see Walker have such a nice on ice moment. I can still see that vividly from the visiting booth in Boston."

Of course, there have been other memorable games in Tracy's broadcasting career, but you'd need a whole other book dedicated to just those games in order to fit them all in.

MESSAGE TO HURRICANES FANS

As is a common theme amongst members of the sports media, it is a well known fact that without the fans our jobs would either A) not exist or B) they'd have a lot less meaning. So, each of the broadcasters in this book took a couple of minutes to address you, the fans, directly.

TRACY: "The Hurricanes fan base, the GREAT CANIACS Nation, at times has been questioned: 'What kind of hockey market is this?' I want to thank each and every one of you for the unbelievable send off that you had for the boys going to the bubble in late July. For me as your long time television broadcaster, it represented all the years of triumph and struggle. And in one electric moment, what all of you mean to me."

CHICAGO BLACKHAWKS

JOHN WIEDEMAN
RADIO: PLAY-BY-PLAY

First Season on Blackhawks Radio: 2006-07
Seasons on Blackhawks Radio (including 2020-21): 15

Birthday: August 16, 1957 Hometown: Kansas City, MO

College/University: University of Kansas

BIOGRAPHY

There's no rule regarding who or what makes the best broadcasters. Some say you're born with the innate ability to be a sportscaster. Others say it's something you choose to become. There's no hard, fast answer and that's what makes all the different personalities and styles of broadcasters so fun to examine.

John Wiedeman was certainly not born a broadcaster. But he definitely has become one of the most exciting in the National Hockey League. So, Blackhawks fans, how about I let Wiedeman tell you about how he first got into hockey.

WIEDEMAN: "When I was about seven, eight-years-old, I was in the basement with my best friend, Jerry and we were just playing around. I can't remember what we were doing, but anyway, he says, 'come on, let's go upstairs. Let's go outside.' And I went 'sure.' He walked ahead of me and he walked past this TV that was on; it just happened to be on. He went around the corner and went upstairs and I turned, looked at the TV and I saw this hockey game being played.

"It was a hockey game between the Montreal Canadiens and the Chicago Blackhawks. The game was being played at the old Chicago Stadium and in that game were men like Stan Mikita, Bobby Hull, Moose Vasko and Glenn Hall.

"On the other side, with the Canadiens, were men like Jean Beliveau, Henri Richard and I think Gump Worsley. It was just an NHL regular-season game on a Sunday afternoon at the Chicago Stadium. CBS used to cover the NHL. The other guy I want to mention on the Canadiens was a man named Jimmy Roberts, who also was playing in that game. That name is significant for me, because that was 1965. About 30-years later, Jimmy Roberts would become my boss in the American Hockey League.

"Being in Kansas City, we didn't get a ton of hockey coverage at the time, but we did get sports reports. We did get highlights from Stanley Cup games. We definitely got to watch Olympic Hockey, which I always found really, really cool. As somebody who just had seen the game and developed a curiosity for it, at that point I really developed a passion. I wanted to see more and I wanted to actually be a part of that.

"I believe it was the next winter, we had a massive snow storm in Kansas City. We got hit with a snow storm that left probably two feet of snow on the ground, not just in drifts. I'm talking about big piles of snow and the way the weather was in the winter time, it could be a massive snow storm for a couple of days and then maybe two days later, the temperatures would be in the 60's and all of that snow would melt.

"Well, that's kind of what happened and the snow melted and all of that snow was in a big football field adjacent to where I grew up. There was a High School not far from where I grew up, all the snow that was on that field had melted and it saturated the ground. It laid in a great big pool over the top of the ground. Well, wouldn't you know it, that night and for the nights right after that, the temperatures got down into the 20's and into the teens. So that water froze and it became like an ice rink. That's where I put the skates on and I skated for the first time in my life.

"I've been playing hockey by the way for the last 53 years now, but that's the first place I skated and it was in the middle of winter with a hockey stick that I basically assembled in my garage.

"The skates that I used were my dad's skates that he had in his box of things from when he was in the Navy in World War II. When he left the ship in Norfolk, Virginia and came home, he had all this stuff packed into this box. I opened up the box one day and I saw these hockey skates in there and I thought, 'well, what's this?' Well, I went and I put them on that day. They were huge on me. I could barely stand up on them. They were wobbling back and forth. Finally, I got wise and I jammed a whole bunch of socks in there to take up all the room and I did my best. I labored around on that. That was 1966.

"A year later, the NHL expanded from six to 12 teams. St. Louis got a team, the St. Louis Blues. They put their minor league affiliate in Kansas City at the old American Royal Arena and they joined the Central Hockey League as the Kansas City Blues. I used to go to their games at the American Royal, which was a rodeo arena and they put ice down in it. The Blues played there and they used to draw great crowds. The building held 6,500 and on some nights they would just have overflow crowds. My dad had season tickets and we used to go a lot.

"Roll the clock ahead a little bit to1971, the Blackhawks were playing the Montreal Canadiens in the Stanley Cup Final and my family went bowling the night of Game Seven. I used to love to go bowling. But on this particular night, I knew that the Blackhawks were playing and I loved watching the Blackhawks and they were playing Montreal in Game Seven of the Stanley Cup Final. I said, 'you guys, go ahead. I'm going to stay home and watch the game.'

"I watched it on a black and white TV. I thought I was going to see the team that I liked, the Blackhawks win a Stanley Cup that night. They got up 2-0 on the Canadiens and then the Canadicns came back and scored three third period goals, won Game Seven and won The Cup. That was my first experience with heartbreak; seeing my team lose. But the addiction to the game of hockey just continued to grow for me and I started to play.

"I wanted to start playing right around 1966. My dad signed me up to start playing. We had a couple of local rinks in Kansas City. My dad had me all signed up to play and I was really excited about it. We had a subscription to Sports Illustrated. So, this one week, this edition of Sports Illustrated arrives and it's got a picture of Bobby Hull on the cover and Bobby has his mouth open. He's yelling something down the bench and you could see all of his missing teeth and you could see the scars on his face. I was just so psyched about this.

"I took that and I ran to my mom and I said, 'mom, mom, look at this. You remember I talked about hockey.' She says, 'yeah,' because my mom didn't know what it was about. I showed her the picture of the cover of Sports Illustrated with Bobby Hall. I said, 'this guy plays hockey.' I thought she'd be as excited as me. She looked at the Sports Illustrated and she said, 'that's hockey?' She said, 'you're not playing hockey. No son of mine is going to end up looking like that.'

"I thought she was kidding. She was as serious as could be and my dad felt terrible. He knew I wanted to play and I was heartbroken. I mean truly heartbroken.

"A couple of years went by, I got into my teens and my mom really couldn't say no, because I would sneak out of the house and I would go and join a friend of mine and we'd go to a local rink. We put on rental skates and played pickup hockey. That was kind of where it all started for me. Then I got more and more involved in leagues and played and played and played. I was feeding the addiction."

That late start into playing hockey might have cost Wiedeman a legit shot at pursuing a professional playing career. Nobody can know for sure, but if he would have had the reps and everything else that goes into hockey training, down as a youngster, he might have been able to follow that path. However, there came a time when he realized a playing career wasn't in the cards.

WIEDEMAN: "Being a guy who played the game during the '70s and in the late-'70s, I wanted to try my hand at College Hockey. But I didn't. I wasn't able to. I wasn't good enough. I gave it a shot. I went up to upstate New York, SUNY Brockport and I jumped on the ice and I tried to make a team of 25 players.

"The coach's name was E.J. McGuire. E.J. ended up coaching in the National Hockey League as the assistant to Mike Keenan in Philadelphia and Chicago and then E.J. went on to be a Head Coach in the American Hockey league. He then became an Assistant Coach in Boston. He was kind of a video guy, but he could break down a game and he had great value. Then he joined NHL Central Scouting as the Director. Unfortunately, E.J. passed away from brain cancer in 2011.

"He was a guy who gave me a shot. And he had to be the one who told me, 'John, nobody worked harder than you, but I just can't keep you.' Essentially I was the 26th man on a 25-man roster.
He let me practice with the team. I hung around for that year and I did get better as a player. But I also learned something that year and it's probably the best that I did.

"That was 1978-79. I learned that I was not going to make the National Hockey League. It just wasn't going to happen. I remember seeing a Canadian Major Junior A Hockey game in Niagara Falls, Ontario. The Niagara Falls Flyers against the Toronto Marlies. I remember these guys playing in an exhibition game in September of 1978 and I knew, at that moment, I was not going to make the NHL. I'm not going to. These guys were not only younger than me, but they could fly and they had this incredible skill.

"I just knew right then and there, as soon as I saw them playing, I said, 'these guys are unbelievable.' They've got a whole league of these guys and they've got actually two whole leagues. So that was kind of a reality check for me."

That reality check came at a time when Wiedeman had to start thinking about what he would do to support himself in life and even though playing was out of the question, he still wanted to remain in the game in some capacity; in a prominent capacity.

WIEDEMAN: "I began thinking, 'I do want to be part of the game, but I don't want to be somebody folding towels and cleaning up after guys in a dressing room or something like that.' I didn't want to do that. I wanted to be more of an integral part of the game. And I remember I used to listen to TV broadcasters because, as much hockey as you could get back in the '70s, which wasn't much, unless you were in Canada, you did hear some of the broadcasters.

"I felt that some of these broadcasters were awful. I thought they were just terrible. I did. I'm listening to the broadcast, watching the game on TV and I'm thinking to myself, 'I could do a better job than that guy. I could do it.' I was so confident at that time that I just wanted somebody to give me a chance. And I never got that chance, until 1980."

That's a lot of confidence for someone who had never held the role of a Play-by-Play broadcaster before. But I suppose confidence is key, so maybe he was indeed meant to pursue this path. Of course, Wiedeman's opinion about who he thought was a good broadcaster was shaped by who he listened to in his youth. And it was those broadcaster's who he considered to be influences on his own career.

WIEDEMAN: "There was Lloyd Pettit with the Blackhawks, for sure. Being from Kansas City, I couldn't really get Chicago games unless they were on WGN. Jiggs McDonald was one of my influences. I really genuinely could take hold of what Jiggs did and kind of make that a part of my repertoire. I could do that because I could see what Jiggs was doing and how effective it was. He was definitely an influence. I mentioned Lloyd Pettit with the Blackhawks. He was an influence.

"Dan Kelly, for sure. Gene Hart in Philadelphia. Gene Hart was a wonderful man and he was just a great counselor. He would listen to what I would do and he would give me feedback. I recall hearing him describe Flyers games during the '70's and thinking to myself, 'that's the way somebody needs to describe a game.'"

Now, Wiedeman actually has a rather heartwarming story that connects to Dan Kelly, so I'll let him narrate before we get back to how he started his career.

WIEDEMAN: "When I was in grade school, I was in the Boy Scouts and we used to go on canoe trips to Southern Missouri and my dad played a big role in that. He would take me down there and maybe a couple of other kids because they had fathers who couldn't take them down.

"My dad, from being in the Navy and also being in the Boy Scouts himself, when he was younger, he knew how to do all those things, make tents, start a fire from scratch and dig a big pit so that you could have an outdoor oven and cook food and things like that. I mean, he knew how to do all those things. He loved the outdoors.

"So I used to go with my dad down to Southern Missouri in the spring and go on these canoe trips. Well, we're driving from Kansas City down to Southern Missouri in the middle of the night and it's pitch black. We were on these country roads that were two lane roads. They were pretty dangerous, but at the time, you're not thinking about that.

"The only thing that we could really pull in on the car radio was KMOX Radio out of St. Louis. There were several times, in fact, I think it was consecutive years, where we could hear Dan Kelly narrating the games of the St. Louis Blues and I think both times they were in the Stanley Cup Final against Montreal -- 1968 and 1969.

"I have clear memories of those games and hearing Dan Kelly. You're driving along on a country road and it's dark and the only thing you can see are the headlights and maybe some of the lights from the dashboard in the old cars. But you could hear the sound of the game coming through and in a way it took me from that front seat of the car, into the arena in St. Louis or into the Montreal Forum.

"I felt like I was there and it was something that really grounded me into the game. It really did. It just cultivated the passion and the thirst for the game. My dad was, in my opinion, the greatest man I ever met."

It's always so wonderful when you can have a bond as strong as the one Wiedeman had with his father. And those early experiences listening to games certainly helped shape his style as he started out as a young broadcaster. Now that we're getting back on track, let's journey back in time to Wiedeman's first gig.

WIEDEMAN: "Back in Kansas City, in 1980, a man opened up an ice rink in Grandview, Missouri and he wanted to promote the rink in different ways. Kansas City had just lost its minor league team. The Red Wings (not the Detroit ones) had moved into Kansas City in 1977 and they lasted until 1979. They left town and they went to Glens Falls, New York. Keep in mind, Kansas City from '74 to '76 had the NHL Scouts. So, after you've had the NHL and then you try to sell Minor League Hockey, I mean, people probably weren't buying.

"So, the man opened up the rank in Grandview and we got together one night. I remember all the guys who played in this Men's League and there were a lot of really good players in that Men's League. There were guys who had played professional hockey, guys who had played College, in Junior. We had a lot of talent. So what we decided to do was, we decided to pool our money and create this Senior team, call it semi-pro and what we did was we contacted similar types of teams in other cities in the Midwest.

"As an example, Des Moines had a team. Omaha had a great team. St. Louis had two teams. Wichita, Kansas, believe it or not, had a team. Little Rock, Arkansas had a team. What we did was, we cobbled together a schedule of about 20-games and we would invite these teams down and they'd come to our building. They'd play two games and we'd sell 1,500 to 2,000 tickets. We would take the money, we'd pay our bills and then split up the rest of the money among the guys who played. It turned out to be beer money, but it was just the way we rolled.

“Well, one day we're at the rink and this man from Jackson County Cablevision comes in. His name was Kevin Shank. He said, 'we have all these community access channels for Jackson County Cablevision and we don't have enough programming to fill them up. How would you guys feel if we put your games on TV?' We looked at each other and were like 'are you kidding? Heck yes!' So we signed a deal and we got it all put together.

“So now he says, 'who do you have who can broadcast the games, do the Play-by-Play?' And I was one of five partners in this business. I threw in $1,000 of my own money, which was pretty hard to come by at that time. I stepped forward and I raised my hand. I said, 'I can do it.' I truly believed I could. I had total confidence that I could do it. And he goes, 'are you sure?' He says, 'have you ever done it before?' I said, 'no. But I can do it.' He turned to the other guys. He said, 'Do you guys have any objections?' And they said, 'no, no. We think John can handle it.' So he said, 'okay, fine.' So he picked a date and he said, 'we are going to need a place to broadcast the games, like a booth.' So the Rink Owner, who happened to be at the meeting, said, 'you know what, we'll buy the lumber. We'll build a booth. We'll get it all done.' So we did.

“We built a booth and Kevin brought the truck one night and he brought one assistant with him. They ended up both being camera people. Then there was a guy in the back of the truck who ran the production. We ran cable through the lower floor of the building, through a hole and ran it up to the booth where we set up a camera on top of the booth. There was another guy, the other guy who came with Kevin, who had a camera that he had mounted on his shoulder. He would roam the rink and get shots from inside the rink.

“We were on and I handled the Play-by-Play. Remember that was my first actual broadcast experience, on any kind of a medium. I knew after that night that was what I wanted to do. And what reinforced it was when we met after the game. We had a crew meeting, Kevin turns to me and he says, 'you have a future in this business.' I was just blown away by that. I said, 'wow, thanks.' He says, 'I mean it. I think you should pursue this. I think you can use what you're doing right now to perfect what you're doing. Any experience that you can get, you need to get and I think you should keep following this.' It was at that moment that I kind of set sail for where I am right now. I got a lot more serious about it."

Unfortunately, things weren't so cut and dry for Wiedeman. As he admitted, life can get in the way sometimes and a lot can happen while you're pursuing your goals. First things first, he went back to school to complete his degree and it took until 1989 for that particular goal to be achieved.

He had originally quit school and by his own admission had a "good time," so once he went back, it took awhile to get the degree completed. After all, he was working full-time so he had to balance school and work; which is never an easy balancing act.

Of course, that full-time work wasn't yet hockey related as Wiedeman was now in his early 30s and moved to Chicago to become a salesman for a company called National Plumbing Supply. At the same time, he also enrolled in the Connecticut Broadcasting School in order to build his rolodex of contacts; which is one of the most important things a broadcaster can have.

It was a six-month course and by the end of it, Wiedeman had developed some contacts as well as put together a demo tape, which he then promptly sent out across the country. It was a rough go at first and Wiedeman eventually quit his job as a salesman to become a bartender at a Comedy Club in Chicago. Lucky for Wiedeman that his boss was an avid Blackhawks fan and allowed Wiedeman the flexibility to take on a part-time non-paying gig that allowed him to cover the Blackhawks and gain valuable experience as a Reporter.

Wiedeman continued to make some contacts within the Chicago sports media during this time and eventually, one of them even helped him put together a new, better demo tape. Again, though, nothing but rejections came his way. Then, after the 1992 season, Wiedeman decided to search for more knowledge and ended up reading Don Cherry's book, "*Grapes: A Vintage View of Hockey.*" It was in "*Grapes*," that

Wiedeman read about Cherry's advice to go to the NHL Draft when looking for a job.

So, after the 1992 season, Wiedeman decided to do as the book said and went on his own dollar to the NHL Draft, which was being held in Montreal at the Montreal Forum. He met some people, handed out some demo tapes and resumes, but got no leads. But that's when inspiration struck.

On the way back from Montreal, Wiedeman decided to stop in Wayne Gretzky's hometown of Brantford, Ontario. While there, he went to a local rink and ended up talking to a man who was involved with the new Colonial Hockey League. That man told him to go to Chatham, Ontario and speak with the new team there; so that's what Wiedeman did.

When he got there, Wiedeman went looking for the General Manager of the team. It didn't take long for Wiedeman to find him. And after giving his pitch about what he was looking for, the GM told him they weren't going to have radio that year but that he should try Muskegon, who had gotten a new team after the Lumberjacks moved to Cleveland. So, persistence being a virtue of Wiedeman, he decided to now drive to Muskegon, only, he was nearly out of cash.

WIEDEMAN: "I was almost out of money. I had less than $20 in my pocket and I still had to get gas. I still had to drive around the bottom of the Lake to Chicago and pay the tolls getting back. And I had to get something to eat too."

Being extremely limited on cash and without a place to stay, Wiedeman ended up pulling into a Church parking lot. And even though the Pastor invited him to stay inside, Wiedeman didn't want to impose and stayed in his car. He got a small amount of sleep and in the morning he woke up, drove to Muskegon, placed a phone call to secure an interview with the team and found a YMCA so he could freshen up. From there, Wiedeman went to his interview and was told that they'd be in touch with him.

Well, during that time it took for the team to get in touch with Wiedeman, he began to grow worried. He had gone back to work at the Comedy Club in Chicago and the summer months were flying by. Eventually, the end of August had rolled around and still nothing. A sense of hopelessness had set in and Wiedeman, out of sheer desperation had taken to repeatedly calling the team to see if they had an update. They didn't.

By that time, Wiedeman had moved to a new house, but he decided one day to go back to see his former place of residence, just to check in with his old roommate to see if any messages had come there for him. As it turned out, one had arrived via phone call earlier that day and it was from one of the Owners of the Muskegon Fury, Bill Cooper.

Cooper, in his message, said he wanted to talk to Wiedeman about a radio job, so Wiedeman immediately called him back and two days later went to see him. After a tour around Muskegon, Cooper offered Wiedeman the job and at last, Wiedeman had secured a gig with a professional hockey team.

Wiedeman spent the 1992-93 and 1993-94 seasons as Muskegon's radio man, but after two-years with the team, he decided he wanted to try and go up a rung. He wanted to move into the American Hockey League. So, he went back to The Draft, this time being held in Hartford, Connecticut. Again, Wiedeman sent out packets of demo tapes and resumes, but he was getting no leads.

Eventually, he was driving out of Hartford and in his copy of *The Hockey News* magazine, he noticed that Worcester, Massachusetts was getting a new American Hockey League team. So, what did John do? Well, he decided to drive to Worcester. He found where the team's office was and headed inside.

Wiedeman went up to the receptionist and asked if he could please speak to Jim Roberts, who was the team's General Manager. She asked if he had an appointment, which he didn't, but she was still polite enough to see if Roberts would speak with him.

Well, Roberts agreed to talk to him. And what a talk they had. Remember, this is the same Jim Roberts, who Wiedeman had watched play for the Montreal Canadiens the very first time he'd ever seen a hockey game on television.

So the two got to talking and talking and talking. After over an hour-and-a-half Roberts told him to keep in touch because the team was going to have to make a decision on who its broadcaster would be very soon. Following the impromptu meeting, Wiedeman and his dog drove to Boston for the night, where he took in a Yankees-Red Sox game at Fenway Park. The next day, Wiedeman and his faithful company drove back to Muskegon, where he waited out the summer hoping to hear from Jim Roberts.

No messages or contact came and again that sense of dread started to set in. However, on his birthday (August 16th), Wiedeman was at the Muskegon office and he received a phone call from none other than Jim Roberts, who promptly offered him the Worcester radio job. He spent two-seasons with Worcester and then moved to the NHL when he got a job with the Philadelphia Flyers in 1996. However, after the conclusion of the 1996-97 Stanley Cup Final, which the Flyers lost to Detroit, Wiedeman chose to leave the Flyers as he felt he wasn't a good fit there.

Looks like it was back to the drawing board. Well, he got a job in the IHL (International Hockey League) from 1997-2001 and then just as he was about to take a job at Culver Academy with his girlfriend (now Wife), the New York Islanders called and offered him their radio Play-by-Play job; which he quickly accepted and started just after 9/11.

John held the Islanders job from 2001-2006 and then landed his current gig with the Blackhawks when Pat Foley didn't have his contract renewed by the team. Wiedeman had contacted a guy on the inside to throw his hat in the ring for the role and once the Blackhawks Owner, Rocky Wirtz heard his tape that was it. Wirtz wanted Wiedeman and Wiedeman has been in Chicago ever since.

FAVORITE PLAYER(S) GROWING UP

WIEDEMAN: "Stan Mikita would be at the top of the list. I remember watching Stan play and I was just in awe of how he was as a player; how in control he was. He was a very intense player. A lot of people think that he was just this small, skinny guy. He made these great plays and Stan was an intense competitor. I used to love watching him."

HOCKEY AFTER DARK -- TALES AWAY FROM THE RINK

In hockey, there's nothing quite like the tradition known as "The Dad's Trip." Nearly every team in the NHL has at least one of these per season; when the players invite their Fathers to come on a specific road trip with the team. For many players it can be the highlight of their regular-season.

Well, that feeling isn't exclusive to just the players as it also pertains to the broadcasters and in this particular instance, John Wiedeman.

WIEDEMAN: "This happened during The Cup year, our first year with The Cup (2009-10).
We had our first ever Father's Trip. I remember taking my dad and how excited he was to go along. My dad, at that time, was in his mid-80's and he was on a lot of medication. He was on medication for blood thinner. He had some other things that had gone awry.

"I was excited for him to go along with me. It was like my way of rewarding my dad for believing in me and supporting me through all the years. We flew from Chicago to Phoenix, Arizona and we stayed in these awesome hotels. We got to go out for a really nice dinner. All of the dads and my dad were just having a great time getting to know the other dads and talking and laughing and whatnot.

"I was just kind of a mess because I was worried about his medication and the timing of everything. I'm texting my sisters, 'when do I give him the white pills? When do I give him the red pills? If he takes a nap in the afternoon, do I have to give him more? Stuff like that.'

"It became kind of hard for me to concentrate on my work because I was so worried about my dad. So I was kind of a wreck as we left Phoenix. I got through that game and we flew to Colorado. We had another nice dinner in Colorado during the day in between. Dad had just a great time going to the rinks and seeing how everything works and all of that and seeing where I work. But I had to keep an eye on his medication this whole time.

"So, it's the last game of the Father's Trip, which is in Colorado and I was worried about him that there was something a little bit off on that evening. I remember showing him where they were going to be sitting. They were in this nice suite. I went over to Dave Ladd, who is the father of Andrew Ladd and to Gary Seabrook, who is the father of Brent Seabrook. I said to them 'Hey guys, would you mind keeping an eye on my dad? He's got some pills in his right coat pocket. If he starts to fade, can you make sure that he can at least take one of these pills with a glass of water, maybe a little something to eat like that?

"I said, 'this whole trip, I've been worried about him. I'm worried about him faltering.' And Dave Ladd could sense that I was a mess and Dave Ladd put his hand on my shoulder and he said to me, 'you go do your work. We'll look after your dad.' I can't tell you the relief I felt at that moment. I knew that those guys would take care of my dad and they could see how much I loved and cared about my dad.

"We got through that game and on the charter on the way home my dad sat there with his rosary and we got back and he stayed with us another couple of days. Then he flew home a couple days after that. But I knew that that was probably going to be the only time I could take him because his health wasn't great."

WIEDEMAN'S FAVORITE BLACKHAWKS GAME HE CALLED

There are so many things that can make a game a "favorite game." For a player it can be a big offensive performance. For a goalie it can be a particularly dominant shutout. And for a broadcaster it can be a game where just everything goes right with your calls. But invariably, Stanley Cup clinchers almost always take precedence over everything else.

John Wiedeman has had the unique opportunity to call not one, not two, but three Cup-clinchers for the Blackhawks but the first will always be his favorite.

WIEDEMAN: "I would say The Cup clincher in 2010 in Philadelphia. I would say that one. We were playing against the Flyers in this six-game series. They were a great team that year. We got to overtime of Game Six and I was thinking, 'if we don't win here, we've got Game Seven back in our building. But, if they win here tonight, the season's over and we won our first Stanley cup in 49-years.' That's the one that's going to stand out for me, really, for the rest of my life.

"I can still see Patrick Kane darting down the left wing and from maybe two-feet above the goal line, firing a real hard, low shot past

Michael Leighton. Kaner knew it went in. Patrick Sharp also knew it and he was standing on the other side of the ice. I didn't know it was in until I saw Michael Leighton lean a certain way. Then I could see the back end of the puck underneath the apron that rides along the ice inside the net. And I knew that we'd won The Cup. So I started screaming, 'the Blackhawks win the Stanley Cup' and all of that.

"Then I started hearing all these stories from all these fans who had been listening on the radio. One of them was from a Cop on the South Side. He was in his car staking out a house and he was listening to the game. And when we won the game, he jumped out of his car and completely blew his cover. He was running up and down the street screaming, 'Yeah!' So he blew his cover and he was sitting on a house, like a drug house or something like that. He said, 'I didn't arrest anybody that night.'"

WIEDEMAN'S MOST FAMOUS CALL

The Blackhawks' 2010 Stanley Cup championship may have been Wiedeman's favorite game to call, but it was their 2015 Cup championship that gave him his most memorable call.

WIEDEMAN: "I remember saying when the seconds were ticking down, 'for the third time in six seasons, it's one goal achieved.' And 'one goal' was the mantra of the team."

That was the first time the Blackhawks clinched the Stanley Cup on home ice since their 1934 Cup win, so you can imagine how emotional it was for all in attendance and listening back home on their radios. And to cap it all off, Wiedeman punctuated the moment brilliantly.

WIEDEMAN: "Lord Stanley, the Blackhawks organization, along with the greatest fans in all of hockey, welcome you back to your new home, Chicago, Illinois, in the U.S. of A!"

MESSAGE TO BLACKHAWKS FANS

As is a common theme amongst members of the sports media, it is a well known fact that without the fans our jobs would either A) not exist or B) they'd have a lot less meaning. So, each of the broadcasters in this book took a couple of minutes to address you, the fans, directly.

WIEDEMAN: "To the Blackhawks fans, I've always said that you were the greatest fans in hockey. And I mean that from the bottom of my heart. Being in the position that I have, being in the position that I'm in and calling the games on the radio for you fans is the most worthwhile thing that I do professionally, is the best way to say it. It's an absolute joy."

COLORADO AVALANCHE

CONOR MCGAHEY
RADIO: PLAY-BY-PLAY

First Season on Avalanche Radio: 2018-19
Seasons on Avalanche Radio (including 2020-21): 3

Birthday: February 2, 1985 Hometown: Breckenridge, CO

College/University: University of Denver

BIOGRAPHY

Colorado Avalanche fans, in case you didn't already know, you have one of your own in the Radio booth calling games with the same passion for the team that he's had since the Avs first arrived in Denver.

Conor McGahey has been as indoctrinated with the Avalanche as anybody and it's been that life-long connection to the team that eventually led him to the Radio booth.

MCGAHEY: "I remember, it was something that my dad took my brother and I to when we were kids and it was all sorts of sports. I mean, it didn't matter what it was. We went to, early on, (Denver) Nuggets games. We went to College Hockey. But it really started to settle in, in 1994, the old IHL, the International Hockey League. We had the Denver Grizzlies for one-season in 1994 and they ended up winning the championship, The Turner Cup. And Butch Goring was the Head Coach of those Denver Grizzlies.

"So, I remember that sort of was the appetizer and then the very next year, the Avalanche moved from Quebec and my dad and I went to the very first game, October 6,1995, versus the Detroit Red Wings. The Avalanche won 3-2 and it just sort of settled in that, being at that game in particular, some sort of switch just went off and I loved it. I loved being around it. I loved listening to it on the radio. I loved watching it on TV and it had announcers of all kinds. Whether it was Public Address in the venue or over the airwaves it really intrigued me.

"So, I went through a ton of other iterations on what I wanted to do. But when it came down to it and selecting the University of Denver, it was because they had a hockey program and I had in my head that I could work in some capacity in and around it and hopefully, eventually, get to the broadcast. And I ended up doing that and then eventually with the team that I've really loved since Day One. And that's the Colorado Avalanche."

Of course, McGahey's fandom extended beyond the players on the ice, all the way to the broadcasters in the booths and that helped to inflame his passion even more. And, it also gave him a template that he could use to help create his own unique style.

MCGAHEY: "On TV we had John Kelly and Peter McNab. Peter McNab is still around. He is still the Analyst for Altitude Sports. So he and I get to work together on a regular basis, which is a true honor for me, because he was a great player; almost 1,000 games in the National Hockey League for Peter McNab with Buffalo, Boston and Vancouver. So it was fun listening to him analyze the game. John Kelly was a voice that was familiar to me early on. He's the Play-by-Play now for the St. Louis Blues, taking over in the spot where his dad, the great Dan Kelly, was.

"So he went home to St. Louis and that opened up spots for Mike Haynes, who was the original Radio Play-by-Play voice of the Avalanche, to go to TV and that allowed Marc Moser to come into the Radio Play-by-Play spot.

"It's sort of been a moving around of bodies, but those were the early local voices I remember. Nationally, Gary Thorne has always been one of my real favorites. He was, for a lot of us, the voice of hockey nationally and really, truly, one of the best. We got to interview him on one of our local shows last year and he was a true pro and I remember his voice and mannerisms really sticking to me as I consumed hockey.

"We got Gary Thorne plenty because, obviously, with the Avs winning the Stanley Cup in their inaugural season and making the playoffs every year going up until 2004. When you make the playoffs and you go the distance, then you get the national attention. And when you're watching the game on the national network, ESPN or ABC, then you're going to get those voices. And I'm not sure exactly if there's a specific reason why.

"I mean, maybe it was just a good balance of A) voice and then B) delivery and the right balance of excitement and delivery of information; which is something that I have always been a proponent of. The balance of personality and professionalism. A guy like John Kelly and a guy like Gary Thorne had the ability to do that. And it made it entertaining to listen to. It wasn't always over the top. I mean, when you're a regional broadcaster for a team, then you can sort of be a Homer a little bit more and that's okay. That's actually what people want. And I think entertainment is a big piece of it. But also, you don't want to be so over the top where it's unlistenable. So I think the balance from those guys early on was one of the things that drew me to them."

All that was left for McGahey to do was to find the opportunities necessary to transform himself from a fan to a broadcaster. And those opportunities were as wide-ranging as could be.

MCGAHEY: "Well, I tried to do everything that I could, even in high school. I did the PA announcing for my High School sports. When I was a sophomore, we got a High School hockey team and we had just finished in the town of Breckenridge, an indoor ice sheet and the indoor rink had stands and it had speakers. So, what I volunteered to do was, I announced the games and also DJ'd. I mixed CDs with certain tracks.

"I knew which one was the goal song and which songs you could play for a power-play and stuff like that. So I DJ'd and did the Public Address announcing for my High School hockey and football games. And then when I got to the University of Denver, I asked the Athletic Department, I said, 'Hey, here's what I did in High School. Is there anything available for me to do that in college?' At first they were kind of like, 'Oh, okay. This 18-year-old kid is coming in and asking to get behind a microphone.' And eventually I got a couple small gigs.

"I got Women's Lacrosse. And then, I was actually playing saxophone in the pep band for the University of Denver at a basketball game and the announcer, for whatever reason, didn't show up. So they were looking for somebody to announce the game. So, I took off the saxophone, I put it down and I went over behind the scores table. So, I announced the Men's Basketball game. I got some gigs after that. And that allowed me to get a couple of hockey games. And that's how I got intertwined with Alan Roach, who recommended me to back him up at the Avalanche.

"And so that led into employment with Colorado after I graduated from the University of Denver, as a Producer for Game Operations, for the Avalanche and the Mammoth at Pepsi Center here in Denver. So as part of that, we sort of instituted an in-game pre-game and intermission show for the fans, just like you would get on TV at home, but we did it for the in-game audience. I want to say that we were one of the first to start doing that. Everyone really does it now. So, we did 41-home games a year, plus pre-season and everything. And during that, I was always exploring options to get more reps in broadcasting. And that's where Altitude Sports was a nice tool because they were right next door and they had properties.

"They started doing D.U. Hockey eventually, which I was able to get in on. I did Play-by-Play for the Colorado Mammoth of the National Lacrosse League. I just sort of did all that I could as far as reps, until 2016, when the Colorado Rapids had announced, because the company had bought a new cluster of radio stations and one of those was going to be a dedicated sports frequency. And so 950 AM was added and then 92.5 FM was the FM frequency. And so at that time, they decided to do a radio specific broadcast for the Colorado Rapids.

"Up until that point, they had just been simulcasts from TV. And so, when I heard that news, I went into both Altitude Sports and the Rapids, I said, 'Hey, if this was going to happen, I'd like to be the one to do it.' Right then and there, they said, 'okay, you got it.' So, I did Radio Play-by-Play for the Rapids for two-seasons, until the fall of 2017, when it was announced that AT&T SportsNet Rocky Mountain, which is also headquartered here in Denver, was going to be the broadcast partner of the Vegas Golden Knights.

"When I found that out, I was just freelancing at the time, I reached out to their Executive Producer and I said, 'Hey, I'm local. I've worked in hockey for a decade. And if you're looking for someone to be a pre-game, intermission and post-game host, let me know.' There were three of us at first who rotated doing games in Vegas and road games were in the studio here. And then eventually I got hired full-time by them.

"So I did Vegas Golden Knights hockey at the desk. And part of that job was also Play-by-Play for the Mountain West basketball and football and then doing pre- and post-game for the Colorado Rockies in Major League Baseball. So I did that for a year and then Altitude Sports came back to me and wanted me to do the Play-by-Play for the Avalanche, which obviously is a dream job. So, after one-year with AT&T SportsNet, I went back to Altitude doing Play-by-Play for the Avalanche. And that's where we stand today."

FAVORITE PLAYER(S) GROWING UP

MCGAHEY: "We had some of the all-time greats (on Colorado). Obviously, Joe Sakic was the Captain. And he's the current General Manager for the Avalanche. And to be able to work around and with him is really a privilege, because he's an incredible human being, one of the all-time greats.

"Probably my favorite player of all-time, was Peter Forsberg. And obviously he was acquired by the Nordiques in the (Eric) Lindros trade with the Philadelphia Flyers, which is one of the bigger trades, probably of the 20th century. And Forsberg sort of just redefined how the power four position was played. It was just incredible to watch him initiate contact while he had the puck. He was able to do things that very few others really could do.

"So, you have those two and it was hard not to love a guy like Patrick Roy when he was acquired in a blockbuster as well. He came in that December, he obviously had that spat with Mario Tremblay publicly on the Canadiens bench after he wouldn't get pulled and that was it for him in Montreal. And we benefited from that. So it was fun to watch Patrick Roy.

"My brother and I would play Shinny, mini stick hockey, in our basement. We had a plastic net down there. I usually played goalie. I had a used baseball glove for a glove and I had a goalie hockey stick and it was hard not to try to be Joe Sakic or Peter Forsberg for him. And it was impossible for me not to try to be Patrick Roy when I was playing goal right there in our basement."

HOCKEY AFTER DARK -- TALES AWAY FROM THE RINK

Since the United States is well over 200-years old, there's so many historical places you can visit and never get enough of. History buffs scour the country to find anything and everything possible so they can learn about the country's history and get a chance to experience part of it for themselves.

So, since broadcasters tend to have some time on their hands during off-days, it makes sense that some would be history buffs; which is a very adept way to describe Conor McGahey.

MCGAHEY: "Marc Moser and I both love history a lot. And so, whichever city we'd be in we'd go and find something to do or something that we have always wanted to see that's historical. I think it was this past year, it was December and we were in Boston and neither of us had ever been on the USS Constitution, which is one of the original six frigates of the United States Navy, from the 1780s, that is still an active warship today.

"It is sort of a museum, but it's actively manned by the Navy. And so, it's in the Charlestown Navy Yard there in Boston. Marc Moser, one of our producers, Peter McNab and I all went down to see the USS Constitution, Old Ironside and we did sort of a walking tour. The person in charge, let us basically go all over the ship, even on decks that the public wasn't allowed to. So we went down to the very bottom of the vessel, which is holed with copper because it used to be the ammunition storage and copper wouldn't ignite. And although most of the ship has actually been replaced over the years, obviously some of the original pieces of wood from USS Constitution are down there at the bottom, which we got to see and touch; crawling through a space that I barely fit through. And I'm just 5-8.

"But we were able to go down there and do that. And so, we crawled through, we did all this stuff and we got up to the top and Peter McNab was standing on the deck. Obviously Peter spent a lot of time in Boston and he's sort of looking around and Moser and I are like, 'Peter, isn't this great? This is so cool. Can't you believe that you're on here?' He goes, 'well, let's see, the last time that I was on USS Constitution, she was under full sail out in the Harbor and Bobby Orr was with me. It was sort of a salute to Bobby Orr.' And we just both looked at each other, like, 'all right we've been had, you win.'

"So Peter McNab, who's one of the best storytellers on the planet, very slyly one-upped us and kept it close to the vest until the very end. We were all geeked about being on USS Constitution, but there McNabb was and the last time he was on Constitution, she was under full sail in the 90's with Bobby Orr onboard. Incredible."

MCGAHEY'S FAVORITE AVALANCHE GAME HE'S CALLED

It's always difficult, whether you've been in the business for two-years or twenty-years to pick a favorite game. There are just so many different games and moments that occur that it's near impossible to have a unanimous decision as to which is your all-time favorite. So, with that being said, Conor McGahey, who has been calling Avs games on radio for only a few seasons, has given us several different games to think about.

MCGAHEY: "Game Six vs the Sharks in last year's second-round because the Sharks were up 3-2 (in the series) and the game went to overtime. Colorado was trying to force a Game Seven in San Jose two days later and Gabriel Landeskog scored in overtime. The call I had, I don't remember exactly what I said, but I remember it was all over the place. I ended up getting calls and texts from everybody -- friends in Canada as well. Ron MacLean from Hockey Night in Canada had done a small segment on it as well.

That was kind of neat for me to have that happen. I mean, it happens all the time with everybody, especially the local guys, in a big game like that.

"But my personal favorite was, I think this past November, the Avalanche were playing on Hockey Night in Canada, in Vancouver and it went into overtime. Nathan MacKinnon's first possession of overtime, took the puck out of his own zone, went down the left-wing, perfect wrist-shot to the far side of the net minder -- I think it was Thatcher Demko -- and the Avalanche won in overtime. It was just, every game, for whatever reason, the past two-years between the Canucks and the Avalanche has been 5-4 or 6-5. They're always high-scoring entertaining games. So that one was a lot of fun. Vancouver is one of my favorite cities to visit and to work in. So that was pretty neat.

"It might be a tie between that one and Cale Makar's debut. He just won the Calder Trophy for the Avalanche this season, but he made his debut last post-season in Game Three versus his hometown Calgary Flames. And on his first NHL shot, he scored his first NHL goal versus the team he grew up rooting for as a kid and it ended up being the game winner. And that sparked, for whatever reason, me to say, 'All Hail Cale' and that has stuck over the past two-years as well."

SIGNATURE PHRASE

Move over John Sterling, you have company. For many years the Radio Voice of the NY Yankees has been known for creating zany calls whenever a player on the Bronx Bombers goes yard. Well, Sterling isn't the only broadcaster who can be that creative.

Enter Conor McGahey of the Colorado Avalanche. Much like Sterling with the Yanks, McGahey gets creative with his calls for the various Avalanche players; although none are quite as perplexing as Sterling's, which is a good thing for Colorado's Radio Voice.

MCGAHEY: "Well, I think with me, I tend to just give identifiers to different players. There are a ton of movie and music references inside my broadcasts. My brother and I communicate (that way). My friends and I communicate that way. So, it's another piece of common ground that everybody can sort of identify with.

"Everybody's seen Slap Shot. Everybody's seen Caddyshack. Everybody's seen Dumb and Dumber. And so, to put those references into broadcasts has been fun. I think it makes it entertaining to listen to and like I said, that's how I communicate. It's not all the time, but it's just a fun way to do it. So when I say identifiers on players, it's like for whatever reason, 'All Hail Cale.' If he scores, that usually is the thing that follows.

"We had Carl Soderberg on the team last year and if he would score, I would say, 'Carl, good to see you,' from Billy Madison. We have Joonas Donskoi, 'My name is Jonas,' which is a Weezer song. Nazem Kadri, 'The Kadri-man can,' which is a play on words with, 'The Candyman can.' There's not just one, but it's having some fun with some pop culture things that people can sort of have fun with and say to each other. There's a local group of fans, a digital artist, who's made t-shirts, cups, pens and stuff. So, they've started to put a bunch of those together and the feedback has been good.

"It's not just, 'he shoots, he scores,' which everybody can do -- which we still do. But it's nice to have that little personal touch on the end, depending on who it is. We have 'Nate The Great.' An overtime win is, 'you don't have to go home, but you can't stay here because this party is over.' Just little stuff from pop culture and elsewhere to put a nice little tag on the end of certain sequences and situations."

MESSAGE TO AVALANCHE FANS

As is a common theme amongst members of the sports media, it is a well known fact that without the fans our jobs would either A) not exist or B) they'd have a lot less meaning. So, each of the broadcasters in this book took a couple of minutes to address you, the fans, directly.

MCGAHEY: "Thanks for listening. The thing is, I have the blessing of being a fan of the team that I cover, which I think everyone tends to be, especially if you're a radio play-by-play announcer or you're a regional broadcaster, you can lean into the homeliness a little bit more.

But like I said, I've been a fan since day one. And I think that connection is extra special with people who have either been fans for that period of time or have been fans for a couple of weeks or a couple of days, or a couple of years. So, I think the fan connection is the most important part. I'm not above anybody. I like to think that we're all in the same living room together. That's how I go about it. And it makes it special for me to have everybody listening and watching on a nightly basis. And we're enjoying our team together. That's really special."

COLUMBUS BLUE JACKETS

BOB MCELLIGOTT
RADIO: PLAY-BY-PLAY

First Season on Blue Jackets Radio: 2013-14
Seasons on Blue Jackets Radio (including 2020-21): 8

Birthday: June 30, 1969 Hometown: Somerset, PA

College/University: N/A

BIOGRAPHY

Whoever said you need to know what you want to do in life when you're little? People change their minds all day and night long about anything and everything. So, why should you be stuck with just one idea for your entire life?

Well, you shouldn't. And Blue Jackets' Radio Play-by-Play man, Bob McElligott is a perfect example of what happens when you allow yourself to have an open mind to the different paths that life takes you on.

MCELLIGOTT: "To be honest with you, I fell in love with broadcasting as a kid from listening to morning radio. And that's what I originally wanted to do. I wanted to be a morning guy. I played sports in school and baseball was my favorite, but by the time I was in High School and I couldn't hit a baseball, I knew that if I wanted to stay in sports, I had to find another avenue.

"(I knew) I wasn't going to be good enough to play sports at a post High School level. (So) I kind of merged those two things.

"I started working at our local radio station back home because I knew they did all the High School sports. I got a part-time job there and I eventually got on the list to do some High School stuff.

"(Now) Somerset is an hour East of Pittsburgh. I was actually born in the city. My parents moved out to the country when I was just a baby. My grandparents lived in the city, so (I) was (a) Penguins (fan) for sure. It goes back to the (Mario) Lemieux Era. It was him getting drafted and turning them into a Stanley Cup powerhouse in the early '90s.

"So, it's really funny, like now, doing what I do, to see Ron Francis in press boxes. Craig Patrick, who actually worked with the Blue Jackets for a couple of years, I know Craig really well now. So it's just kind of funny how it's all worked out over the course of the years, to see these guys who I remember watching when they were playing and they were winning Stanley Cups and never thought I was going to be in the same realm with.

"When I was a kid, we would go, probably one-time per year, my dad would take us to a Penguins game. We went to a lot more baseball games, probably because tickets were a little bit cheaper, I would imagine. There were more games. But we would go to a Penguins game and so that's how I was exposed to it then. And I liked it back at that time. Not every game was on TV. In fact where I lived, the channel that there were some games on in Pittsburgh, we didn't even have where I lived. So, if I would be at my grandparents house and there was a Penguins game and it was going to be on TV, I made sure that I was parked in front of that TV because I wanted to be able to watch that game and listen to Mike Lange.

"Like I said, I enjoyed the game. But when I was younger, I never really thought about working in it.

"(However) Once I got into the game and I started doing games, I just realized that the passion of the game matches my passion personally. The people are great people and it kind of all fell into place. It was almost like somebody knew that I was meant to do hockey way before I knew I was meant to do."

Call it fate. Call it destiny. Call it whatever you want.

MCELLIGOTT: "With my family being from Pittsburgh, there were three teams in my existence (as a kid): the Penguins; the Pirates; and the Steelers.

"They were my favorite teams and that's all I paid attention to. Of course, back at that time, growing up in the '70s and '80s, it wasn't like today where you can be exposed to all kinds of different people. I mean, sure, you could tune in late at night to KMOX or something if you were just dialing around and it would come in. But to be honest with you, it was just the Pittsburgh guys who I listened to and I emulated.

"Of course, Mike Lange has always been that guy for the Penguins. Lanny Frattare was the Pirates announcer who I spent the most time listening to. And Jack Fleming was with the Steelers for a long time. So, I mean, I really wasn't scouring around and listening to a bunch of people. I was just listening to my teams and the effect of those guys, they're the ones who had the effect on what I try to do in my career.

"But, the way that I got into hockey (as a broadcaster) was, I always liked hockey and there was an East Coast Hockey team in Johnstown, Pennsylvania, which was close. They had an owner who bought the team and was doing some different things.

"So, way back in 1993, he was adding a mascot. That was one of the things he was doing to be different. And I went and I auditioned for the mascot job and I got the mascot job that year with The Chiefs. I also, a couple of months later, got a minor league baseball broadcasting offer. So I left and I went to do baseball. My job was over at the end of the season, so, in September I didn't have a job.

"The owner of The Chiefs wanted to bring me back to be the mascot, but I told him I needed a job. I couldn't just do $30 a night on a game night. So he made me the Director of Group Ticket Sales. I would work in the office and try to sell tickets to groups during the day and then at home games, I would do the mascot job.

"What I ended up doing, the guy who was doing radio there at the time, his name was Greg DeVito and he knew that I was doing baseball radio and he had some High School hockey games he had to do as part of his deal. And he said to me, 'you know, if you want to come to these High School games with me, I'll teach you how to broadcast hockey. So I started going and doing those games with him.

"Then, eventually, I started to go to some of the closer games that Johnstown played, like in Wheeling, West Virginia and in Erie, Pennsylvania. And I started doing color with him. So I would go back in the summer and I did baseball in the summertime and all that.

"But a couple of years later, he got a chance to go to the American Hockey League and the Johnstown job opened up. So, I went back as the radio voice and I did that for two-years. And then, there was nobody in Syracuse and I applied for it and I went to Syracuse and I spent 10 glorious years doing American Hockey League all winter and doing Triple-A baseball all summer. And that was up until the time I came here to Columbus."

There's no one way that you have to go in order to become a broadcaster and McElligott proved that. I'm not sure many, if any, other broadcasters ever started out as a team mascot. But hey, he kept an open mind to different things in order to eventually get to where he is today.

Of course, there were a couple of other people who also should be mentioned in helping McElligott along his path.

MCELLIGOTT: "I'll tell you, the first guy who helped me and helped me in the way of baseball was a guy named Kent Derdivanis. He used to work with the Pirates. He was the number two Play-by-Play guy with the Pirates. The Pirates used to have this off-season ticketing campaign thing they would, I think they still do it; where they'd bring in players and they would have autograph sessions and they would have fan forums and stuff. And they had a booth where you could pay to actually go up on a stage, watch a video of an inning of a game or half-inning of a game and call it with one of the announcers.

"The first year I did it, I did it with Jim Rooker, who was doing color at the time. And that was fine. I paid and I went. I did it and I got my tape and I took it home. I went back the next year and they had it again. So, I went and I signed up and the guy who was on it when I was doing it was Kent Derdivanis.

"Personally, I was a little disappointed, because he was a Play-by-Play guy and I wanted to work with one of the actual color analysts. But anyway, I got up there and I did it. The whole time I was talking, he was not saying much of anything, which was surprising to me. We got done and he looked at me and he said, 'you do this better than a lot of guys who are doing this in the minor leagues right now.'

"He said, 'is this what your dream is?' And I said, 'yeah.' So, he did two things for me. Number one, he set up for me to come back later in the day and actually do another session with Steve Blass, who was a color analyst. And then, he introduced me to the Baseball America Directory, which was a listing of every minor league team in the country with the contact information and how to try to get a hold of people. So, he was really instrumental in helping me to do that; to get going with that.

"Hockey wise, I mentioned Greg DeVito, who was in Johnstown before me. I mean, he was the guy. He didn't have to take me under his wing and teach me anything. I wasn't even really interested at that time. That was my winter job, filling the mascot and selling the tickets. I was happy with that.

"He gave me the opportunity to do something else and sometimes I feel bad because he's been long out of the sport working just a regular job and here I am in the NHL; that was his dream. He didn't get a chance to get all the way here and I did. Those two guys were the two most influential guys to me as far as pointing me in a direction and helping me out."

HOCKEY AFTER DARK -- TALES AWAY FROM THE RINK

You never quite know what to expect when broadcasters have some down time. They might go to dinner. They might go for drinks. They might explore a historical sight. The list of possibilities goes on and on.

What probably isn't on the list and if it is, it's not exactly high on the list, is meeting an all-time great in another sport and also going on a tour of a prison.

MCELLIGOTT: "When we were in Vegas, the first year that Vegas was in the league. Jeff Rimer, who's our TV Play-by-Play guy, knows Pete Rose from way back in the '80s when he worked in Montreal. Pete Rose signs autographs at a memorabilia shop on the Vegas strip every day.

"So, Jody Shelley, Jeff and I went down; Jeff took us down there and introduced us to Pete. We did an interview with him that covered, Oh my goodness, it covered everything. We talked about hockey. We talked about baseball. We talked about life. We probably talked to him for at least 30-minutes. The interview was like 30-minutes. And we talked to him for probably another 20- to 25-minutes beyond that.

"That was pretty cool. I mean, especially for a guy who was interested in baseball, early on, to be able to meet somebody and talk to somebody like that and do it with a couple other guys who I work with and then just have it be all encompassing was pretty neat.

"I remember I was kidding with him (before going to see Rose) because Jeff knows all these people and he'll always name drops about all these famous people who he knows. He'll always be like, 'I talked to Jon Miller from the Giants. He might show up when we're in California. Oh, Larry King might come over after breakfast.'

"Well, I never see these people. So I always tease him and I'm always on him. I go, 'Oh yeah, here we go. We're all going to LA, I gotta hear this Larry King story again.' So, the Pete Rose thing, I was all over him as soon as he brought it up, because I was like, 'Oh, this is just like all these other stories.' 'No, no I'm telling you, I'm telling you he's there. We're going to talk to him.' So, that was my reaction. That made it even more fun, cause we got to have a good time with him.

"Another thing that was kind of strangely interesting and fun last year, I went with some of the guys on our Fox Sports TV crew. We went to an old prison in Philadelphia. It's in the city. It's like, you're in a cab driving along and then all of a sudden there's these old prison walls. We went there and walked around and killed a couple of hours on a day-off.

"It was kinda neat cause it's not something that I would go out of my way to do on a normal basis. Although, there was another time, early on when I was here, when we had a day in San Jose and we actually went out to Alcatraz; that's when I was doing color. I went with my Play-by-Play partner, George Matthews. We went to Alcatraz. So I guess I did that two different times, which is kind of weird, but they were both really neat experiences and it was just kind of historical and different and weird in some ways I guess, but it was fun."

Like I said, when it comes to broadcasters and down time, expect the unexpected.

MCELLIGOTT'S FAVORITE BLUE JACKETS GAME CALLED

When your favorite franchise has gone its entire history without that one defining moment, it can weigh on the hearts and minds of the fan base, as well as the organization itself. And that extends to everybody within the organization, not just the players and coaches, but also the scouts, the broadcasters, the ticket reps, etc.

So, when history comes knocking and that one shining moment presents itself, you grab ahold of it and make it your own. You don't let it go because you're well trained to know that these moments are fleeting, not guaranteed and you have no way of knowing when another might come around.

For the Columbus Blue Jackets and their fan base, this is a reality that hits way too close to home. Or, at least, it did prior to April 16, 2019.

For the first 17-years of the team's existence, it never won a single playoff series. Not a single one. They'd only made it to the playoffs three times in their first 16-years. So, you can understand the anguish felt by Blue Jackets fans when this annual topic came up for discussion.

However, Year-17 promised to be different. The 2017-18 Blue Jackets were a strong team, finishing the regular season with 97-points. A playoff date with the Washington Capitals appeared to be a daunting one. But the Blue Jackets rose to the occasion early in the series; claiming an early 2-0 series lead.

That's where it all went wrong.

MCELLIGOTT: "Going into Washington and winning the first two-games and coming back home, being up 2-0 and we were thinking, 'all right, this is the year the team gets out of the first-round. They caught this team by surprise a little bit. And here we go.' And all of a sudden you lose two-games and now it's a 2-2 series and then you lose a third game and then geez, by the sixth game, you're done."

That wasn't a good feeling for the Blue Jackets and their fans.

However, what doesn't kill you does indeed make you stronger as the Jackets learned from that experience and carried that with them during their 18th season -- the 2018-19 campaign.

Columbus again qualified for the playoffs, the third straight season they'd done. And this time they were going up against the history making Tampa Bay Lightning. Tampa had been the best team in the league all year long and had set or tied many records along the way. Many expected them to make more history as they chased down and captured Lord Stanley's Cup.

Wow, hold your horses there. They still had to win the requisite amount of playoff games before they could compete for the Stanley Cup. And they were facing a rather determined Blue Jackets team. Of course, Tampa wasn't afraid and the Lightning took a 3-0 first period lead in Game One against Columbus just to emphasize the fact that this was their year.

Um, about that. Remember all the history Tampa made during the season. Well, they were about to make some more. Just not the kind they wanted to.

MCELLIGOTT: "The first game, being down 3-0 and being completely mad; I call it like a fan so I was not pleased. I could see the rout coming and all of a sudden they came all the way back and they won 4-3. So that was surprising. And that was nice."

It was even nicer when Columbus, not Tampa, took a 3-0 lead; not in a game, but in the series.

So, heading into Game Four, Blue Jackets fans were eagerly dreaming of some history of their own, but not without a drop of reality mixed in.

MCELLIGOTT: "There was nothing taken for granted, because we had fallen prey to that the year before playing against Washington. So there was nothing to be taken for granted, because we knew how good that team was. We talked about it as a group. I mean, if you blow the game at home, now you've got to go back to their place. And once you get to their place, if they win, then all of a sudden it's a 3-2 series and then it's anybody's guess what goes on from there. So, yeah, there was nobody who was taking anything for granted."

Game Four opened with promise for the Blue Jackets. Columbus took leads of 2-0, 2-1 and 3-1. But then came desperate Tampa, tying the game at 3-3. Surely Columbus wasn't about to fold, right?

No they were not. A late second period goal by Oliver Bjorkstrand put Columbus up 4-3 and that's where the score remained until late in the third period. With Tampa in crisis mode, the Lightning pulled their goalie, hoping beyond hope to prevent their season from going down in flames.

Well, with 1:53 to go Artemi Panarin officially made it okay for Columbus fans to hope and dream as he scored an empty-net goal -- the first of three by the Blue Jackets -- to essentially ice the game.

MCELLIGOTT: "Once Artemi Panarin got the empty net goal, that let you know that it was in the bag. It was at home and it was in front of a city that had not seen its team get out of the first-round ever.

"It was a really big deal. The atmosphere was electric and it was a franchise first. When you put all those things together, I think without question, that that has to rank as the best game that I've had the luxury to sit here and call.

"Like I said, when that empty net goal was scored, then you knew the win was coming for sure. Then you could finally breathe a little bit."

Then the clock struck triple zero and Columbus and its fans were breathing all the way to the Second-Round of the playoffs for the first time in franchise history.

SIGNATURE PHRASE

When you think about your favorite broadcaster's many, many phrases and calls, you are probably drawn to the ones that described a memorable moment or that put the finishing touches on a historic game. But those aren't the only types of signature calls that exist.

Some broadcasters have actually found a way to use a phrase, or phrases, on a regular basis that still carry the weight and meaning of those special moments without the moment always having to be something out of the ordinary. And it's these types of phrases or calls that fans can easily latch on to and even use in their own chants, which helps to signify the fan base's affection for their announcer.

For Bob McElligott, his signature call is a simple, yet effective one. No need to overthink things.

MCELLIGOTT: "Whenever we win a game and I know we're going to win, it's much more effective if we win on a final shot in overtime or shootout. But I use it every time we're going to win a game, as the clock is winding down, I say, 'I got two words for ya, Game Over.'"

As far as fans are concerned, those are probably the two best words to hear in all of sports.

MESSAGE TO BLUE JACKETS FANS

As is a common theme amongst members of the sports media, it is a well known fact that without the fans our jobs would either A) not exist or B) they'd have a lot less meaning. So, each of the broadcasters in this book took a couple of minutes to address you, the fans, directly.

MCELLIGOTT: "The message would be: I am you. And what I mean by that is, I get paid by the Blue Jackets. So I travel with the Blue Jackets. I'm part of the Blue Jackets. I'm not gonna pretend that I'm in love with the other team because I don't want the other team to win. When I do games I want the fan to feel like if I was sitting in that chair doing that game, this is exactly how I would do it.

"This is how I would feel about it. I have people who tell me all the time, 'well, I turned the game on, I didn't know what the score was, but I knew we were losing because you sounded pissed.' And again, when you're working for a team, that's fine. If you're working for a network, obviously you have to call a completely different game. But I enjoy being part of the team. And so that's what I would tell a fan. I am you. I'm trying to bring the game to you with the same kind of feeling you have; wherever you are."

DALLAS STARS

JOSH BOGORAD
TV/RADIO: PLAY-BY-PLAY

First Season on Stars TV/Radio: 2018-19
Seasons on Stars TV/Radio (including 2020-21): 3

Birthday: March 18, 1980 Hometown: Los Angeles, CA

College/University: University of Arizona

BIOGRAPHY

As a California boy, Josh Bogorad had a lot of sports influences in his life. But he initially grew up during a time when hockey wasn't really part of the lexicon in Southern California. That all changed when he was eight-years-old, thanks to a man named Wayne Gretzky. As hockey fans know, Gretzky was traded from the Edmonton Oilers, with whom he'd won four Stanley Cups, to the LA Kings, in the late-80's and that one move completely changed the cultural landscape of sports, as well as the NHL, in California.

BOGORAD: "I was a sports fan from as long as I can remember. Just a sports fanatic across the board. I loved playing and watching all sports and growing up in Los Angeles, hockey wasn't really on the scene as much as basketball or baseball. I grew up when the Showtime Lakers of the '80s were taking place and the Dodgers had a pretty great team. The NFL was kind of tap dancing in and out of Los Angeles around those years, but the NFL is still a monster. So, hockey, it just wasn't as widespread in Southern California, but I would watch it occasionally on TV and then I had a grade school friend whose uncle was a season ticket holder to the LA Kings.

"I wound up just going to my first hockey game as a kid. I was instantly hooked on the sport because it's so much fun and it's just such great action. Even at that time, when I didn't know the rules, essentially, the way that you needed to and I didn't know the intricacies and the nuance of the sport; it still was just so captivating immediately.

"So, the fact that I loved sports and loved watching and playing anything I could, this became something that it kind of just, I fell in love with it immediately and then I just gravitated to consuming it more and more. Ice wasn't as readily available in those days in Los Angeles so I actually started playing roller hockey and then just watched as much as I could. I also knew from a very early age that I wanted to be a sports broadcaster and quickly hockey became my favorite sport, even though I still watched and played pretty much every other sport as well.

"But the fact that hockey was my favorite sport and I found it to be the most entertaining and I knew that I wanted to do this, you can't really map out exactly where your career is going to go, but I kind of set out with the goal in mind to be a hockey Play-by-Play broadcaster."

"I don't have this job (if not for the Gretzky trade) because I was eight-years-old when that trade happened. It was 1988. That kind of put hockey on the map in a way that it hadn't been and it was right around the time that I went to that game and I started watching more and more. The Kings had rebranded from the purple and gold to that newer, sleeker look and then Gretzky came and all of a sudden you went from not being able to give tickets away, basically to games at The Forum, to they became instant, hot tickets and people wanted to be seen there.

"So while I don't think that trade directly had an impact where that was the moment where I said, 'Hey, Gretzky's here. I want to start following.' I think just inherently around me, the environment changed where hockey just became much more of a mainstream event in Los Angeles. So even though it wasn't the direct impact where the trade happened that threw me further into the sport, it was right around the time that I happened to just kind of stumble onto it and it piqued my curiosity."

Of course, Bogorad was influenced by more than just Wayne Gretzky. He also loved listening to the voice of the Kings, Bob Miller.

BOGORAD: "Bob Miller was the soundtrack of that team and that sport for my childhood. I thought he called a phenomenal game. He was entertaining to listen to. He was informative and he was just so good and such a nice man as well. I was lucky enough to get a chance to meet him and eventually form a friendship with him."

That friendship proved vital to Bogorad as he would occasionally, without overdoing it, seek advice from Miller on big ticket type items. And that advice undoubtedly helped get him to where he is today. But it wasn't a straightforward road for Bogorad, even with Miller's sage advice.

BOGORAD: "Out of college, I sent out demo reels, they were literal cassette tapes. I took whatever broadcasting experience I had doing hockey Play-by-Play and spliced it together, using a dual deck cassette tape to create an actual three or four-minute demo reel. I sent it out to every team I could find in the minor leagues that was looking for a broadcaster, which wasn't easy, because the internet wasn't the database that it is now.

"I mean, you're talking about 2002, 2003. So, trying to find who needed a broadcaster was a full-time job, because you'd have to do detective work and you'd have to look up phone numbers. You weren't emailing people the same way you are nowadays. It existed, but you'd call people and you'd have to find a number for someone else and a number for someone else.

"And then there'd be outdated listings that you had. So anyway, I sent out demo reels to everyone who I could and then put them in the mail. I was prepared to go anywhere. I had moved back from Arizona to Los Angeles at the time. I was just working whatever jobs I could get to kind of just hopefully fill the time until a broadcasting gig came along. Then I wound up getting an opportunity with the team in Corpus Christi. It was the Corpus Christi IceRays. They were in the Central Hockey League. It took a while to get the job. I was sending out a lot of information.

"I couldn't really get anybody to call me back. So I wound up going to the Central Hockey League, League Meetings. They were in Phoenix, Arizona. I had some friends from college who lived in Phoenix.

I kind of crashed the league meetings and just introduced myself to the GM at the time. He was pretty shocked to meet me in person because he had kind of been avoiding me for a series of weeks because I had called him and I had sent him this demo reel.

"But I knew they needed a new broadcaster because someone at the league had told me, so it wasn't just a dead end. I knew that there was an actual job open and it was so hard to find that, that I didn't give up on that team, because it was one of the few that I knew absolutely needed to hire someone.

"So, I drove from LA to Phoenix, I crashed the league meetings, I found him, I introduced myself and made a decent enough impression. Then I turned around and I drove back to LA and I didn't hear from him for a few weeks. I figured that it didn't work out. But then he called me, somewhat out of the blue, a few weeks later and offered me the job. So I moved from LA to Corpus Christi sight unseen. My interview never took place in Corpus. It was just that period in Phoenix, during that session at the league meetings. So I got in my car and drove. It was a 24-hour car trip and I took whatever I could fit in my two-door compact car. I drove across the country from LA to Corpus Christi and started my professional career that way.

"I couldn't have predicted what would happen. I was there for seven-years and there were other opportunities along the way that could have taken me out of Corpus, but for a host of reasons, the opportunities just weren't the right ones. I wound up meeting my eventual wife there. I knew that she knew and I knew that, eventually, we were going to leave Corpus Christi, but we weren't going to go for just any opportunity, because we had bigger decisions at play together. We didn't get married until we left, as a side note. But we started making decisions collectively and we were prepared to leave, but we weren't going to leave for just anything.

"So I started doing some freelance work while I was the broadcaster for that team. When you're with a minor league team for seven-years, there's so much turnover in the Front Office, eventually your role grows and pretty quickly with that organization I started doing much more than simply broadcasting.

"Then, year-after-year, it just seemed like my plate grew in terms of what was on it. In terms of minor league broadcasters, you do everything under the sun, in addition to Play-by-Play. So I started taking on all of those responsibilities. Some I signed up to do initially. Some I kind of inherited along the way. I would do football games here and there. I hosted my own sports radio show on the local ESPN affiliate for about a year and then kept doing the Play-by-Play there all the way through 2010. Then the team wound up leaving the Central Hockey League. There were a lot of teams who were leaving minor pro hockey and becoming junior teams. They eventually became a member of the NAHL, which is a Junior League.

"At that point in time I felt like I needed to start looking at other opportunities, because now it wasn't just any move. Around that same time, there was an opening with the Alaska Aces in the ECHL. I submitted a demo reel when I found out there was an opening there. Their broadcaster at the time was Jack Michaels, who went straight from Alaska to doing radio Play-by-Play for the Edmonton Oilers. I don't recall very many people, if any, who made the jump directly from minor league hockey to NHL Play-by-Play.

"So it left an opening and Alaska was never anywhere that I had anticipated going to, or even considering going to, but it also had this unbelievable reputation for being a terrific organization. Their broadcasts were top notch. They televised their home games. They televised all of their road games in the playoffs. So it was, from a job standpoint, it was among the best you could find at any level in any minor leagues. It rivaled any job or surpassed it, that you would find even at the American Hockey League level. But it was in Alaska. It was pretty crazy to even entertain the idea of going. But in this line of work, jobs don't open up all the time.

"So when they do, you can only be so selective. I kind of just tossed my hat in the ring, not thinking much about it. They liked the demo reel that I had sent. They called me back and we started doing a phone interview and within a week of sending the reel I had a series of interviews and a job offer. It was lightning fast. All of a sudden, you're sitting there in Corpus Christi, Texas, which is as South as you get -- it's on the Gulf of Mexico -- and you're contemplating a move that's going to be 4,600 miles North to Anchorage, Alaska.

"I was now engaged at that point in time and me and my now wife, then fiance, had a long conversation. We had turned down some other opportunities before because they weren't really great opportunities. They were just opportunities that were different, but they weren't great. This one really felt great and candidly, I didn't want to move to Alaska. I was petrified to move to Alaska. She's a native Texan. I'm from Los Angeles.

"I had spent my entire life in the Southern part of the United States, in warm weather climates. I didn't know what to expect. It's such a different remote world to even think of going up there. And I can tell you, it was the best decision that I ever made, because I went up there and instantly fell in love with the city, the state, the people and the organization. My wife was the same way. Logistically, it was crazy, because it all happened so quickly.

"We had an entire life in Corpus that we had to button up. I took the job and moved up there without her and lived there for a couple months, then she wound up meeting me a couple months later once the season had already started. But I wound up being there for three-years and everything that I wanted it to be professionally, it was.

"It was such a great experience and such a well-run organization. I started doing more and more; all the things I had done in Corpus Christi had prepared me to just kind of land and instantly take over those roles. I wound up becoming a VP of Operations and then an Alternate Governor for the team; in addition to being their Play-by-Play broadcaster.

"I got TV experience, I didn't know it at the time, but it was vital in terms of accelerating my career once I moved down to Dallas. It was wonderful professionally. It was wonderful personally. My wife and I got married during those years. We had our first child up in Alaska and it was an awesome experience, just all around. It was so great. I spent three-seasons there and that first year I wound up being able to call my only championship. The team won The Kelly Cup. That run was incredible to be a part of. I wound up winning the ECHL Broadcaster of The Year Award in my first year in the league. It just couldn't have gone better.

"Then, in the summer of 2013, I wound up getting an offer to be the radio Pre- and Post-game Host for the Dallas Stars.

"It was a tough decision to make too, because I wanted to be in the NHL, but I also knew that when you leave Play-by-Play, sometimes you're leaving it for good. For 10-years I had been a Play-by-Play broadcaster and this would be the first year that I wouldn't. I knew that Play-by-Play was still the eventual goal. So it wasn't a no brainer to take the job, but I weighed this one very heavily, and I felt that after 10-years of doing Play-by-Play and receiving some pretty good feedback, getting some accolades along the way at that point for my career, I felt it was more important to change the scenery and get myself closer to where I wanted to be and bank on, if that role ever became available anywhere else, that I could lean on 10-years of experience and feel comfortable in what I was doing.

"I didn't come here (to Dallas) to eventually be the Play-by-Play broadcaster for the Dallas Stars. In fact, I was told point blank not to expect that, because other people had taken that role and it wound up leading them to not focus on the job that they were hired to do and they didn't last very long. So, I wasn't really planning directly for what it was going to be. I just knew I was going to get to a major media market.

"I was finally going to be in the NHL in some capacity. I figured it would help expand my network and I would just see where it went at that point, because I felt that was the best thing for my career.

"As great as things were in Alaska, I had to think of the big picture. I had a family now and I was thinking about the best thing I could do for the long run. I felt that this new experience, this new city and this new opportunity would be more beneficial than year 11 of essentially doing the same thing, even though I loved it. I had to steer just a little differently than I had been. So I wound up coming down to Dallas and I spent one-season as the radio Pre- and Post-game Host.

"After one-year they wound up moving me. They offered me the job as the television Pre- and Post-game Host on Fox Sports Southwest and that was a huge career move for me at the time. That opened up some additional doors with Fox locally and just a more established role inside the organization.

"I wound up doing that for four-years and then, a couple summers ago in 2018, they wound up offering me the Play-by-Play job. I still kind of have to pinch myself at how it all worked out, because none of this was part of the plan.

"I went from Los Angeles to Corpus Christi without a plan. Then I went from Corpus Christi to Alaska without a plan, just because I felt that was the best move at the time. Then I went from Anchorage to

Dallas without a set plan. It was just the best move at the time. Then I went from radio to television without any guarantees of what would happen. And somehow, it all led to the summer of 2018, where I finally got the Play-by-Play job."

FAVORITE PLAYER(S) GROWING UP

BOGORAD: "Obviously, when you get a chance to watch (Wayne) Gretzky, that was pretty special. And those (Kings) teams also had Luc Robitaille, who was a fan favorite. I used to love watching him. Kelly Hrudey, who was the goaltender, came over shortly after Gretzky did. He was one of my favorite players to watch as well. Those were the three who were just the most fun for me to watch and then there were peripheral guys who probably aren't household names, like Tomas Sandstrom and Tony Granato."

BOGORAD'S FAVORITE STARS GAME HE'S CALLED

Josh Bogorad hasn't been the voice of the Dallas Stars for too long, yet he's already presided over some enormously magical moments. Some of the magic has been personal. Some have been teamwide. But either way, there's no denying the magnitude of some of the games Bogorad has called since taking over as the voice of the Dallas Stars. So, let's let Bogorad relive those magical moments for us.

BOGORAD: "I mean, the first game is pretty high up on the list. That was unbelievable. I had actually called two NHL games prior to the Season Opener in 2018-19. As the TV Host for the Stars over the four prior years, there were a couple of times that the Play-by-Play broadcaster was on television for a national game and so they needed someone, because it's a simulcast, to call the radio. So I had done those two and that first NHL game that I did, which was in 2016, that one will always be so special because that was truly a lifelong goal; to just call a game in the NHL.

"At that point in time, I had no guarantees that I would ever get another one. I'll never forget the feeling when that game ended. It was just so special. But in 2018-19, in a similar, yet somewhat different way, that was the first time I had done a television game and that was the first time that I had done the game really as that defined role; as the Play-by-Play broadcaster of the Stars. I mean, the way my phone just blew up before, during and after that game was just so crazy.

"It was truly a lifelong goal that had been realized. It was just fantastic. I still kind of get chills thinking about it. I hope I never stop. It was so special. I mean, the game itself, it was a 3-0 Stars win. Season Openers are always fun. It was a sold-out crowd. It was a home game. All of those things make it really fun. But for most people there's really nothing memorable about that game that happened. But for me, it'll be one that I remember pretty clearly for the rest of my life. It was just a spectacular thing to be a part of. It was so amazing and so special.

"So that's always high up on the list.

"Then, this year is crazy, because it feels like it was 25-years ago with how 2020 has played out. But on January 1st, I got to call the Winter Classic and that was so cool. I mean, that was just a once in a lifetime experience. You're calling a game from the boards, like ringside, because you're not in a press box. Doc Emrick and Eddie Olczyk are immediately to my left and then Razor (Daryl Reaugh) and I are right there on the boards, near the blue line, right around the top of the circles.

"So you're calling a game from that vantage point, which is so unique and different. And then there's 86,000 people in the crowd and it was at the State Fairgrounds. I had a chance to just walk the Fairgrounds for a couple of hours before the game. It was empty and then it got filled and I was talking with fans. That was such an awesome event to be a part of and to get to call that game.

"It wound up being a comeback win for the Stars and the place erupted when they scored the go ahead goal in the third period. Most people who were there say it's the loudest sporting event they've ever been to. That was spectacular. That one sticks out for sure.

"And then this year in a little bit of a different way, I called some of the most memorable games that I'll ever call. But it goes back to the way that we did them, that we did them remotely. So that made them memorable and pretty unique for that reason.

"To call a Conference-clinching goal in overtime, even though it was off of monitors, even though it was a game in Edmonton involving Dallas and Vegas and I was in Dallas. There were a lot of things that were weird about it. But still, getting to do that is truly something that I'll never forget."

Bogorad's call for that goal was: "up high for Klingberg...fake the shot...one-time...Gurianov...he SCORES! DENIS GURIANOV! The Stars win Game Five! They win the series! They win The West! And the Dallas Stars are headed to the Stanley Cup Final!"

BOGORAD: "And proceeding there was a Game Seven against Colorado in the Second-Round that might be the best hockey game I ever call.

"It wound up being a 5-4 overtime win where a guy who wasn't supposed to play that night. Joel Kiviranta completed a hat-trick in an overtime game on a series-winning goal. He was not supposed to play. He was a last minute roster addition because Andrew Cogliano was hurting and unable to go.

"So it's that storyline, plus it was the first time the Stars had made the Conference Final in 12-years. The first time since I got to Dallas they had gone that far. They had lost in overtime of Game Seven of the Second-Round the year before. So it was kind of avenging that season in the way it ended.

"There were three different game-tying or go-ahead goals in the last 10-minutes of regulation before the overtime-winner. It was just this back-and-forth slugfest of a seven-game series that broke records for how many goals were scored and how it played out. That game was so memorable."

Bogorad's call for Kiviranta's goal was: "The overlap for Sekera...behind the cage now...defensemen's in deep...Andrej Sekera, fed out SCORE! KIVIRANTA! You couldn't script it! Joel Kiviranta a hat-trick, series-winner in Game Seven and for the first since 2008, the Dallas Stars are on their way to the Western Conference Final!"

MESSAGE TO STARS FANS

As is a common theme amongst members of the sports media, it is a well known fact that without the fans our jobs would either A) not exist or B) they'd have a lot less meaning. So, each of the broadcasters in this book took a couple of minutes to address you, the fans, directly.

BOGORAD: "Honestly, I think it would just be, thank you. Thank you for so much. First of all, thank you for watching and thank you for listening and thank you for passionately supporting this team, because none of this happens without them. I think if 2020 has shown us (anything), it's shown us quite a bit, but one of the things that it's shown us, in sports, is that the game isn't the same without the fans. And even with fans not there, none of this happens if they're not watching and if they're not listening, if they're not tuning in. So, thank you for that. And because I still feel like I am a very big sports fan. That's why I got into this industry. I feel like I identify very well with the fans.

"I know how they're living and dying with these games and these moments and I love the passion. I think the fact that you can't pick where you end up in this career and I never, in a million years, thought a hockey broadcasting career was going to take me to Texas for the rest of my life. I always figured it'd probably be somewhere on the East Coast if I was going to do this. But I'm still happy with where I am. Because of where I grew up, in a non-traditional hockey market, I knew what it was like to be a hockey fan and kind of like part of this special fraternity. And to see the way the game is growing here locally, like I've got two small kids and they play youth hockey, here in Dallas.

"You get to see Texas born kids in the NHL and they get drafted every year now. I love being a part of that. And I love seeing that. And I thank them for their passion. And then, aside from that and the way they support the team, I've followed some pretty enormous broadcasters when it comes to their footprint on the sport and on this region and how talented they are and how incredibly beloved they were by this fan base and pretty much even beyond this fan base; just universally. So I know I had huge, huge shoes to fill. And I think that the way that Stars fans welcomed me, it was just unbelievable and I'm so appreciative of it.

"I'd absolutely say thank you to them for that. I know that a lot of people didn't know whether I could call a game or not when I got the job. Most Stars fans knew me as a host and not as a play-by-play broadcaster, because they didn't know about the 10-years that I spent prior to getting to Dallas. It wasn't their job to know that. But I think it's really easy to dismiss someone and not give them a chance when you don't necessarily feel like they're necessarily the pick that was the obvious pick or the one that they would have made -- or the high profile pick. So, when I got this job, I didn't really know what the reaction was going to be from the fans. And part of what made that first game so special that I told you about earlier is the way the fan base reached out to me.

"And after that first year, the way they reached out, it was just completely overwhelming and so special. I think I'll always be forever appreciative of how they accepted me so quickly and welcomed me into their homes. I think that's what you're doing with a broadcaster, especially a regional broadcaster of a team that you follow for six months. You welcome these people into your lives and they become a nightly, weekly, regular part of your routine. And I felt so welcomed from Day One. I felt welcomed as a radio host. I felt welcomed as a TV host. I felt so welcomed as the play-by-play broadcaster. I don't think I'll ever fully be able to say, thank you enough for that."

DARYL REAUGH
TV/RADIO: COLOR ANALYST

First Season on Stars TV/Radio: 1996-97
Seasons on Stars TV/Radio (including 2020-21): 25

Birthday: February 13, 1965 Hometown: Prince George, BC

College/University: Northeast Broadcast School

BIOGRAPHY

The neighborhoods throughout Canada are filled to the brim with aspiring NHL players, as well as aspiring NHL broadcasters. And while it has become fairly commonplace for former players to eventually make the move to the broadcast booth, that usually comes out of a desire to stay in the game, rather than a previous infatuation with broadcasting. Sure, players can and usually do have favorite broadcasters growing up. Back in the day, in Canada, it seemed everybody was a fan of either Danny Gallivan, Foster Hewitt, Bob Cole, Jim Robson or Jim Hughson. Of course, in the United States you also had to include Dan Kelly in that list.

But it wasn't like those aspiring players also had the dream, at the time, to one day join the ranks of the broadcasters. Again, once their playing careers were over, that's when the players usually began to think about the transition, or at least, towards the end of their careers.

Daryl Reaugh was somewhat different. Sure, he wanted to be an NHL player. But he also had a strong affinity for the broadcasters, with Danny Gallivan and Howie Meeker being among his favorites.

REAUGH: "Growing up in Western Canada, all your friends, everybody played hockey. It was the one thing that we did. We played outside. We played on frozen tennis courts. We played on outdoor rinks. My group of friends played together -- organized hockey -- all the way through minor hockey. That just carried on to Junior Hockey and then getting drafted and turning pro.

"As for broadcasting, to be honest with you I was as infatuated with broadcasters as a kid as I was with goaltenders. I loved Ken Dryden. But I also loved Danny Gallivan and Howie Meeker. Broadcasters, for me, were as big a deal as the players on the ice. And maybe that's because there were so few broadcasts that you could watch back then, or even listen to.

"I listened to Canucks games at night going to sleep. We got that in Prince George, in British Columbia. They were piped everywhere on strong AM signals back then. That was kind of the origin of everything. And probably the two most influential guys (for me), because I was a huge Montreal Canadiens fan, were Ken Dryden and Danny Gallivan, who called the games for the Habs."

Reaugh didn't just listen to these broadcasters though.

REAUGH: "We called games as we were playing them in the streets and everybody was Danny Gallivan. You mimicked him. He had such a wonderful vocabulary and this booming voice. Once you move on into broadcasting, one of the first rules always is, don't copy people. You can steal little morsels, but you have to be yourself. And I think for the most part, I've been able to do that. Obviously I'm in a different line as a Color Analyst than being a Play-by-Play guy. But he was the man, no question.

"We would get the midweek Canucks games on television. Howie Meeker did those games. So he was an influence (of mine). And then on the weekend we would get -- I would die if we didn't get Montreal games -- to watch the Toronto Maple Leafs. It was terrible for me in my household. I was like, 'I don't want (them). I don't care about the Leafs. I don't care one bit about them. I don't know who this is calling the games.'"

With all that in mind, Reaugh did eventually make it to the NHL as a player, but his stay in the Big Leagues didn't last very long.

REAUGH: "I got injured quite a bit and then I had a really nasty injury that ultimately, for all intent and purposes did me in, when I tore my hamstring off the bone in Winnipeg when I was playing for Hartford. That was pretty much the end of it. I'd been drafted by Edmonton and bounced in the minors and made it with the Oilers and then back down to the minors and then made it back up with them. At that point it was just like, 'man, I'm not gonna rattle around in the minors.'"

Those injuries had Reaugh thinking about what was next and it was only natural that a childhood infatuation ended up being the solution. And it's rather funny how that childhood love for broadcasting was turned into Reaugh's first Pro broadcasting experience.

REAUGH: "There was an American Hockey League weekly highlight show that was done by Pyman Productions somewhere in Ontario. Jim Ralph, who now does color for the Toronto Maple Leafs radio broadcasts and has forever and myself, would go on and do these skits. That was probably my first foray into it. I was as interested in entertaining and in the broadcast aspect of hockey as I was actually playing my position all the way through.

"I always had an appetite for it and the injuries were likely the tipping point where I just said to myself, 'okay, it's time for you to move on to a different career and see what you can do in that.' I was still in my late-20s, but I had a pretty good idea what I wanted to do after hockey.

"And apparently, 'after hockey' was coming quicker than I had anticipated. So that's when I took a year, my wife was going to school in Boston and I went to a trade and technical school with the idea that rather than just sound like a dumb jock idiot coming right from the ice into a booth, I'll try to give myself some broadcasting tools. It was one of those schools that basically, whatever you put into it, you got out of it. And I got a lot out of it. I really did.

"You learned how to interview. You got rid of oral pauses. You worked on your diction, just all those basic things. And out of that, I used my connections within the game. My first job was in the East Coast Hockey League doing Play-by-Play for the Dayton Bombers. That came out of nowhere.

"So '91, I was in Hartford and then the following year, I tried to come back. It just wasn't right. So, '92-'93, I was going to go and play in Europe and then I was like, 'no, I don't really want to do that either. I just want to move on.' So I went to that trade and technical school, probably in '93. Then, when I came out of that, my buddy was coaching the team (the Dayton Bombers). It was his first coaching job and his name was Jim Playfair.

"He said, 'Well, why don't you come down here and just help me out while you're trying to figure out (stuff).' I made a resume tape and sent all that stuff out. So I went down and did that in like '93-'94. In '94-

'95, I was in Detroit with the Vipers. '95-'96, I was in Hartford with the Whalers for my first NHL gig. And then, '96-'97, I was down here in Dallas. And that was the first year of my run here with the Stars.

Reaugh's run with the Stars has been a wonderful one for him and for the fans, but it's also taken several twists and turns that have seen him go from having a steady partner to multiple different ones in short order. Plus, he'd flipped-flopped between doing the Color and doing Play-by-Play.

REAUGH: "For I think 18-years of this, it was just Ralph Strangis and myself on the simulcasts. And then, when he decided he was done and we were looking to make a change, we went through different names and the timing was perfect for Dave Strader to come in. I'd worked with him before at ESPN and a little bit with NBC. So he was no real stranger. It was a glove fit and he was such an incredible broadcaster.

"It was so sad that it was only a year. But it felt like he'd been here for 10. It was just one of those things. And following that, we weren't sure whether he was going to kick cancer's ass and be able to come back or not. We didn't want to make any changes. I had done some Play-by-Play before and I'd always wanted to do it.

"The organization was kind enough to allow me to just kinda keep the seat warm while Dave was out sick and trying to recover. So I did that for a couple of years and Craig Ludwig was my Color man. Then things had to change again for unforeseen circumstances. With that, they flipped me back round and made Josh (Bogorad) the Play-by-Play guy and that's been it for the last couple of years. So, it was funny. For 18-years we had one guy and then all of a sudden it felt like every two-years I had a different guy I was working with. Such is the nature of the business."

FAVORITE PLAYER(S) GROWING UP

REAUGH: "I lived and breathed Ken Dryden. I had pictures all over my walls. I saw he did a thing with McDonald's where his signature was in a handout and I, to this day, sign my name as close to how Ken

Dryden signed his name. It's crazy. I had no idea. I mean, I was six-years-old. You have no idea you're going to grow to be the exact same size as him. I emulated everything that he did."

AN EVENT NOBODY EVER WANTS REPEATED

Hockey is just a game. Fans and players may treat it like life or death when their team wins or loses, but it is still just a game. Never was that more true than on the night of March 10, 2014. If you are a Dallas Stars fan, you know what happened and how close things came to a very different ending. In fact, if you're a hockey fan in general, you know what happened.

On March 10, 2014, the Dallas Stars were playing the Columbus Blue Jackets in a game that seemed to be just that, a game; until it wasn't.

The Blue Jackets jumped out to an early 1-0 lead, but 6:23 into the game that no longer mattered. After completing a shift, Stars' centerman Rich Peverley went to the bench for a line change. Unfortunately, it ended up being the last of his career.

Peverley, who had previously been treated for an irregular heartbeat, collapsed on the bench onto teammate Jamie Benn's lap.

Immediately, though time seemed to move in slow motion, Stars Head Coach, Lindy Ruff knew something was wrong, as did the team's Trainer Dave Zeis and Dr. William Robertson, who was sitting a few rows back of the Stars' bench. Trainer and Doctor sprang into action, as did several other team affiliated doctors.

Peverley's teammates, none of whom knew exactly what had happened, but who did understand the gravity of the situation, instantly began throwing anything they could find onto the ice to try and get a stoppage in play. They banged their sticks incessantly on the boards to attract the officials. When that failed, they jumped over the boards and onto the ice to attract the attention of the Referees and Linesmen that play needed to be halted immediately.

A lot of confusion ensued as nobody, outside of the select few working to revive a lifeless Peverley, knew what was going on. The broadcasters in the booth, Daryl Reaugh among them, were no more informed than the viewers watching at home or the fans in the stands.

The fans knew something was wrong, this was clearly an emergency situation, but one fan was paler than the rest -- Peverley's wife Nathalie, who was attending the game with the couple's daughter, as well as Peverley's brother-in-law and nephew. Nathalie and her daughter raced down to the hallway where the makeshift medical team was administering life-saving measures to the Stars' centerman.

Stars Head Coach Lindy Ruff, ashen-faced and weeping, stayed by Peverley's side the entire time. After approximately two-minutes -- which seemed like an eternity to all present inside American Airlines Center -- a jolt from a defibrillator restarted Peverley's heart after it had flatlined for roughly 120-seconds.

The first words out of Peverley's mouth were a hockey question, as he wanted to know how much time was left in the first period and if he could get back out there. For the record, only a hockey player could respond that way after what happened.

The game was postponed as Peverley's teammates were in too much shock to continue as he was sent to the hospital where he received further treatment and underwent tests. As for Reaugh and company in the broadcast booth, they too had a role to play.

REAUGH: "The wildest thing I've ever been through, as a broadcaster, was when Rich Peverley's heart stopped mid-game and we were on the air. You have no experience on how to handle something like that and what you're supposed to do and what you're not supposed to do and what's going on.

"You turn, all of a sudden, like in a blink of an eye, into a news organization, which is not something you're prepared for. Yet, when it's over with, you feel like, 'I don't know what I just went through. I hope we didn't embarrass ourselves and I hope it went off the way it was supposed to be and above everything else, I hope Rich Peverley's gonna live.'

"You're getting information and it's just crazy. We sort of ended up being a bit of a template for likewise things happening in the future and what you should and shouldn't do. We were just flying by the seat of our pants that night.

"I'll never forget that night. Never. And then they (the Stars) had to play a game again the next night. We had to fly after the game to St. Louis. There were a couple players who couldn't play. They were just too shaken up (one of Peverley's teammates was sent to the hospital to be treated for shock). They went into St. Louis the next night and won 3-2 in overtime. It was the craziest 48-hours I've ever been involved with in the sport; ever."

Thankfully, Peverley made a full recovery, even though his playing career was cut short. But more importantly, he was able to return to his family.

The incident evoked memories of Jiri Fischer's cardiac episode on the Red Wings bench in 2005. Both players made full recoveries and also caused the NHL to revise its health and emergency protocols so that heaven-forbid another such incident happens in the future, the necessary help will be prepared. Peverley's cardiac episode was able to be handled the way it was because of the new protocols put in place after Fischer's and even more protocols have been put in place since Peverley's.

Hopefully, those measures will never need to be used.

REAUGH'S FAVORITE STARS GAME HE'S CALLED

The Dallas Stars of the late-90s were an exciting, veteran-laden team with Hall of Fame talent up and down the roster. They had some terrific rivalries with teams like the Oilers and Avalanche; so there was no shortage of exciting games when the Stars took the ice.

Daryl Reaugh was on the call for many of those games, some of which, regardless of what happens for the rest of his career, will always rank among his favorites. So, let's discuss a couple of them with Reaugh.

REAUGH: "You could pick any game from those old (Dallas) Stars-Edmonton Oilers series in the late-90s and they would be my favorites. It was just such brutal, phenomenal theater, from '97, '98, '99. You had this young Oilers team and you had the high price veteran Stars team and they would come out and try to kill the Stars and the Stars had execution. They were amazing.

"The '99 Western Conference Final Game Seven at Reunion Arena, in June, is the greatest sporting event I've ever been to. We called it. For the people who were there and I've talked to people after the fact and they all said that they've never been to a better sporting event than that one in '99.

"The roof came off Reunion when Mike Keane scored twice in about a four-minute span in the second (period) to blow it wide open. They'd been building toward that. It was Game Seven and the series was such a spectacular series between two great teams. That's one of my favorite games. I don't care what happens going forward in my career. That'll still be one of my favorite games.

"It's (also) tough to overlook the '99 Cup win in Buffalo, just because it's going to be top-three forever in most memorable Stanley Cups in the history of this league because of the way it unfolded. I remember, we called that game. We had the shittiest seats in Marine Midland Arena. We were basically on the goal line on the radio and the goal was scored at the other end (of the ice)."

For the record, that '99 Cup win in Buffalo is remembered for Brett Hull's controversial triple-overtime. Cup-winning goal that sent the Stars and their fans into a state of euphoria. The Sabres and their fans were instead sent into a state of outrage as replays after the game clearly showed the Refs had missed a violation that should have, by the rule book, discounted the goal.

For much of the NHL's history, Hull charging into the crease to jam the puck past Dominik Hasek would be considered a "good goal." But during the 1998-99 season, the NHL had changed the rule to strictly prohibit goals from counting when the player entered the goalie crease. Hull was most definitely in Hasek's crease when he scored the goal.

It was a stupid rule and the NHL even tried to claim it had adjusted the rule to state that a player could be in the crease if they were getting their own rebound. Only, no team had ever heard of that adjustment until after Hull's goal was scored and Sabres Head Coach Lindy Ruff went ballistic on Commissioner Gary Bettman while the Commissioner was speaking on the ice.

So, you decide if the goal should have counted or not. But since you are likely Stars fans reading this section, party on; it's a good goal.

MESSAGE TO STARS FANS

As is a common theme amongst members of the sports media, it is a well known fact that without the fans our jobs would either A) not exist or B) they'd have a lot less meaning. So, each of the broadcasters in this book took a couple of minutes to address you, the fans, directly.

REAUGH: "When you're around for 20-plus years, you're speaking to a lot of the people who have been here since Day One, but there's a whole new generation of fans who come along too, which is, you have to find a way to connect with them too. Otherwise, you become just a dinosaur or a caricature of yourself and I'm always wary of that.

"I think, that's why none of what I do or even have done really matters or means anything, if not for the embrace of what I do in my presentation and our broadcast's efforts. Because, really, our positions are to serve the people who watch and listen. We're the conduit between the team and the fans. And I know we're there also to sell sponsorships and commercials, otherwise we're not even on the air. But we like to believe we're there for them (the fans). I'm pretty proud that it's not always just unvarnished, or varnished homer-rism we put forth. There's some honesty in our broadcast. We try to be fair. And I think fans have appreciated that through the years. I hope they have anyway."

DETROIT RED WINGS

KEN DANIELS
TV: PLAY-BY-PLAY

First Season on Red Wings TV: 1997-98
Seasons on Red Wings TV (including 2020-21): 24

Birthday: March 18, 1959 Hometown: Toronto, ON

College/University: York University

BIOGRAPHY

If you are a fan of the Detroit Red Wings, then you know Ken Daniels is one of the top Play-by-Play announcers in the NHL. His even pace while calling a game and his straight-foward attitude are a tough combination to beat. Of course, Daniels has been perfecting his style for many years, going back all the way to his childhood as a fan of the Toronto Maple Leafs.

DANIELS: "I began my Play-by-Play career when I was 10-years-old. When my parents and older siblings got tired of me calling the games off our black and white television; maybe even younger than that. I would have been eight, probably.

"I would have been eight when the Maple Leafs were on their way to winning the Stanley Cup over Montreal. Mrs. Townsend was our housekeeper, because my parents were away on vacation and she was from Montreal, a huge Canadiens fan. So, of course, our whole family, my three older siblings and I were all rooting for Toronto and we were giving her grief. Nothing like a Montreal Canadiens fan when you're eight-years-old, staying in your house and the Maple Leafs are about to win their last Stanley Cup; back in 1967. And I was part of it, but I remember I didn't get to stay up and see the end of it.

"What did I know when I was eight? They actually sent me to bed. So I turned on the radio and listened to Foster Hewitt. I was upstairs listening to the Maple Leafs on the radio with it underneath my pillow as they sent me to bed. But, of course, I heard the end of the game and the next morning I got up and she was very upset. But that's my memory of the Maple Leafs Stanley Cup.

"I think I was probably doing Play-by-Play in the living room and they probably got tired of it and sent me to bed. And then just continued to do that. So, I think, from a very early age, eight, nine, 10, I just fell in love with the game of hockey and probably my two older brothers, John and Gary were a big part of that, cause they played a lot.

"I wanted to hang out with them, even though the age difference was seven and 11-years. I wanted to do what they did and they'd stick me in the goal and I'd wind up going in the house, probably crying, when they hit me too hard.

"These were just tennis balls. We used to just shoot on the driveway in front of our house. And once in a while or more than once in a while, we'd miss and the window to our family den would just be smashed. And my mother would have been there reading. We scared the living daylights out of her. So those were always interesting conversations to have after the fact.

"We had a church yard right across the street and in eighth grade, I had made a hockey stick rack in shop class where I managed to keep all my fingers, even though our shop teacher was missing his thumb, but I made a hockey stick rack that I still have to this day, actually it was on one of my Instagram stories I did when this pandemic started about the game used sticks that I have.

"I made it in eighth grade and I still have the hockey stick rack. We lived close to a church yard right across the road, about three doors down, where we'd play street hockey after school every day. So everyone would leave the goalie equipment and the two nets and they'd leave their hockey sticks in my garage on the stick rack that I had built.

"So from eighth grade, all through High School, we'd have ball hockey games probably three days a week after school. Everyone would congregate at my house and bring the nets over, bring the nets back and pile their sticks. So it was like I was the home rink.

"I just always loved the game and played the game, refereed the game from an early age; just to be on the ice."

Daniels' love for the game is and has always been evident and his broadcasting talents are part of that. Of course, he did grow up listening to some of the best to ever do it, in Foster Hewitt, Bill Hewitt, Brian McFarlane and especially Dan Kelly.

DANIELS: "Dan Kelly, for me, was my idol."

Daniels would tune his radio dial to KMOX in order to listen to Kelly do St. Louis Blues games. But he also recalls Kelly doing the 1987 Canada Cup vs the Soviets.

DANIELS: "It's spellbinding to listen to the three games that all had a final of 6-5, 6-5, 6-5. If you listened to those three games Dan Kelly called, it'll make the hair stand up on the back of your neck. His inflection was just perfect. I don't know if there's been a better broadcast of a series than what Dan Kelly did out there."

With those broadcasters as his influences (and of course, there were others too), Daniels set about carving his own career path to the NHL broadcast booth.

He worked as an ice official from age 11 through college, which gave him a unique perspective on that part of the game; you know, the part every fan gets frustrated with on a near nightly basis. But I digress.

After Daniels graduated from York University in Toronto, he went to Oshawa to begin his radio career. He wasn't doing sports at first, but that came in time. From Oshawa he went to CJCL in Toronto and eventually started his Play-by-Play career with the Maple Leafs in 1988. What could be better than being the voice of your childhood team? The answer: nothing.

During that time, Daniels also experimented with television for CBC and eventually carved out a role with Hockey Night in Canada as a Reporter, then as a Game Host and finally as one of the legendary program's Play-by-Play announcers.

During the early-to-mid-90's Daniels also got the chance to cover various other sporting events, including, but not limited to, baseball and the Olympics. So he's quite the well-rounded broadcaster. And finally, shortly before the 1997-98 NHL season began, the Red Wings called him up and hired him to take over as their TV Play-by-Play announcer, a gig he remains in to this day.

He's even written a book, "If These Walls Could Talk: Detroit Red Wings," which was published in 2017. So, he's not just a broadcaster, he's also an author. Is there anything he can't do? Answer: we don't think so.

FAVORITE PLAYER(S) GROWING UP

DANIELS: "I was more a Bobby Orr fan. So, even though I was a Toronto (Maple Leafs fan), I think everybody was a Bobby Orr fan. He was really my idol. And in goal, I guess, because I was a street hockey goalie, I'd only played a couple of times on ice and the puck hurt like hell; I probably didn't have the best equipment. I played in a couple of practices and I thought, 'okay, goaltending on ice is not for me.'

"I was just a little guy and it was going right through me. So, in street hockey though, I loved the fascination of playing goal. And I think my son did too. Jamie started out as a forward, but then gravitated to goal. And he became a goalie. He loved being that guy in the mask.

"And even though Bruce Gamble at the time wasn't wearing a mask, just watching him and being the center of attention, I guess, of that game and so much is focused on you. I just loved watching the goalies. So for me, I would say it was Bruce Gamble. I loved Johnny Bower. I loved Jacques Plante. And I think, probably in Philadelphia, cause I loved the Flyers in the '70s with the Broad Street Bullies; Bernie Parent.

"So, Bernie was my idol. Bobby Orr was my idol. And I think Jacques Plante, Bruce Gamble, or Johnny Bower in Toronto. As a forward, I liked Darryl Sittler a lot and loved watching Darryl. That 10-point night, I'll never forget against the Boston Bruins, but at the time, because Maple Leaf Gardens was so hard to get into, my brother wound up getting season tickets to the Toronto Toros. We were in the second row right above the goal."

As a brief aside, Daniels' was particularly fond of one of the Toronto Toros, a fellow by the name of Tom "Shotgun" Simpson. Simpson could really rip it with his slapshot and after a game one night, Daniels went down to the outside of the Toros' dressing room and actually met Simpson. And even better for Daniels, Simpson gave him his stick. Well, that's one way to make a kid's night.

HOCKEY AFTER DARK -- TALES AWAY FROM THE RINK

When you've been around the game of hockey for a long time, it's rare that you get to see something so impressive that it actually shocks you. But that's exactly what the early 2000's Red Wings teams were. They were a collection of Hall of Famers and it was awe inspiring to watch as they walked by. Whether you were a fan of the team or a broadcaster for the team, it was a sight to behold; even in times of turmoil.

DANIELS: "We were getting on Red Bird. We were down in the series in 2002, 0-2 to Vancouver. The Sedins were strong. Going back there, Brett Hull and his team, the goal was to win. I remember being on the plane at the start of that season and you're seeing everybody get on Red Bird. We started on the road and you're going, 'Holy, shit!'

"You're sitting on Red Bird and on comes Dominik Hasek. And on comes Luc Robitaille, on comes Brett Hull. And everybody you've added now to get this team to win, and you're going, 'Holy crap.' And then there's Nicklas Lidstrom and Sergei Fedorov and Steve Yzerman and Brendan Shanahan; what a team, what a group. So it was amazing.

"And then, later that year, we're down 0-2 to Vancouver to start the playoffs. I remember getting on Red Bird, walking up the stairs to the plane and already seated were Scotty Bowman and Ken Holland at the front. I'm getting on right behind Steve Yzerman and Steve turns to Kenny and he says, 'we're not losing this series.' He goes to the back of the plane and I see Kenny sort of look at Scotty. And to me, I felt comfortable. We weren't losing this series.

"Then we fly to Vancouver and it's the late morning hours, because of the time change and I guess there were three or four cars following the bus. I'm on the bus sitting right behind Ken Holland. As you get on, on the right side, he's the first seat, Mickey (Redmond) and I are right behind him. There are four cars following the bus. They're flying 'Red Wings Suck' flags and Vancouver Canucks flags out the window. And the bus was quiet. You could hear a pin drop. The only sounds you heard were the four cars, Vancouver Canucks fans taunting the Red Wings.

"Ken Holland turned around to Mickey and me and said, 'I love it. This is perfect.' And the Red Wings won the next four.

"The funny thing is, so we go to practice the next day (prior to Game Three) and we're leaving and again, Mickey and I are on the bus and I remember, back then in '02, The West Coast Express was Markus Naslund, Brendan Morrison and Todd Bertuzzi. So, Kenny Holland turns to Mickey and me and he says, 'you guys think Naslund, Morrison and Bertuzzi are pretty good, huh?' We're down 0-2 in the series, so we're like 'yeah, they've been pretty good.' And he said, 'Mr. Ilitch thinks you guys do too.'

"So, of course, Mickey laughs as only Mickey can, right then. And Kenny was sort of laughing too, but we got the message. So I don't really know if they (The West Coast Express) touched the puck the next four games, (at least) in my mind."

When a team General Manager relays that type of message to you regarding what your Owner thinks, that's about as uncomfortable a situation as you can be in as a broadcaster. But at least some nervous laughter is better than the alternative. However, if you want some real laughter, stay tuned for Daniels' other story.

DANIELS: "I do remember, one night, we're out with Bowman and we used to go watch games. So we're in Colorado and we went to The ESPN Zone and it's March Madness. We found a booth, Scotty and I, where you could actually watch a hockey game, because St. Louis was playing that night and we were flying on to St. Louis to play them next.

"So we wanted to watch the Blues game and March Madness was on all the TVs. No one was really giving a shit about hockey except for Scotty and me. So we had the TV on in our little booth and all the big TVs are on March Madness. Scotty and I are having dinner and the place erupts. Scotty looks up at the TV and everyone's going crazy and Scotty looks at me and he says, 'fuck me. Fuck me. It's 5-2. It's 5-2.' And I'll never forget that. It's 5-2 and he's right. It's a basketball game. It's 5-2, who cares? It's going to be 31-27 in about an hour-and-a-half."

That right there is just a brief glimpse into the difference of mentalities between two of the Big Four professional sports in America.

DANIELS'S FAVORITE RED WINGS GAME HE'S CALLED

All broadcasters have a role they need to fill. Whether it's doing the Play-by-Play, the Color Commentary, the pre-game/intermission/post-game hosting, etc. there's just so many things for them to do. And then you break it down even further to doing television or doing radio.

From a sheer X's and O's standpoint, there are some differences in style when you contrast those roles between TV and radio, but, for the most part, Play-by-Play is still Play-by-Play. Color Commentary is still Color Commentary and Hosting is still Hosting.

However, once you get to the Stanley Cup Playoffs, that's when the major discrepancy rears its head. You see, ever since 1995, the NHL's National Broadcast partner(s) has reduced the role of the teams' individual regional broadcasters.

It used to be that a team's TV and radio broadcasters would call all of their team's games until the team was either knocked out or they won The Cup. But starting in 1995, the TV side started to get the shaft as the National Rights Holders began to cut into the regional broadcasts. So, if you were a TV Play-by-Play guy for a specific team, your role began to become reduced, all the way to the point where, today, you only call your team's first-round games and that's it. After that, it's all National broadcasts.

Meanwhile, the radio broadcasters keep plugging away uninterrupted. It hardly seems fair. But every now and again, certain circumstances lead to the TV guys finding their way into some later round games; as part of the radio broadcast. The circumstances around these happenings vary, but the TV guy is always grateful for the opportunity and Ken Daniels is one such guy.

DANIELS: "The favorite game for me would be on the radio in 2008, Game Six against Pittsburgh and the Red Wings won the Stanley Cup. I handed it over to Ken Kal with 15-seconds left, because Schleprock, as I call him, lost his voice that morning and I had to fly down.

"Luckily, the Red Wings' families were being flown down on a private jet at four in the afternoon to Pittsburgh. So I hopped on that. Got there just in time, about a half-an-hour before pre-game, cause we were a little slow getting there. I wasn't sure where I was going at the old Igloo and I ran into Colin Campbell, who was working for the National Hockey League at the time. I ran into Colin and I said, 'how the hell do you get up into the press box' from where I was?

"I was on the Concourse and he goes, 'Oh, I'll show you. You come up here through the concession stands. I was a healthy scratch enough in Pittsburgh. I know exactly where to go.' So Colin Campbell showed me upstairs. I got up to the press box and called the game.

"Ken Kal was actually handing me reads for the radio and that. And then, with about 15-seconds left, I said, 'you're taking the final call.' And he said, 'no, I'm not.' I said, 'yes, you are.' And he said, 'no, I'm not.' I said, 'fuckin suck it up. You're calling the final.' And so he did. Marian Hossa, then for Pittsburgh, as he was chasing the Stanley Cup, was very close to getting to the goal on Osgood. I said to Kenny later, I said, 'if they had scored there, you would have been the biggest jinx in the history of the National Hockey League.' But they didn't.

"So, to me, calling that one-goal win for 59-minutes and 45-seconds was pretty cool. And Henrik Zetterberg put one in off of Marc-Andre Fleury's ass that went into the net. So that, to me, finding out that day, you get to call a potential Stanley Cup victory, even though it wasn't my domain to call it, it had to be Ken Kal's. But still, to be a part of that, flying down and Nicklas Lidstrom, the first European born to hoist the Stanley Cup as captain. That was all very cool.

"So even though it was on radio, because, on TV, we used to do the first two rounds. Now we only do one and who knows what we'll be doing going forward. I'll never get to call a Stanley Cup. So although I didn't get to say, 'the Detroit Red Wings win the Stanley Cup,' to me, being a part of a Stanley Cup-clinching game on the radio, that I'll never get on TV. That was my favorite ever."

SIGNATURE PHRASE

When broadcasters coin a catchphrase or signature saying, it's not always applicable to every player, rather, sometimes, the phrase is meant for just a singular player. And when that player goes to a different team or retires, the phrase leaves too.

For Ken Daniels, Pavel Datsyuk was the player he coined a phrase for and when Datsyuk left the NHL, so too did the phrase. Of course, with the type of player Datsyuk was, it was only natural for Daniels to have a special phrase for him, given all the insane highlight reel moves Datsyuk used to pull out of his bag of tricks. So the phrase, "Datsyukian Deke" was well earned.

DANIELS: "I used to (use a phrase). It's gone now. The Datsyukian Deke. I used it enough over his years from '02 to when he retired in '16. It was Datsyukian Deke, which people still use when they do their Top-10 lists. I did coin that and I know that Pavel loved it. Datsyukian Deke was pretty prominent. My son always said I should have patented it."

MESSAGE TO RED WINGS FANS

As is a common theme amongst members of the sports media, it is a well known fact that without the fans our jobs would either A) not exist or B) they'd have a lot less meaning. So, each of the broadcasters in this book took a couple of minutes to address you, the fans, directly.

DANIELS: "Patience. Be patient. I think we've been spoiled in Detroit for a number of years and we were. There's a lot of teams that don't even get into the playoffs and have high draft picks; look at the Buffalo Sabres for one. Columbus, a lot of decent years, finally getting a playoff win upsetting Tampa a year ago. It's tough to win the Stanley Cup. There's soon going to be 32 teams. If you get one every 32 years, as many will tell you, the St. Louis Blues have been around since '67 and finally won (in 2019).

"The Toronto Maple Leafs haven't won since '67. People think it's easy and it's not a three- or four-year rebuild. Ottawa went to the Conference Final, thought they were close, made some deals and look at the disaster they've been in since and now are just coming back. But until they're in a position to win again, how many years is it going to be? The last Canadian team to win the Stanley Cup was Montreal in 1993 for God's sake. Think about that. It takes time."

PAUL WOODS
RADIO: COLOR ANALYST

First Season on Red Wings Radio: 1987-88
Seasons on Red Wings Radio (including 2020-21): 34

Birthday: April 12, 1955 Hometown: Hespeler, ON

College/University: N/A

BIOGRAPHY

Stop me if you've heard this before. Canada is a hockey crazed country and so are most of those people who grow up there. I know. I know. It's no surprise, rather, it's a known fact. Well, Paul Woods is one such person who indeed grew up in hockey-crazed Canada and ended up working in the Hockey World for much of his life.

WOODS: "Well, in Canada and where I came from, that's just what everybody does. You just start at a young age. My hometown had a hockey stick factory, so it was like hockey crazy. We just started playing at a young age and just kept going. You're just playing endlessly; playing and practicing with your team. You're skating on homemade rinks and lakes in the winter time. It was just a passion.

"In Canada, hockey is like football in America. Saturday night is Hockey Night in Canada and Wednesday nights are the other games. So, you're just constantly watching hockey every Wednesday night and every Saturday night. And then there's the Minor Leagues too. I took to it right from the start. I just loved it.

"Skating is interesting because it's almost like cycling, where you have to work hard to get your speed up, but then there's this other area of time where you're gliding and it's effortless. You're just floating. When you combine that with stickhandling and passing the puck and put all that together, there's so many different elements to the game. But it's really easy to fall in love with it."

Woods not only fell in love with playing the game, but also listening to and watching the game as the three main voices of his hockey upbringing were none other than: Foster Hewitt; Bill Hewitt and Danny Gallivan. Of course, his playing career and subsequent broadcasting career brought him in contact with this magnificent trio as well as many others within the close knit hockey family.

While his NHL playing career was undoubtedly not as long as he would have liked -- it lasted just seven-years -- Woods was and is eternally grateful for the opportunity he had to play the game at its highest level; especially since he was able to play entirely for the Detroit Red Wings, a team who he has been affiliated with in one way or another for most of his life.

Shortly after his playing days ended because of an injury, Woods was approached by the Red Wings about the possibility of becoming a broadcaster for the team. And while initially decided to try it just for a year, there's no doubt he enjoyed it, because over 30-years later he's still doing it and with the same unbridled joy and enthusiasm as he had on Day One.

FAVORITE TEAM(S)/PLAYER(S) GROWING UP

WOODS: "The Toronto Maple Leafs were close to my hometown. There were only six teams back then. So, they were my favorite team and there was a player named Dave Keon, who was on that team. I liked all of them, but he was the one who stood out. He was a centerman. I really liked him. Later on in life, I got to play against him, which was something I never expected. And then I got drafted by Montreal and that became my favorite team, obviously. I spent two-years there in the minors and I learned a lot in Montreal. And then I went from there to Detroit. So that's where it ended up and obviously that became my last favorite team."

WHAT IT MEANS TO BE A RED WING

In hockey, sometimes there's a connection between a player or broadcaster and a team that runs so deep that it doesn't matter what level of hockey you're in, but that team follows you throughout your life. It's like, no matter what you do, you're always associated with this particular team, even if it's a different level of hockey.

For Paul Woods, the Red Wings have been a part of his life since his youth and no I don't mean the Detroit Red Wings; although they certainly have been a large part of his career. But even at the lowest levels of hockey, the Red Wings have been part of Woods' life, as the team logo, or crest if you will, has been emblazoned on Woods' sweaters for as long as he can remember. Basically, if you cut him open, you'd see the Red Wings insignia on his heart. And that has held true even after making the transition from player to broadcaster.

WOODS: "The best thing for me, is that the two guys who I've worked with, Bruce Martyn and the guy I presently work with, his name is Ken Kal. And both those guys are outstanding broadcasters. The biggest part for me is that the game's always been exciting in my headset. It's a big advantage for the Color guys that when it really sounds exciting, what you're listening to, you're wrapped up in the game. We've had lots of fun.

"Both those guys have made my job a lot easier because the game sounds very exciting. My first team in Hespeler, when I first started playing in the Squirt House League, it was a six team league and my team was the Red Wings. I had this bright red sweater that I wore for two-years and it just seemed funny to me that when it was all said and done, that it ended up the same way it started. It was really important to me. The Red Wings' crest has always sort of been in my life."

WOODS'S FAVORITE RED WINGS GAMES HE'S CALLED

Ah rivalries! In sports you can't get enough of them. And even though divisional/conference alignments change over the years, as do the cast of characters, there will always be something that really lights the spark between two bitter rivals. Even if one team goes through a down period, you can always count on a heated exchange when a bitter rival comes to town.

Over the course of their history, the Red Wings have had many rivalries; several of which are still in effect to this day. There are the Original Six Rivalries, although perhaps none burns hotter than the one with the Blackhawks. There's also their rivalry with the Colorado Avalanche, that even though it's been quite a few years since they shared a division, the blood still gets pumping when these two teams meet.

WOODS: "When the Red Wings played Colorado and they had a really bitter rivalry back in the '90s, those were just really intense battles.

"There was a genuine dislike back in those days between the teams and that was an element. There were so many narratives and I think, sometimes, that's what's missing today. There's not enough narratives. There were just so many storylines and so many different things that could happen during the course of the game. And then the intensity of the crowd. Back in those days, especially in Colorado, we were right in the crowd. You (the broadcasters) were just part of it. It was just a very intense time."

MESSAGE TO RED WINGS FANS

As is a common theme amongst members of the sports media, it is a well known fact that without the fans our jobs would either A) not exist or B) they'd have a lot less meaning. So, each of the broadcasters in this book took a couple of minutes to address you, the fans, directly.

WOODS: "Never, ever forget that we're an Original Six team in the National Hockey League. We have won the second most Stanley Cups. Only the Montreal Canadiens have won more. But again, we've had this historic franchise and just so many great players. I played for the Detroit Red Wings. And even during my time in Montreal, I felt that history, being part of something very, very special. And then when it came to Detroit, it's the same thing.

"There's just so many great players who have played before you. It's almost humbling in a way when you look back and see these names and think that you're somewhat a part of that group. So I'm just very happy I guess that I've been able to do that. To be part of an Original Six team and never, ever forget about our franchise's deep history."

EDMONTON OILERS

JACK MICHAELS
TV/RADIO: PLAY-BY-PLAY

First Season on Oilers TV/Radio: TV: 2020-21 (Radio: 2010-11)
Seasons on Oilers TV/Radio (including 2020-21): TV: 1 (Radio: 11)

Birthday: January 23, 1974 Hometown: Meadville, PA

College/University: Ithaca College

BIOGRAPHY

It's not unusual for a passionate sports fan to eventually wind up working in the sport they love. What IS somewhat unusual is finding somebody working in the sport who DIDN'T grow up with an undying passion for it.

Now, that's not to say that every single person in the sports industry was a fantical fan growing up, but it at least gives you a solid idea of why they chose to work in the industry. Of course, you could be just a casual fan, which would still make sense, although you might question why they have gone down this career path. For Jack Michaels, he would even tell you he fell more into the casual fan realm then into the fanatical one. It's not that Michaels didn't love sports, because he did. It's just that hockey wasn't as much of a priority.

MICHAELS: "We got a fuzzy station out of London, Ontario. CBC Channel 10. And every once in a while we got a playoff game featuring the Montreal Canadiens, but I really didn't get into it from a fan perspective until Pittsburgh got Mario Lemieux. That's when I started following it.

"You could make an argument that my favorite announcer was Mike Lange, the Penguins' Play-by-Play guy. I thought he was awesome and I still do. Mike is great at what he does. He's a great guy. I got into the Penguins and as I entered High School, they were getting good. So, I became a fan and started to follow the sport a lot more closely. Pittsburgh kind of triggered my interest in hockey from just a kind of a casual, 'Hey, what's this kind of deal,' to kind of must-see TV."

Michaels eventually took that fandom of Lange and used it to help craft his own career as a hockey broadcaster.

MICHAELS: "Most of us Play-by-Play announcers were frustrated athletes, more to the point of being frustrated non-athletes. I think I quickly realized that the sports I was decent at was certainly not going to be enough to make a profession out of it. And I was most interested in sports of any subject matter out there. So, I set upon finding a way I could pursue a career in the business and follow it. While I was a decent writer, I thought broadcasting might have some perks that writing didn't. So, I went after it. Really, you look for ways to stay in sports and being a broadcaster seemed like as good an idea as anything.

"I will say this. I also was fascinated by horse racing growing up and horse racing announcing. There was something about the way a horse race is called that I still believe translates to a hockey game; kind of building to a crescendo throughout the race, throughout the game and then hopefully, you bring your best stuff, your most energy, your most excitement, for the last couple of minutes. I think hockey, I think it translates well, because much like a horse race, a hockey game is often very close at the end; decided by one goal at the most.

"So, probably when I was about 15 or 16, a year or two out from going to College, I started thinking that broadcasting might be for me and let's find a school where I can get some experience. I had called my local radio station, but they wouldn't really put anyone on the air who was still in High School. They wanted at least College experience. So, because of that, I went out and got that experience in College and that's one of the reasons I chose Ithaca, which unlike Syracuse, they were a broadcasting school that would put you on the air right away and you didn't have to wait until your third or fourth year of College. I found that tremendously appealing.

"After College, I ended up not setting the world on fire like I wanted to. I crawled back to my hometown radio station, again, this time with extensive experience, having done a variety of sports in College on the radio and was able to get a radio job where I covered small College football, basketball and baseball and High School hockey.

"I used my High School hockey tape and that's an interesting story. The High School hockey I was covering was in Western Pennsylvania. And the team I was covering was a perennial challenger for the State Championship and the Western Final. The Western Final was played in Pittsburgh and the Eastern Final was played in Philadelphia. Well, the Western Final was played at The Igloo and the Eastern Final was played at The Spectrum. And I happened to do a Western Final in 1999 that went to double-overtime, so much so that the Penguins announcers were starting to set up for their game that night.

"One of them was a guy by the name of Matt McConnell, who's now the voice for the Arizona Coyotes. But back then he was the radio voice of the Penguins. Matt McConnell came up and said, 'you should pursue a hockey job. Anyone can do basketball, football, or baseball, but there's less qualified people who can do hockey.' So that got me applying for hockey jobs and a few months later, I was able to get a job in Colorado Springs for a team called the Colorado Gold Kings of the old West Coast Hockey League.

"After three-years, that team folded abruptly in the summer of 2002. So, I had two choices, because most of the jobs were already filled. I mean, the team folded operations in August, which is not a good time to lose your job if you're in hockey because Training Camp was a month away.

"So I had a choice of going to Anchorage, Alaska, or Greenville, South Carolina. I chose Anchorage because Anchorage had been in the league that I was already in, the West Coast Hockey League. They were one of Colorado's opponents. So I went up to Anchorage hoping. I had a hunch that if they ever got a winning team up there, it was kind of the only game in town. It was the only pro sports team in Alaska. So I went up there and sure enough, we hired a good coach and the team turned things around and was always in the playoffs.

"Then a year after that, the ECHL, which is the AA League, absorbed the West Coast Hockey league teams and all of a sudden I was in a feeder league to the NHL. I was doing games for a very high profile team. It was always in contention for a league championship. And we were doing games on television. In addition to radio, they did a number of TV games, including all the ones in the playoffs.

"So, now I had that platform and the ECHL selected me to do their All-Star game, which was also on television and on the NHL Network and carried by a few other higher profile stations. So, I was able to build together a pretty good resume tape. So much so that along with maybe the cache of being in Alaska and some of the mystery surrounding that, but in 2010, when the Edmonton Oilers had an announcer retire after 38-years with the hockey club and they had never hired before. So, they were looking at anyone and everyone and thought the kid from Alaska might be worth a shot."

FAVORITE BROADCASTERS GROWING UP

MICHAELS: "Well, I mean, Mike Lange could string together 10 or 11-minutes of rapid fire Play-by-Play without a stumble, without a mistake; making it completely clear as to what was going on. He had a great style and I'm not talking about the 'Michael, Michael motorcycle,' stuff that Mike Lange is known for now. He just was great at Play-by-Play. He had a sharp voice and he was always on it. It seemed tireless, with the energy completely up all the time.

"Then the other two guys were: Mike 'Doc' Emrick, who I'm very proud of, eventually became a reference of mine and a guy who advocated for me in terms of getting the Oilers job. Then the other guy would be Gary Thorne. And it's been a long time since Gary has done hockey regularly, but I thought he was very good. I liked the way Gary Thorne called a game. Those were the three guys in terms of announcers who immediately come to mind in terms of who I really liked."

HOCKEY AFTER DARK -- TALES AWAY FROM THE RINK

Traveling around the continent and getting to experience so many different things is just one of the many perks afforded to professional sports broadcasters. And it's always nice to hear about the various different places and activities that these broadcasters get up to when they have some spare time.

MICHAELS: "Well, I mean, not that it's necessarily high culture or anything, but one of the interesting coincidences is that we happened to be in the same city as the (College Football) National Championship Game two out of three years. So, I've seen two Alabama-Clemson games just by pure luck, in terms of being in that exact city with having an off-day and being able to see the game both times was pretty lucky.

"I went to the 45-40 Alabama win in Glendale, Arizona. And then, a couple of years later, we were in the Bay Area and it was the game where Clemson won 44-16 and they blew them out. So, that was pretty cool being there for a couple of games.

"When you travel around the league, you usually knock out a lot of the touristy things. The Arch in St. Louis. The Book Depository in Dallas. I mean, I've had a day where it was so nice in Pittsburgh, we were able to golf in the morning and catch a Steelers-Bengals game in the afternoon, wearing shorts in the middle of November. When I think back about all the different things, I saw Phil Collins in Boston.

"We get out and do stuff; whether it be concerts or other sporting events. The two National Championship Games are pretty funny just because what are the odds that we're going to be in the same city and actually have an off-day where we can see the game and then obviously attend the games in person. That's pretty cool."

MICHAELS'S FAVORITE OILERS GAME HE'S CALLED

The Calgary Flames and Edmonton Oilers have never liked each other. Their shared history is often a brutal and sometimes violent one; which is no surprise given the geographic proximity to each other. Besides, hockey is often a heated game and by its very nature, you can expect fights to break out; although, true heavyweight bouts are far rarer now than they were a couple decades ago. But that doesn't mean you can't still get an exciting fisticuffs when the situation warrants it.

What you can never expect is for the two goalies to start fighting. These aren't the days of Patrick Roy seemingly looking for a fight on a nightly basis. No, goaltenders usually stay far away from each other during the course of a game. And that's why, what happened on Saturday night February 1, 2020, was so stunning.

Edmonton's Mike Smith and Calgary's Cam Talbot took things to another level in what was already a highly combative affair. These two teams had been on edge after Calgary's David Rittich seemingly disrespected the Oilers a few nights prior with a "stick-flip" celebration following a shootout victory. So, when the Oilers knocked out Rittich in the second period of the rematch, having already scored four-goals, the tensions of the teams were mounting.

All that was needed was the final spark. That came when Sam Gagner poked at the puck underneath Talbot's pads and pushed the puck across the goal-line even though the play had been waved off. Several fights broke out and Talbot was involved in the scrums.

Smith, not one to run from a fight, skated to center ice and essentially dared Talbot to do the same.

Ding, Ding, Ding! Talbot came out to meet Smith and the fight was on! Smith won by way of a knockdown and it left an indelible memory for all; including, Jack Michaels.

MICHAELS: "That battle of Alberta game, February 1, 2020, that was a very memorable game. I mean, the Oilers won big, but there was a goalie fight. It was fun to see Edmonton and Calgary get back to the old days where they really used to hate each other when I was a kid. So that was a lot of fun."

MICHAELS' MOST FAMOUS CALL

There's no better feeling for a broadcaster than knowing that a call you made has taken on a life of its own. And the funny part is, you might not think that highly of the call yourself. But that doesn't matter.

What does matter is how the fans feel about it. For Jack Michaels, his call of a goalie fight between the Oilers and Flames is one such example of this.

MICHAELS: "There was a goalie fight this year. There had been a bunch of fights at a game between Edmonton and Calgary. And at the end of it, I said, 'this is the battle of Alberta we've been waiting for, for three-decades.' I think a lot of people, especially locally, took that to heart and liked that call."

MESSAGE TO OILERS FANS

As is a common theme amongst members of the sports media, it is a well known fact that without the fans our jobs would either A) not exist or B) they'd have a lot less meaning. So, each of the broadcasters in this book took a couple of minutes to address you, the fans, directly.

MICHAELS: "Hang in there. Hopefully we're getting closer. With (Connor) McDavid and (Leon) Draisaitl, hopefully we'll be knocking on the door for a Stanley Cup in the next year or two and eventually get over the hump. I think the biggest thing the Oilers have to do is establish themselves in the playoffs as a playoff contender year in and year out. I think you take a look at the last three Stanley Cup champions and they all were contenders for years before finally breaking through.

"Washington, St. Louis and Tampa, were knocking on the door and (came) really close and (were) just not able to get over the hump (until) they finally did. And I guess I'd say to Oilers fans, hopefully we're close. Hopefully we're getting there. This year, their playoff stay was a pretty short one, but hopefully there's a few more playoff years while we have McDavid and Draisaitl that will eventually lead to a breakthrough."

FLORIDA PANTHERS

STEVEN GOLDSTEIN
TV: PLAY-BY-PLAY

First Season on Panthers TV: 2007-08
Seasons on Panthers TV (including 2020-21): 14

Birthday: January 20, 1970 Hometown: Brooklyn, NY

College/University: Syracuse University

BIOGRAPHY

Turns out, you don't need to be from Canada to grow up a rabid hockey fan. And while there are plenty of electric hockey markets in the United States, New York has also had an extra special feel to it. I'm sure there's many reasons why, but that's a story for another day.

Steven Goldstein grew up in Brooklyn, NY, in the neighborhood of Canarsie (South Brooklyn) and boy did he LOVE his New York Rangers. Let's be honest, when he was at the age where he could start picking his team loyalty, the Rangers were THE TEAM in New York. The Islanders, with all the tremendous things they accomplished during their dynasty, didn't start winning soon enough to capture Goldstein's fandom.

GOLDSTEIN: "I was a huge sports fan growing up. I really liked all sports, but hockey just had that energy and growing up when I did, it was an incredible rivalry between the Rangers and Islanders.

Obviously, going to Madison Square Garden was absolutely off the wall. I mean, going to Giants Stadium for Giants games was phenomenal too, but Madison Square Garden, back in the 80's (was just incredible).

"I don't understand how anybody doesn't fall in love with the sport (of hockey) and growing up, I used to listen to all the games. When I grew up in Brooklyn, we didn't have cable. So most of the games weren't on TV. I always listened to Marv Albert on the radio and wanted to be a sportscaster from the time I can remember. So Marv was a huge influence and I was just as happy listening to it on the radio as I was watching the game on TV because I just loved his calls.

"I think the first game I went to was probably in the late-70's, Rangers at Islanders at Nassau Coliseum. We had the last row behind the goal and it was very hard to get those tickets. My dad got them and there were girls, Rangers fans, sitting next to me. I think one of them had a Pat Hickey jersey on and one of them had a (Ron) Duguay jersey on. They had all kinds of signs and the place was just absolutely rocking, it was nuts.

"From then on, I absolutely just loved it. There were a lot of games where the Rangers, back then, used to play Sunday nights at home at Madison Square Garden. And my dad had Giants season tickets.

"So, there were quite a few Sundays as a kid, I remember Giants kicked off at one, four o'clock we're out of Giants Stadium. We were in the city by five. We'd go to dinner right at The Garden. They had the old BeefSteak Charlie's, (I'll) never forget it. There was all you could eat shrimp. Then, me and my dad would go to the Rangers game at seven o'clock. It couldn't have been tailored any better for the greatest Sunday ever for a little sports fan like myself.

"I remember one week, I think the Giants beat the Cowboys, upset Roger Staubach and those great Cowboys teams and that night the Rangers played Edmonton. I think Don Maloney scored the winner in overtime. He might've even had two or three goals that game. It was Edmonton when (Wayne) Gretzky had just gotten there. Gretzky and (Mark) Messier, before they started winning Cups. That's one of my earliest memories; one of the great sports days for me and obviously without my dad, it never would have happened. He's the one who took me to all these games."

Of course, Goldstein did a lot more than just watch hockey and attend games as a fan. He also played street (roller) hockey with his buddies, even if they had to get a bit creative. As Goldstein recalls, there was a hardware store on Avenue L where he and his friends would buy a roll of electrical tape for 69-cents. That roll of tape would then be used as their puck and should the puck go down a sewer drain, or disappear into some other crevice, they would skate back to the hardware store to purchase another roll. Now that's dedication.

Getting back to the NHL, Goldstein, as a Rangers fan, had some top-flight broadcasters to listen to or watch and they certainly had an impact on him. From Marv Albert to Sal Messina to Jim Gordon and Bill Chadwick, their colorful personalities and sweet styles captured Goldstein's heart and imagination.

They lit a fire in him that saw him eventually blaze a path towards his own career as a broadcaster and what a path it's been!

Goldstein started as an intern with WFAN, but not on the air. No, he was a promotions intern. He was tasked with taking The Fan Van all over the place and stopping people who had WFAN bumper stickers on their cars (the station used to give them out all the time) in order to give them lottery tickets. (WFAN had a sponsorship deal with the New York Lottery).

After giving people their lottery tickets, Goldstein would then do a quick little interview with them and that helped hone his skills, even if it wasn't quite the Play-by-Play he would eventually get to do. Although, it did take some time for those Play-by-Play roles to come to Goldstein.

Shortly after graduating from Syracuse, he moved back home and actually took a job with CBS Radio to help with Sunday Night Baseball and Football. It didn't pay particularly well, but it did lead to a full-time job in broadcast operations, so without that grind work, Goldstein wouldn't have been able to advance his career. And during that same time, Goldstein also did part-time work with the CBS Evening News and worked at Sports Phone as well.

There were other freelance roles as well and one such role saw Goldstein do work for a radio station in Miami, Florida, right around the time the Marlins were coming into Major League Baseball, the Panthers were coming into the National Hockey League and the Heat were establishing themselves in the NBA. So, after covering some games as a stringer, Goldstein decided to move to Florida to take a chance on himself. And as it turned out, all the places he was freelancing for in New York, they wanted him to provide coverage of stuff going on in Florida, so it was the perfect set-up.

As it turned out, the station, WQAM, also had the rights to the Panthers, unfortunately, Goldstein was behind a couple broadcasters on the depth chart; including Bob Wischusen. However, after a couple years, the Pre-Game/Intermission/Post-Game role opened up and Godlstein jumped at the chance to do hockey radio. And if that wasn't enough, a missed flight by Chris Moore, who was doing the Panthers' Play-by-Play at the time, led to Goldstein getting a chance to fill in on the broadcast. He was able to call the first two periods of the game (which, ironically was against the Rangers) before Moore finally made it to the arena for the third period.

But that game gave Goldstein the confidence he needed to do the job. And even though he was passed over in favor of Jiggs McDonald a few years later, once Jiggs retired and the 2004-05 lockout had been resolved, Goldstein finally got the full-time gig. He did the Panthers' radio Play-by-Play for two-years and was then shifted over to TV and has been there ever since.

FAVORITE PLAYER(S) GROWING UP

GOLDSTEIN: "You could write letters to players and I did this incessantly, believe it or not, in all sports. I used to write letters to all kinds of players. There were actually nights, believe it or not, I'd be watching the Rangers on Channel Nine.

"I was a big fan of Steve Vickers and I was a Mike Allison fan, 'Big Red,' number 14. I had a Reijo Ruotsalainen jersey because he was one of the first guys to come over from Finland. The way he skated with the puck going end-to-end, I was like, 'wow, this is just phenomenal.' I actually wrote some of those guys letters and I can recall that when I was 10 or 11 writing and saying, I'm watching you right now on Channel Nine, taking on whoever.'

"I remember Steve Vickers sent me back a nice picture with a little note, 'Steve, thanks for your letter.' Mike Allison sent me something back. I want to say Barry Beck probably sent me something back too. I was such a big fan and I loved those guys.

"I was also a big Tony Granato fan. His rookie year, I think he scored 36 (goals), which I think is still a record for a Rangers rookie. I actually had a Tony Granato Jersey. That summer after Granato's rookie year, I had gotten an internship with WFAN. And at the WFAN golf tournament, Tony Granato came and I brought my jersey to show it to him and take a picture.

"I still have the picture. He was so gracious when I met him and I'll never forget, he looked at me, looked at the jersey and said, 'I thought I was the only one who had one of these.'"

HOCKEY AFTER DARK -- TALES AWAY FROM THE RINK

I know you have to really love hockey to be a hockey broadcaster, but that doesn't mean you can't love other sports too. And being from Brooklyn, NY, would it really surprise you to find out that Steven Goldstein loves his basketball? New York is a basketball city after all.

So, when given the opportunity, Goldstein goes to basketball games, regardless of who's playing and he'll even drag his broadcaster partner along for the evening.

GOLDSTEIN: "I remember one night, my buddy used to work for the NBA, we went to a Hawks-Cavs and we were right there in the front row for LeBron James. So that was a good story. I had another night when Jeremy Lin was making his run with the Knicks that one year and I got tickets.

"We got to New Jersey, like at six o'clock one night from Florida, playing the Devils the next night and I got tickets for Knicks-Lakers. Bill Lindsay was my partner at the time on TV and they were up in the Blue Seats. I think we were like second row Blue Seats behind the basket way up there. And I'm like, 'come on, I'm going to take you to The Garden.'.

"So I took him and Kobe (Bryant) had a great game too, but Jeremy Lin lit it up that night. Like, I don't even know how many points. So I remember doing that with Bill Lindsay."

Basketball isn't the only thing Goldstein likes to do in his spare time though. He also loves hot, spicy chicken wings and what's the best place to go for those? You guessed it, Buffalo, NY.

GOLDSTEIN: "When we go to Buffalo, we have a mandatory wing night with all of our crew. We go to a place called Gabriel's Gate in Buffalo on Allen Street. That's my go-to spot in Buffalo. I know there's more famous places and things like that, but that's what we do in Buffalo."

GOLDSTEIN'S FAVORITE PANTHERS GAMES HE'S CALLED

The Panthers haven't exactly been a Stanley Cup-bound team during Steven Goldstein's run as the TV Play-by-Play announcer, but that doesn't mean they haven't had some memorable games and series. For Goldstein, there are two such playoff series that come to mind; even though neither ended with a Panthers victory.

GOLDSTEIN: "The 2012 series against the Devils, there were a couple of games. It was the first time I ever did Play-by-Play in the playoffs. The Game Two win at home was the first ever in that building. The Panthers' first home playoff win since '97, in the series against the Rangers when they lost in five. So it had been a long time coming.

"So, announcing that game and just getting a playoff win, the first I'd ever announced, first in the new building, which wasn't so new anymore and the first since '97 was incredible. The other thing in that series, even though we lost the game, was Game Seven against New Jersey. We were down one late in the third when Marcel Goc scored and tied it.

"Believe it or not, I'll tell the story. Bill Lindsay was in the broadcast booth and he lives and dies with the Panthers; the same way Randy Moller does now. So, Goc scored to tie it and Bill Lindsay, physically, as I'm making the goal call, lifted me up, grabbed me and lifted me up, hugging me as I'm yelling, 'Goc has tied it!'.

"Then, of course, it goes double overtime and anytime you do an extended overtime game, it's incredible. Unfortunately, Adam Henrique ended it and the Panthers lost in seven, but that was an incredible game; probably a big, 'what could have been,' because the Panthers had a pretty good team that year.

"If you recall, the Devils went on to make the Stanley Cup Final that year after the Panthers pretty much had them. I mean, the Panthers were up three-games-to-two. Game Six in New Jersey went to overtime and the Panthers lost and then Game Seven in Florida went to double-overtime and the Panthers lost. So those two certainly stand out to me.

"(Also) the whole Islanders series in '16 (was memorable too). After one of the games, we were in Barclays, so there's no broadcast booth and someone dumped beer on (Denis) Potvin and I during the post-game and I said it on the air. That was in all the New York papers. They had extra security standing next to Denny (after that). That whole series was a great series."

SIGNATURE PHRASE

There are a lot of broadcasters who don't like to be boxed into a corner in always having to use the same phrase in certain situations. They feel it comes off as contrived and disingenuous. Meanwhile, others feel, as long as it comes off naturally, that it's alright to have some fun with your calls; even if it means having to use the same one over and over again.

Steven Goldstein falls somewhere in the middle of these two ends of the spectrum. He doesn't like the idea of having to say something over and over, but he doesn't mind having a little fun when the situation warrants it. And it was his creativity, plus a childhood love for a certain cartoon that led to the berth of one of the funnier signature calls in the National Hockey League.

GOLDSTEIN: "Well, I don't do it all the time, but Jonathan Huberdeau has been with the Panthers since he's a teenager. And I get along with him pretty well. So, I wanted to come up with something fun. I thought maybe he could be a star. It's a cross between being a Scooby-

Doo fan when I was growing up and the Sinatra song. So I kind of came up with something when he scored, one time. I just went 'Hooby Dooby Doo,' on the air and he loved it. He likes it a lot. His family likes it. He's told me that. It kind of caught on. I don't do it every time. Certainly some people think it's hokey, but, when it's a big goal, sometimes it just comes out."

MESSAGE TO PANTHERS FANS

As is a common theme amongst members of the sports media, it is a well known fact that without the fans our jobs would either A) not exist or B) they'd have a lot less meaning. So, each of the broadcasters in this book took a couple of minutes to address you, the fans, directly.

GOLDSTEIN: "My message would be, (I) greatly appreciate the support because they've supported me personally, an incredible amount. So, personally my message would be one of incredible appreciation for everything. The love they've shown me, honestly, it's been remarkable. From a team standpoint, it would be, I do believe the team is going to win. I do believe the team is on the right track and they've been so loyal through a lot of changes and a lot of tough seasons.

"I do believe the loyalty will be paid off one day and just hang in there with the team. I believe the Panthers fans get just a terrible rap, (which is) so unfair because they are great fans, knowledgeable fans. (They) may not be as big as some other fan bases. And when people criticize the Florida fans, it really bothers me because they are as passionate and they love their team as much as anybody."

RANDY MOLLER
TV: COLOR ANALYST

First Season on Panthers TV: 2015-16
Seasons on Panthers TV (including 2020-21): 6

Birthday: August 23, 1963 Hometown: Calgary, AB

College/University: N/A

BIOGRAPHY

What was a young boy to do, growing up in Western Canada at a time when the internet didn't exist and the capabilities of radio and television weren't anywhere near what they are today? Well, he could play sports. But what sport? Come on, do you really have to ask that? It's hockey, of course!

Randy Moller was a Western Canada boy just like any other. He, as well as his brother, played hockey during much of their spare time and much of their planned time too.

MOLLER: "My father and my mother, they encouraged my brother and I -- my brother also played in the NHL. Back then, in the early-70's, late-60's, there wasn't much else to do in Canada for about seven months out of the year, but play hockey.

"My parents gave my brother and I an opportunity to play high level hockey and sacrificed just like everybody's parents did; sacrificing a lot financially and time-wise for us to play. I was able to play at a high level, basically a Triple-A level, in Red Deer, through Peewee, Bantam, Midget. And then, I was able to play Junior Hockey as a 16-year-old.

"I played for the Red Deer Rustlers and we ended up winning the Centennial Cup, which is the Tier Two equivalent of the Memorial Cup. The next year, I went and played for the Lethbridge Broncos with my brother and the Sutter brothers.

"Brent was there. Richie and Ronnie were there. And then I got drafted in the first-round by the Quebec Nordiques. (I) went back to

Junior for one more year and then I turned pro the next year. I wasn't even 19-years-old. And I was able to play 13-years in the league."

Moller was able to carve out a niche for himself in the NHL as a strong, tough defenseman and played for four teams during his 13-year career. There were the early years with Quebec. Then that was followed by stints with the Rangers and Sabres. And lastly, came a brief stop with the Panthers before his body told him it was time to hang up the skates and pursue something else.

MOLLER: "When I came down to Florida, I only played 17 games for the Florida Panthers before I was forced to retire. I took a half-a-year off and then the next year I got right into broadcasting; doing radio and then it became radio and television. I was an Analyst, but I also did (some) Play-by-Play on radio and was the first and only former NHLer to do full-time Play-by-Play. It seemed like it was just natural (to do broadcasting) after I retired."

As Moller put it, he guessed he had a good relationship with Panthers' President, Bill Torrey, because the job was offered to him when Alain Chevrier couldn't commit to doing radio full-time due to his insurance business and his kids. So, Moller basically fell into the job and he's been there ever since -- spending over 20-years in various broadcasting roles.

FAVORITE PLAYER(S) GROWING UP

MOLLER: "My favorite player growing up, as far as I can remember, Hockey Night in Canada and that was Bobby Orr. But, I was also a big fan of Darryl Sittler of the Toronto Maple Leafs and Lanny McDonald. And I loved defenseman Larry Robinson of the Montreal Canadiens as well, cause I was a defenseman."

HOCKEY AFTER DARK -- TALES AWAY FROM THE RINK

Traveling is a big part of the sports industry. Teams and broadcasters go from place to place for each of their games and get to see so many different sights that it's easy to lose track of just how wonderful those experiences are. And forget the sights for a minute, there's also the local restaurants and entertainment scenes that also are worth trying out.

Some people take all this for granted as just another part of the job. But not Randy Moller. Moller LOVES to see each of the different cities across the NHL. It's probably his favorite part of the job; aside from calling the games of course.

MOLLER: "I've enjoyed my time. I've had and continue to have the best job, I think, in the world. I totally enjoy it. And one of the reasons why is because we do get to travel. We travel with the team and we're fortunate to be on the team charters.

"Since day one that I've been broadcasting, that affords you a lot of opportunities. I love to travel. I love to see things. And remember, we go into places, new places like Nashville, Anaheim and Arizona. All these places that have joined the league. Minnesota and Columbus (too). I love going. People ask me, 'where's my favorite city to go to?' I can't put a finger on it because I love them all.

"Vancouver's incredible. Going back to Montreal and going to Toronto where it's the heart and soul and iconic buildings. They're such rabid hockey markets that everybody's just totally consumed with the Leafs and the Canadiens. There's so many great places. I mean, Dallas is a wonderful place to go to.

"I'm a big restaurant guy and I love to eat in different restaurants and taste the local menus at all the restaurants. So it's been fun. Tampa's a great spot as well. I love going to Denver, going to the mountains. I've been afforded a great opportunity to do that and with some of the best friends that I've ever had in our broadcasting group. Whether it's part of the crew or broadcast partners; that's really been the highlight and what I look forward to."

MOLLER'S FAVORITE ARENAS TO CALL GAMES

There are so many unique buildings across the National Hockey League. The history in cities like New York, Toronto, Montreal, Detroit, Boston and Chicago is off the charts. The energy in places like Vegas, Colorado, San Jose, Edmonton, Calgary, etc. is enough to blow the roof off a building and perhaps set new indoor decibel level records.

For Randy Moller, there's no question that each arena and city has something special to it. But there are a handful that perhaps stand out above the rest.

MOLLER: "There's so many. Obviously broadcasting back home, Red Deer's right between Calgary and Edmonton, being able to go back and my family's there and to be able to see them. It's a special place to go back to Calgary and Edmonton. That's special for me. (Also), my first time broadcasting in Montreal and Toronto. Madison Square Garden is one of my favorite places to go to as well, just because of how iconic the building is."

MESSAGE TO PANTHERS FANS

As is a common theme amongst members of the sports media, it is a well known fact that without the fans our jobs would either A) not exist or B) they'd have a lot less meaning. So, each of the broadcasters in this book took a couple of minutes to address you, the fans, directly.

MOLLER: "Stay patient and stay loyal. We are going to someday, hopefully qualify and get into the Stanley Cup Final. It's been a long time since '96. I love the passion of our fans. The dedication, the loyalty of our fans down here, we've got a great fan base and I'm just hoping and I know, one day, hopefully sooner than later we'll be one of the top teams in the National Hockey League. And congratulations to Tampa Bay. Hockey works in Florida. If you win and you're successful, you're going to get supported very, very well. And Tampa is a true Testament of that."

LA KINGS

JIM FOX
TV: COLOR ANALYST

First Season on Kings TV: 1990-91
Seasons on Kings TV (including 2020-21): 31

Birthday: May 18, 1960 Hometown: Coniston, ON

College/University: N/A

BIOGRAPHY

Growing up in Coniston, Ontario, which is a small town in Canada, Jim Fox was just like any kid with a love for sports. He played hockey, because his friends played hockey. Everybody played it. They played it anywhere they could.

In the small town Fox grew up in that even included playing at an outdoor rink that was located up a hill. But it wasn't just playing hockey that captured the attention of a young Jim Fox. It was also watching the sport. From watching the "old-timers" who Fox estimated to be around 50, to watching the one Hockey Night in Canada broadcast per week, everything revolved around the frozen sport.

Now, technology being what it was back when Fox was growing up, that meant tuning into either the Montreal Canadiens game or the Toronto Maple Leafs game every Saturday night. And it wasn't his choice. It was whatever the Hockey Night in Canada program had on tap.

So, naturally, Fox grew up a big fan of Montreal's announcers, Danny Gallivan and Dick Irvin Jr.

Eventually, Fox's hockey skills progressed to the point where he was playing Junior Hockey and then, at the age of 20, he went straight to the NHL as a member of the Los Angeles Kings.

As a first-round pick by the Kings in the 1980 NHL Draft, the right-wing Fox jumped right into the lineup and was a steady secondary scorer for the team. In fact, in Fox's first eight-seasons with the Kings, he registered 60 or more points five times. Unfortunately, injuries curtailed him and the 1989-90 season (his ninth in the league) proved to be his last.

So, what was the 29, soon-to-be 30-year-old Fox going to do now that his playing days were over. Well, I'll tell you one thing. Broadcasting certainly wasn't on his mind.

FOX: "I never ever thought of being a broadcaster. I was injured and had to retire due to knee injuries. I actually worked in the Community Relations Department with the Kings for a year before I was asked to go into broadcasting."

That's right, he didn't decide to become a broadcaster. He was asked to do it. And being the team player he had always been, Fox jumped in; without a single drop of prior training. You might find yourselves asking, "why would the Kings ask him to be a broadcaster without prior training?"

Well, as Fox put it, it was the Wayne Gretzky Effect. Back then, a lot of teams did simulcasts of their games. But with Gretzky's popularity off the charts and hockey becoming a more prominent part of the Los Angeles culture, the Kings decided to take advantage of the situation and reap the benefits of the new revenue streams that were opened to them. So, the Kings split their simulcast into a more traditional TV and Radio setup.

That meant putting Fox on camera as a Color Analyst, which wasn't so usual back then. Nowadays you see plenty of former players becoming Analysts after their playing careers are over. But when Fox was asked to make the transition, it was a lot rarer.

FOX: "So, my first three-years, basically it was learn on the job. It was a very difficult experience. It was something where I was quite embarrassed of how bad I was doing, jumping from being a professional athlete where you're on the top of your sport to another walk of life where I was certainly learning even how to just get by. It was a struggle. It was a huge struggle."

After that, the Kings hired Andrea Kirby, a media consultant, to help not just Fox, but the players, coaches, executives, etc. within the organization learn to deal with the media. And Kirby was able to give Fox a starting point, solid critiques and more in order to help him grow into the confident broadcaster he is today.

Of course, Fox has also learned from some of his contemporaries. No, not by asking them for tips, but rather, by just watching and listening to how they handle their respective jobs. And the three broadcasters he likes to credit most are: Johnny Miller, Troy Aikman and John Davidson.

FOX: "John Davidson in hockey was certainly the guy who was a nice guy to listen to. He broke the game down, but he never seemed like he was breaking the game down. It was just his conversational style. He was just absolutely easy to listen to. And then at the same time he was able to offer the analysis of the game."

Looking back on everything, Los Angeles Kings fans have been able to grow along with Fox over the past 30-years (as a broadcaster) and while there might have been some struggles early on, he's now a well oiled machine of an Analyst; which means the fans are in good hands.

FAVORITE PLAYER(S) GROWING UP

FOX: "For me, it was Bobby Orr. Basically, I was six, seven-years-old when he was a rookie in the National Hockey League. And, of course, when the Bruins won in '69-'70, I was nine, 10-years-old. Bobby Orr was the guy who caught my attention and really allowed me to fall in love with the game. I was a Bruins fan. I was always a Boston fan because of Bobby Orr, but I followed the whole team and, of course, they won two Stanley Cups in three-years. That was huge."

LEARNING THE TRICKS OF THE TRADE

Back when Fox was first breaking into the broadcasting business, things were done quite a bit differently. For one thing, they usually taped pre-game interviews with players for the purpose of playing them back during the game. And as Fox recalls, there were two players he interacted with who stood out to him -- for opposite reasons -- when he was first getting his feet wet as a broadcaster.

The first was Wayne Gretzky, who according to Fox, would stroll into the room for the interview -- which usually was about an hour-and-a-half before game-time -- with a newspaper in his hand. And while the camera crew often took a minute or two to make sure the lighting, audio and visual settings were all good to go, Gretzky would be casually waiting there reading the newspaper. And then, "like the flick of a switch" as Fox put it, the interview would begin and Gretzky would be good to go.

FOX: "You get the five-second countdown and he's still reading the paper. Then it's like, 'welcome back. We're here with Wayne Gretzky' and he turns it on like a flick of a switch. He just turns it on. He was so good. He was personable. His answers had depth, they had analysis.

"Five-seconds before he goes on, he's reading the newspaper. You would think he's not even thinking about doing an interview. I think that quality tells a lot about him just as a player and his ability to focus and concentrate, because he could flick a switch and boom, go from reading a paper to doing an interview and not missing a beat within five-seconds."

On the other hand of the spectrum was Larry Robinson, who once had some fun at Fox's expense.

FOX: "In a previous game, Larry cut his nose. So I made a joke on TV like, 'the cut looks like it's only an inch, but it's really a six-inch cut because of the size of his nose.' Well, someone told him about it. So, the night Larry was coming on, we were actually doing a Live interview during the first intermission.

"He had talked to our Producer and everyone on the team, so they all knew what was going to happen, except me. So, I ask him the first question and he just answers "no." And back then, I would have my questions taped on the wall across.

“So I ask the second question and he goes, "yes." So, he's just giving these one-word answers and I'm about ready to swear, which I can't do because we're on air. I ask the third question and he again just says, "no." Then, before I could ask the fourth question, he just erupted in laughter. The camera man and the Stage Manager were laughing. I even had to give a little chuckle because I knew he got me back.”

FOX’S FAVORITE KINGS GAME HE’S CALLED

As a former player, Jim Fox is uniquely qualified to speak about what it’s like for players going through tough times in the playoffs. He’s been there. He’s done that. And that has helped him as an Analyst, being able to get inside the mind of the players.

So, it’s no wonder that two of his favorite games that he’s been on the call for were two Game Seven’s; 21-years apart.

The first was Game Seven of the 1993 Clarence Campbell Conference Final versus the Toronto Maple Leafs. The Kings were down 3-2 in the series when they headed home for Game Six. Los Angeles won Game Six 5-4 in overtime before traveling all the way back to Toronto for Game Seven. And as Fox recalls, Bob McKenzie, then writing for a Toronto paper, wrote a piece stating that Gretzky was playing like he had a piano on his back.

Well, clearly The Great One didn’t like that comment because he went out and netted a hat-trick against the Leafs, including scoring what ended up as the game-winning goal. And as Fox recalls, “just that overall atmosphere, to be in an historic building like that and with the type of players who were involved and it being a Game Seven, with a trip to the Stanley Cup Final on the line, that was huge.”

Of course, doing the locker room interviews post-game was also a blast for Fox as many of those Kings players were former teammates of his, so it was a special moment for him.

The other Game Seven that stands out to Fox was in 2014, when the Kings came back to beat the Sharks 5-1 at the Shark Tank after first trailing the series 0-3.

FOX: "I'll never forget the goal scored by Anze Kopitar. He took a pass from Justin Williams, he picked it up and he's coming down the middle of the slot, basically receives the pass and it looks like he's going to shoot, but he just holds on. He beats out Martin Jones. And by the time he ends up scoring, it's like Jones is in the corner and it's a wide open net.

"The feeling of being around a team who comes back from 0-3 to end up winning a series like that, in a building known as one of the loudest buildings in the league because of its construction. It's kind of a smaller building and it doesn't have a lot of room for the noise to get lost. Everything is just pounded. The sense of accomplishment is huge."

MESSAGE TO KINGS FANS

As is a common theme amongst members of the sports media, it is a well known fact that without the fans our jobs would either A) not exist or B) they'd have a lot less meaning. So, each of the broadcasters in this book took a couple of minutes to address you, the fans, directly.

FOX: "I hope that they enjoy hockey the way I was able to live it, which is the ultimate team game. And I know most team sports probably try to make an argument for why their sport is the best team game, sport. But in hockey, where basically your best player only plays half the game, it is a back and forth sport. Meaning, unlike baseball and football, where you're not necessarily playing offense and defense on the same shift, basketball and hockey have that back and forth.

"But just to understand how many things, how many players, how they have to work together. How they have to understand that there are little things to be done as well as the big things. And then, if you work that way and find out that way that I think that they can, as fans, I hope we can bring that to them. I hope we can help them feel that.

"And when you win the championships, I think this comes through more than anything, they can feel the fact that they're a part of it too, because there are so many elements that need to come together and the building and the energy and the fans are part of that. The last thing I would say to them is, I would applaud the fans of the Kings and hockey in general, because, live and I'm a broadcaster, there's nothing like a hockey game.

"There's nothing like a Stanley Cup playoff game live, inside a building to let the fans know...I'm not going to say the players appreciate it. They certainly do. But the players enjoy it. The enjoyment you derive from being in that type of environment, that type of energy and that type of atmosphere that is brought about by the fans, so don't ever think it's not important because it is hugely important to the game of hockey to have that experience live in the building."

NICK NICKSON
RADIO: PLAY-BY-PLAY

First Season on Kings Radio: 1990-91
Seasons on Kings Radio (including 2020-21): 31

Birthday: December 21, 1953 Hometown: Rochester, NY

College/University: Ithaca College

BIOGRAPHY

Mr. Sports. That's what Nick Nickson should have been called when he was growing up. Is that unique to just him? No. But it is a highly accurate way to describe how Nickson occupied his time. Cliche nicknames aside, Nickson was a multi-sport athlete growing up as he played baseball, football and basketball in High School. He even played on a traveling bowling team.

Now, you might notice the one sport not listed there is hockey. That's not because Nickson didn't play hockey. It's just because his High School didn't have a team. So, Nickson played organized hockey for a city league in Rochester.

I'm sure -- not that he;s likely to admit it -- that Nickson, at some point while growing up, had aspirations of playing sports at a professional level. Let's face it, most athletically inclined kids have that dream at some point in time. I know I did.

But when he graduated High School, Nickson wasn't sure what career path he wanted to pursue. Yes, he went to Ithaca College and yes, he was a Communications Major. But no, he didn't immediately think about becoming a sports broadcaster. Sure, you might be asking why go to Ithaca and why be a Communications Major?

Well the answer to that is simple. Nickson's dad was a longtime radio Disc Jockey (and eventually was elevated to a management position). So, as a kid, Nickson would visit his father at the radio station and he got to, "see how it all worked. It was kind of magic," for him. But even with that as a starting point, it wasn't until his Junior year of

College that Nickson chose to heed the siren's call of a career in radio. That's where the student run radio station at Ithaca College came in handy. It provided valuable experience for Nickson.

NICKSON: "I was able to do some sportscasts on the air; a five-minute sportscast. A couple shifts as a Disc Jockey. We'd get the remote equipment, go do some Ithaca College games: basketball, football, baseball, whatever and the College station would air them."

Then, his Senior year of College, he got a weekend job in Rochester as a Disc Jockey, doing the all-night shifts. So that was how he spent his Friday, Saturday and Sunday nights. Then it was back to Ithaca for classes during the week before repeating the cycle the following weekend.

Nickson carried that job through his Senior year and then some as he continued to work the all-night shift as a Disc Jockey after graduating from Ithaca College in February of 1976. He hoped it would lead to a permanent position. What he wasn't expecting was for his father to call him with some unexpected news.

NICKSON: "My dad called me and said the guy who was doing the Rochester Americans hockey games -- the AHL team in my hometown -- was leaving. He got the job with the Pittsburgh Pirates. My dad said 'if you're interested, give them a call.' At the time, I was working as a Disc Jockey and I said, 'okay, thanks, dad.'

"I hung up the phone and really didn't think much about it. Then, a couple of days later, I said (to myself), 'I don't even know if I have a tape of a hockey game.' I had one reel-to-reel tape of a game I did at Ithaca and it wasn't labeled. I put it on my machine and it was a hockey game. I listened to it and I said, 'I can't turn this in. This is not very good.'.

"So, using my brain and my resources, I went into the radio station where I worked at night, went into the production room and I spliced up the tape, got rid of all the bad stuff and sent them about five-minutes of decent Play-by-Play. And they hired me.

"Eventually, I moved on to New Haven, Connecticut, in the American Hockey League and then, in '81 joined the Kings in the NHL. So, little did I know that those two-hours in that production room that night, back in 1976, would define my professional career basically for the next 45-years."

It's a nice story how just, by chance, Nickson was able to get his Play-by-Play career started and it's made even more so by the fact he's been with the L.A. Kings for so long. He's as much a part of the Kings' family as anyone.

Of course, Nickson's style has developed quite a bit since he began his career and as he puts it, "I was blessed with a good voice." That was something he had in common with one of the broadcasters he used to listen to on a portable radio as a kid. And that broadcaster is the late Bob Wilson, who used to call Bruins games. Granted, it wasn't just Wilson who he listened to. Nickson was often able to pick up the signal for games being called by Lloyd Pettit in Chicago, Dan Kelly in St. Louis and Bruce Martyn in Detroit. But it was Wilson whom Nickson felt influenced him most.

Now, Nickson continues to forge ahead as he enters yet another new decade with the Kings, all while carrying with the lessons he's learned throughout a very fruitful career; including how a broadcaster should be as descriptive as possible on radio. As Nickson told me, "a player has two names. The first is his name and the second is wherever the puck is."

FAVORITE PLAYER(S) GROWING UP

NICKSON: "I remember I was in High School and this was about the time, or maybe a couple of years before, where the players started curving their sticks. Bobby Hull and Stan Mikita were two of the first to experiment with this. They figured out that they could put the blade of their stick into water and then they would put the blade of the stick in the door jam and bend it. So they tried it with a curved blade and went out and shot some pucks.

"They said, 'the puck is doing some funky things here. Maybe let's try this in a game.' And they did. Of course, Bobby Hull could shoot the puck probably faster than anybody at the time. So I remember getting a hockey stick and back then they were about eight bucks a piece, all wood, of course. I got a Bobby Hull model hockey stick and the curve on it was like three-inches. It was like a banana, which of course is illegal. You can only have like a half-inch curve on your stick.

"They made that rule on the curvature of the stick only because the pucks would dip and dart and it would give goaltenders fits. It was basically to protect the goaltenders. I remember going to a rink at the backyard of one of our neighbors and I got this Bobby Hull stick with a huge banana curve on it. I wound up to take a shot and the puck went straight up in the air. I had no idea how to control this puck on a stick with that bend in it."

NICKSON'S FAVORITE KINGS GAMES HE'S CALLED

If you go back to the early and middle part of last decade, you'll find that the Kings had quite a nice run for themselves. In fact, had a couple more games gone their way against Chicago, they might have even had a dynasty.

You see, while the Kings won the Stanley Cup in 2012 and 2014, they almost managed to make it three in a row, unfortunately the Blackhawks had something to say about that. During the 2012-13 and 2013-14 playoffs, the Kings and Blackhawks twice met in the Western Conference Final; with each club winning one series each.

They were bitter rivals during this stretch of time and there's nothing like a good rivalry in the playoffs to get the blood pumping and the vocal cords going.

NICKSON: "How often do you get the atmosphere of two teams, who were probably the two most dominating teams in their conference for a number of years; the Kings and Blackhawks over that six, seven-year period, up until a couple of years ago, playing each other. And you know that if we can knock the other team out, you've got a good chance of winning it all. So the Kings-Chicago series, both in '13 and '14, certainly stand out in my mind as games where I felt my energy was just a little bit higher. My focus was a little bit better. It's only because the game is that important and you want to try and present it as best as possible."

FAMOUS CALL

"The long wait is over...after 45-years, the Kings can wear their crown!"

Los Angeles Kings fans, if you are old enough to read the prior sentence then it likely gave you goosebumps to relive the moment that took you so long to get to. The Kings came into the NHL at the start of the 1967-68 season. At that time, nobody knew it would take until 2012 for your favorite teams of monarchs to at long last ascend to the throne. But when they did, Nick Nickson, who had been with the team as long as anybody, was there to deliver the words you'd longed your whole life to hear.

There wasn't much expected of the Kings when the 2012 playoffs began. After all, the team went into the Stanley Cup Playoffs as the lowest seed of the eight Western Conference teams. Plus, they'd never won The Cup before, so why should this year be any different?

Ah! But it was different! A five-game knockout of the favored Canucks got the puck rolling in LA's favor and the Kings swiftly followed that up with a four-game sweep of the Blues. So, it was onto the Conference Final to take on the surprise team of the playoffs, the Phoenix Coyotes.

As Nickson recalls, he was approached by Chris Cuthbert after the first period of Game One of the Western Conference Final and Cuthbert had a rather interesting question to ask.

NICKSON: "We saw each other in the hallway and he asked me 'what are you going to say when the Kings win the Stanley Cup?' I said, 'Chris, we're halfway through. We have a long way to go here.'"

Well, that innocent exchange got Nickson thinking and lo-and-behold, the Kings dusted the Coyotes in five-games to set up a date with the New Jersey Devils. The Kings won the first three games of the Stanley Cup Final -- two of which were decided in overtime -- before falling in Games Four and Five to send the series back to Los Angeles for Game Six; a possible Cup-clincher.

Three first period goals by the hosting monarchs took the early suspense out of the game and it allowed Nickson a little more time to think about his answer to Cuthbert's question. He knew he wanted to say something that would stand the test of time and with the final dozen seconds draining off the clock, before Nickson could get to what he planned to say, he spontaneously added, "the long wait is over" before letting the final couple ticks of time drain off the clock. And then, it was time to celebrate. "After 45-years, the Kings can wear their crown!"

MESSAGE TO KINGS FANS

As is a common theme amongst members of the sports media, it is a well known fact that without the fans our jobs would either A) not exist or B) they'd have a lot less meaning. So, each of the broadcasters in this book took a couple of minutes to address you, the fans, directly.

NICKSON: "Thanks for your loyalty. I know many of you fans have followed the Kings since the club began playing back in 1967, and your patience was finally rewarded 45-years later in 2012. We thought we would never see one Cup. We saw two Cups in three-years. Now, we're kind of retooling the whole system, getting younger, fresher bodies players involved and stay patient again. It will come back and the Kings will be on top of the NHL once again, hopefully sooner than later."

FRANCISCO X. RIVERA
SPANISH TV/RADIO: PLAY-BY-PLAY

First Season on Kings Spanish TV/Radio: 2018-19
Seasons on Kings Spanish TV/Radio (including 2020-21): 3

Birthday: 1982 Hometown: Mexico City, Mexico

College/University: Long Beach State

BIOGRAPHY

Who knew that a simple video game could have such an impact on somebody's future?

For Francisco X. Rivera, his introduction to hockey was a video game. "I remember playing ice hockey on Nintendo with my dad when I was eight-years-old," Rivera told me. "I really got attracted to the game. The characters would actually fight each other. They would bump against each other. So I thought that was very interesting. That was my first connection to hockey."

It's interesting to think about how a video game, especially one who's graphics were nowhere near what they are today, was able to convey so much about the sport of hockey that it got a young Rivera to fall in love with the frozen game.

Of course, Rivera had family he would visit in Los Angeles every summer, so he was also a big L.A. Dodgers baseball fan. Baseball, along with soccer and hockey were Rivera's main sports while growing up in Mexico. He played the first two quite a bit and had dreams of one day playing them professionally. But his love for hockey wasn't to be ignored either; even if it was initially based on a video game. Lucky for Kings fans, that love for hockey also managed to grow when Rivera would visit his family in L.A. as those trips exposed him to the Kings.

Rivera's dad and several other family members were athletes in their own right and the young kid quickly took to sports. And for his own amusement, he'd call his own games by doing the Play-by-Play for himself. Eventually, when he came to California for College that love for sports led to him pursuing a career in sportscasting.

First came an internship with FOX and out of that was born opportunities to work as a Production Assistant and to then call baseball games for the Spanish Language broadcasts. On top of his baseball broadcasts, Rivera was also given the opportunity to call other sports; including doing a few hockey games off a monitor during the Vancouver Olympics in 2010 for Directv Latin America. He found it to be challenging to do hockey games off a monitor, but he persevered.

Eventually, Rivera found himself doing some work for ESPN Deportes Radio calling Angels and Rams games. And it was during a casual conversation with a Programming Director that the subject of hockey was broached. As Rivera recalls, he was informed that the station was going to be doing L.A. Kings games and they wanted to know if he had any knowledge of hockey. So, after informing the Program Director about his childhood love for the sport and mentioning how he has a couple of cousins who are working their way through the hockey minor leagues, they put together a demo reel of Rivera's hockey work and got the ball -- or puck -- rolling towards him calling Kings games.

However, Rivera's community work also appealed to the Kings, so they made a deal with him. He would call games for their Spanish Language broadcasts, but they also wanted him to be a consultant for the team to help lead their outreach initiatives in the Latino communities around Los Angeles.

Rivera agreed and has been a driving force behind many of the Kings' various community outreach programs. And all the while, he continues to call games and loves every minute of it.

FAVORITE PLAYER(S) GROWING UP

RIVERA: "Because of my L.A. connection, I grew up a huge Dodgers fan. Even before I was born, my dad, when coming to L.A. to visit his siblings, would go to games and they were friends with Fernando Valenzuela. So, there was Dodgers memorabilia, photos, autograph balls, things like that, all over the house. That connection with

L.A. teams started with the Dodgers. And the Kings were part of it, I guess by default. At that time it was The Gretzky Era. There was all this buzz about Wayne Gretzky. And then, obviously, I knew about Rob Blake. Luc Robitaille too. Tony Granato. Those were the guys who I remember playing as on Super Nintendo. I remember actually calling those games, like broadcasting it for myself."

HOCKEY AFTER DARK -- TALES AWAY FROM THE RINK

When you're young you often dream of one day getting to meet your idols. They can be actors/actresses, athletes, rockstars, etc. Most every kid wants to meet the famous people they are influenced by while growing up. Unfortunately, that's not always possible. And sometimes, it's better to not meet your idols. But that's the extreme other side of the spectrum.

Francisco X. Rivera always had big dreams and when he was hired by the L.A. Kings to be a Consultant for the team to help lead its hispanic outreach initiatives -- in addition to calling games for the Kings' Spanish Language broadcasts -- it ended up being the opportunity of a lifetime.

Through his two roles, Rivera has been able to come into contact and develop relationships with people such as Dave Grohl and Nick Turturro. That in itself would more than satisfy most people, but Rivera is a diligent worker and because of that he was also able to conduct some highly interesting interviews with former NHLers like Lubomir Visnovsky and Miroslav Satan; all while being on vacation with his wife.

Rivera and his wife were planning a nice trip to Poland, Hungary and Romania and decided to stop in Slovakia to make time to do a digital interview series with Visnovsky at an empty arena in Bratislava. (Rivera had cleared this with the Kings previously). Visnovsky welcomed Rivera with open arms and even introduced him to Satan during a chance encounter.

For Rivera it was "the time of his life." And there are many more such experiences just waiting for Rivera as he continues to grow as a broadcaster.

RIVERA'S FAVORITE KINGS GAME HE'S CALLED

Francisco X. Rivera is no ordinary broadcaster. In fact, he's much more than a broadcaster. On top of having to call games, he also consults and helps with the production and in-game entertainment -- specifically as it pertains to the Latino Kings fans. So, for him there could be no fonder game to remember than when the Kings played host to the Blackhawks on "The Day of The Dead" in 2019.

RIVERA: "My favorite would have to be the game on El Día de los Muertos (Day of The Dead) in 2019, because we planned that Spanish TV broadcast and I led basically the production effort too. It was hard to get a hockey analyst who speaks Spanish, so we went a little out of the box and I got a good friend of mine and colleague (to do it).

"His name is Henry Briones, he's a former UFC Fighter, but he played hockey all his life. He actually still plays for a semi-pro team in San Diego. Also, that night, I helped plan a lot of the in-game entertainment, because it was a very typical Mexican celebration. So I helped the whole team plan everything.

"We brought in a lot of guests, a lot of Latino (Mexican specifically) celebrities. The game itself was going to be an event and we made it an event, but the outcome of the game was nuts. It was November 2 2019 against the Blackhawks.

"The Kings were leading 2-0 on quick goals, then they lost the lead. So it's 2-2 and we ended up going to overtime tied 3-3. Then, 17-seconds before we would have gone to a shootout, Drew Doughty shot the puck. The goalie (Corey Crawford) rejected it. But he lost sight of it. The puck was loose right in front of him.

"So, Doughty, who was already behind the net, comes back quickly to score. I remember they actually put the call on the English broadcast as well and they put a GoPro right in front of us. So they actually had the image of Henry and I calling the goal. It was incredible. I shouted 'goal' as if there was no tomorrow; as if it was my last game."

SIGNATURE PHRASE

"GOOOOAAAALLLL!"

Oh, are you wondering why the word "goal" is so drawn out? Well that's a little bit of the soccer influence that Francisco X. Rivera brings to his hockey broadcasts. You see, the very first hockey goal Rivera ever called, he drew out the word "goal." And that call went viral. So, as they say, "if it isn't broken, don't fix it."

Rivera's "gooooaaaallll" call has become so popular amongst Kings fans that the Kings entertainment team decided to record a video of him doing an extra elongated version of it. They then use that on the scoreboard as part of a fan challenge where fans have to try to hold their call longer than Rivera does. It's quite a nice way to get fan engagement and also pay homage to the Latino soccer fans who have become drawn to hockey.

MESSAGE TO KINGS FANS

As is a common theme amongst members of the sports media, it is a well known fact that without the fans our jobs would either A) not exist or B) they'd have a lot less meaning. So, each of the broadcasters in this book took a couple of minutes to address you, the fans, directly.

RIVERA: "I might be biased, but I can tell you, I've been to arenas and stadiums all over the U.S. and a few in Europe as well. And I can tell you, hockey-wise, they are the best fan base that there is. And again, I might be biased, but I can tell you, these guys are very welcoming. They're a family.

"I remember one of the biggest experiences I've had was going to the NBA Finals back in 2007, when I was working for the Lakers. 2007-08, they played against the Celtics and going into TD garden and the whole environment and the guys going at it against the Lakers players and the officials, things like that. It really, really blew my mind. And then when I first went to Staples Center for a Kings game in 2012, this environment was very similar. I mean fans are telling other fans off, they're talking crap to the referees. They are really getting into it. And for me, going to games in Southern California for so long, I wasn't used to it. I mean, fans in New York are actually harsher, more critical, but here things are a little bit more mellower, more relaxed, laid back.

"But going to hockey games, man. It was just incredible. My message would be, I am so proud to be part of the family. I appreciate how fans have welcomed me into this great family. I've had a lot of people come to me during autograph sessions or meet and greet sessions with players and broadcasters. People come to me and say, 'I don't speak a lick of Spanish, but I appreciate what you guys are doing. And I've heard your calls. And I think they're entertaining even though I don't speak Spanish.' And I appreciate the Kings trying to go out and find more diversity within our fan base. So I can tell you I've never heard a negative comment about not only my work, but about what we're doing with Kings fans.

"So I am very proud to be part of the family. I hope we are on the right track to getting the Stanley Cup back to Los Angeles. And, at least on my end, I don't play, but in terms of bringing more fans to the arena and trying to entice more people to come to the Staples Center or being hockey fans, believe me, that's my job. And they actually paid me for that as a consultant. It's something that I love, trying to get more people to fall in love with the game of hockey, the same way I fell in love with it the first time I went to see a hockey game myself, which I can tell you, it's not just a gimmick, but I could tell you the first time I went to a game myself, I thought it was the most entertaining sport to watch live."

MINNESOTA WILD

TOM REID
RADIO: COLOR ANALYST

First Season on Wild Radio: 2000-01
Seasons on Wild Radio (including 2020-21): 20

Birthday: June 24, 1946 Hometown: Fort Erie, ON

College/University: N/A

BIOGRAPHY

How often do you get to make something out of nothing? Probably not as often as you'd like. It could be in regards to crafts, or anything. It could even be in regards to your entire life. Sometimes, you just have to keep pushing and plodding along and eventually you'll get rewarded, even if you're not looking for it.

In Tom Reid's case, he didn't grow up with any grand ideas of one day making it to the NHL. But he stayed involved with the game he loved and eventually the National Hockey League came calling. Oh and by the way, he's never left.

REID: "I grew up in Fort Erie, Ontario and, of course, Canada was a pretty good hotbed for hockey back in those days and I started just playing in my local community in Fort Erie, which is a border town across from Buffalo, New York. And I just started playing organized hockey.

"My dad always built a rink for myself and my brothers in the backyard. And then, when we got older, we started to maintain the rink ourselves. When we were a little bit older all the neighborhood kids would come down and be a part of that. And then, when I was 11-years-old, I was at the local arena one day, which was torn down many years ago and I got a job there as a rink rat. I spent most of my waking hours at the rink; really all of them.

"In those days we had to scrape the ice with the big scrapers. We had big metal scrapers and then we would flood it with a 55 gallon drum of hot water with rags on the back end of it to smooth it down. Then I started to work in the recreation department and just elevated my career, going through the Peewee program, into the Bantams and then into the Midgets. And then when I hit the Midgets era, I played a few games of Junior C, back in those days and got a chance to go to St. Catharines, which was the farm team of the Chicago Blackhawks, back in 1964, and played three-years there.

"The first two-years, I was not a very good player. I was growing. I was uncoordinated. But I made it work in the final year in the OHA. In those days, all the Junior teams were actually spinoffs of the NHL teams. It was kind of your stepping stone to get to the NHL and there were guys there before me, just a few years ahead of me, like Stan Mikita and Bobby Hull and Denis DeJordy and Pierre Pilote. The list goes on and on of players who played there. And then I finally made the All-Star team along with Brian Glennie from the Toronto Maple Leafs.

"I didn't really expect to play in the NHL. There were only six teams at that time. I actually wanted to go to the University of Michigan to get a scholarship. We didn't have a lot of money back in those days for schooling; no direction. So I had applied there, but they didn't feel that I could make their team. So, I got into recreation and then I got a chance to get a call from the Chicago Blackhawks and went there and made their team. So that tells me the University of Michigan must have had a very good team back in those days.

"I played in Chicago for a couple of years and, of course, I was the fifth defenseman. We only had five in those days. You had Pierre Pilote, Pat Stapleton, Doug Jarrett and others. I mean, we had a number of players back on that blue line and I just had to wait my turn. And then

I was traded to the North Stars on February the 14th of 1969 and I've been here (in Minnesota) ever since."

Several years after the trade that sent Reid to Minnesota, a gentleman named Walter Bush approached him and that meeting gave birth to Reid's broadcasting career.

REID: "Walter Bush, who was one of the founders of the North Stars in '67 was an attorney here. He came to me after the '77-'78 season and he asked me if I'd be interested in doing the radio color with Hall of Fame broadcaster, Al Shaver. Al Shaver was from Tillsonburg, Ontario, and had been the North Stars broadcaster since the beginning in '67, when they were one of six teams that came into the league. And I said, 'I'll give it a shot.'

"Al really kind of walked me through the whole thing. He was very gracious. It really showed me that in order to be successful in this business, you have to work at it. You just don't sit down because you played the game and think, 'Oh, I can do this.' You can't. You really have to work at it.

"When you talk to different people around the league, you can tell who's worked at it and who has not worked at it. It really does make a difference. So he asked me if I would do the radio because they were changing radio stations at that time. So, I did that for the first two-years with Al Shaver and then they contacted me, the team did. Walter Bush, who was the head of USA hockey for many, many years. He passed away a couple of years ago. A wonderful, wonderful man. He asked me if I would consider doing television.

"Well, I wasn't very good in front of people or a camera when I was a kid. I was terrified. I thought, 'well, if I don't try this and at least give it a shot, I'll never know and I will always regret not trying.' I tell kids that today, 'just give it a shot. If it doesn't work out, it doesn't work out. But at least you can say 'I tried."

"So, I started doing TV and I was fortunate to work with Bob Kurtz, who had been doing TV for a while. He grew up in Livonia, Michigan. He was doing stuff at Michigan State. He kind of helped me through this whole thing. I had no idea when I put the headset on what an IFB was or who was talking to me in that ear piece. Nothing at all. And they told me from the station I worked at, which was KMSP, that you'll learn on the job and that's how it was.

"I was fortunate to work with Bob for many years and they changed stations. I've had a multitude of different broadcasters who I've worked with over the years in: High School Hockey; in College Hockey; Women's College Hockey; NCAA and the NHL.

"The biggest thing is preparation. In hockey we're always prepared. And in broadcasting. It takes me a long time to set up for a game. Even now when I do the broadcast. It's not just something where I sit down and can do it in one or two hours. It takes hours. I enjoy doing it. And I think that's part of it. It's not a job when you enjoy what you're doing. So, I wanted to just stay with it as long as I could.

"Fortunately for me, the Wild have been very gracious to me. I've been with this organization since they started back in the year 2000. I'm still employed by them. I love doing the games. I love to travel. I don't get as close to the players as I used to, because I have to sometimes say some things on the air they may not like. But you never say something that is going to be detrimental to the player. If a guy makes a bad play or a bad pass in any way, you don't go after the player, but you do say that was not a good move on that player's part or whatever it may be."

FAVORITE PLAYER(S)/TEAM GROWING UP

REID: "My favorite team was Montreal. We didn't have the ability to watch games like they do today. Obviously you saw the game every Saturday night in Toronto and those games didn't come on until the second period because they thought if they started in the first period that people would stay home and wouldn't come to the game. So they always started in the second period.

"But my favorite team was Montreal and my favorite player of all-time was Mr. (Jean) Béliveau and still is today one of my all-time favorites. To have the opportunity to play against him when I broke into the league back in 1967-68, was just a treat for me. Scary moment to be honest with you."

REID'S FAVORITE WILD GAMES HE'S CALLED

Color Analysts have a very different job than Play-by-Play announcers. Instead of calling all the action as it happens, they are tasked with breaking down and further analyzing specific moments of action that occur within the game. These moments can happen at any time and the Color Analyst needs to be ready and on their toes. So, it's not unusual for a particular player's performance to stand out to a Color Analyst as opposed to an entire game.

REID: "When I think of players, one player comes to mind. It was a terrific night. It was Marian Gaborik, it was back in 2007, that he scored five-goals in a game. Those are one of those nights that you remember forever. And he could have had 10 goals that night. It was against the New York Rangers. I mean, he was on fire and I wish he would've had 10-goals. But they won the game and he was absolutely terrific in that hockey game. And that's the one player who really stands out in my mind."

Of course, there are certain games or series that do stand out in their minds as well and for Reid, none stands out more than when the Minnesota Wild caused the Colorado Avalanche to choke away a 3-1 series lead and then followed up with an encore performance against the Vancouver Canucks.

The year was 2003. It was Springtime. And for NHL fans that means one thing -- the start of the chase for Lord Stanley's Cup has begun in earnest as the playoffs are underway. Only one team can scale the mountain. But that doesn't mean others can't etch their names in history for a variety of reasons.

In a best-four-of-seven series, it is difficult to come back from a 3-2 series deficit. And it's even more difficult -- try improbable -- to come back from a 3-1 series deficit. Sure, it happens every once in a while. But it's not a situation you want to find yourself in; especially not twice in back-to-back series.

Well, that's exactly the situation the Minnesota Wild found themselves in during the first and second-rounds of the 2003 playoffs. To pull off that type of comeback once is amazing. To do it twice; well that's downright historic.

People say lightning doesn't strike twice in the same spot, but people are wrong and Tom Reid was there to witness every last second of it.

REID: "As far as a game that I would remember the most, it would probably be in 2003, in the playoffs when Minnesota beat out Colorado in seven-games, in Colorado, by winning Games Five, Six and Seven; three in a row. I remember the broadcasters on the other side were saying, 'well, where do you think we're going to go next? Or who are we going to play?' And I was saying, 'be careful what you wish for guys.' We ended up winning that and then going on to play against Vancouver and winning in seven-games there as well, by winning Games Five, Six and Seven.

"It was a treat for me to be a part of that. The closeness of that hockey club that year and they had Jacques Lemaire who was instrumental in giving those guys the credit and giving them direction to make it work for them."

MESSAGE TO WILD FANS

As is a common theme amongst members of the sports media, it is a well known fact that without the fans our jobs would either A) not exist or B) they'd have a lot less meaning. So, each of the broadcasters in this book took a couple of minutes to address you, the fans, directly.

REID: "It's called patience. I mean, the one thing is, this is a very, very tough business. There are 31 teams, soon to be 32 and 30 other teams right now want to win the Stanley Cup. So, it's not an easy road and I admire the players and how hard they work today. You only see them on the ice for the games themselves, but these guys work hard.

"I go to most of the practices at home and on the road and they don't let up; they're relentless. And they have strict rules they have to follow also about how they have to conduct themselves and how they have to perform. In sales, if you don't perform, you lose your job. And it's the same way in hockey. If you don't perform up to the expectations expected of you by management, you're going to lose your job, or you're going to be traded to somebody else.

"So, I just tell the fans, be patient with these guys. We've had a number of changes here lately. Billy Guerin is coming in and it looks like he's going to be able to turn this thing around. He certainly has worked hard at it. He comes in at a very difficult time with everything that's been happening with the pause and the pandemic. And he didn't come until late August. So he hasn't had a lot of time where he could put things together. He's had to do it very quickly."

MONTREAL CANADIENS

DAN ROBERTSON
RADIO: PLAY-BY-PLAY

First Season on Canadiens Radio: 2014-15
Seasons on Canadiens Radio (including 2020-21): 7

Birthday: February 15, 1970 Hometown: Trenton, Nova Scotia

College/University: St. Mary's

BIOGRAPHY

Close your eyes and imagine for a second that you could take a lifelong passion and turn it into an unexpected career. Now, keep them closed and tell me, what do you see? And not only what do you see, but how would you plan on going about doing it? Now, open your eyes.

When you first started this exercise of the mind, you probably had a lot of thoughts and very few actual answers. Well, if that's the case. You're not alone. That's how it is for most people. Now, if you happen to be a fan of the Montreal Canadiens, you'll probably enjoy hearing that your radio Play-by-Play announcer, Dan Robertson, is just like you. He too had a passion for something and no idea what to do. So, how about we dive into his story and maybe you'll find some answers to your own questions.

ROBERTSON: "I was like millions of us here up north. I started playing at a really young age. I was a good player. It was my whole life.

I absolutely loved it. And I played right into Junior. I played a little bit of Junior A and whatnot. I kind of lost the desire to play at a certain point, maybe 15 or 16, I got a little burnt out. But I always liked it. It was just a part of my life.

"I mean, I would watch Hockey Night in Canada, when I was young and begged my parents to let me stay up as late as I could. I can remember always, after the first period was over, I would go down to the basement, shoot pucks and sort of do Play-by-Play, as if I was the Montreal Canadiens or the Toronto Maple Leafs, while I was taking shots. I was probably eight or nine-years-old at that point. It was a big part of my life and then, as I said, I kind of cooled off from it a little bit. But I always thought that I understood it pretty well. And I think I do and I think that helps me in what I do now.

"I went to University and wasn't really sure what I wanted to do. I majored in English. I always liked to write and I thought, maybe I'll teach someday. And then, looking back, I tried to get into an education program and I couldn't get in. I kind of wandered a little bit in my life for a couple of years and then I remember watching SportsCenter and thinking I could do that.

"So I went to broadcasting school for a year. It was called the Atlantic Broadcasting Institute; just a small school. The goal was to be a Sports Anchor. And then that didn't work out. I actually got married and moved to Colorado, didn't work for a couple of years and went back to Nova Scotia. Then, I started volunteering at a cable TV station and I was actually doing Color Commentary for a Major Junior team in Halifax.

"And then, one night, I tried Play-by-Play and I liked it. I thought I was reasonably good at it and I might be able to do it. That's basically where it started. I kept kind of moving up the ladder, for lack of a better term and getting a couple of higher profile jobs and then eventually that led me into getting the Canadiens job back in 2014."

See, Robertson didn't have a clearly defined path, but he took what he loved and eventually found a way to do something with it. It wasn't easy, but he did it and so can you. Now, about that whole, "trying Play-by-Play" thing that he just talked about. Let's delve deeper into how exactly that happened.

ROBERTSON: "It was really a small production kind of thing. We (at Eastlink TV) were calling games as they happened, obviously, but they were showing them on the cable station the next day, at like seven in the morning.

"So, I wouldn't think anybody was watching those games and one day, the guy who normally did Play-by-Play, he couldn't go, he had another engagement. I called the game and as you can believe it, when the game took place, about halfway through, a player slid into the boards and he kicked a hole in the boards. So I had to fill in for about a half-an-hour. I mean, we didn't have a host. We didn't have anything to throw to, so I just kind of talked and filled in and my boss thought that was pretty good.

"And again, it was just volunteer stuff. I think I was making 50 bucks a game. But it seemed to come easily to me. Even watching hockey as a kid I would kind of, in my head, do Play-by-Play. So I was glad to get that opportunity. And then, from there, I got more hockey games in. With Eastlink, that's who I volunteered with, I did basketball and football and soccer and a little bit of boxing and a whole bunch of different things. So it really helped my progression, I think."

I guess you'll never know what can happen until you just try it; who knows you might even stumble into something you never thought about. Of course, Robertson's story resonates with me because I never liked to write, nor was I particularly adept at it. But I loved sports. And somehow, those two paths converged and now here I am, bringing you written stories from some of the people who you love to listen to.

Getting back to Robertson, it might shock some of you, it certainly shocked me, to learn that he didn't exactly get to go to a lot of hockey games growing up.

ROBERTSON: "Growing up in Nova Scotia and I moved around a lot, the closest team was Montreal and it was a 12-hour drive. It's not anything my Father ever suggested that we do. I never even really thought about it. It just seemed to be so far away. It wasn't anything that I missed. And then when I moved to Vancouver when I was I guess 20 or 21, I went to a game. I just went to a Penguins-Canucks game. I (actually) went to a couple of games in Vancouver and then I lived in Denver and I think I went to one game in Denver. And then that was it until I did the audition for my job.

"(So), Before I got my job calling Canadiens' games, I probably went to, I would say, three NHL games, which is kind of funny when you think about it.

"I can (still) remember getting there (to my first game) early and going down to ice level for the warm up and watching Paul Coffey skate. To me, he's just the best skater ever. And I was blown away by watching him at ice level. He went into the corner, pivoted and skated backwards; just flew back up the ice going backwards. And I thought, 'Wow, it's so different to see them live than it is to see them on TV.'"

I told you it was shocking. But perhaps you disagree. Anyway, now that you know about Robertson's upbringing and early hockey days, let's delve into some of his thoughts on broadcasting; specifically, other broadcasters who he was drawn to.

ROBERTSON: "There certainly were Play-by-Play guys and broadcasters in different sports who I admired. I mean, Al Michaels, who, yeh he did the 1980 Olympics and we remember him for that, but we remember him for so much more with football and basketball and the like.

"Bob Cole was a legendary Play-by-Play man here in Canada. But to say that I consciously tried to model myself after him, I'd be lying to you. I guess, back then when I was watching, I wasn't thinking, 'okay, I want to be a Play-by-Play guy when I grow up.'

"Today, Chris Cuthbert is my favorite. I think Chris is the best of All-Time to be honest with you. And I've gotten to know him just a little bit and picked his brain a few times. But it's more watching and listening and trying to learn what I like about what he does. And not just him.

"I think subconsciously, when you watch and listen to so much hockey, the guys who you like, I think you probably take some elements of what they do and you incorporate them into your broadcast, I think and into your own style. But ultimately, you can only be yourself and sometimes that's an amalgamation of what other guys have done. Ultimately, it's got to come from you."

That's excellent advice and hopefully it helps any of you who are thinking about pursuing a career in broadcasting. But you also need to know that you'll likely be in for a long, winding road before you get to your preferred destination.

ROBERTSON: "I worked at Eastlink TV in Halifax and that would have been, I would say, 1999, when I started to volunteer there. As I said, I did color commentary. I actually was there for several years. And then, in 2001-2002, I got a job with the Moncton Wildcats in the QMJHL. And I did their road games.

"So, I was living in Halifax and I would drive three-hours to get on the bus with the team and then go and do the road games. Corey Crawford was a 16-year-old rookie on that team. Of course, Corey's won a couple of Cups with the Blackhawks. So that helped a lot. And then, all at that same time, I was still volunteering at Eastlink. And basically, I was at Eastlink until I got the (Montreal) job offer in 2014.

"There was a year, I believe it was 2010-2011, that I did six or seven American Hockey League games on CBC here in Canada on television. It was something that I got an opportunity to do through someone who I knew. So that was a good step in the right direction. And not to get too far off topic, but his name was Joel Darling and he used to be the Executive Producer of Hockey Night in Canada. And in the mid-2000s, (when) CBC fired Chris Cuthbert, I had sent a tape to CBC and Joel Darling, who (again) was the Executive Producer of Hockey Night in Canada called me and I was pretty surprised.

"In the end, he said, 'you can say you were shortlisted for this job, because you were.' They gave it to Jim Hughson, which made sense. But it was at that point, I sort of thought, 'okay, if I got shortlisted for that job then I must be kind of going in the right direction.' So those were the main jobs that I had: with Eastlink; with the Moncton Wildcats for one-year and some piece work here and there with the AHL on CBC."

And now Robertson's been with the Montreal Canadiens for seven-seasons and hopefully there's many more that lay ahead.

FAVORITE PLAYER(S) GROWING UP

ROBERTSON: "I was a fan of the Canadiens. My brother didn't push me into (playing) hockey, but he pushed me into being a Canadiens fan. I looked up to my brother, who was nine years older and that's who he liked. I was born in 1970 and when I was seven, eight-years-old, I mean, the Canadiens, those were some of the best teams ever. So it was easy to kind of root for the Canadiens.

"But then, around December 1983, there was a Hockey Night in Canada intermission. They did a profile on Mario Lemieux, who was playing with the Laval Voisins in the Quebec Major Junior Hockey League. And right away, I looked at him and I thought, 'wow, this guy's magic.' From that point, I was transfixed and a Penguins fan from that point.

"It's kind of funny being a Nova Scotian. Eventually, Sidney Crosby goes there. That's kind of a neat link too. So, a Canadiens fan and then a Penguins fan. But now, it doesn't really matter. But it's always better for me if the Canadiens win, for a lot of reasons. It generates a lot of interest in the city and it's just good for everybody around Montreal.

"I can also remember being a big fan of Guy Lafleur when I first started to like hockey, because he was such a superstar. I mean, he was the best player in the 1970s with due respect to Bobby Orr, who was, by the time you know '74 came around, I suppose, or even earlier, declining because of his knees. But there were six straight seasons there where Lafleur was clearly the best player in the league and he had a superstar quality about him.

"And I've met Guy a few times in my role now and every time I see him, he's just got that special quality about him. He's a star and I look at him and think, 'man, it's Guy Lafleur.' But then as I said, when I saw him, it was really something. I kind of tried to be like him on the ice, which didn't work, obviously. There were other guys who I admired. I was a big fan of Peter Stastny, who played for the Quebec Nordiques back then. But I would say those three guys, but certainly (Mario) Lemieux, was head and shoulders above everybody else."

HOCKEY AFTER DARK -- TALES AWAY FROM THE RINK

Having a career as a sports broadcaster means getting to experience things that nobody else can. It's like being the ultimate fan. And even though you're doing a professional job, there are still some moments that touch you in a way where the fan inside of you gets to shine through. For Dan Robertson, he's been presented with several of these moments during his career with the Canadiens.

ROBERTSON: "I mentioned Chris Cuthbert and how much I admire him. And a few years ago, I want to say, I guess it was two-years ago. I would have done and I still do them. I do a handful of games on TSN television every year. So I filled in one night in Buffalo. And the next game or a couple of games afterward in Montreal, I saw Chris and I didn't know him then and I said, 'Chris, I'm Dan Robertson. It's really nice to meet you.' He said, 'Listen, I caught the game the other night. I thought wow, this guy really knows his stuff.' And I don't say that to boast. I just about fell down. I felt so good about it. It's so nice when people can pick you up like that from time to time.

"Guy Lapointe, who's in the Hockey Hall of Fame, came up to me my first year on the job and he said the same thing. He said, 'I listen to you all the time. I think you're really good.' And I was pretty blown away by that. My first year on the job was just so cool because I met so many people. And I mean, Montreal is such a hollowed arena and place for hockey that even at the age of 44, it was pretty overwhelming. But overwhelming in a great way.

"Saku Koivu, they had a night for him that season. Of course, he had come back from cancer years previous but they honored him and being a rights holder, I got a chance to sit and do an interview with Saku. It was pretty special when he recounted all the love he got from the Canadiens fans after he returned after being diagnosed with cancer."

These are all terrific moments and ones that Robertson is sure to never forget. But he would have never gotten to this point if not for a whirlwind couple days in the Fall of 2014.

ROBERTSON: "The way that I got hired, it was very late in the preseason. September, I want to say 25th, 2014, I went up and I did an audition. And then, I called my last game with Eastlink TV on a Friday night, my last hockey game. The next afternoon, I called a football game for them. That was a Saturday. The next day I put all my stuff in my car and drove to Montreal. And on Monday I went in and met my new boss. And then Tuesday we went on like a five-game road trip. That was how I got thrown into things. My head was spinning. It was really an amazing time. And that was really a magical first season for me. And there's a lot that I'll never forget about it."

ROBERTSON'S FAVORITE CANADIENS GAMES HE CALLED

It does not matter whether your career has lasted two-years or 20, there are always going to be a handful of games that will stand out to you; for varying reasons of course.

Sometimes these games can stand out for singular moments and other times they can stand out for the entirety of the game. Either way, these memories are usually near and dear to the person's heart. And since joining the Canadiens' radio broadcast team, Dan Robertson has encountered three such games.

ROBERTSON: "My first home game at the Bell Centre, they did the pre-game ceremony and it was just Goosebumps City. I can't remember what happened during the game. But before the game was pretty amazing.

"(Then), In 2014-15, they beat Ottawa in the first-round and then they ended up losing to Tampa in six. But in Game Five at home, it was tied and P.A. Parenteau scored late to give them the win. And again, it was just so loud and I still think this, if I'm ever in the broadcast booth, if they ever go on a run, maybe to a Conference Final, or a Stanley Cup Final, I can't imagine just how much fun that'll be.

"(And finally), Three-years ago, they were in the playoffs in the first-round against the New York Rangers and they had home ice advantage. They lost the first game. And then in the second game, they were down, I'm quite sure it was 3-2 late and Tomas Plekanec scored. I can't tell you when, but it was late in the third to tie it. And then Alexander Radulov scored.

"Listen, it wasn't a must win. But if you go down 2-0 (in the series), especially if you lose the first two at home, it's not good news. We ended up losing in six anyway. But Alexander Radulov scored in overtime and it was incredible. I know there's countless great arenas in the league to see a hockey game. I've been in all of them. But it was just incredible. The atmosphere when he scored. And then we went to New

York the next day and NBC was promoting the game. I was in my hotel room, they were promoting the game and my call of the Radulov goal, the audio was on. And I thought 'Wow, that's pretty cool. It's going coast-to-coast here in the United States.' So that was neat."

MESSAGE TO CANADIENS FANS

As is a common theme amongst members of the sports media, it is a well known fact that without the fans our jobs would either A) not exist or B) they'd have a lot less meaning. So, each of the broadcasters in this book took a couple of minutes to address you, the fans, directly.

ROBERTSON: "We have a pretty loyal following at TSN 690. Twitter can be a bad thing and Twitter can be a good thing, too. Social media is that way, as you know. But I get a lot of positive reinforcement from fans and it really means a lot. People who go out of their way, whether it's just during a game or after a game, maybe they heard a call they liked or whatever, but you get those things from time to time. And so, for anybody who's ever reached out that way, I would just like to let them know that I really appreciate it, that it means a lot."

NASHVILLE PREDATORS

WILLY DAUNIC
TV: PLAY-BY-PLAY

First Season on Predators TV: 2015-16
Seasons on Predators TV (including 2020-21): 6

Birthday: February 9, 1971 Hometown: Boston, MA

College/University: Vanderbilt University

BIOGRAPHY

How does a professional baseball player, who also played basketball in College end up as a hockey broadcaster? All you're missing is football at that rate, but I digress. It does seem to be an odd mix though. However, I believe Willy Daunic would prefer the term, unique.

You see, Daunic was your prototypical sports junkie growing up (his words) and even though he made it much further than most people ever do in baseball -- he played some minor league ball for the Blue Jays -- he always had an appreciation for hockey. That appreciation by the way stemmed from watching the dynasty Islanders in the early-80s as well as the competitive Rangers.

This Boston born, Purchase, NY, raised boy has been well-traveled during his life and career. So let's let him tell us how he got to where he is today as the voice of Nashville Predators television broadcasts.

DAUNIC: "Well, I've always been a sports junkie, for all sports, following and playing. For hockey, living in New York in the early-80s, that was Miracle on Ice, that was New York Islanders four straight Stanley Cups. Those were some really good Rangers teams. Great rivalry. That was pre-cable, so you just kind of had to watch whatever games were on TV, locally, in New York. Fortunately we got a lot of games. So, we watched a lot of Islanders and Rangers games.

"That's where I first got connected to the sport. When I moved to Florida, I kind of lost connection with it, to a degree, for a good long time, because we never had a team down in Florida. And then moving to Nashville, obviously, no team in my College years and post-college years. But when the team came to town, the Predators were an expansion team.

"My background, even though it wasn't extensive, was more than most of the local media at the time and that sort of gave me a leg up. I wanted to dive in and be a big part of one of our first major league franchises. So that's what made me want to be a big part of the Predators."

Along with his love for sports, Daunic also loved the big-game feel that certain broadcasters brought to the games they called; specifically on national broadcasts.

DAUNIC: "I was probably drawn to more of the national scene for broadcasters. I moved away in early-1983, to Florida and that's where I probably got a little detached from hockey for the next decade or so. So I don't think it was any one hockey announcer. I was always drawn to the big broadcasts with Al Michaels, Keith Jackson, Howard Cosell and Vin Scully. Dick Enberg would be another one. I always wanted to play first and foremost."

Ah yes, Daunic's desire above all else to play sports. Well, that desire led him further than most who share that dream, but even he had to eventually make the switch from being down on the field to being up in the booth.

DAUNIC: "I went to Vanderbilt on a basketball scholarship in 1989. That was my freshman year. I ended up playing basketball and baseball at Vanderbilt. So, I was very consumed by playing and that was what I wanted to do. I ended up playing two-years of minor league baseball for the Blue Jays. I got drafted after my senior year. As I got through school, I was doing better at baseball than I was at basketball. So, I juggled both for three-years.

"I only played baseball my senior year and I got drafted by the Blue Jays. So with all that being said, it started off as when I stopped playing basketball, we had a really good basketball team, I asked my coach if I could go up into the press box and keep stats for the radio announcer, who at the time was Wes Durham, who is now the voice of the Atlanta Falcons.

"He calls a lot of ACC games. He was a pretty young announcer at the time and he was nice enough to let me just kind of sit there and keep stats. I knew the team really well, obviously. I knew all the plays they were running and it kept me connected to the group.

"Up there, I was fortunate enough to meet some of the other Nashville media who were there and a guy named George Plaster was up there all the time. We struck up some conversations. He could tell that I had the sickness of being a sports junkie. He had a sports talk show at the time. So he was the guy who really took the initiative from there and said, 'well, why don't you tag along? If you're interested in announcing, why don't you tag along to some games that I'm doing. Come over and watch my sports talk show, I'll show you how it works.'

"He really took me under his wing. So, when I got drafted by the Blue Jays, it ended up being sort of a side gig, just sort of interning and making minimum wage and chipping in on his sports talk radio show, which at the time in the early-90s, was sort of a budding success. That's how I sort of dipped my toe in there, still thinking that I was going to be succeeding John Olerud as the first baseman for the Jays someday.

"But of course that dream didn't last very long. Then it became a point a couple of years later, I had to decide, 'am I staying with this or am I going to go into coaching or am I going to still try to play?' At that time, that's when I made the critical decision to stay in broadcasting.

"I got released by the Blue Jays in 1994. About a year later, I'm doing regular sports talk radio with George Plaster who has been extremely valuable in opening up opportunities for me. So what happened then is our show kind of took off because in the next year, the Oilers decided to move to Nashville to eventually become the Titans.

"So we have the NFL all of a sudden. Nashville builds a beautiful downtown arena. They're looking for a team and the NHL announces they're going to have hockey. So, Nashville goes from being a city that's never had a major league franchise to all of a sudden we have two. At the time, I was chipping in on some Vanderbilt broadcasts, George and I were the announcing team for Vanderbilt's men's basketball team.

"I did the sidelines for football. So when the Predators came, our radio station happened to be part owners of the team, along with Craig Leipold, the first Owner of the Predators. Gaylord Entertainment was the name of the company. So, since our radio station was owned by it and our radio show was doing very well, we were the flagship station of the Predators and our ownership said, 'well, we want our main sports talk show guys to be a part of this.' Also the Predators decide at the beginning, they're going to have a simulcast.

"They're not going to have separate TV and radio teams. They've got Pete Weber and Terry Crisp, an awesome broadcast team and they want to have them do both. So they need a Radio Host to tie it together on the radio side for Pre/Intermission/Post. I was the one guy who was young enough. I had the time. I had the desire for that gig. I didn't really have to try out with anybody else. I just happened to be there. So it was a really big stroke of luck for me.

"I probably didn't know a whole lot more than the average fan, but I knew I knew enough. And then I just stuck very close to Pete and Terry and asked a lot of questions so I could get up to speed on what I needed to. I knew the top players in the league and I knew the basics of the game, but what you quickly find out is how much you don't know about the rank and file players and about the nuances of the game that you don't really get.

"I didn't know very much, but I tried to connect my knowledge of sports, playing other sports and trying to make some analogies; what translates and what does our audience in Nashville, how can they relate to what we're learning about how hockey is played? So it ended up being a good match, even though nobody could've ever predicted it. I just happened to be the guy who said, 'I'll do it. You need a Pre- and Post-game show Host. I'll stay here in the studio. I'll do all the games.'

"(Then) in 2006 they decided they're going to split the radio from the TV and they hired a guy named Eli Gold, who is the long-time voice of Alabama football.

"He's kind of a legend in the South. He was hired to call the Predators games, but because of Alabama football and NASCAR, there were a handful of games that he couldn't make. So again, me being just a guy who had worked on it behind the scenes, listened to Pete, done some practice games. I was able to do those six or seven games on radio that Eli was not able to make. So that's where I started. So I was a little bit of a utility man. If the Color guy wasn't there, for whatever reason, I filled in on the Color. So I got to the point where I was qualified to do it.

"So then, we move up to 2013, the Play-by-Play announcer at the time for the Predators had to resign. It happened suddenly and it happened just like nine-games into the season. The team was about to go on a really long road trip. And again, right place, right time. I was there. They knew I had done some games. I could, at least in the short term, fill the gap. I got the chance to go on that road trip. They liked what they heard enough to where they just said, 'well, why don't you stay for the rest of the season on radio?'

"The rest of the season became indefinitely, the Play-by-Play guy and then, eventually, onto TV in 2015."

FAVORITE PLAYER(S) GROWING UP

DAUNIC: "I probably jumped on the bandwagon of the Islanders, just because they were so successful at the time. So that was Mike Bossy, Bryan Trottier, Clark Gillies and all those guys. I think I was probably attracted towards the goal-scorers as much as anything else. So I would say Mike Bossy and Bryan Trottier were the two."

HOCKEY AFTER DARK -- TALES AWAY FROM THE RINK

When you think about sports and celebrity appearances, you probably immediately think about A-list Hollywood types, sitting in a suite drinking an expensive glass of wine while fulfilling some social obligation. Sure, you get the occasional celebrity who is there for the love of the game, but more often than not it's about appearances.

Well, sometimes it doesn't matter why they're there. Sometimes, the fans and the team are just so caught up in the atmosphere they've created that the reason for the celebrity being there goes out the window and their appearance actually serves to just rile up the crowd even more (in a good way).

This is where Willy Daunic comes into play. Take it away Willy.

DAUNIC: "During the Stanley Cup Final against the Penguins, Nashville became this crazy place where people were lining up in the streets, shoulder to shoulder, thousands and thousands of people outside the arena. So it became a place where a lot of people were coming in. The TV guy doesn't get to do the Play-by-Play.

"So we're doing anything and everything. We're doing Pre- and Post-game coverage for Fox Sports Tennessee, but we're also just trying to do whatever we can to help the radio team. Pete's (Pete Weber) calling the game. So I'm roaming around before the game and it's a who's who. Wayne Gretzky is there. Paul Coffey is there. Among these people, Charles Barkley is there.

"So I got a chance to interview on the same night: I got Paul Coffey and Charles Barkley. I didn't get Wayne that night. That was a really interesting night where it went so far beyond the game itself. Just the spectacle of the whole thing. Charles Barkley, he heard it was a good time. He wanted to come to the game. So I did a great interview with him.

"He was talking about just soaking up the energy. He didn't know a whole lot about the game, for sure. But he was really impressed at the atmosphere in particular. The Predators (and the fans) ate it up. They kept showing him on the jumbotron during the game. The Predators won the game and evened the series two to two. It was rocking. So they milked it."

DAUNIC'S FAVORITE PREDATORS GAME HE'S CALLED

For many years the Chicago Blackhawks were a thorn in the side of the Nashville Predators. No matter what the Predators would do, they just could not get over the hump and beat the Blackhawks when it mattered most; in the playoffs.

The teams met in the 2009-10 Conference Quarter-Finals and the 2014-15 First-Round, with both series being won by Chicago. So, when the teams met for a third playoff encounter in the 2016-17 First-Round, the Predators fans had a lot of pent up anger and hostility towards the Blackhawks. But fear not, for the third time's the charm.

DAUNIC: "The regional TV guys do get to do the first-round. I'm thankful for that. But in 2017, the Predators played the Blackhawks, who have eliminated them twice in some heartbreaking, gut-wrenching series; both of which led the Blackhawks to then go on to win the Stanley Cup.

"So the Blackhawks and a lot of people from outside, maybe wouldn't realize this, but the Blackhawks are still probably the most hated rival for the Predators. So when the Predators swept them in 2017, in the first-round, as the eighth-seed and the Blackhawks were the one-seed that was really, really satisfying to the fan base.

"Game Three, I got to call that one. The Predators were down 2-0, came back to force overtime and then Kevin Fiala won it in overtime. That is probably my most favorite moment calling the game, because I knew what it meant, in that moment, to the fan base. That made it three-games-to-none. You knew you were in pretty good shape at that point. And then they went ahead and won Game Four. But the Game Three moment was the best."

SIGNATURE PHRASE

The one thing that's constant for broadcasters who use catchphrases is that they feel the phrase has to come about organically. It can't come off as contrived because then they'll sound phony. But once something does come organically, then it can really take off if used the right amount.

During the course of his baseball player-turned-hockey broadcaster career, Willy Daunic has actually had two such sayings come about. Both of which are really loved by the fans who tune in to Predators games on a nightly basis.

DAUNIC: “It wasn't intentional, but there are two that have sort of gained traction, I would say.

“I played for the Blue Jays in the minor leagues and we had a really funny, charismatic Manager named Omar Malavé. He's from Venezuela. He has a great accent, great personality and instead of saying, 'Oh my goodness,' or 'Oh my' or something like that, well, Omar's was 'Oh my laundry.' He would say it in his accent and all the players just loved him. If you could get him to say it, you knew it was something good. Everybody would laugh.

“So, if a puck hits the post or something happens, a real close call, you're holding onto a one-goal lead, it's an ‘almost’ moment; I'll throw in an 'Oh my laundry.' You don't do it every game. But if you plan it in the right spot, I've gotten some really good reactions from fans and stuff. So I think they liked that one.

“The other one is really simple. It's a punctuation for a game-clinching goal. I only say it if you know the game is over. I'll just say, with a lot of passion, 'Yes, sir.' It's a little bit of a Southern tradition, I guess. So that fits a little bit from a secondary standpoint. That's just kind of taken off.”

MESSAGE TO PREDATORS FANS

As is a common theme amongst members of the sports media, it is a well known fact that without the fans our jobs would either A) not exist or B) they’d have a lot less meaning. So, each of the broadcasters in this book took a couple of minutes to address you, the fans, directly.

DAUNIC: “When I'm up there calling the game, I have experienced it, because, when I was the pre- and post-game show host, while the game was going on, for home games, I would sit in the stands with the fans, for the first several years. I learned a lot from the fans, just sitting around them. A lot of those original fans, who went through the tough times, it wasn't like the Vegas Golden Knights, who immediately have been a really good team from the day they opened up. The Predators had five- or six-years of being scrappy, earning everything they got; not winning a whole lot.

"But in doing that, you get this great fan base cultivated that went through the tough times together and they appreciate the good times. So, that is what has always stuck with me, as I always remind myself when I'm doing the game, I want to deliver for the fans. I know how passionate they are. I know how bad they want to win. And so I want to deliver that passion for them. I want to deliver that desire. So, I kind of try to channel them. That's what I think about when I do a game."

PETE WEBER
RADIO: PLAY-BY-PLAY

First Season on Predators Radio: 1998-99
Seasons on Predators Radio (including 2020-21): 23

Birthday: January 1, 1951 Hometown: Galesburg, IL

College/University: Notre Dame

BIOGRAPHY

It's not often that a fan base can say today that it has only ever had one voice of its team. Broadcasters, like players, tend to move around quite a bit, especially early in their careers. But sometimes, you get a match made in heaven between a broadcaster and team. Now, you also need the team to not be terribly old, because even if a broadcaster stays for the duration of their career, eventually age is going to catch up with them. Father Time is undefeated after all.

However, the Nashville Predators have been lucky in that sense, as Pete Weber has been calling the team's games since their inception and he's not leaving anytime soon. He's a Midwest boy who fell in love with sports due to a radio, newspapers and the voices of some All-Time great broadcasters. But that's putting it too simply. So let's let Weber himself tell you how he became the voice of the Nashville Predators.

WEBER: "Well, I fell in love with all sports. Really, from the outset, I guess what attracted me most to the business was, as a kid, I had a Zenith radio on my nightstand and I used it to listen to Harry Caray, Jack Buck and Joe Garagiola Sr. do St. Louis Cardinals games. Here I was, seven, eight-years-old, listening to these guys and discerning that they were having fun doing what they were doing.

"Later on, I found out they were getting paid for what they were doing. So that sort of attracted me to the business to begin with. (As for) falling in love with hockey, at that point in time, there were only six teams in the NHL. And the Chicago Blackhawks had Lloyd Pettit doing their games.

"Lloyd was a spectacular craftsman and listening to him as a kid caused me to, first of all, fall in love with the Blackhawks and then fall in love with the game. It was a special point in time. Just a few years later, by the time I was a junior in High School, the NHL doubled in size and the St. Louis Blues came in.

"They had Jack Buck doing their games the first year and the next year, they imported from Canada, the wonderful Dan Kelly. Jack Buck went back to his Cardinals duties on KMOX radio. So, I think I had some pretty good artists to follow on that little Zenith tabletop radio.

"I came across (sports) because of the radio. And then it got reinforced. We usually had a minimum of five daily newspapers at our home. Chicago, Peoria, Galesburg and on occasion, from St. Louis. So reading about the game I had just listened to the night before and then hearing the excitement in Lloyd Pettit's voice when Bobby Hull would score or Glenn Hall would come up with a spectacular save or Stan Mikita with a great pass. In those earlier days, Stan Mikita was also a pretty good penalty minute guy and listening to those guys just captured my imagination."

The flame of passion had been lit, but as we all know, Weber still needed to get some experience before he could turn that passion into a reality.

WEBER: "We didn't have a broadcast journalism curriculum at Notre Dame. But we did have a campus radio station that was really administered by us, the students. So we had like 40 guys on the sports staff. We did five-minute sportscasts on the half-hour, virtually 18 to 19 hours a day. And then, as you got more senior in standing on the staff, you got to do Play-by-Play.

"So I got to do some College hockey Play-by-Play on the student station and some football. We did virtually everything, other than baseball. Because of the way we were wired, the baseball stadium was across the street. We couldn't get the signal over there. So I did hockey and then I graduated and I had an opportunity to get a Graduate Degree in Communications, because my undergrad degree was in Modern Languages/German.

"So I applied for the job, because the guy who had been doing Notre Dame hockey on the commercial station had decided to go run a restaurant in Niles, Michigan. I lined up my interview. I got to the station and I found out, all of a sudden, the guy who was supposed to interview me had also left and also quit. So they quickly arranged for someone else to interview me.

"While we were awaiting the interview, the TV monitor in the lobby broke through with an update from NBC News. 'Hank Aaron has just tied Babe Ruth, hitting his 714th home run against Jack Billingham of Cincinnati.' So here we were, it was April of 1974, interviewing for a job to start, effectively that Fall.

"I got the job and as an extra, I got to work in radio operations for that station, WNDU AM, over the course of that summer, leading into the next hockey season. I was there the next two hockey seasons. While I was doing Notre Dame hockey, on the student station, I ran into the guy who had been doing Wisconsin hockey, Bob Miller.

"Bob had moved on to become the voice of the Los Angeles Kings. He needed a Color Commentator and I happened to send my resume in at the right time. They called and I moved from Buffalo, New York, where I was working on an all news radio station, to Los Angeles to join Bob Miller and the Kings for the next three-years. And it just sort of developed out of that.

"I also went to Albuquerque and did baseball for a summer. I did the Seattle Supersonics for a year on their new regional sports network in '81-'82 and then went back to Buffalo and started doing everything there; including hosting Buffalo Sabres cable and then Buffalo Bisons baseball. Doing the Buffalo Bills football games, including their four straight Super Bowls.

"Then, in the late spring of '97, I was hooked up in my home office in Kenmore, New York and saw this notice from the National Hockey League that four expansion franchises had been provisionally awarded to Atlanta, Nashville, Columbus Ohio and St. Paul Minnesota. So I talked to my wife very quickly, because her parents at that point in time had been moved to Knoxville, Tennessee for awhile. And I thought, 'geez, if I could hook on with Nashville, how much easier would that be on family life around the holidays and other celebratory times?'

"So I immediately contacted Craig Leipold, who was the Founding Owner of the Predators, who were not yet named and FedEx'd my materials to him the very next day and then kept following up. Ultimately, Gerry Helper, who had been in the NHL office, but who had worked in the Sabres PR when I was doing games there, I found out he was named Vice President of Communications for the team and then kept following up with him.

"So that was in '97. In '98, the team began and by August of '98, with my follow-ups and so on, I got hired to be the voice of the team. So that's how I got to Nashville. It's been a circuitous route to be certain, but it's been a happy one."

FAVORITE PLAYER(S) GROWING UP

WEBER: "I always wanted to be Bobby Hull. But when I was in my later stages of my college career and attending summer school at Western Illinois University, I went to the newsstand there and picked up and got the story from Bob Verdi and the Chicago Tribune that Bobby Hull and the Chicago Blackhawks were no longer. He was signing with the Winnipeg Jets. So that's when the business aspects of the game seeped into my consciousness."

HOCKEY AFTER DARK -- HILARIOUS TALES

While it can be a dream come true to broadcast a live sporting event to the masses, you have to remember there is a downside and that's the potential for misspeaking; saying something you can never take back. Not to get too doom and gloom, but there are times when a misspeak can cost you your job. So that's something you always have to be on guard against.

However, there are times where a misspeak luckily won't cost you anything other than a little joyful humiliation from your colleagues. Well, it just so happens that Pete Weber was present for one of those hilarious type moments and it was his partner Terry Crisp who committed the untimely misspeak.

WEBER: "Myself and Terry Crisp (were working a game together) when Terry misspoke. The game was in San Jose many years ago and it involved our defenseman Cale Hulse. His stick had been tied up, we came back out of commercial break and Terry said, 'well, let's just see here, Cale Hulse, with a nice cock……er, soccer kick was able to clear the zone.'

"So that makes it on the air and I'm basically rendered useless for about the next 90-seconds. But at that point in time we were doing a simulcast. So I quickly realized I better say something for the radio audience, but I wasn't able to say too much. I mean, that was painful. Thankfully Denis Arkhipov scored a goal to sort of stamp us back toward reality.

"Our Stage Manager in San Jose wouldn't laugh at Don Rickles or any comedian. And yet she was standing between us -- behind us -- and she was bent over at the waist laughing so heartily. Since it was a simulcast our Radio Engineer was right next to us. He took off his headphones and put his head down on the desk, convulsing in laughter. So that made it a little bit more difficult (to get back on track)."

WEBER'S FAVORITE PREDATORS GAME HE'S CALLED

When a team has never advanced to the championship round of its sport and it is over a decade old, the fans start to get very distraught. On the flip side though, those feelings of despair quickly become feelings of joy when the team finally puts itself in a position to go where it hasn't gone before. The fans throw their undying support behind the team and a magical energy fills the arena night in and night out.

By the time the 2016-17 NHL season had begun, the Nashville Predators had never even sniffed the third-round of the playoffs, let alone the Stanley Cup Final. For 17-years, when the NHL got down to its Final Four, Predators fans turned off their televisions, shut off their radios and went about waiting for next season.

However Year-18 (2016-17) was different. The regular-season gave no indication that this year would be any different; although the Predators were a superb team, especially on defense and in goal. But once again they faced their hated rivals, the Chicago Blackhawks in the opening-round. Historically, this was never good for the Predators as the franchise was 0-for-2 in this playoff matchup.

But, Lo-and-behold, things were different and after four-games the Predators had swept Chicago aside. It was on to round-two and a matchup with the St. Louis Blues. Well, six-games into the series Nashville said “sayonara” to St. Louis and “bonjour” to the Anaheim Ducks as the teams squared off in the third-round of the Stanley Cup Playoffs.

This was uncharted territory for the Predators and their loyal fans. A deep Spring playoff run meant Country music and hockey were intermixing, to great affect. They were partying in the streets outside the Bridgestone Arena, but as happy as the fans were that their beloved Preds had gotten this far, they knew work still needed to be done.

Through five-games the Predators held a three-two series lead and headed home for Game Six with the chance to advance to their first ever Stanley Cup Final. Nashville scored twice in the first and twice more within the first 14-minutes of the third to carry a 4-3 lead into the final six-minutes of regulation. The fans were on their feet, as were the broadcasters who had been with the team from the very beginning 18 long years ago.

Time continued to drain away and two empty-net goals by the Predators had everybody inside Bridgestone Arena -- except the visitors -- in the mood to celebrate. All that was needed was for the clock to hit 0.00. And when it did, Pete Weber, the team’s longtime broadcaster, uttered the phrase he had so longed to shout.

WEBER: “At the end, I got to say, 'sit down if you need, the Nashville Predators are going to the Stanley Cup Final!’”

SIGNATURE PHRASES

Most broadcasters don’t worry about their legacy until well after their careers are over and they get a chance to look back on everything they accomplished. It’s just the nature of the job. You enjoy everything in the moment but you can’t really appreciate what you’ve done until it’s all over.

Well, Pete Weber has been enjoying his career with the Predators for a couple decades now and has shown no signs of slowing down. However, he's already created quite a nice legacy of calls in the annals of NHL history.

One such call took place after one of the most emotional and crazy moments in Predators history and the another such call is one that keeps the Ice Officials on their toes. What might these calls be? I'll let Weber tell you for himself.

WEBER: "After Mike Fisher scored his triple-overtime goal, I sort of did a tribute to Jack Buck. If you recall his call of Ozzie Smith's home run, 'go crazy folks, go crazy.' So, when Fisher scored that goal at the end of the triple-overtime, I just said, 'go ape everybody. Go ape,' without adding the other word on there and people did go ape during that period of time."

Fisher's goal was an iconic moment in Nashville sports history. And I think you can all figure out what the word was that Weber left out off the broadcast. As for the call that keeps Ice Officials on their toes? Here we go.

WEBER: "The one that perhaps more people associate with me than any other, is when I think there has been an Official trying to atone for a previous error in judgment or in carrying out the rule book. Well, I will say 'it's Mary Kay time here.' In other words, it's makeup time. And people seem to really appreciate that one. I've had some Officials come up to me and say they hope to never be on the end of a 'Mary Kay' call."

MESSAGE TO PREDATORS FANS

As is a common theme amongst members of the sports media, it is a well known fact that without the fans our jobs would either A) not exist or B) they'd have a lot less meaning. So, each of the broadcasters in this book took a couple of minutes to address you, the fans, directly.

WEBER: "I never could have imagined, because I traveled here for 10 baseball seasons doing Triple-A baseball in the summers. I remember saying to myself, 'I cannot imagine living here, this place is so hot.' And then a few years later I moved here and 22-years later, I remain and intend to continue remaining here. I can't believe how welcoming they were, how tremendously neighbor-like they have been to us. Because, remember after 20 some years in Buffalo, when we first moved here, I said to Claudia, 'what is it with these people? Why are they so nice? What's their angle? What are they trying to get from us?' And then we just realized that is their nature. So thank you Nashville for having embraced us with open arms."

NJ DEVILS

MATT LOUGHLIN
RADIO: PLAY-BY-PLAY

First Season on Devils Radio: 2006-07
Seasons on Devils Radio (including 2020-21): 15

Birthday: February 11, 1958 Hometown: New York, NY

College/University: Seton Hall University

BIOGRAPHY

Ever since the Devils came to New Jersey in the Fall of 1982, there has been one constant. And that has been the presence of absolutely fantastic broadcasters, both on television and radio.

Names such as: Larry Hirsch, Mike "Doc" Emrick, Stan Fischler, Glenn "Chico" Resch, Steve Cangialosi and so many more, have populated the Devils' airwaves for going on 37 seasons.

And one name who has been around for close to 90% of the Devils stay in New Jersey, is Matt Loughlin. Loughlin has been featured on Devils' television and radio for several decades now and he's still going strong as the 2019-2020 season approaches.

For Loughlin, it has been a dream come true to cover a professional sports team, in his home state, that actually embraces its' Jersey home. And he's had quite the impressive journey to get to where he is today.

LOUGHLIN: "I went to Seton Hall University and the plan was to be an accountant. I loved math. Quick side note, I had a wonderful math teacher in high school and her name was Dorothy Holiday, she's since passed away; 'Dot' Holiday. And when I told her I was planning to go to Seton Hall to study accounting, she said, 'you'll hate it.' And I said, 'why?' She goes, 'it's not mathematics, it's arithmetic and then law. It's addition, subtraction, multiplication, division and then it's law. You're not going to like it.' Well, what does she know? So I went to Seton Hall, primed to be an accountant and she was absolutely right. I absolutely hated accounting, it was very boring. That being said, I wasn't going to get out of school in anything more than four years.

"But during that time, so now it's freshman year (1975), I really haven't started my real accounting courses and, of course, I was a big sports fan. I watched and listened to sports all my life and loved all the local teams. So I'm listening to my team, Seton Hall. The games were broadcast by the school's radio station, WSOU. And sometime during my freshman year, there was a notice in the school newspaper, 'Hey, if you want to be a part, we're always looking for people.' I never thought where it would lead, but I thought it sounded interesting. So, at the end of my freshman year, literally I finished my last exam of freshman year and I walked across campus from the business school, up the steps of Walsh Auditorium and into the radio station.

"I knocked on the door and asked how I could get involved. The incoming Sports Director for that following year was there along with the Station Manager, who was a faculty rep and they both welcomed me with open arms and said, 'listen, come on in, you're a student here. Whatever you do, whatever you put in, you'll get out. Work here a little bit, you'll get a little out of it. Work here a lot. You could potentially get a lot out.' And from that moment on I was just absolutely in love with the media and the radio. I walked in, the noise, the energy, it just felt like home.

"So anyway, I did finish with a business degree, but I switched from accounting to marketing because that following year when I started taking accounting courses I hated them. But I wasn't getting out in more than four years. So, I switched to marketing. Anyway, I just worked my way up. I just kept doing more and more at the radio station. And when I got out, I started to apply to a lot of places and I began working for a radio station in New Jersey, WCTC, it's in New Brunswick, near my home. While I was at Seton Hall, Bob Lee, ESPN, was working for a local cable company called Suburban Cablevision. He came by the radio station and said, 'Listen, why don't you come?' And it was located in the next town over; the headquarters. He said, 'why don't you come over, I'll teach you some of the ins and outs of television and I can always use some free labor,' which is exactly what it was. So I started to do some television.

"A year after I graduated, I spent a year doing news and this company, Suburban Cablevision, has an opening in their sports department. Bob had left to go to ESPN and Bruce Beck became the Sports Director and he said, 'we have an opening. Do you want the job?' Then I got the job and I turned to TV. And then, I just started knocking on doors and eventually SportsChannel hired me and I started covering a lot of things; college football and college lacrosse to start. That was the regional network break that I got and then I just kind of progressed from there.

"It was the late-80's when I was starting to do a couple of events here and there for SportsChannel. As I said, it started with me doing Hofstra Lacrosse and Hofstra Football and I guess I passed whatever muster they had and I started filling in for Stan (Fischler). There were two sports channels, the main channel and the backup channel. They had the Nets, the Devils and the Islanders in the Winter. There were many conflicts, so they had this overflow channel. So, whatever hockey team was on the main channel, Stan would do it and there were two of us who were filling in for him. So when the Islanders were on the backup channel, Carl Reuter, a Long Island based journalist, would fill-in. When the Devils were on the backup channel, me being a Jersey Guy, I would fill-in.

"After a couple of years, I wound up getting hired to do it regardless, Islanders and Devils. And so that was really the beginning, filling in for Stan. And then it just parlayed as SportsChannel decided to increase its budget and wanted to up its ante a little bit. I just eventually worked that into a full-time job, but not with hockey. It became a full-time job with basketball, the New Jersey Nets. But I was still fill-in, going back and forth, but I was Nets, Nets, Nets. And then when there was an opening that matched an opening in my schedule, I would do a

Devils event. But then in '96-'97, it became a full-time gig. I moved away from basketball and was doing Devils full-time."

That's a really incredible journey for the Jersey native. And his journey isn't complete just yet.

LOUGHLIN: "This will be my 14th year, coming up, doing radio. What had happened was, 2004 was the lockout year and then I came back and did one year (2005-06) and then 2006-07 was my first year doing radio. I was doing all my stuff with the Devils, loved it, but I had also been doing the Mets as well. They then left to their own network and so I was just doing the Devils and I enjoyed it. It was great. The Devils were winning and they were a championship team. I was working with Doc Emrick and Stan Fischler. Roland Dratch, our producer, was an awesome guy to deal with. Just a lot of fun. I'm in my home state, the team wears the Jersey logo; all that sort of stuff was good.

"But, going back to when I got into the business, I really, I loved radio. I loved everything about it. I'm still more of a listener than a watcher. But, you follow whatever path you need to follow to get where you can. And it happened to be television. So this job opened up and I thought about it long and hard and a couple of people, including the guy, John Hennessy, who was let go, told me I should apply for it. He thought I'd be great. And it sat there. I always wanted to be the play-by-play guy and I wasn't getting much of an opportunity. It was nobody's fault. It just wasn't not my role.

"SportsChannel morphed into Fox Sports Net and Fox Sports Net New York and then ultimately into MSG. But Doc Emrick was going nowhere. He's an Emmy Award winner. He's the best there's ever been. And he loved doing that gig. So there didn't seem to be any way for me to get a play-by-play job. I was filling in for him when he would have national assignments, but I never was going to get the job. And I thought, 'you know what? This is really where I want to be.' I want to be the play-by-play guy.

"I had a family, three boys, two who were in high school, one who was in grammar school. I wasn't going to traipse them all over the country with my wife. I'd established a family here. I'm from here. So I wasn't going to try to scratch that itch so to speak, by finding a job elsewhere. But here it came. A team I know. The team I'm covering. The team I'm working with and so, I applied for the job and I got it. And so now, 14 years later, I'm more radio guy than a TV guy."

HOCKEY AFTER DARK -- TALES AWAY FROM THE RINK

LOUGHLIN: "We went to a (Bruce) Springsteen concert in Hamilton, Ontario. The Devils were in Toronto. We happened to obviously have an off day. Sherry Ross is a huge Springsteen fan. She's gone to well over a hundred of his concerts; probably approaching 150. Tom Gulitti joined us and I'm trying to remember if Rich Chere went. But it was definitely Tom, Sherry and myself. We drove to Hamilton from Toronto to see a concert at The Copps Coliseum. That was pretty cool. Sherry always had good seats. So we had very good seats for the show.

"Interestingly, she was only able to get two and one as the breakdown. So I sat by myself at the show and she was with Tommy Gulitti, but that's okay. We had a lot of fun. That was probably 2006 or 2007."

LOUGHLIN'S FAVORITE DEVILS GAME HE'S CALLED

The 2011-12 Devils were a team on a mission. That mission? To win a FOURTH Stanley Cup championship. But before New Jersey could earn its way into the Stanley Cup Final, it had to first earn its way into the playoffs.

And before the Garden Staters could earn their way into the playoffs, they had to first make it through the grueling marathon that is the NHL regular season.

Now, there are some games that stand out more than others when it comes to the regular season. Some games bring more electricity. Others act as vessels for historic achievements. And some even act as a prelude for things to come.

So, whenever the New Jersey Devils crossed the Hudson River to face their blood rivals, the New York Rangers, or the Blueshirts crossed into Newark, you could be damn sure that the fans in attendance would be treated to an experience they'd never forget. And, of course, that sentiment extends to the players, writers, broadcasters, etc. as well.

With an archive full of memorable games and moments between these two teams, you almost have to stop and ask yourself, "what more can these teams do to each other?"

Well, how about a good old fashion line brawl?

The date was March 19, 2012, and the Devils were getting ready to face the Rangers inside The World's Most Famous Arena. Little did they know what was about to occur. And for one Devils broadcaster, this game was going to be one he would talk about for years to come.

LOUGHLIN: "It was March 19, 2012, at Madison Square Garden and the Rangers were a first place team. The Devils were going to be a playoff team. And in a rough and tumble series, it was the sixth game of the regular season series, a line brawl breaks out at the start of the game. And it was just great. I loved it, not because I'm a man who supports physical violence, but in our game we still need to have that element and it's slowly eroded to the point where it's almost nonexistent.

"But at that moment, that game, even though the Devils lost, spoke to me about the rivalry. There had been many fights in the five games previous, including another line brawl, which was only two guys involved; this was a full three. But the scene was incredible. Brandon Dubinsky, who had his nose broken earlier with the Rangers, had just recently returned. But because he's got a broken nose, still, he can't fight. He steps in to take the draw against Ryan Carter.

"And we found out later he said to Ryan Carter, 'good luck.' And he backs out. So now, Sherry Ross and I are sitting in our perch at The Garden getting ready for the game and it's just this roar at that moment, where those two teams, at that point in their seasons and what had transpired, it was just there, like there was a fire. And we know something's up because Stu Bickel had just come in to take the face-off.

"What is going on here? Well we kind of knew what was going on and it didn't take long. They dropped the puck and fights broke out. It's three guys just pounding each other. The crowd is going crazy. John Tortorella was barking at Pete DeBoer and Pete DeBoer was barking back at John Tortorella. Ryan Carter wound up being taken down to the ice ultimately. He got in a couple of really good punches on Bickel, but they got taken down and wound up breaking his nose on the ice.

"Bryce Salvador came over to try to help him out and instead of being a third man in and being kicked out, the officials kind of looked around and said, 'well you were just really helping a teammate. There was a lot of blood. We were busy elsewhere.' They only gave him a 10 minute misconduct, but it just was fantastic. And in many ways it set the tone for that 2012 Eastern Conference Final, because there were so many memories. The institutional memory of the Devils-Rangers rivalry and all that had transpired previously in '94, even though it was 18 years ago, it was still there.

"They beat the Devils in the Conference Final and won their first Stanley Cup in so many years. The Devils never really were able to beat them enroute to a Cup. So it was like, when are you going to put 'Big Brother' in his place? And while that night didn't do it, it set in motion what happened two months later when the Devils went in and beat them in six games. And even though they didn't win a championship, to me, that exercised their demons."

Even for two teams who really didn't -- and still don't -- like each other, this was a night that really brought the rivalry up another notch or two. In fact, it kind of harkened back to the days of the Original Six, when line brawls were more commonplace and fights would spill into the stands. Now, that's not to say this was a regular occurrence, rather it was just something that happened from time to time when it was needed.

LOUGHLIN: "There were 11 fights between the teams that year. This year (2018-19), the Devils as a team, all season long, had 15. So that was when the game still had that element of physical toughness that has eroded. The roar. The reaction afterward where Tortorella was pissed that Pete had put out his tough guys, his fourth-line at the start, but Tortorella had done it earlier at The Rock.

"And so, Pete came back with the classic line, 'Well, either he's got a short term memory issue or he's a liar.' So, to me, even though it didn't result in a Devils win, it spoke about hockey, the rivalry and the rawness of it. And I talk about it all the time, because you'll never see it again. And I'm not a violent guy. But I just think that's an element of the game we still need. And on that night, in that venue, the Devils stood up for themselves, even though they lost

"Well, you knew in the previous games there had been a lot of fights. Again, it was still a part of the game. You knew the Rangers were holding onto first place. The Devils were still clawing their way into a playoff spot. They were in a playoff spot. They didn't need the win so much, but certainly it would have helped. And they hadn't secured anything. So, going in, it was a chance for the Devils to reestablish themselves. That season's series ended 3-2-1 in favor of the Rangers.

"So it was even going into that game. The Rangers wound up winning to take their third win. And you knew they could very well be on a collision course. So how was what was going to take place tonight, going to impact any potential meeting down the road?

"And this was Marty Brodeur near the end of his career. This was (Ilya) Kovalchuk putting the previous year behind him, where Johnny Mack gets fired and Jacques Lemaire comes in. The Devils were somewhat of a mess the year before. Kovalchuk wasn't playing any kind of a team game. Lemaire was able to convince him, 'Okay, well you can score 30 goals, but we need, just once in a while, for you to get back here.' And he bought into it. It was one last kick at the can for Petr Sykora who had come back. The bank was reunited with Patrick Elias. So all of those things are there.

"David Clarkson was having a great year. Zach Parise, you knew the backdrop there. He was playing out his contract. He's the captain. He's the homegrown kid. He's that first round pick in 2003. Fan Favorite. Now he's in the last year of his contract. Is this the last we're going to see him play for the Devils? So there were so many things that went into that season. It was Pete DeBoer's first year. You knew something was going to happen, inevitably.

"Cam Janssen was going to fight. Eric Boultoon was going to fight. That's what those guys did. They brought that energy level. It was going to happen. Nobody knew it was going to happen, until warmups were over. Everybody skated off, we were waiting to get handed the lineup sheets and then we came back from a commercial and were ready to go. The Anthem had been played and low and behold -- we knew when the Anthem was being sung, who was out there -- I'm looking at

Sherry going, 'we're going to see something now.' She was not as in favor of it as I was, which is fine, but I was like, 'here we go.'"

While Sherry's trepidation was understandable, this was -- and is -- the type of rivalry where the bad blood is not contained to just the ice. Of course, I'm not saying that the media or the fans are going to fight each other, far from it. (Well, maybe the fans will if they've been drinking). But there is always a palpable tension when rivals like the Rangers and Devils meet. Even the reporters who cover the teams get a little more jacked up than they usually would.

LOUGHLIN: "This is hot. This is a rivalry. This is what it's all about, right here, at this moment. This puck gets dropped and they know what they're going to do. We know what's going to happen and the crowd was in a roar.

"Eventually, things did calm down a little bit. I mean, once that energy dissipated, it was not going to happen right away again. It was just too much energy that was used up in those first three seconds. So you know now, okay, now let's play the game. But you have guys in the penalty box. Bryce Salvador, he's gone. So the Devils are really short-handed.

"One of their key defensemen was not available for 10 minutes. The Rangers took some early control. And really, the Rangers, thinking back on that game, they were pretty much in control the whole way. After the game, Marty Brodeur wasn't too happy. Again, it was him and Lundqvist and that side story. But he was like, 'that's not what we came for. We came to win the game and we didn't win the game.' And I understand that, because that's what an athlete is doing. But, it's still, to me, a night that I talk about.

"That being said, the Rangers kind of controlled things. The Devils never pushed them to the point where they were sending a message, 'when we meet, we've gained the toehold, we're the better team. We beat you up.' And you could argue that Carter having his nose broken, they won the battle. I think it was pretty much probably even. So there's no gain made by the Devils in the fight or the fights themselves. Again, the Rangers won. And it was kind of like they said, 'okay, you brought out your tough guys. You brought out the nuclear option. We went toe-to-toe and we came out with a victory and we won the season series and we're still the Rangers and you're still the Devils.

"So I do remember leaving that game, a combination of disappointed, pissed, because I am a fan, trying to be objective as I can be, but such a moment that it didn't work out where the Devils could leave the arena heads held high. And that's why the "Adam Henrique, it's over!" was even more special, because they hadn't gotten over the hill that night.

"And I do remember a sense from Cam and Eric that, 'well, we didn't win the game, but man, that was fun.' Especially for Cam Janssen, that to him, that's what hockey should be like. He could still find a way to play this game and stay in this game because of the element he brought. And they all were like, 'hey, nobody left. Nobody went for a hot dog. We know it was early in the game, of course. But they were all on their feet.'

"And you know, the Devils and Pete made a statement by putting those guys out there. He knew Tortorella had one of two responses. He could put out as top-line and try to take advantage of their skill against the Devils' ruggedness. Or he could take the bait, which he did, and say, 'you're not going to do that in my home rink. You think I'm not gonna take a chance. You might do something to our more skilled guys. So here we go, let's have at it.' And to the Rangers' credit they won. But it's still, just that roar, that feeling, that energy, it's something that won't happen again. And that's okay. It's okay in a way. But just to be part of that and around that was pretty cool."

MESSAGE TO DEVILS FANS

As is a common theme amongst members of the sports media, it is a well known fact that without the fans our jobs would either A) not exist or B) they'd have a lot less meaning. So, each of the broadcasters in this book took a couple of minutes to address you, the fans, directly.

LOUGHLIN: "You are part of something special. You're an organization that came from two cities actually, Kansas City and Denver, but found a home in New Jersey and became an elite, respected franchise led by Hall of Famers. And not just Hall of Famers, but All-Time Hall of Famers in Scott Stevens and Marty Brodeur. No knock at Scott

Niedermeyer, but if he did just a little bit more sometimes he might be one of the All-Time greats. But there's no question Stevens and Marty take their place at the top of that Hall of Fame Mountain.

"So you are a part of something good and real in Jersey and it's our thing and the red and black and the Christmas tree colors are all part of that and will never go away. And you have every right to put your chest out and say, 'I am a Devils fan.' That's it. I mean Lou (Lamoriello) put this team on the map. Lou made being a Devils fan important and satisfying and this ownership group now is going to continue that and there's going to be ups and downs. But the Number One thing is just this organization. This organization has some history that makes it very special. Three championships, five appearances, more good things on the way. And again, everyone from that first year fan to somebody more recent is a part of something special."

NY ISLANDERS

GREG PICKER
RADIO: COLOR ANALYST

First Season on Islanders Radio: 2012-13 (Full-Time began 2015-16)
Full-Time Seasons on Islanders Radio (including 2020-21): 6

Birthday: June 18, 1991 Hometown: Dix Hills, NY

College/University: Boston University

BIOGRAPHY

Anytime you get to live out a childhood dream, it's something that will always stick with you, regardless of how old you get.

For Islanders Radio Color Analyst, Greg Picker, the Boys from Long Island have been a part of his very being for as long as he can remember and that's something that has been a constant throughout his career as well as his personal life.

PICKER: "I can remember wanting to be a broadcaster before hockey was even my number one sport as a fan. I remember being as young as five-years-old and playing video games with my brother and annoying the heck out of him. I'd be broadcasting whatever sports game we were playing, whether it was hockey, football or anything really.

"That kind of predates even my hockey (fandom). I never like to kind of say that this is the entire reason, but it's impossible for me to be honest, without saying that my father did work for the Islanders beginning in 2000. And so, as a result of that, I was going to probably 20-games or so a year beginning that year. And that was where I really fell in love with hockey and the Islanders; more than any other team, any other sport. (He was one of the business overseers. He wasn't in the hockey operations at all.)"

That love for broadcasting and for the Islanders helped mold Picker and it wasn't just his fandom, but also his being a student of the game and the art of broadcasting.

PICKER: "(Howie Rose) was obviously number one, because he was the guy who I heard more often than anybody else. I was watching close to 82 games a year, I can't promise that I watched every single minute, but probably about 60 games a year on television, without a doubt (I was in attendance for roughly 20 per year).

"Watching the games on television, without a doubt, you're gonna fall in love with the broadcaster who's bringing you your team, especially when he does a tremendous job like Howie.

"Interestingly enough, one of the other guys that I always had an affinity for is Jim Houston, because he, during my primary youth playing video games lifetime, was the voice of NHL and probably from 2002 to 2008, those NHL games. So, that kind of became an influence. And then we had the NHL package. If I was staying up to watch a late game from the West coast, more often than not, I would just choose the Canucks games because he was doing the Canucks games. So, because I kind of knew who he was from the NHL video games. They were never my number two team, but if I couldn't fall asleep and I was like, 'alright, I'll put on a West coast game,' I would always choose the Canucks because of Jim Houston. Again, I was never a fan of theirs at all. It was just, I could watch and be neutral and just enjoy their games more than I would other team's. I would seek their games out because of that."

"I can think more of signature calls that whenever I would hear them, it would give me sort of a joy from being a fan of broadcasting. It's Howie's whenever the Islanders were in overtime, it was so simple, but I can still hear it in his voice, 'the Islanders win it in overtime.' And for Houston, sort of his signature call, I think it was always the, 'great save Luongo,' type of thing. And whenever you hear that, it's like, 'that's a broadcaster!' That's something that you love to hear. I was probably 14-

or 15-years-old at the prime of watching those West coast games where I could stay up. And I could always hear Houston's 'great save Luongo!'"

If there's one thing in particular to be learned from Picker's story, it's that if you truly dedicate yourself to what you do, even at an early age, it will eventually benefit you greatly.

Of course, the amount of hard work that it takes to actually make your desires come true cannot be understated.

PICKER: "So I wanted to go to BU (Boston University) for two reasons. The Communications School and obviously they're a huge hockey school. I knew that if I went there, there was a really good chance that I could get on air right away. There are some other great communications schools in the Northeast, Syracuse being one, but everything you hear is, 'yeah, you'll be lucky if you can broadcast games by your junior year.' So when I went to BU I signed up right away for TV and radio, the two separate clubs and just signed up for as many games as I could call, especially from the hockey side of things. Now, obviously as a freshman at BU you're not going to get on the men's call right away, but they had a great women's team. It was only in its fifth year of existence, but they had started to really build.

"And so I broadcast a whole lot of their games that year, my freshman year. They ended up, surprisingly, winning the conference tournament. So, they ended up going to the NCAA Tournament, which is an 18 field. And that was my spring break with the person who I met there, who ended up becoming my best friend, who's still my best friend to this day. My broadcast partner in college, we spent our freshman spring break in Erie, Pennsylvania, to cover the women's hockey tournament. They ended up losing to Mercyhurst, but it was their first ever game in the tournament. Then my sophomore year, I wasn't broadcasting for the men's team, but I was the beat reporter for our radio website. But basically we were the main two broadcasters for the women's team. They were really good that year.

"They ended up going onto the Frozen Four, which coincidentally enough was in Erie, Pennsylvania. So I think we are the only two people outside of, I guess the ones who played for the team who can say our freshmen and sophomore year spring breaks were spent in Erie, Pennsylvania. We ended up as sophomores calling the National Championship Game between BU and Wisconsin on the women's side of things. Unfortunately BU lost, but I mean, it was tremendous getting to call that. And then junior and senior year, we were on the men's side of things. The team wasn't as good as the women's team was. They only made the NCAA Tournament once in our four-years and we didn't even get to go because it was in Minnesota. They lost in the first-round. So I never got to call a men's NCAA Tournament game.

"Oh, one more crazy game. Junior year, I wasn't really on the women's broadcasts for the most part, but they ended up winning Hockey East again, which was a surprise. So they went to the tournament and they were playing against Cornell. I was supposed to drive a buddy of mine from high school who also went to BU, home to Long Island. When they ended up playing at Cornell, I said to him, 'Hey, let's spend the weekend (in Cornell).' We had a couple of friends in the Cornell and Binghamton area, so why don't we go? I ended up going by myself to call the BU-Cornell women's quarterfinals in the NCAA tournament. The game was absurd. The night before they had a men's ECAC game, which went to double-overtime. It was the longest game in Lynah Rink history.

"The next day was BU and Cornell's women's hockey. I think BU was up 3-0, down 7-4 and tied it 7-7 in the last minute of regulation. So it was 7-7 at the end of regulation and it finished 8-7 with like eight-seconds left in triple-overtime. So we called 14 goals in regulation and played essentially eight-seconds shy of another full game. It took that long to score the deciding goal. I called that game by myself and it was absurd. That was the most ridiculous game I think I've ever called; certainly in college without a doubt. That was unbelievable."

That indeed was some game! And for a broadcaster-in-training it helps to get experiences like that to physically prepare your body, namely your vocal cords, for the stress that calling a game can put on you. But it's also important to know more than just how to broadcast a game. You really need to learn the little nuances of the game and of the organization you do games for in order to truly bring out the best in your calls.

PICKER: "I interned, actually in high school for the Islanders. I guess you could call it the radio team. Basically it was me just shadowing Chris King and Steve Mears, who was his partner at the time. And basically all I did was go down during the intermissions and the communications person at the time would tell me a player and I would basically just hand the microphone to a player. And that was it. But I still got to see what was going on and learned a little bit of the behind the scenes. That was my junior and senior year in High School and it was just for the home games.

"Then, in June going into senior year of college, I interned in the PR department for the Islanders. So that's how I really got to know everybody in that department. Then I finished up college a semester early, so December 2012, which ended up being just perfect timing for me because of the lockout and three weeks after I graduated, the lockout ended and the Communication Department basically said, 'we're trying to do an Islanders TV thing, why don't you come be the Islanders' TV Host?' And that's what I did.

"I also worked in the Communications Department where I also helped with press releases and whatnot. That was the lockout shortened year and then in 2013-14, in addition to Islanders TV stuff, my main thing was actually controlling the social media for the team. So I did that for the two seasons, the last two-years of The Coliseum. I ran social media in addition to broadcasting."

From an eventful college career to multiple internships and a do-whatever-you're-asked attitude, Picker has shown that he's prepared to be one of this generation's long standing broadcasters.

FAVORITE PLAYER(S) GROWING UP

PICKER: "I could tell you the three guys who I remember having a Jersey of. When I was like 10-years-old, I had a Michael Peca and Alexei Yashin and then, when I was a little bit older, probably 15, I still think I was the only one who had a Marc-André Bergeron jersey. He was not there that long, only a year-and-a-half, but there was something about this 5-foot-10 guy who could blast it past anybody else from the point. At that point in time, I was like, 'if I'm going to have a favorite player, it's going to be somebody who is a little bit more unique, that you're not going to see a million jerseys out there.' So for some reason, I just kind of liked something about Marc-André Bergeron and I don't know if any other Islanders fan would say that name."

HOCKEY AFTER DARK -- TALES AWAY FROM THE RINK

Getting to travel around the continent broadcasting games for a professional sports team, is probably high on the list for many sports fans. With that being said, the real joy is also getting to have unique experiences away from the game that you wouldn't necessarily get in your normal everyday affairs. For Picker, he's managed to accumulate a couple of these.

PICKER: "The thing that I like to do the most when we're on the road is find out if there's a game going on there. So if we get to a city two days early, sometimes there will be something. For example, our first time in Vegas, we had like four nights in Vegas. I was actually really sick at the time. We had a three-game road trip. It started during the game we were in Chicago. Then we went from Chicago to Arizona and Arizona to Vegas.

"I must've had the actual flu. The only thing that I did at all for fun was going to see the Knights play the Blue Jackets two days before our game. So like, I just put myself up in the press box, away from everybody else and just took in that atmosphere. And it's not so easy to take in the atmosphere all the time when you're broadcasting a game, just because you have the headset on. So you don't get the true crowd sound and that was unbelievable, to see that for the first time and sometimes I'll take my headset off for big moments, whether it's at home or pre-game on the road -- like in Montreal. You want to always hear that crowd because it's unbelievable. But that's what I love to do, is see games that I wouldn't necessarily get to see just because we're traveling and it extends to other sports.

"For example, we were in Vancouver and we had an off-day and we saw a Vancouver Whitecaps vs Montreal Impact game. Going to a random MLS game like that was a great experience.

"There's also a funny story, which is quick. Back when we were traveling with the team, because obviously we don't do that with Lou (Lamoriello) anymore. But back when we were traveling with the team, we were at the hotel in DC and Kinger and I were often the first ones on the bus, because obviously we never wanted to be the last ones. So we're outside the hotel, we get on the bus and we sit down and the bus driver says something about going to the White House.

"And we're like, 'we're not going to the White House today, what are you talking about?' So we looked at each other and we realized, 'Oh my God, the LA Kings are in town because they won the Stanley Cup last year.' I think it was the lockout year; I could be wrong but I believe it was the 2012-13 season. They weren't coming to play the Capitals, so they had to find an off-day where they played one of the Eastern most Western teams, like the Blues and then travel from St. Louis to DC.

"I think they played at the Blues, flew to DC, happened to be staying at the same hotel, which we had no idea about and we got on the bus. Thankfully we didn't get on and see Jeff Carter and Anze Kopitar sitting there. We were the only ones there, but the bus driver said something about going to the White House and it was the Kings going to have their day at the White House. It just coincidentally was the same day that we were in Washington. So, we quickly got off the bus, rushed around the corner, saw the Islanders' team bus and got on that one."

PICKER'S FAVORITE ISLANDERS GAME HE'S CALLED

While Picker primarily does the Color Analysis for Islanders radio broadcasts, he has occasionally gotten to live out his boyhood desire of doing the Play-by-Play as well.

PICKER: " So, although I am the color broadcaster, I still, growing up, always wanted to be a Play-by-Play. And I've been lucky enough to do five Play-by-Play games. A couple of times Kinger was filling in for Howie on TV. A couple of times there were medical things going on actually. My first two Kinger was on TV. So that was a Western trip. And I did the first two games, I think, on that Western trip, which involved an overtime win. So my first ever game was Michael Grabner scoring an overtime winner in Colorado -- my first ever Play-by-Play in Colorado. It would have been the 2013-14 season.

"That's the only game we played in Colorado that year and we won at Dallas the next game. I'm 5-0 when doing Play-by-Play. The most wild of those was probably in 2014. I think it was October 2014, at the latest November 2014, where the Islanders were playing in Boston the next day. The night before I was about to leave the office, which was at The Coliseum. I got a call from our PR guy, Kimber (Auerbach). He said, 'you've got to get up to Boston. Get Cory (Wright),' who's our writer, 'the two of you drive up right now.' But, we didn't have our stuff. So it was like five o'clock.

"We had to both go home and we said we'd meet at The Coliseum in like three hours or something like that. So we left at like eight o'clock at night and drove up to Boston to broadcast the game the next day. Kinger did TV. One of the Hofstra kids was up there, cause they were still doing those local road games at the time. So Cory and I stayed in a hotel room and a couple of Hofstra kids came up to us like, 'Hey, we're staying with you tonight.' He was like, 'all right, I guess that's what you have to do.'

"So we stayed in his hotel room and then broadcast the game the next day. So that was kind of a last minute type of thing. There was a game in 2017-18, where we were out of the playoff hunt, it was just towards the end and Kinger threw me a bone and said, 'this game doesn't have the same importance, so we'll get you some Play-by-Play in here. So we won that game in Ottawa. Then, unfortunately in 2018-19, Kinger had some chest pains so he missed a game to get some tests and was okay thankfully. But it was sort of like, 'Hey, Greg, you're doing Play-by-Play tonight.' And I got that notice probably five-hours before the game. So, basically, I already knew I was broadcasting, I had done plenty of the prep. It's just a little different style of prep for doing Play-by-Play versus doing the color. That was a shootout win. So I'm 5-0-0 on the Play-by-Play."

MESSAGE TO ISLANDERS FANS

As is a common theme amongst members of the sports media, it is a well known fact that without the fans our jobs would either A) not

exist or B) they'd have a lot less meaning. So, each of the broadcasters in this book took a couple of minutes to address you, the fans, directly.

PICKER: "On behalf of both me and (Chris King) Kinger, I think he'd feel comfortable with me saying that, we're just too huge Islanders fans who we're lucky enough to be in this position to have a microphone. We're not people who jumped around and had this opportunity that came to us when we could have gone to...Not to say that we would've ever turned down working for any of the other NHL teams, but, we just feel like we're two fans who have a microphone and can kind of bring those emotions that all the fans are feeling to our broadcasts. I think when we did the playoffs from the studio this past summer and we went on this amazing run, it allowed us the opportunity to record some of it.

"You can really just see the raw emotion of the two of us, how much this team means to us. And we get to see them in every single game. And if you're not in the arena, if you're in the car or wherever you might be, if you want, you can listen to us. We just feel that we bring those emotions, that all the fans are feeling to the broadcast. Whether it was a high moment that everybody loves, or even on the low moments. We kind of bring that through. We feel the highs and lows of this team no matter what happens."

NY RANGERS

DON LA GRECA
RADIO: PLAY-BY-PLAY

First Season on Rangers Radio: 2005-06
Seasons on Rangers Radio (including 2020-21): 16

Birthday: February 13, 1968 Hometown: Hawthorne, NJ

College/University: Ramapo College of New Jersey

BIOGRAPHY

Growing up a huge sports fan in New Jersey, Don La Greca made it his business to know everything possible about sports (and still does to this day). And without a doubt, his three favorite teams were: The New Jersey Devils; New York Giants and New York Mets (not necessarily in that order). In fact, for anyone who has ever tuned in to The Michael Kay Show, where La Greca is and has been for years, a Co-Host, his passion for the Giants and Mets is still unmistakable.

But La Greca didn't always intend to make his mark in radio, rather he, like many young men growing up sports-crazed, wanted to be a baseball player. "I was trying out to be a college baseball player," recounted La Greca. "But I got cut and I walked into the radio station at Ramapo College and I thought, 'well, I'm not going to be a baseball player, so I may as well try the communications route.' They had a radio station on campus and I figured, 'well, if I can't play it, I'll cover it.' So I did the baseball and basketball games for Ramapo's radio station."

Of course, that walk to the college radio station wasn't completely out of character for La Greca, as his passion for the broadcasting side of sports had been evident for quite a while.

"I was a Mets fan and a Devils fan. I'd listened to Gary Thorne and I loved him. And I loved Bob Murphy too, doing the Mets. But from hockey, it was Gary, since there was that connection between baseball and hockey. And when the Devils made their run in '88, just listening to every game and his calls was awesome. And then the next year after '88, I joined the Devils Fan Club and you were supposed to sit with a player and the player I'd picked was Jim Korn, but Jim Korn didn't show up.

"They were very apologetic and they said, 'look, would you mind if we sat you with the announcers?' And so they sat me with Gary Thorne and Chris Moore. Chris Moore was doing the radio at the time. So it was like a dream. It was better than like any player on the team, to be able to sit there and have a conversation with Gary. And I picked his brain on how to get into it. How did he do it? And that's when I realized that I'd love the chance to do that. And I just followed the broadcasters and listened to games. Then, the Devils had a bunch of them after that and I remember Mike Miller and talking to him. I was covering the team a little bit at the time and I'd always sit with him and talk to him about how he got into it. How did he get better? But I think it really started with Gary Thorne."

Don't worry Rangers fans, La Greca may have rooted for New Jersey back then, but he thoroughly earned his Blueshirts License years ago and has maintained it ever since. But back to the story.

"From college, I went on to intern at K-Rock, which was the classic rock station in New York in 1990. That's where I met Maria Milito, a DJ at K-Rock, whose husband, Pete Walker, worked at Sports Phone. And I got the job at Sports Phone, the 976131 number, to get scores. A lot of people started there, including; Howie Rose, Al Trautwig, Bob Papa, Michael Kay and I did updates there from 1992-2000. But in the middle of working there, I got an opportunity to meet a guy named Andy Roth, who knew Steve Malzberg, who got me a part-time gig at 1010 WINS.

"From 1010 WINS, Mark Chernoff heard me on The Fan and I started doing updates on The Fan. And then, when ESPN Radio started, Steve Malzberg, who was the one who got me the gig at 1010 Wins, was doing the hiring at ESPN and he recommended me, so I started working at ESPN and the rest is history.

"I kind of had a crazy way of getting from Point A to Point B."

After moving around a bit early in his career, La Greca has since found a steady home at ESPN Radio, where he has done the NY Rangers' radio broadcasts with Kenny Albert and Dave Maloney since the 2005-06 season. And in true La Greca fashion, there's a story behind him getting the gig.

"It was as simple as being the hockey guy at the station when we got the Rangers," said La Greca. "They wanted to expand. When the Rangers were on FAN, they just did a 10-minute pre-game and post-game, and it was always done by Kenny (Albert) or whoever was doing the play-by-play. There wasn't a lot of thought put into it. But, when we started, they wanted to do a 30-minute pre-game show and a 30-minute post-game show.

"I was the hockey guy, so they offered it to me. I did that for a few years and then Frank Moretti, who was the producer at the time, called me up and he said, 'Bob Wischusen, who was the main backup to Kenny, had to quit because he was getting a lot more college football and college basketball games.
So his availability was very limited.'

"So he said, 'would you want to audition since you're around anyway all the time doing the pre and post and we know you know the team well. Would you be interested in auditioning?' So I said, 'yeah, that would be great.' They had me go to MSG.

"They took a random Rangers-Devils game from the previous season and they put it on the TV and Pete Stemkowski was my color guy and I did a period. I figured, 'all right, I don't know how many people were auditioning. I don't know how many people they were considering, but I did it.' And I really didn't think too much of it.

"Then, the next day I got a call saying, 'okay, well, second game of the season in Philadelphia, you're on the schedule. And here's 14 more games you're going to have during the course of the first-half of the season.' So I bolted right in and Game Two was in Philadelphia. My third game was a Friday at home against Toronto and then a Saturday I went with the team to Detroit to do the Red Wings game. So it was crazy, like out of the box I did three of the first four games of the season. I got thrown right into it."

I guess it's only natural that the game that landed La Greca the Rangers gig had at least some tie-in to his previous Devils fandom. But regardless of that, he obviously aced the audition and has been on the Rangers' side of the "Battle on The Hudson" for many years now and Blueshirts fans are glad to have him.

FAVORITE PLAYER(S) GROWING UP

"Ken Daneyko. I loved Jim Korn. I loved Pat Verbeek. Sean Burke when he came up and helped them make that run in '88. John MacLean. Those were the guys I really liked."

HOCKEY AFTER DARK -- TALES AWAY FROM THE RINK

We all know that one of the perks of being part of the sports media is going to games for free. And yet another perk is the constant travel; unless you don't like to fly, in which case you might want to try a different profession.

While the work is both hard and fun to do, it also carries with it some unexpected encounters. And that's where Don La Greca's "Hockey After Dark" story comes into play. Don, the mic is yours.

"Because I do The Michael Kay Show, I don't get a chance to travel with the team a lot," explained La Greca. "I have to catch up with them and fly commercial. So, because I always seem to do Saturday games because of Kenny doing football, there was a game we were doing in Toronto and I took a commercial flight after The Kay Show.

"I ended up getting into Toronto, I got to the hotel at like 11 o'clock at night and I was exhausted, but I was really hungry. So I left my bag in the room and I went down to the bar to get a burger. I sat down in the hotel bar and Billy Jaffe was there. And Billy Jaffe was talking to John Rosasco, who's the PR Director for the Rangers.

"I obviously know both of them. So, I'm sitting down and I order my burger and Kelly Chase walks in and Kelly walks in with Mike Modano and they sit down with us because they know Billy Jaffe. So, I'm talking to Mike Modano, who actually followed me on Twitter; that was an ice-breaker.

"I'm talking to Mike Modano and I know Billy Jaffe. I'm talking to Kelly Chase and we're just bs'ing. And then John got off the phone, he had been on his cell phone. John puts the phone down and he says, 'he's coming.' Everybody shook their heads, but I didn't know. because I had gotten there a little late. So, I didn't know what they were talking about. And it was (Wayne) Gretzky. Gretzky walks in and he sits down.

"So, there I am, it was like one of those like lounges where it's like a couch and a coffee table, but the food was on the coffee table. So you've got Kelly Chase, Mike Modano, Billy Jaffe, John Rosasco and then right in front of me is Wayne Gretzky.

"I'm talking to Wayne Gretzky and what happened was, there was a card-signing that weekend in Toronto; that's why Modano and Chase were there. A lot of them were coming to Toronto and it might've also been around the same week as The Hall of Fame (Induction). So they were killing two birds with one stone. So they're all there and I'm sitting there and I'm having a hamburger and drinking a beer with Wayne Gretzky.

"The amazing thing is, all these people are coming up to him wanting his picture. They were in the bar and he took everybody's picture. He couldn't have been nicer. It was a nice little meeting. He'd say, excuse me and he'd take the picture with all the fans, which I thought was amazing.

"Then he paid for the meal and he left. He paid for my hamburger and I was like, 'I had a hamburger with Wayne Gretzky.' I could have just gone to bed and instead I was hungry and ended up hanging out with Mike Modano and Kelly Chase and in walks Wayne Gretzky. It was so amazing. I told Dave Maloney the next day at the morning skate, because they always asked what time did I get in? I said, I got in at 11 o'clock and Dave always goes to bed early. So there was no chance to catch up with him.

"So I told him the story. And then coming out of a commercial break (during the game), there was a stoppage of play or something, Dave goes, 'so, Don La Greca had quite the night last night over at the bar.' He made me tell the story on the air. And it was like the coolest thing. As much as I have been in this business a long time and have gotten the chance to meet so many famous people, I still never get over little things like that. I still get a kick out of talking to famous athletes and having that moment. And listen, I've seen Wayne Gretzky before that and since then in casual little encounters. But to sit down and break bread with a guy out of nowhere, at like 11:30 at night, the night before a game, that's probably the one that jumps out at me."

You've gotta love a job where an encounter like that can happen anytime, anywhere.

LA GRECA'S FAVORITE RANGERS GAME HE'S CALLED

What's the old saying, "you never know what's going to happen?" Well that's especially true for La Greca as his favorite game is one where the "impossible became possible."

For you fans who think you've seen everything, well, guess again for La Greca's favorite game of his career is one where "two-goals" were "scored" in one overtime period. Let that sink in for a minute. And for those of you who are confused or bewildered, or adamantly saying that's not possible, just remember, context is key.

I take you back to the 2013-14 season, to a time when the Rangers were considered to be one of the top teams in the NHL. They had a new Head Coach -- Alain Vigneault -- a new style of play -- uptempo as opposed to The "Black and Blueshirts" -- and some new pieces they hoped would be the final ones in their pursuit of a Stanley Cup championship.

But to get there, they'd first have to get past the two teams from Pennsylvania. Up first were the Philadelphia Flyers. It took seven grueling games, but mission accomplished. Next were the Pittsburgh Penguins. The Penguins and Rangers had been bitter rivals for years and recently the Pens had been a particularly consistent thorn in the side of the Seventh Avenue Skaters.

Game One took place in Pittsburgh, but had a distinctly New York feel by the time it was over.

As is the case in any hockey game, but especially in the playoffs, it's crucial to score first. So, when Benoit Pouliot put the Rangers on the board 5:03 into the first period, things were looking good for New York. And things only got better near the end of the period when Brad Richards scored with under three minutes to go in the opening frame to put the visitors in the driver's seat -- up 2-0.

Unfortunately for the Blueshirts, Pittsburgh's superstar players weren't going to let the Rangers win the game without a fight. And in the middle of the second period, roughly six minutes apart, the Penguins scored two-goals to tie the game. The first came from Lee Stempniak and the second from James Neal.

With their two-goal lead a thing of the past; New York tried to regain control of the game, but to no avail. So the teams continued to battle for that elusive third goal and when the final horn sounded at the end of the third period, neither the Rangers nor the Penguins had added to their score sheet.

So as the saying goes, "Ladies and Gentlemen, please stand by for overtime."

And here's where I'll let Don La Greca take over.

DON LA GRECA: "I had called playoff games before. And I had called some cool moments, but I'd never had an overtime game. So, I was in Pittsburgh doing the game and we're going to overtime and I'm nervous. I was like, 'geez this is crazy,' and there's no commercials. This is going to be a big moment, win or lose; it's going to be a call that could very easily be remembered.

"So I'm calling the game with Dave Maloney and in the overtime, Derick Brassard scored. But they waved the goal off, so they kept playing. And then, Benoit Pouliot put in the rebound and scored the game-winning goal.

"I called it as Brassard scoring the goal, but I followed the play and the official waved it off. Then, Pouliot scored and the replay showed that I had it right, Brassard had scored. It's kind of known as the 'Two-Goal Overtime;' you're not supposed to score twice in overtime.

"But I also remember that Dave had gotten so excited and you could hear him yell when Brassard scored. And then the play continued. But what people don't know is that Dave actually hit his hand on the parabolics. We were high-fiving each other and I was like; I can't believe that after growing up a Devils fan, I was celebrating an amazing Rangers' game against Pittsburgh.

"Just everything that went into that series, and it being my first overtime, the way they scored and for me to be on top of the call, it was just one of the craziest things I ever was involved in. And to be able to call it too and being on top of the action, it was really amazing.

"So, on that play, we're not exactly dead center at the new building in Pittsburgh, so that's the far side of the ice that I'm calling it from. And I remember Brassard comes in, takes a shot from the slot and when I'm calling the game; I usually go by the sound. Sometimes it's tough to tell if the puck goes in unless you're standing above it. Like, at The Garden sometimes, you can tell because you're right on top of the action.

"But in Pittsburgh, it's a big building and you're far away. So my little indicator is, did I hear a ping? The puck came out hard and I didn't hear the ping, so I said 'goal!' I said, 'he scores,' but I immediately saw the official, who's to the right of the goal, wave it off -- immediately.

"So I was able to incorporate that into my call. Dave yells, so there's this feeling like they won the game, but they've got to continue to play. Some of the players were kind of half celebrating. The play was continuing but there was this surreal feeling of, is the game still going on? Is it not going on? Did anybody see? I saw the official wave it off. But sometimes a lot of people don't see that. The light never went on, but there's that indication of celebration and then the puck's loose to the right and Pouliot picks it up and it hammers home the rebound.

"So you know they won the game. It's either Brassard's goal is going to count or Pouliot's is going to count. But either way, you know they won the game. It was just that surreal feeling of, when did the game end and is there going to be some kind of controversy, because there were some guys who stopped playing. But in my mind I knew the game was over. It was just a question of who scored the goal.

"So Dave and I are analyzing it and I'm sticking to my guns saying I think Brassard scored the goal, but we weren't sure. And then they got the replay, but obviously replay didn't matter; it just determined who scored the goal. And usually what strikes me about that is that the goal is scored, the game's over, everybody runs to the guy who scored the goal and he becomes a part of history.

"I mean how many guys score overtime goals in the playoffs? And especially in the second-round, especially against Pittsburgh and to not know who the heck scored the goal was just one of the more surreal moments that I remember."

SIGNATURE PHRASE

Over the years, fans, if you listen close enough, you'll realize many broadcasters will become synonymous with a particular saying of some sort. Now, not every broadcaster has one, but for the broadcasters who do, it will sometimes become something that fans will greet the broadcaster with anytime they meet them.

For La Greca, his "Dagger" goal call follows whenever the Blueshirts score an empty net goal; which essentially means the game is over and the Rangers have won. And if you think about it, the imagery is appropriate for the situation. Blueshirts Faithful, here's to hoping for many "Dagger" goal calls in the future.

MESSAGE TO RANGERS FANS

As is a common theme amongst members of the sports media, it is a well known fact that without the fans our jobs would either A) not exist or B) they'd have a lot less meaning. So, each of the broadcasters in this book took a couple of minutes to address you, the fans, directly.

DON LA GRECA: "Just appreciate it. It's an amazing organization with a tremendous history. To walk into that building, which is now officially the oldest building in the National Hockey League, and to see the numbers in the rafters and see the connection the fans have with those players. I saw it from being a Devils fan growing up, to now working with the Rangers. I've seen it from both sides that it's not a fly by night kind of, 'oh we're hot, people love us. Or, oh we stink, nobody cares.' The building is always full. The fans are always passionate.

"They've always connected with the players; whether it's (Eddie) Giacomin to (Adam) Graves, to (Mark) Messier, to (Mike) Richter, to now, Henrik Lundqvist or Mats Zuccarello. They just appreciate that this is a family that's connected to its history; not just to their own history, but the history of the League and whether it's in a losing season or a winning season. It's a tradition that continues to march forward that really connects family and generations. And there are not a lot of organizations that can say that. And as much as you want to win, ultimately you know that when you're a fan of that team, you're part of a family and a tradition that's lasted for going on a hundred years.

"It's easy to follow a team that's going to win a championship every decade, or a couple. But it's one thing to say you can be that passionate about a team that's literally won one championship in 70-plus years. You're not going for the winning and you're not going because it's an easy team to root for. You're going because you appreciate the history and you appreciate the organization. Think about it, Kenny's (Albert) been doing games forever. Sam (Rosen) has been doing games forever. This is just a very comfortable organization to be around; at least for me anyway. They welcomed me with open arms and they treat me very well."

OTTAWA SENATORS

GORD MILLER
TV (TSN 5): PLAY-BY-PLAY

First Season on Senators TV (TSN 5): 2013-14
Seasons on Senators TV (TSN 5) (including 2020-21): 7

Birthday: June 21, 1965 Hometown: Edmonton, AB

College/University: N/A

BIOGRAPHY

Have you ever wondered what your life would be like if not for one specific event that took place when you were growing up? Come on, raise your hands, we've all done it.

Well, for Gord Miller, even though he had a love of sports and broadcasting, who's to say whether he embarks on his decades-long career or not, if not for a little divine intervention on the part of Mother Nature?

MILLER: "I lived in Edmonton and was going to High School in the early 1980s. The Oilers had just started and to be honest, I got into broadcasting because I don't like the rain. Our school had a high-end track and field set up and we had to work there when other schools had their track meets. I was raking a long jump pit in the rain and the announcer didn't show up. The announcer booth was covered, so I went and did that instead."

Perhaps it was fate giving Miller the nudge he needed to start down his career path.

MILLER: "I'd do the announcements in my High School. And then, a guy came up and he said, 'there's a high school basketball tournament, 'would you like to do (it)?' I said, 'Sure.' And I wound up being the PA announcer for the University of Alberta, Golden Bears basketball and hockey. The Edmonton Trappers were a Triple-A team. I did their PA announcing and in 1983, in the summer, CBC hired me to help out on the weekends doing highlights for them.

"That was '83 and in '84 TSN started. Two of our guys left to go to TSN. They replaced one right away, a couple people auditioned for the other job while I was filling-in. I was only 19 then. And eventually they hired me in 1986 full-time after I filled-in for almost two-years.

"I did enjoy doing the PA announcing for my High School and I did love sports. But I didn't know you could make a living doing it. I remember watching Vin Scully calling the 1982 NFC Championship game and thinking, 'wow, what a great job. I wonder what he does during the day?' And someone said, 'no, that's his job.' 'Really? You can do that full-time?'

"At the time, when I started working in Edmonton, I mean, the Oilers were one of the best teams in the NHL. There was a lot going on and it was a great introduction to it. The CBC network used me a lot for reports on the Oilers and everything else. TSN first offered me a job in 1988. I turned it down. And then, in 2000 they offered me a job and I took it."

It's a job he's held in one form or another to this very day.

Of course, you need to go back to his days as a kid and as a teenager to find the origins of his love for hockey; beyond just the Oilers being a winning team.

MILLER: "All the kids in the neighborhood played; so I played. Now, those days, you only saw the Vancouver Canucks once in a while (on TV). I mean, you didn't have hockey on TV all the time. But, the one thing was John Davidson's wife's family is from my area in Southern Alberta and he was a big deal. John was a big deal back then. He was a big Junior star in Calgary. When he came back in the summer, that was a big deal.

"I played hockey until I was 16. The Oilers entered the NHL in '79, but before that they were in the World Hockey Association. (Wayne) Gretzky came in '78, I think. So, I was always interested in hockey. I loved it. The Oilers, in the early '80s kind of exploded onto the scene. In '81, they upset Montreal. In '83 they went to The Final. '84, they won The Cup for the first time and I was just starting out then. It was just an amazing time to be around them."

John Davidson of course, later became a Hall of Fame Broadcaster and eventually, a highly respected President with several different NHL teams. So, while JD was an influence on Miller, so too were some of the biggest broadcasters of the time.

MILLER: "There were three I listened to growing up. Danny Gallivan, Dan Kelly and Bob Cole, were who I really admired and liked.

"They called all the big moments. Dan Kelly's call of Bobby Orr's goal, I still remember. Bob Cole was calling the big games. Danny Gallivan, Montreal was such a great team in the '70s, so I heard Danny Gallivan a lot. They were the voice of the big moments. That's why you were kind of drawn to them."

Miller carried those moments with him throughout his career and was eventually able to get to know, meet and learn from those broadcasters in a one-on-one setting.

"When I started out, the late Don Wittman was terrific to me. Don did a lot of games in Edmonton and was very supportive of me and encouraging. Bob Cole was great to me early on in my career. I was lucky enough to be around him a lot. And I was lucky to meet Danny Gallivan. I became friends with Bob Cole and even had dinner with Dan Kelly when traveling to Philadelphia.

"It was incredible. Those guys were so helpful to me and I've always tried to be that way with young broadcasters, because those guys were that way with me."

PLAYER(S) MILLER GREW UP WITH

MILLER: "Ken Daneyko actually broke my collarbone in a game. There were a lot of players in our area, like Ken Daneyko and there was a goaltender named Darrell May. Lyndon Byers was a guy in the neighborhood. Gord Donnelly. Kelly Hrudey was a little older. There were a lot of good players around there."

HOCKEY AFTER DARK -- TALES AWAY FROM THE RINK

Sometimes a story is more about remembering a specific interaction than about an entire lengthy set of events. But just because it's not lengthy doesn't mean it doesn't hold the same weight to the person who experienced it.

For Gord Miller, there have been two interactions in his career -- away from the broadcast booth -- that stand out to him.

MILLER: "I think about the late Johnny Bower and what a gentleman he was and just running into Johnny at an event. It was a dinner in his honor in Mississauga, Ontario, that I was emceeing. He pulled me aside and said, 'I really like watching you on TV.' He said, 'you talk about the goalies a lot.' Johnny was always teased about that.

"So I think about that, because when you do a legacy team like that, there's a long line of history and those guys were around a lot. And to know that Johnny Bower was watching and enjoyed my work, meant a lot to me.

"(There was also) a national game I did. Prime Minister (Stephen) Harper, I ran into him at a game and he said, 'Oh yeah, I saw you doing a game the other day.' When you realize he's watching, you don't realize the numbers, but you realize that someone like that's watching; that's pretty cool."

MILLER TALKS DEALING WITH NHL'S LONGEST GAMES

In today's day and age, everybody wants things faster and faster. People are no longer content to wait for information or to take a long time to get somewhere. It's all about instant gratification and the advancement in technology has fueled this.

Yet, even as the world speeds up and some sports leagues make the mistake of trying to do the same -- yes, I'm looking at you MLB and Commissioner Rob Manfred -- there is still a time and place for some never-ending, edge of your seat, marathon-style sporting events.

The National Hockey League, during the regular-season, has implemented new rules over the last couple decades to attempt to prevent games and the schedule from becoming even more grueling than it already is. Take three-on-three overtime and the shootout as examples. Both were implemented to prevent games from dragging on and on.

But come playoff time, those restrictions go out the window and that's when hockey fans can be on high alert for something special. Overtime playoff hockey is one of the most exciting and dramatic sports events a fan can witness. And without the limits of the regular-season, it is straight five-on-five for 20-minutes; or more, depending on the situation.

There is no limit to the number of overtime periods a game may need to determine a winner in the NHL's playoffs. That is when things can get wacky. And Gord Miller knows this all too well.

MILLER: "Well, I just did the five-overtime game between Tampa and Columbus. I've done some long overtime games. I mean, I did the five-overtime game between Dallas and Anaheim in '03. I've done some really long overtime games. I would say those are the ones that stand out.

"You never know how long the game is going to be. I mean, it could end at any moment. So, you're just staying in that moment and not really thinking about whether it's going to go three, four, or five-overtimes. I've had experience with them.

"You're going to hit a cluster where it's the 10th longest game, the ninth-longest game, moving up that list. I mean, in terms of doing a long game like that, at things like the Olympics and the World Championship in the World Junior, I do multiple games in a day. So I'm used to calling six, seven periods in a day. That doesn't bother me. I'm used to it. That doesn't bother me at all. I'm quite used to that.

"The great thing about my job is you go to the rink and you don't know what's going to come next. You have no idea what's going to be next.

"(My Color Analyst) Brian Boucher played in the Keith Primeau game. So, (during the Columbus-Tampa game) I was just joking with him and talking to him. But I think, secretly, he wanted their game to remain the longest in modern history. He was happy the Flyers win still stood. And of course, we called the Keith Primeau game. But, he's the guy who made 57-saves in that game. So, just joking with Brian Boucher about it. The difference between calling a game like that and broadcasting it is quite something. But I mean, it is interesting that he had sort of the experience of both."

MOST FAMOUS CALLS

When you've had as long of a career as Gord Miller, you're bound to have made a few calls that are just a cut above the rest. And it's those calls that regardless of how much time goes by, will always be remembered by hockey fans.

The first of which was Miller's World Junior call on a Jordan Eberle goal that has since managed to take on a life of its own.

MILLER: "Can you believe it?!"

According to Miller, that one, "gets played a lot up here (in Canada)."

The other is one that essentially announced the arrival of Sidney Crosby as a superstar in the NHL.

MILLER: "Crosby scored against Montreal in his rookie-year, early in the year; scored in a shootout. I'll always remember that. 'Welcome to The Crosby Show, Canada.'"

MESSAGE TO SENATORS FANS

As is a common theme amongst members of the sports media, it is a well known fact that without the fans our jobs would either A) not exist or B) they'd have a lot less meaning. So, each of the broadcasters in this book took a couple of minutes to address you, the fans, directly.

MILLER: “I think what I appreciate from (the Senators fans) is the passion they feel for their team and the roots their team has in the community. And I think the message I would give them is it's a long term love affair and it can be painful. And that's part of the joy of it, right? The pain is part of the joy of it. And that's part of being a sports fan -- the highs and the lows. And that's why we love it. It's unpredictable. I appreciate their passion for their team and for the game. And Ottawa fans, just be patient, because our team is building.”

NICOLAS ST-PIERRE
FRENCH RADIO: PLAY-BY-PLAY

First Season on Senators French Radio: 2008-09
Seasons on Senators French Radio (including 2020-21): 14

Birthday: March 2, 1970 Hometown: Sept-Îles, Québec

College/University: Collège La Cité

BIOGRAPHY

When you do what you love, you'll never work a day in your life. It's an old saying but it's completely true. And in Canada, after your family, what most everybody loves is hockey. To put it another way, late-New York Yankees owner, George Steinbrenner once said that winning was only second to breathing.

Well, in Canada, hockey is second only to breathing. And Nicolas St-Pierre is no exception.

ST-PIERRE: "Basically I'm from a small town and what we did in the winter (was we played) hockey and (in) the summer, if you were lucky you were playing for the ball team. Since I can remember, I've had skates on my feet; like basically two, three-years-old.

"My dad, when I was a kid, I remember having stories. My dad used to tell me stories about him. Stories from the old hockey games, like the Richards and The Punch Line. I had a few uncles who were playing. My dad kept saying that he would be playing with two of his brothers.

"I loved those stories. And watching Hockey Night in Canada, on Saturdays, those are things that you're basically born with. I guess I was born with the sport. I'm born with hockey."

He may have been born with the sport, but he certainly didn't get his team fandom from his family.

ST-PIERRE: "The Quebec Nordiques were my team. My parents, my family were Habs fans, I can remember, they were winning Cups every year. I don't know what happened, but the moment I heard about the Quebec Nordiques, I fell in love with those guys."

That love for hockey eventually became concentrated on the radio broadcasts and that's where the story of St-Pierre really gets going.

ST-PIERRE: "The love was foremost for radio. I always loved that medium. Since I was very, very young, I've always been, well, in love with that medium. The hockey part and the sports part came after I got some experience within the radio business.

"I started at a radio station called CJRC. I basically started doing traffic and weather on the morning and midday shows. I was basically doing everything I could.

"I remember a time where I was at the Montreal Forum. That was my first time at the Montreal Forum, 1983, I think. I was 13-years-old. And at that time I was in the nosebleeds and at the press box, there was some sort of passage where you could see the journalists going there and all that stuff. A little bit like the new one. I could see the three guys, main guys for Hockey Night in Canada.

"At that moment, when I saw those guys, I said, 'man, if one day I could do that. That would be awesome.' And I knew those guys were on radio, TV and all that stuff.

"So, going back to my love for radio, I always had that back in my mind; like being Play-by-Play. But it was so far away that you don't really know if one day you'll be able to achieve it. But the further you get, like the closer you get to the medium, which is radio, you say, 'wow, well, maybe one day.' You always get that back into your mind.

"The story basically that I want to tell is, when, in hockey, you call up a kid and you always say, you have to be ready when they call you up, because you never know. Well, it was the same thing for me. I always had that in the back of my mind, like, you're doing Play-by-Plays for fun. Like playing video games and watching games and all that stuff.

"While you're doing a journalist job, while you're doing traffic, you're replacing people and going to that station, CJRC. Throughout, a few months, I became a journalist and at one point, there was a Play-by-Play guy doing the Junior team, the Gatineau Olympiques. And he basically quit in the middle of the game, in the middle of the season.

"It was a February day and the Gatineau Olympiques were basically blank. So the General Manager was looking at someone and said, 'Hey, Nick, do you ever do Play-by-Play?' And I said, 'yeah, I did Play-by-Play a lot.' Lie! I'd never really done it before. I'd done a few minor games and all, but never on radio. So that's how I became the Play-by-Play for the Gatineau Olympiques out of the blue.

"My first night that I did the play by play, that was Charlie Henry beside me. He was the General Manager. Here, he's an icon. So, after my game, the guy looked at me and said, 'what the hell is that dude doing here?' Like, 'he's worthless.' Just swear words.

"I said, 'Holy crap, man, dude, you don't know who you're talking to.' In my head, I said, from that moment on I'm going to show him that I'm not useless. So I did three-years with the Gatineau Olympiques and after that, there was the guy who was doing the Play-by-Play for the Ottawa Senators at that time, he left for Montreal and then, the guy who replaced him, basically came and did a season and a month before leaving for Montreal.

"So that's when they basically asked me if I could do Play-by-Play for the Ottawa Senators. It was barely at the beginning of the season. Then I got the job. I remember that day because it's one day after my first son was born. I was having him in my arms and my dad was there with my parents. Everything was happening at the same time. So it was my first day with my newborn and I got the call from the station saying that I got a job doing the Play-by-Play for the Ottawa Senators."

FAVORITE PLAYER(S) GROWING UP

ST-PIERRE: "I tried very hard to do whatever (Wayne) Gretzky was doing. I thought I had something because I was playing a lot behind the net. I was trying lots of wraparounds and stuff like that."

HOCKEY AFTER DARK -- TALES AWAY FROM THE RINK

The dark underbelly of sports broadcasting is the highly volatile nature of stations and teams constantly shifting the broadcasting rights around like a game of hot potato. And when the rights get shifted, the former rightsholder usually cuts ties with a lot of its staff because they are no longer needed.

Like I said, it's a dark underbelly of the industry and one that St-Pierre experienced the hard way.

ST-PIERRE: "In 2012, I was with CJRC. They were negotiating with the Ottawa Senators at that moment for the (radio) rights and for signing a multi-year contract. That's in the 2011-12 season. So in 2012, February or March, I was told by the General Manager of the station, 'don't worry, everything's going to be fine. You'll have a job, or you'll be our guy for the Play-by-Play and all that stuff.'

"So (they're) negotiating and nothing's happening. I'm waiting and I'm asking while summer's coming. They're saying 'don't worry, they're going to sign.' All right. So at a moment, I think it was August 8th, the General Manager called me and said, 'we just cut ties with the Senators. You have no more jobs. There's no more broadcasting rights in French.'

"So, (now) it's August and by that time nobody's hiring because everybody did their stuff and hired their people. So, I'm basically jobless and I don't know what to do. So, they're announcing that there's going to be a lockout. By the time we're announcing the lockout, to the time they're launching the new season, I had gotten myself a personal loan. I got myself a company, the equipment and I had signed the French Radio broadcasting rights for the Ottawa Senators. By January 19th (I believe), they started, I was on the air with my crew, myself and negotiated the broadcasting rights with a local radio station.

"I wasn't going to let some suit in Toronto decide I was done doing what I loved. And we held those rights for two-years."

From being stuck in the dark to going into the light, St-Pierre showed he was determined to keep his passion alive and in doing so, created one of those more unique stories you'll ever hear in regards to NHL broadcast rights.

ST-PIERRE'S MOST FAMOUS CALL

In the Spring of 2017, the Ottawa Senators and New York Rangers met in the Eastern Conference Second Round to determine who would move on to the Conference Final. It was a series Ottawa fans had waited five-years for as the teams had previously met in the playoffs in the Spring of 2012, when the Rangers took their Conference Quarter-Finals series in seven games.

Come 2017, there were a handful of players on both sides who remained from the first series and fans North of the Border had no desire to see New York skate away with another victory.

After winning Game One at the Canadian Tire Centre by the score of 2-1, the Senators looked to make it a 2-0 series in game Two.

The teams traded goals in the first period, with Michael Grabner scoring for the Blueshirts and J.G. Pageau for the Senators. Then came a three-goal outburst by the Rangers in period two, which was slightly mitigated by a lone Ottawa goal from Marc Methot. So, after 40-minutes of play, the scoreboard read 4-2 Rangers.

On to the third period and what a period it was!

Mark Stone scored early to bring the Senators within 4-3, but that was soon negated by a Brady Skjei goal to make it 5-3 New York. And that's where the score stood as the period entered its final 3:30.

Pageau soon scored again -- his second of the game -- to make it a one-goal game. But the Rangers still controlled their own destiny, at least until the final 1:30, when their defense was caught in a bad matchup and Henrik Lundqvist was placed under siege.

With 1:02 left in regulation, Pageau scored his third-goal of the game to complete the hat-trick and more importantly, tie the game. Ottawa had come all the way back and now it was off to overtime. Who would be the hero?

Well, nobody wanted the mantle of hero in the first overtime, so a second extra period was needed. It was then that Mr. Hat-Trick (J.G. Pageau) decided to further etch his name in the history books by scoring his fourth-goal of the game; this one the double-overtime, game-winner. And the moment was punctuated by St-Pierre's call.

ST-PIERRE: "Pager, the game-changer, four for 44!"

MESSAGE TO SENATORS FANS

As is a common theme amongst members of the sports media, it is a well known fact that without the fans our jobs would either A) not exist or B) they'd have a lot less meaning. So, each of the broadcasters in this book took a couple of minutes to address you, the fans, directly.

ST-PIERRE: "In 2017, we made it to the Eastern Conference Final. And since then, yes we've struggled a little with attendance and on the ice. And I get some of the complaints people have about our ownership and about The Barn. But don't forget there are kids out there on the ice bleeding their hearts out for the team. Even though the team is struggling in some areas, there's still things to look forward to."

PHILADELPHIA FLYERS

JIM JACKSON
TV: PLAY-BY-PLAY

First Season on Flyers TV: 1995-96
Seasons on Flyers TV (including 2020-21): 26

Birthday: March 23, 1963 Hometown: Cortland, NY

College/University: Syracuse University

BIOGRAPHY

While there are an innumerable amount of broadcasters who have to travel to the farthest reaches of the sports world to gain experience before finally, after many years, landing their dream job, there are far fewer who get lucky enough to avoid the many winding twists and turns that are a staple of the broadcaster's journey.

Jim Jackson is one such broadcaster who, thanks to being in the right place at the right time, managed to carve out a much straighter line from the start of his career to where he is now. And that's not to say he didn't deserve it, because he worked just as hard as anyone else. Rather, there's always a little bit of luck that's needed to successfully navigate a career as a sports broadcaster and Jackson had luck on his side.

Of course, Jackson didn't necessarily think his path would take him into hockey. That was sheer circumstance.

JACKSON: "It's interesting because I really was a four sports person growing up. I didn't have a specific love for hockey. I loved hockey. It was one of my four, but my goal was to do any of the four major sports; at the time soccer wasn't a major sport.

"To me, it was basketball, football, baseball, hockey and I was in upstate New York. So I was a big fan of the New York teams. The Mets, for some reason in baseball and then the traditional teams, Knicks, Rangers and Giants in the other sports. I became a huge sports fan. The hockey (love), specifically, probably came from the minor league team there. My father got half-season tickets one-year for the Mohawk Valley Comets.

"So I got to see the sport up close and personal and I fell in love with it. Now, we didn't have a hockey team at my school, so I couldn't play the sport, but a kid up the street from me had an outdoor rink, so we'd always go up there and play. It wasn't like I had this dream to become a hockey announcer. I had this dream to become a Play-by-Play announcer for a major sports team. I loved Jim Gordon, but my absolute favorite, I had one for each sport, and my guy for hockey was Dan Kelly. He was the national guy then, basically. I loved Dan Kelly's goal call. I loved his enthusiasm for the game.

"I went to Syracuse starting in '81 and graduated in '85. It was huge to why I'm where I'm at, because I grew up in Utica. I think probably, when I was in High School, my goal was to do sports for sure, but I would have been satisfied with being Sports Director at WIBX in Utica. And that would have been a career goal for me.

"After about two-months at Syracuse, you're around all the kids from New York and all the kids who come up and have these bigger dreams, so your dreams kind of change. It definitely pushed me and I roomed with Dan Hoard, who does University of Cincinnati sports and the NFL's Cincinnati Bengals. Mike Tirico was there and Todd Kalas too.

"There were so many people during that time who were at school with me. It's just amazing. Some people who didn't go to Syracuse kind of think of us as arrogant because we're everywhere, but it is kind of neat, especially in sports, how many people went there and moved on and were successful in the business.

"It just so happened that when I got out of college, I went to the station in Utica and I was able to create a position for myself by proposing a role as a Weekend Sports Talk Show Host.

"So I went from intern, to full-time employee and then, wouldn't you know, six-months later, the Sports Director, who was Tim Roye (he's now the voice of the Golden State Warriors), decided to leave to go to Birmingham. So I became the Sports Director and about six-months after that, the Utica Devils came to town when the New Jersey Devils moved their AHL team to Utica.

"For six-years I worked at that station. The teams I did were: The Utica Devils and one-year with the Mohawk Valley Comets, who were in the ACHL at the time. There was one-year of that (doing the Mohawk Valley Comets) and then I did six-years of the Utica Devils from '87-'88 through '92-'93. While I was there, I also did Utica Blue Sox baseball, who were in the New York Penn League during those years. (I managed to turn that experience into doing the Phillies too). I've been lucky enough to grow up in a town, go to college then go back to that town for six-years and then go straight to my dream job. So I lucked out.

"There I was doing AHL hockey at about 22 or 23. So I ended up in hockey largely because of the way fate had it. I ended up one step below the NHL at 23. So I got six full years of AHL hockey and then I moved to Philadelphia when I was 30. So, I think I ended up in hockey more by chance than by design. Not that I didn't want hockey. It's just what came my way.

"So it was not just one sport for me. It was any of the sports and it just so happened that it was hockey. I love the sport. So I'm happy it is. But, it could have very easily been basketball or football if circumstances had been different."

FAVORITE PLAYER(S) GROWING UP

JACKSON: "My very first favorite was Eddie Giacomin. I just remembered Eddie Giacomin from when I was really young. Jean Ratelle became a favorite as well. I was getting older as they made that trade and they brought (Phil) Esposito and other guys in. John Davidson had an unbelievable year in '79. And I loved Don Maloney."

HOCKEY AFTER DARK -- TALES AWAY FROM THE RINK

Sometimes it takes a well respected coach to change how a broadcaster says things. I mean, broadcasters have been honing their speaking skills for years, so what exactly would an NHL Head Coach find that would need to be changed? Well, you're about to get an answer.

JACKSON: "Roger Neilson is one of the All-Time hockey characters. He was the coach here for three-and-a-half-years. Roger was such a unique individual and such an easy going guy. But I got this call from the PR guys saying, 'Hey, Roger wants to talk to you about something.' And when a coach wants to talk to a broadcaster, it's never good.

"So I'm racking my brain as to what I might've said on recent broadcasts that could have made him upset. I just couldn't come up with anything. The team was winning. So, I go in there (to Roger's office) and he's sitting there, he's got his sandals on; typical Roger in shorts, a t-shirt and sandals by his desk.

"He says, 'Come in and sit down.' He shuts the door behind me. I'm like (to myself), 'what is this?' He says, 'you have a good call. But there's one thing you say when the puck goes into the zone and a player preceded it. What do you say it is?' I go 'it's offsides.' He said, 'it's what?' I said, 'it's offsides.' He goes, 'it's one. It's offside. How can it be plural?' He says, 'you say offsides every time. It's really just offside, not offsides.' He's having this whole meeting over offside vs offsides. But he got his point across. I never say offsides anymore. Since that day I say, 'offside.'"

JACKSON'S FAVORITE FLYERS GAME HE'S CALLED

When it comes to the games and moments that Jim Jackson has been on the call for, you can never go wrong with high drama affairs. They are the most exciting types of games and moments and when your team comes out on top it's all the sweeter.

As Jackson recalls, there are two games he's done where the drama was unmatched. One was the Flyers season-ending shootout victory over the Rangers in 2010. And the other is the longest game in modern NHL history, you know, the one that went five-overtimes between the Flyers and Penguins before Keith Primeau finally put an end to things.

Well, let's dive into each.

JACKSON: "One moment I go to is the 2010 shootout between the Flyers and Rangers in the last game of the season. There were two rivals. One goes to the playoffs. One goes home. Into a shootout against, at the time, the best shootout goalie around, Henrik Lundqvist. It was just an unbelievable moment and the Flyers won and the fact that they went onto the Stanley Cup Final from that, I guess adds to the moment of it. The moment itself was unreal because there were these two rivals, one goes home, one goes to the playoffs. You can't beat that kind of drama."

That's correct, you can't beat the drama that unfolded on April 11, 2010, inside the Wachovia Center. The Rangers and Flyers each entered the game eyeing a spot in the Stanley Cup Playoffs. But there was only one spot remaining. So, the two teams battled it out for 60-minutes with Jody Shelley (Rangers) and Matt Carle (Flyers) providing the only regulation scoring.

Then the game went into overtime and when that wasn't enough, it went to a shootout.

Daniel Briere started things off on the right foot for the Flyers as he scored against Henrik Lundqvist to put his team in the lead. Erik Christensen led off for the Rangers and was denied by Brian Boucher. Then it was Mike Richards' turn for Philadelphia, but he was unable to build on the Flyers' lead. Richards' miss loomed large moments later when P.A. Parenteau beat Boucher to even things up at a goal apiece.

So, with the shootout even after two rounds, it all came down to the third and final round. Claude Giroux stepped up for the Flyers and put the team and the city on his back as he scored against Lundqvist to move Philadelphia to the doorstep of the playoffs. Giroux had done his part and now it was up to Boucher to stop Olli Jokinen. Jokinen broke in on Boucher but couldn't find the back of the net and the Flyers were off to the playoffs while the Rangers went home for the off-season.

That was definitely a drama filled affair, but you can't compare that to the five-overtime madness that ensued between the Flyers and Penguins on May 4, 2000, at Mellon Arena.

JACKSON: "That was the longest game, still is by not much, in the modern history of the NHL. The Lightning and Blue Jackets almost beat us, but they fell a few minutes short. When you're part of history, that kind of has to be one of those moments. The game was great. The goal by Keith Primeau was a good goal. The whole moment was great."

The moment was indeed great and tiring too. Let me set the stage. It was the Eastern Conference Semi-Finals. The Flyers and Penguins have had a long and storied rivalry. The Penguins won Games One and Two to take a two-games-to-none lead heading into Game Three. Games Three and Four were being played in Pittsburgh, so it was the perfect opportunity for the Penguins to close out the series against the Flyers. Only, that's not what happened.

Philadelphia won Game Three 4-3 in overtime as a precursor for what was to come in Game Four. In the fourth game of the series, Pittsburgh's Alex Kovalev scored 2:22 into the game to put his team up 1-0. It was a good start for the home team. But that wasn't enough. The score remained 1-0 until the 4:47 mark of the third period, when John LeClair tied things up for the Flyers with a power-play goal.

That's when things got really interesting. For the second straight game overtime was required to determine a winner. But unlike Game Three, this wasn't going to be decided with just a single overtime period. Although, a John LeClair steal and Daymond Langkow shot off the crossbar 31-seconds into the extra period almost ended the game before things could get crazy.

In reality, that type of close call should have been a warning of what was to come. When the first overtime expired and a winner hadn't been decided it was on to double-overtime. Soon, double became triple and triple became quadrupole. Somewhere around the fourth extra period all of the players' locker room supplies ran out. The standard pizza and power bars were long gone. Multiple players were being hooked up to IVs to keep themselves going.

Eventually, the game entered rarified territory as a fifth overtime period was needed. For perspective, an NHL playoff game hadn't needed five overtimes since 1936! That's 64-years without a single five-overtime affair. And yet, there the Flyers and Penguins were. Finally, with 12:01 gone by in the fifth extra period, Keith Primeau beat Ron Tugnutt to win the game for the Flyers and tie the series at two-games-apiece.

Wait?! There were more games left to play in the series? Yes, indeed there were. Luckily for both teams no more overtimes were required as the Flyers closed out the series with regulation wins in Games Five and Six.

MESSAGE TO FLYERS FANS

As is a common theme amongst members of the sports media, it is a well known fact that without the fans our jobs would either A) not exist or B) they'd have a lot less meaning. So, each of the broadcasters in this book took a couple of minutes to address you, the fans, directly.

JACKSON: "I would thank them because of the passion of Philadelphia sports fans, which is talked about a lot and sometimes it's talked about from the outside, at least in a negative frame. I love, obviously it can go overboard at times, if you take it to the extreme, but for the most part, the passion of Philadelphia sports fans helps drive everybody around the team, whether it be the fans or the broadcasters; because that enthusiasm is there.

"I would much rather be with a fan base who's going to follow it's team, read about them and yell at them. I'd much rather be with a fan base that does that than a fan base where there's not much noise at all; it's just apathy. And there is no apathy in Philadelphia. It's great. Being here for such a long time, it motivates me. It's just that passion is pretty much unmatched. I mean, I know Boston has and in New York it has. It's the Northeast corridor. But in Philly it is unique and it is something that I've loved being part of."

JASON MYRTETUS
RADIO: PRE-GAME/INTERMISSION/POST-GAME HOST

First Season on Flyers Radio: 2006-07
Seasons on Flyers Radio (including 2020-21): 15

Birthday: March 30, 1972 Hometown: Westchester, PA

College/University: Penn State

BIOGRAPHY

Some careers happen intentionally, while others come about by accident. Growing up, you can say you're going to do one thing with your life and potentially follow through. Or, you might fall into something else entirely.

Jason Myrtetus wanted to play hockey. That's the simple part. He loved hockey and played it all the way into College. The logical next step would be to play Minor League Hockey or get drafted. But fate had other plans.

MYRTETUS: "I have two older brothers who are twins and are five-years older than me and they started playing when they were 10. So I started skating and doing 'learn to play' programs when I was five.

"I started playing organized (hockey) at Mite age. So, I started playing at six, seven-years-old. And I've played my entire life. I played all the way through Mite, Squirt, PeeWee, Bantam, Midget, Junior and then into College.

"There was a kid in our neighborhood who played, so my brothers got interested in it. We played street hockey all the time. Then, when the signups came for that one-year, my dad was taking my brothers and he was like, 'do you want to sign up if there's a program for you?' And I was like, 'sure.' So it kind of happened at the same time and we've been a hockey family ever since. My dad never played growing up, but he was into the sport and watched it. We all just were totally into it. One of my brothers played in College at the University of Hartford. The other one didn't play beyond high school."

Of course, for Myrtetus, there was one player in the NHL who he really wanted to be like in terms of what position he played and that's Ron Hextall.

MYRTETUS: "He was really the first guy to come in with a couple of things. Number one was just his attitude. He was really brash. He was physical too. He was really intense and had a lot of compete in his game. Most times, back then, goalies were really passive in the way they approached the game. He wasn't. He initiated contact and he would get after guys. And obviously through his career we saw that. Then, the other thing was the ability to play the puck."

So, Myrtetus played goalie and that got him a taste of the career that lay ahead of him. He just didn't know it at the time.

MYRTETUS: "Well the guy who did the radio and eventually moved to TV was one of the great Play-by-Play voices in Philly history in Gene Hart. He was tremendous and such a gifted broadcaster and great guy. And there was a guy named Bobby Taylor, who was his Analyst for a lot of years, who was really good as well. They used to do this thing at The Spectrum called the Pepsi Shootout. It was a breakaway competition and then a two-on-one and a three-on-two.

"You'd go against the other youth teams in the area. I guess it was 1982 when my Squirt team was in it. And when you got to the Semi-Finals and The Final, Gene Hart and Bobby Taylor actually would do the Play-by-Play and Color Commentary of it. It would air in between periods of the Flyers game. We won it. It was phenomenal to have those guys calling your name and they actually didn't butcher my name."

The two legendary broadcasters called Myrtetus' competition and while he loved listening to them, he didn't think he'd ever be joining their ranks. That is, until fate stepped in.

MYRTETUS: "My growth kind of stopped at 5'8" and even though goalies weren't huge back then, that probably hindered me a bit.

"It was weird. I was never a kid who, growing up, had any thoughts or aspirations of being on the radio. It totally happened by accident.

"I went to Penn State to play hockey and I hadn't declared a Major that would get me into the main campus, because I wasn't a great student. And the way to do that was to declare a Major of Forestry. But then, when I got there, I realized that there was way too much math, way too much science for Forestry and that wasn't going to work.

"I had a Teacher in High School who had a big impact on me as a Public Speaking Teacher. I did really well in his class and he was always like, 'you should think about doing radio.' And I was like, 'whatever.' I never really thought about it. And then when I had to switch my Major, I had to figure out what to switch it to at Penn State. So I switched to what was called Broadcast Cable Journalism.

"And still I wasn't really even thinking about radio a whole lot. Sports Radio had come in about five-years before that. I was intrigued by it. I thought, 'Hey, that'd be a cool way to make a living.' But once I switched my Major, I was working at a beer distributor that was a drive-through beer distributor. A guy came in one day and bought a case of beer and we were beer runners. We ran it out to his car and he paid with a check.

"I saw his name and he was a morning radio guy on a rock station at Penn State. I said, 'Hey, I just switched my Major to Broadcast Journalism. I was thinking about doing an internship.' He's like, 'I'd love to have the beer guy as an intern. Come to the station tomorrow after the show. And we'll meet. I went in there, we met and they offered me an internship on the spot. That was 27-years-ago and I'm still doing radio.

"So the station that I interned at, it was a rock station. So I did Rock Radio for the first portion of my radio career. I was doing Commercial Radio, not College Radio while I was still in school at Penn State. And then, I stayed there for a couple of years after I got done with college and did Rock Radio. Then I came to Philly in '99 and worked at a station, WYSP, which was one of the biggest rock stations in the country.

"They had Howard Stern in the morning. They were the first station to syndicate Stern. So I came down and I worked there. They were owned by Infinity Broadcasting, which also owned WIP Radio in Philadelphia and had a bunch of stations in their cluster. WIP was one of the first sports stations in the country.

"Eventually, I ended up going to WIP because the Program Director, who voiced all their commercials, had triple-bypass surgery and they needed a voiceover guy to do commercials. So I would just go there a couple days a week, they'd have a stack of scripts there for me to read and I would read their commercials and their promos. And then that was it. One thing led to another and I ended up working at WIP and they were the Rights Holders of the Flyers.

"So I ended up working there and I was in management there. I was actually running the station. I was the Program Director. The Flyers were the first team to have a radio guy, outside of the Play-by-Play guy and the Analyst, who handled Intermissions or Pre-game. It was always the radio crew who did that prior.

"But I thought we could take it up a notch by having somebody else do that, free those guys up and interview players as they come off the ice. Now, I think 29 of the 31 teams do it that way. It was the idea I came up with one day in a broadcast meeting with the Flyers -- around 2004 -- to say, 'how can we make the broadcast better?' Well, to me, TV's doing walk-off interviews. Why can't radio do it? So we figured out the mechanics of it, where to set me up in there and that's how it happened."

FAVORITE PLAYER(S) GROWING UP

MYRTETUS: "I grew up a Flyers fan, just because I was in Philadelphia. They were definitely my favorite team. Through the years I was a goalie. So, I was always really enamored by the position and that's where my idols were. So the guys when I was really young were Pelle Lindbergh, until he died in 1985 and then (Ron) Hextall came in. There were other guys around the league too who I was always kind of intrigued by. But it was Hextall, and Pelle here for those years. Some guys around the league were Grant Fuhr and Patrick Roy."

HOCKEY AFTER DARK -- TALES AWAY FROM THE RINK

As a broadcaster for a professional sports team, you're going to occasionally experience things that just don't happen to the average fan. Consider them to be like super fans. They get to do things normal people can only dream about. Well, if you're an average Boston baseball fan, you might get very jealous at what Jason Myrtetus was able to do one day back in 2010.

MYRTETUS: "In 2010, the Flyers played in the Winter Classic at Fenway Park against the Bruins. So, we were there a couple of days before New Year's Day, which is the actual Winter Classic. There was a practice the day before. So we're at the practice and we're in Fenway Park. It's just Flyers media and a bunch of people. But there's no crowd or anything. Then, after that, me and a couple of the guys we went up and were just kind of walking around Fenway Park, because it's such a spectacle. We managed to get our way into a suite that was loaded full of alcohol. We might've sat there for a little while and unloaded it full of alcohol, in Fenway Park by ourselves. It was awesome."

Notice the wording used by Myrtetus, that way he has plausible deniability in case the Red Sox ever come asking questions.

Another thing that can happen to broadcasters while traveling is actually something that many fans who travel to see their favorite teams play also go through. And that's dealing with a language barrier in a foreign country.

MYRTETUS: "In 2010, in the Conference Final, the Flyers were playing against the Montreal Canadiens. So, I'm staying in a hotel about a block away from the Bell Centre and I don't speak French. I can't read French. I remember the hotel was on the street where there was a market, kind of like the Reading Terminal Market in Philly where there's a bunch of vendors and food places and flowers and gifts and all that stuff. So that's right there in downtown Montreal. I went in there to get something to eat for lunch one day and I'm walking around. I go to order my food and I go to pay and she says, 'Oh no, we only take cash.' And I didn't have any cash on me.

"I was like, 'well, is there an ATM machine?' So she points me down to it. So I wait in line, I get up to the front of this machine and I'm trying to figure it out. It's all in French. I can't figure this thing out, there's a line of people behind me and they're getting impatient. I just turn around to the guy behind me, with my card and I'm like, 'I don't speak French.' And he's like, 'this isn't an ATM machine. This is a train ticket machine.' So I'm like, 'Oh my God.' I just walked out of there. So it's kind of the odd things in your travels that can happen."

It was also during that series against Montreal where the Flyers were "victimized" by some sand. You see, according to Myrtetus, during the first period of one of the games at the Bell Centre, the Flyers players kept coming off the ice with skate issues. Normally, that wouldn't raise much of a red flag, except for the fact that it was basically every Flyers player who was having an issue and nobody on the Canadiens' bench seemed to be having a problem.

A little quick detective work uncovered the culprit. Somebody and we're not going to point fingers at who put sand down on the carpet that led from the Flyers' bench to their dressing room. The sand was adversely affecting the skate blades of the Flyers players, so after the situation came to light, some Flyers staff people put down mats over the carpet so the players would avoid the issue for the rest of the game.

Just a little gamesmanship from the Canadiens. Don't worry, there are plenty of teams around the league who do stuff to gain a "competitive advantage." But we're not going to out all of them right now.

MYRTETUS'S FAVORITE FLYERS GAME HE'S CALLED

As a broadcaster, you're not playing in the game. That's the players' job. Your job is to entertain and inform the fans who are watching or listening back home. But just like the players, broadcasters also get to bask in the glory of victory when their team archives something monumental. After all, they are, for all purposes, part of the broader "team."

So, it's no surprise that Jason Myrttetus looks back rather fondly on his role during the Flyers' 2010 celebration after the team knocked off Montreal to advance to the Stanley Cup Final.

MYRTETUS: "It was such a great season. They were reeling. John Stevens got fired in, I believe, December. Peter Laviolette came in. The team gets into the playoffs on the last game of the regular season in a shootout versus the Rangers. Brian Boucher vs (Henrik) Lundqvist in the shootout to go to the playoffs. It's a magical ride. They get past the Devils. They come back from down 0-3 in the series against Boston and come back and win that series in seven after being down 3-0 in Game Seven. And that's still not the best one.

"It was in Game Five when they beat Montreal to go to The Cup. The reason is, just being on the ice after the game, for the presentation of the conference trophy and knowing you're going to The Final and getting to interview Ed Snider, the Owner, in the Post-game show and just how excited he was to go back to The Final. He is as competitive as any player and wanted to win so badly.

"To be able to talk to him for a good four- or five-minutes while he was just beaming at this unlikely group that everybody left for dead. They came back in that series against Boston and got past Montreal in five games to go back to The Cup. It was incredible. The atmosphere was so insane. It was just great to be a part of and The Final was great too. But, obviously, it didn't end the way Philadelphia sports fans wanted. So, the night when they won the Conference Final was probably the peak of my career, from an individual game standpoint."

MESSAGE TO FLYERS FANS

As is a common theme amongst members of the sports media, it is a well known fact that without the fans our jobs would either A) not exist or B) they'd have a lot less meaning. So, each of the broadcasters in this book took a couple of minutes to address you, the fans, directly.

MYRTETUS: "One player in a team sport cannot win you a championship. It takes a team to win a championship. That's number one. And there's much more to hockey than the offensive blue-line to the goal-line."

TIM SAUNDERS
RADIO: PLAY-BY-PLAY

First Season on Flyers Radio: 1997-98
Seasons on Flyers Radio (including 2020-21): 24

Birthday: December 19, 1962 Hometown: Grosse Pointe Woods, MI

College/University: St. Clair County Community College (Port Huron) & Eastern Michigan University

BIOGRAPHY

What is a kid to do when he loves sports but isn't part of the one-percent of the population who is gifted enough to play at the professional level? Well, you could just be a fan for your whole life. That's what most people do. But Tim Saunders isn't "most people." He wanted more; more than just being a fan. He wanted to be involved with sports at the professional level. So, what did he do? He took his love for sports and merged it with a well-timed opportunity to kickstart a career as a sports broadcaster that's lasted close to three-decades and counting.

SAUNDERS: "Well, growing up, in Detroit, it's not unusual to be a hockey fan. Actually, my grandmother was the hockey fan and she actually started taking me to games before I was big enough to see over crowds when they stood for a goal. I used to go to Olympia stadium all the time. In fact, over the years, growing up, I probably spent more time at Olympia Stadium than I did in school. And I had the grades to prove it. I was a lifelong Red Wings fan growing up. I played some hockey and baseball, but it became fairly apparent pretty quickly that I wasn't going to have the ability to play.

"I had the heart, but I didn't have the skill. So it was a matter of trying to find another way to stay involved in sports. I was writing for school newspapers about sports and in my senior year, the journalism teacher got in front of the class and said that WXYZ in Detroit, one of the major stations in Detroit, had reached out and they were looking for interns to work on a sports talk show. And it was actually one of the first sports talk radio shows in Detroit. I jumped at the opportunity and after school, four days a week, I would drive to the station and was an intern on that sports radio talk show.

"That kind of set me on the path that was more interesting to me than being a hockey writer or a sports writer. So radio quickly became the goal. It wasn't long after working on that show that I kind of fell in love with radio, to be honest with you. So, I did that throughout my senior year, went to Junior College and after my first year in College, I got a job at WWJ in Detroit as a Board Op Engineer type. So I wasn't on the air yet, but that exposed me to another major station in Detroit. My love for radio just grew from that."

Saunders' love for radio grew not just because of his personal experience, but also because of the voices of Detroit Sports at the time, with Bruce Martyn standing out from the rest. Martyn of course was the legendary Red Wings radio announcer and he touched the hearts and minds of sports fans and aspiring broadcasters alike.

Now, let's get back to Saunders' journey into radio.

SAUNDERS: "After two-years of college I'd already worked for a couple of major market stations. So, at the end of my sophomore year, all the kids who were graduating and were two-years ahead of me, were talking about getting this job or that job. And I didn't think any of them knew a damn thing because none of them had any practical experience. It quickly became apparent that the practical experience was going to get you further quicker than sitting in class. That might've been shortsighted, but after my sophomore year at Eastern Michigan, I decided I wasn't going to wait.

"I started looking for a full-time radio gig. So I was working at Sports Phone in Detroit. I was working at WWJ in Detroit. And I just decided to start sending resumes, because, by then, as I said, I had more practical experience than any of my counterparts who were older and graduated. So, long story short, I got a job at WOOD Radio in Grand Rapids. Grand Rapids is the second biggest city in the state. You don't really start in a major market.

"As most broadcasters will tell you, you've gotta be willing to go anywhere. So Grand Rapids was a pretty good option. I went there as both an Engineer Board Op, but also with some On-Air responsibilities and that grew in a couple of years into me becoming the Sports Director at that station.

"So I spent 10-years at WOOD Radio. I met my wife. We had two kids. Bought a house. And after a while, people started asking me, 'what really is your ultimate goal in broadcasting? What are you trying to accomplish?' I hadn't really been forced to consider that. It was always in the back of my mind to work in a major market, but when I really forced myself to answer that question, it would have been to do hockey Play-by-Play.

"So it occurred to me that I wasn't really doing much to make that happen, because it doesn't take long to realize that those jobs are not filled by radio stations. They're typically filled by teams. So after 10-years at WOOD and, by now, I'm over 30, I started sending tapes all around the country. I had done some work at WOOD. I did a year of broadcasting for the Muskegon Fury in the old Colonial Hockey League. That was close enough where I could commute and keep the WOOD Radio job and do hockey for a year.

"That gave me tape and convinced me that, 'yeah, that's really what I wanted the most to do and where I could be at my best.' So I started sending tapes around to every minor league team in the country. I had a few interviews, drove to the NHL Draft in Quebec City one year in the early-90s and eventually, after a few interviews, I got a job in Tulsa in the Central League, to work for the Tulsa Oilers. And when you start in the minors you don't go just as a broadcaster.

"You're a PR Director. You're doing sales. You wear several hats, because no minor league teams, at least back then, could pay you to just do a broadcast. So that was both exciting and frightening. I put my house up on the market, convinced my wife that we were gonna move and when I got the job in Tulsa, the idea was that I was going to leave her back in Michigan to sell the house while I go ahead and get started on the job and find a place to live; hoping that that house would sell pretty quickly.

"It took six-months. So I was without my kids, who were babies at the time, for six-months. And that was really hard. Had I known it was going to be six-months I might not have done it. So I'm glad I didn't know that. But Tulsa turned out to be a great place to cut my teeth. I developed some great relationships, particularly with the General Manager and the Owner of that team.

"I spent two-years in Tulsa, went to Cleveland in the IHL and spent two-years in Cleveland as the Director of Broadcasting and did radio and TV in Cleveland for the Lumberjacks. And then, after the second year in Cleveland, I got the Flyers job in 1997."

FAVORITE PLAYER(S) GROWING UP

SAUNDERS: "I played more baseball than I did hockey growing up. But I was always a huge hockey fan and I was probably more emotionally vested in hockey than I was baseball. It was after Original Six. I mean the Original Six ended in '67. I was born in '62. So my memory doesn't go back before expansion, of course. But Marcel Dionne was a big Red Wing. Danny Grant. Later guys like Reed Larson came in. And during my whole childhood, the Red Wings had awful teams. They missed the playoffs, I think my entire childhood.

"Those were the guys who I idolized in Detroit. But My favorite player growing up was Eddie Giacomin, because I was a goalie and he was the flashiest goalie in the league at that time; still with the Rangers. And then Eddie ended up being waived by the Rangers around Halloween in the mid-70s and went to Detroit. So I loved that. My favorite player in the league suddenly became a Red Wing. He was the guy I probably idolized more than anybody else."

SAUNDERS'S FAVORITE FLYERS GAME HE'S CALLED

There's no game more taxing on broadcasters than one that goes historically long. Back in the 1930s, the two longest games ever played in NHL history took place. But there were no television broadcasts back then and there wasn't really any radio either. So no broadcasters had to suffer through those two games.

But fast forward to the year 2000 and television and radio broadcasts carried games from start to finish; no matter how long they went. You never know when an extra long game is going to take place, so there's no preparing for it. You just do what you can to make it through. And that's the situation Tim Saunders found himself in on the night of May 4, 2000, when the Flyers and Penguins met for Game Four of their Semi-Finals matchup in Pittsburgh.

SAUNDERS: "It is, to this day, the third-longest game in NHL history. After doing some research, the two previous games that were longer were actually before stations would do an entire radio broadcast. In other words, back then they would actually join the game in progress.

"So I think we figured out that the five-overtime game against the Penguins was probably the longest radio broadcast of All-Time. And it felt like it while doing it. I remember doing everything I could to keep my voice; drinking tea and honey and just trying to get through it and praying that I don't blow it when the final goal gets scored.

"That's really what's going through your mind when you're doing a game like that, 'just don't blow the call. Get a clean call.'

"When Keith Primeau finally ended it I think I was more relieved than anybody. I remember my partner at the time was Brian Propp, the former Flyers great. He would do intermissions and he would interview somebody in the press box, a writer or whoever; somebody from the other team or whoever he could get to fill the intermissions.

"I can remember after the fourth overtime, we're going into another intermission and he's already done six intermissions at that point. I remember going to the commercial after the fourth overtime and I was exhausted. I said, 'and Brian Propp will be up next with whoever the hell he hasn't talked to yet.' It was just one of those nights. I think it ended at 2:35 in the morning or something like that."

Saunders' long night wasn't quite done yet though. Even though Keith Primeau had ended the game, Saunders still had to catch a flight out of Pittsburgh, back to Philadelphia. You see, during the playoffs, teams carry so many extra players and personnel that usually the broadcasters get bumped from the team charter and have to fly commercial.

SAUNDERS: "So it turns out, we were supposed to fly home the next morning from Pittsburgh after the game and we had to leave the hotel ultra early because we were on the first plane out of Pittsburgh that next morning. When we got out of the game that night and got back to the hotel, I think we had 45 minutes before we had to be back downstairs to catch the shuttle to the airport. So it was a long night."

MESSAGE TO FLYERS FANS

As is a common theme amongst members of the sports media, it is a well known fact that without the fans our jobs would either A) not exist or B) they'd have a lot less meaning. So, each of the broadcasters in this book took a couple of minutes to address you, the fans, directly.

SAUNDERS: "My goal is to broadcast to the little kid in every Flyers fan who's listening to me; no matter how old you are. In my mind's eye, I remember myself as a kid growing up, loving a specific team and the guy I listened to reflected my same passion level. And that's my goal. That's the guy I'm trying to reach on any broadcast. I want to be objective, but I want to be entertaining. I want to be fun to listen to, because if it's not fun to listen to, then you're not going to have a guy listen to you for very long. So that's the audience I'm after. I want it to be very apparent that I'm as passionate about the Flyers as the Flyers fans who are listening to me. And if you're not a Flyers fan, I could care less."

PITTSBURGH PENGUINS

JOSH GETZOFF
RADIO: PLAY-BY-PLAY / STUDIO HOST

First Season on Penguins Radio: 2015-16
Seasons on Penguins Radio (including 2020-21): 6

Birthday: October 8, 1988 Hometown: Dresher, PA

College/University: Ithaca College

BIOGRAPHY

I'm a firm believer that your environment has a big impact on how you grow up. And I don't just mean personally. I also mean professionally. So, if you're exposed to a lot of sports, you're highly likely to want to work in the sports industry.

Josh Getzoff is a perfect example of this as he grew up in a very sports-centric home and surrounding area.

GETZOFF: "Hockey has always been my favorite sport. I grew up in a family where my brother played in the college. He actually played for Trinity college in Hartford, Connecticut, Division III, as a goalie. So, when I was really young, he was rising up in the ranks and I was exposed to the games, I wouldn't say at the highest level, but I was exposed to it at a pretty high level with him being a pretty good minor player and then, obviously, going into the college ranks.

"My dad, weirdly enough, still to this day, doesn't even know how to skate. But I would credit him for being a big reason why I got into the game. We had season tickets growing up and we would go to a lot of games, a lot of hockey games across all levels.

"My earliest memories when I was playing youth hockey would be getting in the car early in the morning and going to those Mite games, Atom games and then, obviously, moving up to Squirt, Pee-Wee, Bantam, Midget and all through the ranks. But, for me, I just always loved the game.

"I guess just being around it from when I was really young, it was always a big part of my life and then, I kind of realized when I was about 12-years old that playing the game for a career was probably not in the cards for me. I wasn't a bad player, but I definitely wasn't going to be taking my game to any kind of professional level or even like my brother, to be playing in college.

"I did end up playing at Ithaca for a couple of years on the club team. But, the operative word there is 'club.' As for the ability to get into broadcasting, I was pretty fortunate that I was able to grow up in a pretty sports-centric household in a pretty sports-centric area. I made it a habit every morning to read the newspaper, glance over the sports section and everything.

"What I kind of realized around the time that I realized that hockey as a player wasn't going to be my future, was that I could probably stay in the sport if I worked on the media side. Again, I was young when I realized this, so it kind of steered me in a direction where, what I started to do, when I would watch games on TV, was that I would really study the broadcasters. Oh sure, I had my favorite players and my favorite teams, but I also had my favorite broadcasters. So, I would study how they would deliver games and how they would come across on camera. And on the radio side, which really became a big part of how I grew, is, I was kind of like a sponge and just absorbed what I was hearing.

"I would lay in bed a lot and listen to baseball on the radio, like very cliche things to hear, but it was the reality for me. That's kind of how I got into broadcasting, grew a love for broadcasting. As I got older, there started to be more opportunities to actually do it. In High School, I was fortunate enough to start, with a couple of my best friends still to this day, a broadcasting club. We were calling games off a camcorder that we bought at Best Buy, doing High School football on Fridays. We were wearing shirts that were too big for us and ties that were not tied correctly or straight. But Hey, it was a part of the experience and it was a great experience to kind of get that.

"And then, obviously, getting into Ithaca, I kind of hit the ground running right away with the opportunities they afford their students to get into student run broadcasting organizations and stuff of that nature. So I was really able to hone my craft there and also grow on many different levels as a person and as a professional, with the experiences that I was given and the opportunities that I was given while I was there. So I would say the love of hockey has always been a constant.

"The broadcasting aspect, I would say it really has been a constant as well, because I started to really get into it when I was fairly young -- 11- or 12-years-old. Those two things kind of have been at my core for as long as I can remember and have really been the only things I've ever wanted to do. So I consider myself very lucky and fortunate to be where I am right now. And I can only hope that it'll continue moving forward."

It's interesting to note how Getzoff studied the various broadcasters he watched or listened to, because you don't normally see at such a young age. But he was a realist, which certainly helped his case. And among the broadcasters, Getzoff studied were a trio of All-Time greats in Mike Lange, Harry Kalas and Gene Hart. Of course, his studies with Lange are still ongoing as they are now colleagues at the Penguins, which sort of brings everything full circle for him.

Granted, he did have aways to go between Ithaca and Pittsburgh, so let's follow his roadmap.

GETZOFF: "When I graduated from Ithaca, I was fortunate enough that in my senior year, we had a Career Day and I ended up meeting a guy who was a Sports Director at a station in Elmira, New York, which was about 30 minutes down the road.

"He was at Ithaca just for networking, we got to talking and he said to me, 'everyone has a goal to get to a big market, but very few people realize that it starts in smaller markets. And it starts in these little areas where you can make your mistakes when no one's watching.' It was a simple comment, but it kind of resonated with me. We started talking and he said 'if you're interested, we could have some internship opportunities. You get some hands-on experience. Why don't you think about it?' Of course, I was interested. I was happy to do anything.

"So, the Spring of my senior year, I interned for the station in Elmira and just by a stroke of luck, after I graduated, they ended up expanding their sports staff and my internship essentially served as my interview, because I knew everyone there. It was a super small station. They knew they could bring me in right out of college. I'd be gung-ho for everything. And I was able to get a job. I graduated on May 22nd, I think and I started on May 25th, which, in the broadcasting world, is kind of unheard of. I got very lucky in that sense that I was able to jump right into something, right away.

"I started as a Tape Operator there. But I worked my way up to eventually doing Sports Anchoring, reporting there for two-years. From there, I moved on to Champagne, Illinois, where I took a job as a Sports Director for the ABC and Fox affiliate there, which was a great step forward in my career. Getting to cover the Big-10. The University of Illinois athletics were, for the most part, on the main stage with basketball and football, terrible. But some of the opportunities that I was afforded and the venues that I was able to go to and the teams and players who I was able to cover, gave me the experience in these bigger stages and these elite athletes and mega settings that, I think, really helped me grow as a broadcaster as well.

"But I always kind of had my eye on hockey and I couldn't really figure out how to crack into it. I would constantly be doing any kind of hockey story I could to put some stuff together on my reel. Constantly emailing teams to figure out 'what are you looking for?' Around the time -- 2013/2014 -- when teams were starting to bring in these team reporters and everything, how could I become one of those? And it was a process. I mean, I would say almost every team got back to me, but there weren't necessarily opportunities. Then, as I was working in Illinois, my contract was coming up at the end of the summer of 2015.

"I was aggressively applying to any and all sports broadcasting jobs and I came across on Teamworkonline.com, a job with the Pittsburgh Penguins that was a Pre-game/Post-game Radio Hosts, andPensTV Internet Reporter. I thought, 'wow, this is exactly what I want to do to break into the NHL. Like this would be unbelievable.'

"So I applied very formally on Teamworkonline and I looked up the Penguins communication staff on their website. Basically, I just sent my application, because I wasn't sure how things worked on Teamworkonline. As I sent my application, I had the emails queued up to all these people and I basically hit submit on the application, clicked in the next window, hit send to the email, send to the email, sent to the email, not even sure if I'm sending them to the right people, but I thought that they were, maybe, because they were under the communications umbrella. And sure enough, a couple of those people were involved in the hiring process.

"They did say that the timing worked out, they saw my application and they saw my email and they gave it a read and then they gave it a closer look and they liked what they saw. I got a call about a week later to come out to Pittsburgh for an interview. I did.

"Part of my interview actually was that I had to record a sample Intro and Outro to the Pre-game and Post-game Show. I remember sitting in the Pittsburgh airport, Because I didn't want to wait on this. I wanted them to have it. I was sitting on my iPhone in the corner of the Pittsburgh airport by the Starbucks and I was barking into my phone the Intro for a game the Penguins had beaten the St. Louis Blues in and Thomas Greiss had played well in goal. Beau Bennett had scored a couple of goals for the Penguins in the win. I remember it very clearly and I got it to them before I got in the air. So they had everything they needed.

"A couple of days later, they called me, offered me the job and it was a whirlwind. My wife, at that time she was my girlfriend, we figured out that we were going to Pittsburgh. We didn't know where we were going to live. We knew the season started in about four-weeks and I had a lot to get caught up on. So, I finished my job at the end of September, which kind of coincides with the end of Training Camp and the Pre-Season on the NHL schedule. We jumped into the U-haul, drove the eight-and-a-half-hours from Champagne to Pittsburgh and have been here ever since."

FAVORITE PLAYER(S) GROWING UP

GETZOFF: "My all-time favorite player and still to this day is John LeClair. He was a guy who I always tried to play like as far as playing in the blue paint, being around the net and trying to get goals that way. A great American-born player. A guy who scored 50-goals multiple times in the league and was a member of the Legion of Doom, which, for me growing up, with him, Eric Lindros and Mikael Renberg, was a big part of my youth in that run to The Final in '97 against the Detroit Red Wings."

HOCKEY AFTER DARK -- TALES AWAY FROM THE RINK

Traveling is one of the many perks of being a professional sports broadcaster. But the real perk is getting to explore and see some of nature's most beautiful scenes; as well as getting to experience things related to your job that you wouldn't normally even think about.

Usually, it takes multiple road trips during the course of a season or seasons to get all those various things in. But for Josh Getzoff, there was one road trip with the Penguins that afforded him multiple experiences, as well as tremendous scenery.

GETZOFF: "This would have been the 2018-19 season. One thing that has become an unbelievably, circled, highlighted, bolded part, every time I do games and get to travel, because I do all the road games now, for radio.

"One of the things that really is something I look forward to every year is the Western Canadian trip. A couple years ago we had just an awesome trip. It started actually in Toronto and it was, probably still to this day, my favorite trip I've ever had with the Penguins. It helped that the Penguins went 4-0 on the trip. They were unbelievably good. When you look back on that '18-'19 season, it was the high point and it was the end of October. Things were never as good for the team the rest of the year after that run they had right around Halloween time.

"So, we basically started in Toronto. The Penguins beat the Maple Leafs and then we actually had a couple of days in Toronto before we went West to Calgary. We got to spend a night in the NHL's War Room; the Hockey Ops room with replay review and all that stuff. We got to sit up there and watch how the referees communicate with the Replay Officials back in Toronto. We saw it inside the room in Toronto and heard the conversations with the officials talking to them on the headset and everything. All the TV feeds are up and they have all these different stats and simulators going.

"That was such a cool experience for myself, but also for any kind of hockey fan or hockey nerd. You're on the edge of your seat the whole time. On a regular NHL night, you have 10 or 12 games going on. There's action all over the place. There's constant communication. That was a really cool thing to be able to see up close and personal.

"The rest of that trip, we obviously went out to Western Canada, but one of the nice wrinkles was, because of how the trip was designed. We had a couple of days in between games in Western Canada and the team went up to Banff National Park, which I had never been to.

"For anyone who has never been there, if you can, find a way to go, because there is no more beautiful place I've ever seen in my life; in the Canadian Rockies up there. I remember we got so lucky that the weather was like 40-50 degrees, which, up there, you never know in October. It could be 10 degrees.

"We took a bus up through the mountains and it was just beautiful scenery. You see all these animals. All this running water. I can't even describe it. You don't even realize that you're there for work at that point. It's just crazy to see all this stuff. You just kind of have to pinch yourself. And I love being outside, outdoors, hiking, going to parks and stuff. So that was like a metropolis for me.

"We spent a couple days in Banff. We went on the incline to the top of Mount Sulphur. We did a sunset up there. Of course I had the Alberta beef. We had some good meals. We got to go to a couple breweries. I love to sample breweries when I'm on the road. It's something I made a point of doing and got to go to a couple there that were pretty cool.

"We were also doing some side work for the Penguins TV programming. A cameraman and I, a friend of mine named Mark, drove down to Calgary one of the days we were up there; which is probably about an hour-and-a-half from Banff. We were doing an interview with an old Penguin, Jean Pronovost, who was a member of The Century Line for the Penguins with Lowell MacDonald and Syl Apps; one of the early productive lines for the Pens.

"So, we were able to meet him in his home and do that interview. That was kind of cool to just rub shoulders with a guy who had accomplished so much in his career and obviously meant a great deal to the Penguins when he was playing in Pittsburgh. It was just an experience that you wouldn't get unless you were out in that area. This also was the same road trip where we got (Sidney) Crosby and (Connor) McDavid in one of the best games I've ever seen, where Crosby scored on his backhand in overtime after dancing through defenders."

GETZOFF'S FAVORITE PENGUINS GAME HE'S CALLED

It's a little ironic that for a team with as much success as the Penguins have had in the past decade, that one of their broadcasters would choose not one, but two games as being among his favorites and yet Pittsburgh lost both of them. Call it quirky. Call it whatever you want. But the fact remains that there's a good reason for each game being so highly regarded by Josh Getzoff.

GETZOFF: "One of my favorite games is a loss. But it still is up there from the experience factor. I grew up outside Philadelphia. I'm still an Eagles fan and last year I got to call the Stadium Series game for the radio network. The Penguins and the Flyers. The Penguins blew a lead late in that game and lost in overtime. Actually, I think it ended up being Wayne Simmonds last game as a Flyer. But, for me, that game was surreal, to be able to be a guy who grew up cheering for the Eagles and to see the Super Bowl banner up there at Lincoln Financial Field.

"The night before we played a media game on the ice there. Pittsburgh beat Philadelphia. I had some points and factored in on that. So, we at least won that game. But to be able to call that, be there and get that opportunity. For Mike Lange to trust me to call that game and then obviously to have the chance to do it, just the spectacle of the game in general is amazing. But for what it meant for me to be from there and to have it be (at the stadium for) one of my favorite pro sports teams in the

Eagles, to be able to be in there and call that was just pretty incredible and something that I will never forget.

"I can (also) tell you a story about my first game I ever called. This is one of my favorites just because it was my first, but it wasn't a game that was memorable by any stretch of the imagination. It was actually the first game that Steve Mears also called for the Penguins; not his first NHL game, obviously, but first game as the voice of the Penguins. I was doing my first game filling in for Mike Lange. It was the second game of the season in 2017.

"This was October 2017. We were playing the Chicago Blackhawks. It was their Home Opener. It was their Season Opener. The Penguins had just played the St. Louis Blues the night before, after they raised the banner in Pittsburgh and lost in overtime. We flew that night to Chicago. The Penguins lost 10-1 to the Chicago Blackhawks in that game. Antti Niemi started that game for the Penguins. He was yanked. And I remember walking out of the booth after the first period, I want to say it was 5-0 Chicago. Steve Mears was in the booth a couple down from me with television and he looked over at me. I still remember he said, 'is it us?' And I said to him, 'yep.'

"We both just laughed. That's all you could do. I mean, God, it was embarrassing that was how the Penguins played that night. But in a way, it almost calmed me down, because the game was over and it was at hand at that point. You kind of just focused on calling the game and not be so worried about anything stupid that you might do throughout the course of the broadcast. So that one's up there."

SIGNATURE PHRASE

What do country music and the National Hockey League have in common? Well, outside of the Nashville Predators, probably not much. Sure, there are probably plenty of NHL players who love country music, but it's not like they make it part of the game.

Pittsburgh's Josh Getzoff, though, has found a way to make country music part of the game. How you might ask? I'll let him tell you.

GETZOFF: "Josh Turner is one of my favorite country music artists. I just love his sound and his voice. I did a nod to one of his songs. Anyone who looks it up will figure out which song I'm talking about here. When the Penguins win a game in overtime, my call, consistently is, 'Lock the doors. Turn out the lights. Penguins win in overtime.' So if you hear any game the Penguins have won, including that Crosby goal against Edmonton a couple of years back, that's my call every single time.

"It's not all the time, because it can only happen after the Penguins have won the game in overtime, not a shootout, just overtime. So, when that does happen, that's become my call. There have been people who have caught onto it in Pittsburgh. I'm still working on getting the t-shirts printed, but hopefully that'll be a thing that does catch on more. And obviously, since it does lend itself to some dramatic moments with the team winning in OT, I think that it will. So, that's my call, 'Lock the doors. Turn out the lights. Penguins win in overtime.'"

MESSAGE TO PENGUINS FANS

As is a common theme amongst members of the sports media, it is a well known fact that without the fans our jobs would either A) not exist or B) they'd have a lot less meaning. So, each of the broadcasters in this book took a couple of minutes to address you, the fans, directly.

GETZOFF: "I would say that one thing I've come to appreciate living, working and being part of the community in Pittsburgh is that this is a fan base, but it's also a family. This has a bigger city side to it, but it has a small town feel to it. And these are people who really care about this hockey team and really care about the city. And I've grown to love them, the community, the people who make up the community. And their passion is really, I mean, it's easy to say this when you work in a city, but I've lived in a couple of different places. I've seen sports at a couple of different levels and the passion here, from the Penguins to the Steelers, it's unique, it's special.

"And I know that they are disappointed with how the last couple seasons have ended. But I think they also realize how fortunate they have been to see what they have seen from fan perspectives. From just the championships, to the players they've been able to watch live and in person for so long and throughout much of the history of these great organizations. You can only hope that the great times will continue moving forward.

"I am so appreciative of these people and I've grown to really, they're not just fans to me, they're kind of like an extension of your family when you spend so much time at the rink and at events and around these people, you get to know the faces, you get to know the names and they become pretty special to you. So, I definitely think extremely highly of them and look forward to being alongside them for all the ups and downs in the future."

STEVE MEARS
TV: PLAY-BY-PLAY

First Season on Penguins TV: 2017-18
Seasons on Penguins TV (including 2020-21): 4

Birthday: January 22, 1980 Hometown: Pittsburgh, PA

College/University: Bowling Green

BIOGRAPHY

How often do you get the chance to live out a childhood dream when you're an adult? Probably not often. There's a reason why it's called a childhood dream, hence it's probably something that's not really all that feasible in the real world.

However, every so often, you hear a story about somebody who's childhood ambition was to do something that, while extremely unlikely, was indeed possible and they actually made it happen. That in a nutshell is how Steve Mears ended up calling games for the Penguins on television. But we don't deal in nutshells here, so let's dive into the full story.

MEARS: " I grew up in Pittsburgh as a lifelong Penguins fan. And at the time, when I was growing up, at that very impressionable age of 10 or 11, the Penguins had the best player in Mario Lemieux. They had a team that won back-to-back Stanley Cups and they had the best announcer in Mike Lange, a Hall of Famer.

"I just simply wanted to be like him. I thought it was the greatest job in the world. He got in for free. He got paid to be there. He got to talk about the games and bring the games to life; to a live audience. And that was the appeal for me.

"From that age on, it was all about taking the necessary steps to try to do this for real, to do it for a living. I was able to go to a good broadcasting college -- Bowling Green -- and work in Minor League Hockey.

"I was in the Central Hockey League, which was a Double-A league that no longer exists. But it was a very good league. It was in Louisiana. I went from college, I graduated, packed up my car and moved down to Louisiana after I got the job. And it was the best four years I could ever ask for.

"It was like getting my Master's (degree) in hockey and sports, because you learned every aspect of what it means to be in the sports business. Broadcasting was actually a very small part of that job. So I had the chance to learn about the business side. I did sales. I did media relations, community relations and team relations.

"Then, when 7 o'clock rolled around, there was a little bit of time to prepare and I called the game. It really helped sharpen all of my skills; everything that I needed to become a good broadcaster and just a sports business person. At that point, I was then lucky enough to get my big break, which was getting a job doing radio for the New York Islanders. And that was a perfect first NHL job.

"Even though I was really young -- 26 during the 2006-07 season -- it was a perfect place to start out in The League, because the team was young and just living on Long Island, it was wonderful. And I was with the Islanders from 2006-07 to 2008-09.

"But then, the Islanders went to a simulcast. They decided they didn't want to have an individual radio broadcast anymore, in 2009. And it was devastating news. It was the worst thing that could happen at the time. But in hindsight, it actually was the best thing, because it brought me to Pittsburgh.

"At the moment, you don't realize that, but it's a perfect case of turning a negative into a positive and the three-years that I spent with the Islanders were a wonderful stepping stone. I met a lot of wonderful people. But right around that time, when I got the news that the Islanders were discontinuing their radio broadcast, it turned out that the Penguins, who had just won the Stanley Cup in 2009, were enhancing their radio broadcast.

"They were starting a new 24-hour radio channel and they were looking for a Host who had some experience in the league. And they knew of me because they knew there was a kid from Pittsburgh who was in the NHL and was announcing for the Islanders. We had some great conversations and then they offered me the job as the Radio Host.

"I would also do some things for PensTV, for their website and host a couple of other shows. So it really was a perfect way to get indoctrinated with the Penguins organization. A lot of the people who I met or hired me or I worked with back then in the early Pens radio days of my career, they're still there and I'm still friends with them. It's nice that it's become this family that we've kind of grown up together now and looking at that as 11-years ago. But what a blessing I got to go to the Penguins, my childhood team.

"I got to work in the final year of The Igloo, which was an incredible thrill. To have that type of access in the building where I had walked in as a child, wide-eyed and dreamed of one day being able to set foot in the press box at The Igloo and now I was working there on a regular basis, it was surreal.
Then, the following year, they opened the new building across the street and it was awesome to be a part of that as well.

"So I did Pens radio and the hosting job for three-years. From there, I went to the NHL Network. They offered me a job as a Host for NHL Live. I moved to New York and hosted that show with E.J. Hradek in one form or another for five-years on the NHL Network. That was a blast because I got to live in New York, living in the city, which is something I always had dreamed of. I think, just for a hockey fan, like myself, that I don't think you could have a better seat than the one that I was sitting in for five-years, because I was covering every big event.

"I covered every major storyline. You didn't know what you were going to get when you walked into work every day and what trade was going to take place or what team was going to make a big announcement of some kind. We got to go to all the events: the Stanley Cup Finals, the All-Star Games, the outdoor games. It was a dream for a hockey fan and to be on the ice when The Cup was being awarded, getting ready to do interviews afterward, it was just absolutely incredible. So I'm very thankful for the five-years that I had there in New York.

"After that time, eventually in 2017, the Penguins, or rather, the people at their TV Network, called me up and said they were making a change on the TV broadcast and offered me the position. So I had a tough decision to make. But, I'm glad I did, because I couldn't be happier doing TV for the Penguins now."

FAVORITE PLAYER(S) GROWING UP

MEARS: "Mario (Lemieux) was the only one. He was the one and there are a lot of kids who would say the same thing. As much respect as I had for (Jaromir) Jagr, Ron Francis, Larry Murphy, Paul Coffey, Mark Recchi and all the great players, Phil Bourque and my current partner Bob Errey, Troy Loney and Tom Barrasso.

"There was only one hero and that was Mario. It was evident in the way that I held the hockey stick, the type of hockey stick that I had, the type of helmet that was shaped like a bowling ball, that was the exact same one that he wore. I had the exact same skates that he had. I taped my stick exactly the same way that he did. I had the same gloves.

"I tried, although failing, to play like him and to have the same kind of demeanor. I always make the joke that at like age 13, I somehow developed a French-Canadian accent living in Pittsburgh, which is very strange. I didn't know that was possible. But it all gets traced back to him.

"He was the guy. He was the same idol, whereas, if you lived in Chicago in the '90s, Michael Jordan was your guy. If you lived in New York and were a Yankees fan in the '60s, Mickey Mantle was probably your guy. If you lived in Boston in the '50s and '60s, Ted Williams was your guy. So, when it came to Pittsburgh, it was Mario. He was the superstar. He was the best player in the world.

"You just wanted to be like him, the way he carried himself. The way he played. But also, there was such a dignified quality of the way that he conducted interviews and the way that he led his team. He was a member of the community.

"He's French-Canadian, but is now a Pittsburgh native and resident. I think his charitable approach and all the great things he's done, I think I've said before that I don't think you could find one athlete who has meant more to a single city in any sport than what Mario has meant to Pittsburgh in terms of saving the franchise multiple times, but also all of the charitable endeavors. I don't think there's any comparison with any athlete in any one single city and the impact that one athlete has had on one local region. I don't think there's anybody who exceeds his impact here in Pittsburgh."

HOCKEY AFTER DARK -- TALES AWAY FROM THE RINK

The Penguins as a team, including their production/TV/Radio crews, have had quite a few memorable road trips over the years. Just like any team in the league, or in sports for that matter, there are bonding trips on top of your standard road trips where you go from game to game, city to city.

For Steve Mears, it is one of these bonding trips that will always stand out to him.

MEARS: "One, as far as road trips are concerned, it was two seasons ago at the beginning of the year. We had the Western Canadian road trip and because it was the beginning of the year, the team wanted to have some type of team bonding experience and a little bit of an excursion. So the schedule worked out that we had a couple of days off in between games against the Calgary Flames and the Edmonton Oilers.

"So, we were able to take a couple of days in that little window and go up to Banff, Alberta, which is one of the most beautiful places in the world. And to go there in October when it's not freezing cold, we actually got so lucky with the weather.

"That's the most memorable road trip that we've had and the team won every game of that trip. But the two days in Alberta, in Banff, that we spent in the Rockies, walking around and the weather was unbelievably warm. You didn't even need a jacket.

"I remember walking on the golf course, seeing elk and all these other animals and the Rockies are right next to you. You're at the base of this mountain looking straight up and you can go hiking. We went to the top of one of those mountains. We took a gondola ride way up to the snow capped area of another mountain. Looking down, you felt like you were on top of the world."

MEARS' FAVORITE PENGUINS GAME HE'S CALLED

It's funny how one person can have two fond memories that are on complete opposite ends of the spectrum. One can be of a thrilling victory and one of a blowout loss. But they are both looked back upon fondly by the person. It doesn't make sense. Then again, sports don't need to make sense. They exist to provide entertainment. And what one person finds entertaining another person may not.

That being said, there's nothing hockey people love more than to debate till they're blue in the face, who they feel is the best player in the world. And just like how different people find different things entertaining, different people will also have varying opinions on who the best player in the game is.

Today, some say it's Connor McDavid, a superstar on the Edmonton Oilers who does things with the puck not seen since Wayne Gretzky last called Edmonton home. Others say the best player is still Pittsburgh's Sidney Crosby, a superstar on the Penguins who has made a career out of doing things not seen since Mario Lemieux in his hayday.

So, what did you get when these two supremely talented players met in the same game? Well, you got a thriller and I don't mean a copy of the Michael Jackson album.

MEARS: "I think the most memorable moment in-game and goal of my three-years with the Penguins was two seasons ago. I think it was the same road trip, the Western Canadian road, when we went to Banff National Park. Sidney Crosby scored in overtime against the Oilers and the Penguins won 6-5 in a really thrilling game.

"He scored a signature goal, just a beautiful goal in overtime to win it. And it was just the confluence of all the factors where, it's in Canada, it's in overtime and it's him against (Connor) McDavid. Going into the game a lot of people were saying, 'well, who's better? Has McDavid now supplanted Crosby as the best player in the world?' And it was just an emphatic statement from Crosby that he still owned the throne as the best in the world with the goal that he scored.

"The way the game unfolded too, it was just such an exciting game. So that was my favorite call and my favorite moment and probably from start to finish, my favorite game. I like goals too. So a 6-5 game is one I'll take any day of the week."

That was one enjoyable game, at least if you were a Penguins fan. Oilers fans probably don't recall it so fondly. But now, let's delve into the other side of things to get Steve Mears' other favorite game.

MEARS: "Another of my favorite games is and it's in a completely different direction, my first Penguins TV broadcast. It was 2017 and it was in Chicago; the Blackhawks Home Opener. It's the butt of a lot of jokes with our crew. But my first game was a 10-1 loss to the Chicago Blackhawks. It's something that we can laugh at now. They really had no chance.

"I mean, Chicago, that was their Home Opener. We had just played the night before. Chicago had a lot of pent up anger because they had had a disappointing playoff loss the previous year. They still had a lot of talented players on their roster and they just came out and just smoked the Penguins.

"It was not even close. We had no shot. So my first game pretty much turned into a talk show because of the score. I wasn't exactly calling tape-to-tape Play-by-Play by the time the score got to 7-1, 8-1, 9-1, 10-1. But, it is a funny joke, that was my first game. I still hear that Chelsea Dagger goal song that the Blackhawks play; it's seared into my brain to this day because I had to hear it 10 times.

"But it's just something we can kind of laugh at now. It's also a good reminder that we have no control where we do the Play-by-Play. We have no control on any given night. You could have a 10-1 loss or 10-1 win and you gotta be prepared for it. You gotta have enough material."

There you have it. One broadcaster. Two games on opposite ends of the spectrum. Both are fond memories; at least for Mears.

SIGNATURE SAYING

Some so-called "signature calls" are really just a phrase broadcasters like to throw into their calls to help the fans connect with what they're saying. In fact, there are plenty of times where referring to these calls as "signature" is a bit much. However, for our purposes, we're going to stick with this terminology.

Steve Mears is one such broadcaster who doesn't really have an iconic call or catchphrase, but he does give a subtle nod to Penguins fans quite often during his broadcasts.

MEARS: "The one little phrase that I do try to incorporate a lot in the Penguins broadcasts and especially in bigger moments, 'black and gold' because Pittsburgh is the only city where all the sports teams have predominantly the same colors; which are black and gold. They are so identifiable with the Pirates, Penguins and Steelers and always have been during my lifetime. So I try to incorporate that in some way and I think it's very relatable. When you say 'black and gold' people know what that is in this area.

"If you're a Western Pennsylvania native, I think that phrase and those colors, that's who we are. That's what this area is all about, which is sports and those uniform colors and the history behind them, the success of all three major sports teams and the pride in the fact that it is the only city which has the sports teams with predominantly the same colors of black and gold.

"So, I try to incorporate that whenever I get a chance to, because it's kind of my own little nod to Pittsburgh Pride and I think it's something that fans can relate to. I think the people who are listening and watching, they have a lot of pride too and not just for the Penguins, but also the Steelers fans and Pirates fans. There are very few cities in this country where sports are that much of the fabric.

"It's a fantastic sports town. There are plenty of great sports towns in the country, but here, Steelers football, Penguins hockey and Pirates baseball have such a rich history. So, just sneaking in a 'black and gold' reference whenever I can, I think it's a nod to all that rich history and the fact that we're all proud that we have the teams we do."

MESSAGE TO PENGUINS FANS

As is a common theme amongst members of the sports media, it is a well known fact that without the fans our jobs would either A) not exist or B) they'd have a lot less meaning. So, each of the broadcasters in this book took a couple of minutes to address you, the fans, directly.

MEARS: "Thank you. Thank you for your loyalty to what we do and all the support. I'm so fortunate that I get the chance to live in Pittsburgh, a city that I know so well and on a daily basis, whether it's at the grocery store or the post office, or even at Penguins games, when we're at the arena, to have the opportunity to interact with so many fans and to share stories. I love the fact that I meet somebody and I can ask them, where are you from? And a lot of times, I don't think they realize that I'm from Pittsburgh. They say, 'I'm from Pittsburgh, I'm from here.' And that doesn't answer the question for me, because I want to know where, which suburb, like what part of Pittsburgh, because I know them all. It's not like I'm some outsider that Pittsburgh is an answer that's going to suffice.

"So I like when I can hear about where in the region people come from. And I love having those conversations with people about where they were when they watched a certain goal on a broadcast that we were doing and they liked something that I said, or I made them laugh, or even if they have some type of a gripe with the way that we do the telecast. I'm all ears. I enjoy hearing from all of those fans and their memories because I lived it. I was a part of a different generation, the Lemieux-Jagr generation. But now we have this new generation with Crosby and Malkin. I have been there before and I also know that it doesn't last forever. So I try to impart that. That'd be another message for the fans. Just enjoy this.

"We're so blessed here to have at one point 15 Art Ross trophy winners, scoring champions in the NHL. 15 in 30 years, when some franchises like the Flyers have never had one. We're so blessed to have five Stanley Cups and three since 2009. To have these, what you would think is a once in a lifetime talent like Lemieux, Jagr, Crosby, Malkin. To have that many in my lifetime, it's ridiculous. We've been unbelievably fortunate. We've been blessed. And in the case of this generation with Crosby and Malkin, I would just say, soak it all up and enjoy every second of it, because it does not last forever. I can tell you firsthand, that it's a sad day when one of your heroes like Mario retires or Jagr moves on to another team. It's a short window. It doesn't last forever.

"So make sure you enjoy every game, every second. The privilege that it is to be able to watch two of the greatest players of all-time in Crosby and Malkin and just realize how fortunate we are and have been to be in this city and to have the tremendous hockey talent we've had now for a good 30 years, where it's a perennial playoff team and the thrills that they provided and the way the organization is run.

"It's an entertaining brand of hockey. It's definitely not boring. It's offense and it's thrilling and it's back and forth. And that's Penguins hockey. That's kind of the phrase we have for it. It's Penguins hockey after a crazy game. That's the best thing you could ever ask for. So just to have one of those players would be a blessing and we've had at least four and countless other supremely talented athletes. So I would say just cherish every second of this. And I'm honored that I get the opportunity to bring those games and those broadcasts into your living room."

SAN JOSE SHARKS

DAN RUSANOWSKY
RADIO: PLAY-BY-PLAY

First Season on Sharks Radio: 1991-92
Seasons on Sharks Radio (including 2020-21): 29

Birthday: December 31, 1960 Hometown: Millford, CT

College/University: St. Lawrence University

BIOGRAPHY

Sometimes things work out the way you plan and other times things happen for a reason. Technically, both can be true at the same time. If that confuses you, please pay attention to Dan Rusanowsky's story of how his broadcasting career took off and then you'll understand.

RUSANOWSKY: "It's kind of an interesting story because, in the beginning, I was really enjoying the idea of performance art. When I was a youngster, I was in school plays and a couple of musicals and so forth and I enjoyed that.

"I liked the performance art. I liked the idea of being an MC or announcer. I always watched everybody who did that, but, more than that, I was taken to my first hockey game when I was about 11. (My mom's brother worked for Exxon and they had season tickets at Madison Square Garden). It was a weekend, I'm pretty sure. The Rangers were playing the Penguins and the reason why we got that game was because that was one of the games that the big, top executives didn't want. So we got a chance to go see them play and I'm going to say it was October of '71 and it was a tied hockey game.

"I always remember that. I always remember being fascinated by the spectacle of it all. Captivated by the intensity and the beauty of the game. We had seats in the Yellows at Madison Square Garden. There were good seats and we had a great time. It was one of the chances for me to just sort of get out on my own.

"It wasn't with my parents. It was with my mom's brother and we had a good time. The thing that I remember was we were slightly late coming in, because of traffic coming to Manhattan. So we threw the radio on and the pre-game show was on. They had warmed up and we drove into the parking garage before making our way up into The Garden.

"What ended up happening was we walked in and they had just dropped the puck, maybe a minute into the first period. So we really didn't miss anything. Although we did miss the Anthem. We walked in and we saw the game. I was captivated, not only by the game itself and how beautiful it was and how intense it was and how it was really a combination of everything in sport; but also the idea that the performance art portion and the radio was something that I had never really listened to.

"I had listened to some baseball, so I already knew what Play-by-Play was, but I had never really listened to a hockey game. So, then we listened to the post-game show on the way out, listened to all the replays of the goals and everything else and I just found myself really captivated by it all. And I really started following it very closely.

"Back in those days, of course, Rangers' hockey was not on television all the time. In fact, as I remember, they were on channel nine for just the road games and an occasional home game. But most of the home games were radio only. So, in my house, my parents at the time weren't really hockey fans. They'd be with the rest of the family and they'd watch something else at night; back in the days when families watched TV together.

"There was one TV in the house and for us, it was a black and white TV. And so what I did was, I just went back to my room, did my homework and turned on my radio and listened to the games. I used to really enjoy staying up late at night when everybody was supposed to be sleeping and take a transistor radio and listen to the games in Oakland and in Los Angeles when the Rangers traveled out there.

"And then, of course, during that time, I became not only captivated with that, but also started tuning my radio dial around to find other teams. With 50,000 watt clear channel Am stations, you could get a lot of games in my house in Connecticut. I could get Detroit. I could get Pittsburgh. I could get Philly. I could get Washington. I could get Chicago. I could listen to Dan Kelly do St. Louis games, although KMOX faded in and out. But I could get it. When the Bruins were on BZ, I could get them and I got Montreal in French, so that was always interesting. And also Buffalo, they were on WKBW, which was really strong at night. So, I mean, think about all of those NHL teams and all those NHL broadcasters I could listen to.

"Of course, today, you can listen to all 31 NHL Play-by-Play guys by just flipping on your computer and listening to the radio stream. So everybody gets it now. But back then, it was a little bit more challenging. It brought the romance of the crackle of distant radio stations that also definitely got into my psyche in terms of being romanticized by the sport. That's how I got really interested in actually calling games.

"It's kind of interesting, you have a sort of a grand scheme of how this is all gonna work and it rarely goes that way. But my journey was actually pretty close to the way I kind of mapped it out. My thought was obviously there was no place to actually get any experience; I just thought it was another world when it came to that.

"Maybe I was insecure or scared or whatever, but I just never really reached out when I was in High School. What I used to do was flip the sound down if I had a chance to watch the game and actually try to call it myself. I would occasionally do that if I was sitting in a rink at a college game or something, or at least imagine it in my mind of how I would actually call the game.

"I really had no idea about how to physically do it and what the elements were to prepare and what tools you use to help you. I really didn't have any idea about any of that. I just sort of listened to as many announcers as I could to get the idea of how it was done. And then, when I went to St. Lawrence, I was maybe a week or two into my freshman year, I had an opportunity to walk up to the people who were actually broadcasting the games.

"I walked up to a gentleman who has since become a great friend. He was actually the Play-by-Play guy at St. Lawrence that year and I said to him, 'listen, this is what I want to do. I don't want to go through my life and say, I didn't try this. If it doesn't work, I'll do something else. If I'm not good, I'll do something else. But I really want to try this. This is really what I want to do. I would like to see if you could help me or guide me?'

"It was kind of interesting because the choices that many people make in terms of trying to get experience and choosing a place to go to school and so forth, often is one that's vocational rather than educational. What I mean when I say that is some people go to school to train to get a particular job.

"So that would be the method I would suspect if you say I went to the NewHouse School of Communications at Syracuse University, where Marv Albert, Dick Enberg, Marty Glickman and so many other great broadcasters went to school.

"But my thinking was, number one, Syracuse didn't have a hockey team. Now they have an AHL team in Syracuse. So at least there's something there. But there was no men's hockey team in Syracuse at the Division I level. Secondly, my thinking was, if I go there, everybody in my class is going to want to do what I do. So the opportunity for me, or the odds of my actually getting to do games as early as possible might be lower.

"I might not be able to do it until I'm a Junior or Senior there because of the way that the system works. But there's no hockey team anyway. So I want to learn how to do that. I could learn a lot of other Play-by-Play sports and since certainly have, but that was my thinking.

"So I picked St. Lawrence, 2,500 students, Division I hockey and a radio station. And instead of majoring in broadcasting, what I did was I looked at another bit of math. I said, 'what's the population of the United States? And how many teams in the NHL are there?' My odds of getting one of those jobs was not very good. So I'd better be prepared to have the skills to do something else if this doesn't work out.

"So that was kind of my thinking of why I picked a great school with a smaller population and with a hockey team and a radio station. I said, 'why don't I do this as an activity instead; get a well-rounded education that gives me a lot of skills to be able to do a lot of different things.' As it turned out, that worked out in both areas. It worked out both in that moment that I walked up to the Play-by-Play announcer early in my college career to also everything else I've done in my career on the other side, away from the microphone.

"Back to the so-called present. I spoke to this gentleman and he basically validated everything that I was thinking, because he said 'I've got one or two games later in the season that I can't do and I don't really have a lot of people who are capable of doing this. If you're good I may give you that opportunity. So here I am, a Freshman in college and I'm over the moon thinking, 'this is fantastic.' I said, 'okay.' He said, 'what we'll do is we'll set you up in the press box. We'll have you call some games and we'll listen to them and we'll see if you can develop.'

"Well, I did a game, I think it was against Queens College or Queens University. That's a Canadian University that they had an exhibition game against. I called a couple of periods of Play-by-Play and we sat down after the game and he listened to it and he said, 'number one, you know the game. Number two, you have the skills to do this.'

"That was really validating for me. He said, 'I really believe that if you just continue to develop and work on this, then by the time this game comes up later in the season, you'll be able to do it and you'll be able to fill in for me.' Well, now I was really excited. Fast forward about a week, 10 days later and it's the opening of the ECAC regular-season and St. Lawrence is playing Harvard at Appleton Arena. So it's a pretty big game to start the year. It's the first intermission and I was up there doing my Play-by-Play like usual, into a tape recorder, practicing and doing everything that I had done in High School when I turned the sound down and tried to call the game myself, or just imagined it in my head while I was doing it.

"Here I am practicing like that and the first period ends and this Play-by-Play announcer came and walked up to me and he said, 'it's the intermission and I've got a guest coming on from The Hockey News and you have to do the interview.' I was just getting ready to do something at the end of the year. This was not Play-by-Play. It's something totally different. I haven't prepared for it. And he said, 'you have to do the interview.'.

"Bob said to me, 'you have to do the interview.' And I said, 'why aren't you doing it?' He said, 'because I have to go to the bathroom and this is my only chance to go. I'm not going to make it through the game. So here he is, his name is Tom Burke. You're on the air. When it says 30-seconds, you're on the air. Good-bye.' And he was gone and I was there and I had the microphone. I had a guest who I just met and I had to be on the air.

"Well, it's kind of interesting because that was an ideal test in many ways. I still to this day don't know if it was deliberate. I think he really did have to go to the bathroom, but what it really was, was a test of something that we have to face every day on the radio or on television and that is, you have to expect the unexpected. You have to be able to react to something that you don't expect to occur and you have to adjust to it and you have to do it in a professional way.

"So in a way, it was a baptism by fire. I got on the air and it was only a week into the season. I don't have a tape of the interview. It was probably the worst interview in history. But still, I got through it. I went through the process of the mechanics of throwing it back to the studio for a quick news break and all that other sort of stuff. And after that we resumed and I went back to my tape recorder and did the rest of the game. I was told I did a good job and then I actually started doing some Color Commentary for the team and went on a road trip."

On that road trip, Rusanowsky would experience something no broadcaster can ever prepare for. A player in one of the games was checked into the glass and the glass pane shattered. Now, that's not all that unusual. At the NHL level it takes a few moments to get that fixed. But in College it's a different story. The game was taking place in Providence, Rhode Island and the arena crew didn't have a glass pane to replace the broken one with. So, they had to go to another nearby rink and get glass from them. Luckily, there were several collegiate rinks within close proximity to where the game was being played.

However, it still took close to 30-minutes (Rusanowsky recalls it as taking 26-minutes) to get the new glass in place and seeing as how the college radio station was a commercial free station, Rusanowsky and his partner had to freelance and adjust for a lot longer than they would have liked. So, for 26-minutes they went off script (not that hockey games are scripted, but broadcasters always have some notes they can use) and talked about ECAC players, teams, whatever they could to make the time pass and keep the audience tuned in.

Eventually, the game was able to resume and afterwards, Bob told Rusanowsky he'd be just fine by the end of the year and he'd be able to do the games that Bob couldn't for St. Lawrence as the Play-by-Play announcer.

That game took place in Troy, New York at RPI and Rusanowsky went at it solo for the first time; operating the equipment and calling the game. He was nervous (who wouldn't be) but he aced it and by the time he was a Junior he was doing all the games for St. Lawrence. And by that time, the college radio station had undergone some changes and he was getting experience doing games for a professional station. Eventually, he wound up graduating and like he had thought back when he was a Freshman, there were no jobs available.

He thought about going to the AHL and working his way up to the NHL just like a player or coach, but there were no American Hockey League jobs open. However, he had the opportunity to continue his education and went to Clarkson for his MBA. And while there he managed to continue to stay on the air and hone his broadcasting skills. That's when things finally started to go his way.

Rusanowsky graduated from Clarkson and the next day received a job offer. That summer there were multiple AHL Broadcaster job openings and the one he went with was with a team called the New Haven Nighthawks.

RUSANOWSKY: "That's when my real apprenticeship began, because I spent five-years with the Nighthawks; five great years. A lot of work. A lot of hours. A lot of bus rides and really understanding that hockey as a broadcaster was as much of a business as it was a performance profession.

"The expectation was that I would be good at my job on the air; that was expected. However, what was also expected was I had to sell advertising. I had to sell season tickets. I had to do promotions with the team. I had to go on the ice between the first and second period to do the 'Shoot the Puck contest.'

"I had to do all of these other things in addition to being on the air. And so I learned how to adapt to that. At that time I also learned how to call a game all by myself, which was something I hadn't really done in college. So that was really great training and I have a lot of unbelievable memories."

Among those many "unbelievable memories" was the Calder Cup Final in 1989 against the Adirondack Red Wings. It was a series New Haven lost four-games-to-one, but the drama throughout the series was such that it will always stick with Rusanowsky.

Eventually, after five-years in New Haven, it just so happened that the San Jose Sharks were coming into the NHL as part of a new wave of expansion and somebody had to fill the role of broadcaster for the new franchise. Enter, Rusanowsky.

RUSANOWSKY: "When the Sharks came into being, as is the case usually when expansion occurs and I'm sure it's happening in Seattle, just about every American Hockey League broadcaster was interested in the opportunity and maybe even some NHL people might've had some interest in making the move out there too. But, I believe that because I had the business background I had, I was able to assist in a lot of those other areas.

"I really knew the hockey business quite well. And so I had the qualifications and I certainly had improved continuously each year with what I did on the air. So I was finally ready to think about it. I had gone through the process once before about getting to the NHL. I was pretty far down on the list for a couple of teams; pretty late in the process.

"But as it worked out, I ended up getting the opportunity to come to San Jose. I moved here with the intention of making it my home and making the city my home and to be part of something really special. And for the last, just about 30 years, it has been everything I've dreamed of and the fans are fantastic. It's the dream of a lifetime every time I wake up and put the headsets on."

FAVORITE TEAM(S) / PLAYER(S) GROWING UP

RUSANOWSKY: "The two teams I really liked were the New York Rangers and the Chicago Blackhawks. I loved the Blackhawks uniforms. And the other thing that happened was, I had a newspaper route back in the day and I would stop in at some of the family's homes when I was delivering the papers. But on Sunday, what was really cool was that I'd have to go around and collect.

"You would collect and basically be running a small business in a way where people would have to pay you for the newspaper and then you'd get a bill from the newspaper. You would pay that off and so forth and you kept your tips. But what was really fascinating was there was one kid who I was in the Scouts with that played hockey. And I couldn't play because we didn't have a rink anywhere near where I lived. It was probably 10, 11 miles away from the closest place where they had organized hockey at that time when I was 10-, 11-years-old. And as we all know, hockey is rather expensive. So I wasn't able to do that. What ended up happening was we used to play ball hockey out in the streets.

"I would stop by this one of my customer's house who I was in the Cub Scouts with and we would shoot the puck at nets and play ball hockey in the driveway. Then, it would usually be Sunday afternoon by that time and I would end up flipping the TV on in the house with them and they'd have the NHL on NBC back then with Tim Ryan and Brian McFarlane and Ted Lindsay. So we got a chance to actually see some other teams once a week or so back in those days in the early days of network TV. But primarily my attachment and my real push toward the game was the radio and that's how I listened to most of the games.

"I had to picture all of it in my mind. We had a chance to play ball hockey outside, but we also had a chance to watch some NHL games. I didn't watch the Rangers all that often, but I did get a chance to do that. So, I got my share of both Marv (Albert) and Sal (Messina) on the radio and Jim Gordon and 'The Big Whistle' Bill Chadwick on television.

"A lot of those games are in my memory. That was the team I really liked, but I also really liked the Blackhawks too; because of their uniforms. I thought that watching those games on NBC, one of the really cool things about that era, and that's not quite as evident today, is they would have this really rudimentary open and then they would kind of fade into the arena and all you would hear would be the sounds of the arena and you would see the site of the arena on NBC.

"I don't know what it was, but back then, you could tell exactly where you were within a couple of seconds, without even any graphic telling you where you were. And it was just because each arena was so different. I always remember the Organ at Chicago Stadium and what Olympia Stadium sounded like when they had a game with the Red Wings.

"Stan Fischler used to say that one of the things with Olympia was, you could smell the hot dogs and you almost could carry that through the arena and imagine that whenever you heard all of the noises and the sights and the sounds of the background. Montreal Forum, Maple Leaf Gardens, the same kind of thing. Now, obviously, you need an extra couple of seconds to look for the logos on the ice and to see a couple of other things; maybe you recognize the advertisements. But back then it was something really visceral about it.

"My favorite players back then, it's kind of funny, but I ended up working with one of them, Pete Stemkowski, who played for the Rangers. He was my broadcast partner here in San Jose for four-years. I got a chance to be very good friends with him. I think my favorite player on the Rangers in those days though was Jean Ratelle. He was the epitome of what I thought a great hockey player was. He was a class act, just an amazing talent. And I always felt that he was one of the guys who made his teammates better.

"I was embedded in that Rangers Era that Emile 'The Cat' Francis had set up the team. You had the GAG Line, which Ratelle was part of. And then you had the Tkaczuk Line with (Steve) Vickers and (Bill) Fairbairn. Stemmer played with (Ted) Irvine and (Bruce) MacGregor. I mean, I can still remember it to this day. And it's kind of funny. I remember that better than some of the teams now, because there are so many more of them and because the lines aren't exactly static all year; they keep changing them, even with the Sharks themselves.

"It was kind of a different era. Ed Giacomin and Gilles Villemure in the nets and of course, Brad Park and Dale Rolfe as the top D-pair. That was a great hockey team and was probably one of the best teams during my lifetime that never won the Stanley Cup."

RUSANOWSKY'S FAVORITE SHARKS GAME HE'S CALLED

The word “Classic” gets thrown around too often in professional sports. Yes, there’s no way to truly quantify what makes a game or moment a “Classic” and yes, it’s similar to how “beauty is in the eye of the beholder.” However, that doesn’t mean the term should just be thrown around so casually.

I say all that and then realize I’m about to do what I just admonished everybody else for doing. I’m going to call a game a “Classic.” But I must preface this by saying that if this game isn’t a “Classic” in the eyes of 99% of hockey fans in the world, then I don’t know what is. (I say 99% because I know the fans of the losing team are going to argue otherwise).

In the San Jose Sharks' entire history, the team has never won the Stanley Cup. They’ve had plenty of memorable moments, but some stand out above others. And for Dan Rusanowsky, who by the way has been around for ALL of the Sharks moments, there is one that will always stand the test of time.

I’m of course talking about April 23, 2019. Game Seven. San Jose vs Vegas at the SAP Center in San Jose. For Sharks fans, you know what I’m talking about. For Golden Knights fans, I’ll give you five seconds to turn away before I continue. One...Two...Three...Four...Five.

Okay, times up. If you’re still here I have to assume you’re here willingly.

The 2018-19 Sharks were a veteran-ladden team with some youth mixed in. A nice blend of talent, speed and skill. The previous season had seen the team bow out in the Second-Round of the playoffs. So, a lot was expected in ‘18-’19 and the team mostly looked up to the challenge throughout the regular-season.

Then came the playoffs and a First-Round matchup with the NHL’s new darlings, the Vegas Golden Knights; the expansion team who, in its inaugural season the year prior, had gone all the way to the Stanley Cup Final. Two teams. Both with high expectations. Only one possible winner. Who would it be?

Well, through the first four games it looked like this was Vegas’ series as they were up 3-1 and in complete control. But then, the Sharks’ resilience showed through. San Jose won Game Five 5-2 and followed that up with a 2-1 win in Game Six to force a Game Seven in front of one of the most rabid fan bases in the entire NHL.

That's when things got interesting. The Golden Knights built up a 3-0 lead by the 3:36 mark of the third period and were well on their way to the next round. That's when fate intervened.

At 9:13 of the third period, Vegas' Cody Eakin was controversially assessed a five-minute major for cross-checking San Jose's Joe Pavelski. Eakin was also given a game misconduct for the hit. On the ensuing power-play the Sharks scored not one, not two, not three, but four goals to take the lead and stun the Golden Knights. This was an unfathomable power-play display and it put the Sharks moments away from knocking out the Golden Knights.

Then, with Vegas essentially down and out, Jonathan Marchessault scored with just 47-seconds left in the third period to rejuvenate the Golden Knights and force overtime.

The overtime period went back and forth and just as it seemed like a second extra period might be needed, San Jose's Barclay Goodrow scored with 1:41 left in the first overtime to send the Sharks and their fans into a state of delirium. It was as stunning of a game as there has been in recent memory and it is one that won't ever be forgotten, though Vegas fans will undoubtedly try. And for Dan Rusanowsky, it will always rank at the top of his list, even if the Sharks one day win the Stanley Cup.

RUSANOWSKY: "I could have answered this in a couple of different ways, but since April 23 2019, it's going to be hard not to pick Game Seven against the Vegas Golden Knights; the most incredible thing I've ever been able to call. I felt like I got it right. Just everything seemed to fit and go well. It was the most incredible scenario I've ever seen on the ice, in the National Hockey League in my life.

"I know that it's going to be regarded as the greatest night in San Jose Sharks history until they win the Stanley Cup. And maybe even after that, just because of the unbelievable nature of what happened that day. It was a special, special moment to be part of that. It was just incredible. Only on a couple of occasions, have I heard what's already a very loud and raucous building get to another level. And it was the most amazing thing I had ever seen. There are a few people who left when the score was 3-0 and they'll never admit it now."

MESSAGE TO SHARKS FANS

As is a common theme amongst members of the sports media, it is a well known fact that without the fans our jobs would either A) not exist or B) they'd have a lot less meaning. So, each of the broadcasters in this book took a couple of minutes to address you, the fans, directly.

RUSANOWSKY: "I would just say to them that I think their love for the sport of hockey and their love for the Sharks is something I will always appreciate and that their devotion to the sport and the fact that they're listening on the radio and that they're listening to our broadcast on the web and using the apps and everything else we're doing. But however they're listening, it really means a lot to me personally, that we have that opportunity to share the relationship together.

"Radio is an especially personal medium. It's a medium in which many thousands of people are listening to a broadcast at any given moment, but it's so intimate that all there is, is somebody's voice and your imagination as a listener. And so that's a very personal and very intimate relationship. I appreciate the opportunity to have that with so many Sharks fans and fans of the NHL when they tune in. It's just something that I appreciate very much."

ST. LOUIS BLUES

CHRIS KERBER
RADIO: PLAY-BY-PLAY

First Season on Blues Radio: 2000-01
Seasons on Blues Radio (including 2020-21): 21

Birthday: May 28, 1971 Hometown: St. Louis, MO

College/University: Miami University (Oxford, OH)

BIOGRAPHY

There's something about St. Louis that just breeds tremendous sportscasters. Maybe it's something in the water? Who knows. But with the lineage of all-time talent they've had on the microphone, it's no wonder that current Blues radio man, Chris Kerber, grew up to do what he currently does.

KERBER: "My generation, you were listening to Jack Buck and Mike Shannon do Cardinals baseball. You were listening to Dan Kelly and Ken Wilson on Blues hockey. You were listening to Jack Buck and Bill Wilkerson on Cardinals football. We still had the St. Louis Cardinals at the time. You had Mike Kelly, the longtime voice of Missouri sports doing the University of Missouri. You had Bob Ramsey, who for 25-years has been the voice of Billikens Basketball.

"Dan Dierdorf on Monday Night Football is a local St. Louis guy, having played for the Cardinals. Bob Costas' history in St. Louis is enormous. His ties to KMOX. It's just the amazing history of sports broadcasting in this town and the quality of sports broadcasting in St. Louis. I don't think it's second to anybody. Nobody could call a game better than Dan Kelly. Jack Buck was as good as it got, in sports, in both the football he did and the baseball he did. Ken Wilson was as smooth of a broadcaster as there was; period."

That's a very impressive lineup of broadcasters to be introduced to you when you're growing up and their voices definitely had a huge impact on Kerber.

But it goes beyond the voices Kerber listened to. There was so much more to his sports fandom.

KERBER: "When you grew up in St. Louis, you grew up a sports fan. It's such a spectacular sports town. I think it has to start there. My dad introduced me to sports. We always had sports on the TV. Sports on the radio.

"We'd always listened to sports on a Sunday morning, a staple of radio on KMOX. I was just a sports fan. I didn't play hockey. I'm the second oldest of nine kids. Soccer and baseball were the sports I played. The challenge in St. Louis was that I didn't grow up in a hockey family.

"My dad first got introduced to hockey when Highway 70 was closed down. He was driving back from Columbia, Missouri and the highway got shut down because of an accident. They sat there, stalled on the highway and he listened to Dan Kelly call a game from cover to cover. That was his introduction to hockey.

"In St. Louis, there were so few rinks. It was the acquisition of Brett Hull and the popularity that came with Brett Hull as his career took off that led to the building of more rinks. So the introduction to playing was never really given to me, or really much of an option.

"Again, when you're coming of age it was the Blues and Brett Hull, who was about as exciting a player as there was in the National Hockey League. Even younger than that, you had Bernie Federko and Brian Sutter. The way Dan Kelly could say Jorgen Pettersson on the radio was just cool."

That's what you would call a sports household. Kerber knew that one day he'd be trying his hand at a career as a sportscaster, so he soaked it all in. And once he reached College, he was able to start putting his future plans into motion.

KERBER: “In college I started calling games. I did all sorts of games. I did football, basketball, baseball and soccer. Any work I could do behind a microphone or practice I did. Then, the honest to goodness truth is, when you graduate in May, you need a job before your college loans are due and baseball teams are already in their season but hockey teams are hiring.

“I made a great contact through Doug Kirchhofer, who at that time was the Owner of the Cincinnati Cyclones. He sent my tape down to the Owner of the Birmingham Bulls in the East Coast Hockey League. That owner's name was Art Clarkson, who just passed a year or so ago.

“I got my first job right out of college with Art Clarkson and the Birmingham Bulls in the ECHL in 1994. Phil Roberto, the former St. Louis Blue, was our Head Coach my first year-and-a-half there. I spent two-years in Birmingham, then I moved up to Springfield, Massachusetts in the American Hockey League for four-years and then got the job in St. Louis in 2000.”

Kerber has been in St. Louis ever since, but if you delve deeper, not only is he the radio voice for his childhood team, but he also took over for the son of one of his idols.

KERBER: “When the Blues decided to not simulcast in 1997, Ken Wilson was the TV guy and they hired Dan Kelly Jr., John's younger brother and Dan's youngest son, to do the Blues. So, Dan Kelly Jr. did 1997 to 2000 and the only reason he left is he got the television Play-by-Play job for the expansion Columbus Blue Jackets. So he left to chase the TV spotlight and that opened the door. Then I came in 2000.”

FAVORITE PLAYER(S) GROWING UP

KERBER: “Bernie Federko. Brian Sutter. Jorgen Pettersson was always one of my favorites, just because I loved the way his name sounded when Dan Kelly called it. I'd say Mike Liut. And then, of course, you hit the era with the rock stars when they came in. You're talking Brett Hull, Brendan Shanahan, Curtis Joseph, Kelly Chase and those guys. Those guys ruled this town.”

HOCKEY AFTER DARK -- TALES AWAY FROM THE RINK

When you've been around the game of hockey for as long as Chris Kerber has, you're bound to pick up a wide variety of stories along the way. It's just the nature of being a respected broadcaster for one team for so long.

With that caveat in place, it's near impossible to choose which one of his stories stands above the others. He couldn't pick and neither can I, so the task is now up to you. Fair warning, if you're a golf fan or really love food, you'll really have a tough time choosing.

KERBER: "Going to dinner with Bernie Federko is an experience. Bernie Federko can eat. He loves his food. So, one of the favorite things that we do, there's a Chinese restaurant called the Blue Willow in Edmonton. And Bernie Federko used to go there when he was a player.

"Well, when Bernie was traveling with us as a TV Analyst, Bernie would introduce us to that. He took us there and we went all the time with him when he was a broadcaster with us. Honestly, every year you couldn't wait till we were going to Edmonton.

"It was, 'Do we have the night off before? Or are we staying in afterwards? Because we're going to the Blue Willow with Bernie Federko. And when we'd go in there, you didn't look at the menu. The owner of the place still knew Bernie and he'd come over and start talking hockey.

"He'd always tease him. He'd always think Bernie played for the Swift Current Broncos, which he didn't. But he used to say that. And then he'd say, 'didn't you play for Quick River or something like that?' The Owner was just great with how he would talk hockey, tease Bernie and have some fun with it.

"But the rest of us, we never ordered. We never opened the menu. We'd just say, 'Bernie, you order.' Bernie would open the menu and would basically just order for us. 'We need this number of orders for the almond chicken. We need this order of spare ribs.' And then we'd eat and if we needed to order more, we'd order more.

"(For me, I was lucky) I did 18-years with Kelly Chase as my partner. He took me under his wing, right from the start and showed me what the National Hockey League was about and how things are done. When you have the chance to work with someone who put his heart and soul into the sport and became the player, the person and the broadcaster that Kelly Chase (became).

"For someone who was un-drafted and had to fight his way through everything, that was pretty doggone special. On one road trip, we went to Pebble Beach. The whole team went out there to play. They were going to have the rookie dinner the next night. So we got out there, we played Spanish Bay the first day and then Pebble Beach, the next morning. Chaser, myself and the then General Manager at Pebble Beach played a round early in the morning that day.

"The night before, we're playing Spanish Bay and I'm not great at golf. I'm better now than I was 18-years ago when this happened. But, somehow, I managed to shoot a 44 on the front nine at Spanish Bay. 'What in the world is going on?' I followed it up with a 66 on the back nine. I don't think I've ever seen Doug Weight laugh as hard as I saw when he heard that I put a 44-66 split up there. And Doug Weight, I mean, I still just remember, like it's in high definition, him laughing so hard. I don't remember what my score on Pebble Beach was that next day. I did par the Par Three seventh hole. I remember that. My first shot was just off the green. I chipped on and putted. So I'll claim that bit of victory there.

"That was just one of those cool things where I was supposed to room with one of our athletic trainers, I believe. And one of our athletic trainers decided not to come. So I get up to the room, we're in the villa right there on the course.

"It was either my first or second year with the team. So, you've got all these Hall of Famers and future Hall of Famers, like Chris Pronger on the team. So, I walk into my room and I go out to the balcony, I open it up and I'm overlooking the 18th fairway in the Bay, right there at Pebble Beach. About a hundred yards to the right is the 18th green. And I went, 'Dude, what am I doing in this one?'

"I called up Chaser and I said, 'Hey, you gotta get me out of this room.' And he goes 'are you serious?' I said, 'I don't belong in this room. One of those other guys should have this room. I am not in the right room. You gotta get me out of this room.' He goes, 'dude, just enjoy it. Have fun.' I'm sitting there going, 'listen to me, you call (Chris) Pronger. You call (Al) MacInnis right now and you tell them that they got to switch rooms with me. One of those guys should have this room, not me.' I don't know if he ever did call them, but he called me back about 10-minutes later. He said, 'I called them and they said, 'shut up and enjoy the room.'

"I was like (to myself), 'no way should a rookie broadcaster have this room on this kind of trip when you've got the likes of Pronger or MacInnis or Pierre Turgeon and some of the other greats that we had. Like, Holy smokes!' So I tried to give the room up, but they wouldn't take it.

"(Also) a few years back, when Marty Brodeur was playing with us, at the end of the year, we went out to play golf in Phoenix. Darren Pang and Martin Brodeur were in the group ahead of us with a couple of Blues players. John Kelly, myself and a couple of our TV guys were in the group behind. So we played 18 holes. John's a good golfer.

"Obviously Panger and Brodeur are really good golfers. We got done and it was like three o'clock in the afternoon they're in Phoenix. So they had already started to pull the flags on the second course. There were two courses there. But the (course manager) said, 'if you guys want to go play, go play.' So John Kelly and I then went to join Panger and Brodeur. They said, 'yeah, let's play.'

"Now, they've already taken the flags out. So we start playing and you don't know where the hole is on the green as you're hitting towards it. And look, I'm still about a 16 handicap.

"So we're going through this and I swear to God, the first four holes, I hit pro shots that were right in the dead middle of the greens. I am literally putting for par or birdie on each of the first four holes. Brodeur is just giving it to me. 'Yeah, sure. A 15.' I go, 'I swear to God.' At that point in time I quit worrying about where the flag was. I just started shooting out of the middle of the green, because if I can just get it on the green, then I'll putt okay.

"I was getting chirped, called a sandbagger and all that stuff, because, on those first four and I'm telling them 'guys, wait for it. It'll come around. The real game will come around.' I told Martin Brodeur I'm a 16 handicap and I was putting for birdie or par on like the first four or five straight holes to open up the round. He thought I was just feeding him a line of bull."

KERBER'S FAVORITE BLUES GAME HE'S CALLED

There's nothing quite like having all your hard work and dedication pay off in a big way. And there's no better way to punctuate the moment than by having one of your role models, one of your rocks in life, be there to share it with you.

Chris Kerber has been calling Blues games since the early part of the new millennium and the Blues have had plenty of memorable games and moments during that span. But the one game that stands out the most to Kerber is his first home game.

KERBER: "The first ever regular-season home game I did for the Blues, back in 2000, was obviously a big one, because even though we had done some pre-season games, that was the first regular-season home game.

"So, after working at it through College and I was a marketing major in College; I didn't study broadcasting in College. After doing that and then six-years in the minor leagues, that was a big one.

"What made it really cool was my dad was able to spend the game in the booth with me. So, that first game of the 2000-01 season, it'll always be a really, really important game for me, just because of that.

"We opened up with a road trip that took us from Phoenix to San Jose to Anaheim to LA. Then we came home and played Minnesota. We won that game 2-0. I couldn't tell you who scored in that game at this point, but I can tell you, my dad sat in the booth with me and that meant the world to me."

SIGNATURE PHRASE

Sometimes all it takes for a call or saying to catch on is the right moment. That moment needs to happen naturally and when it does, it usually doesn't take long for the fans to catch on and throw their support behind it. For Chris Kerber, his signature win call happened out of the blue, but it was a natural fit for the situation. And then, even though an Owner didn't like it, the fans did and that's all that mattered. So Kerber kept it.

KERBER: "At the end of every Blues win, I say, 'bring out the Zamboni.' (It started when) I was doing a game in Birmingham, Alabama. It was a home game. The game went into overtime. And at that arena, from our broadcast position, the Zamboni entered at the end zone behind the goal to our right.

"This was the goal that we were attacking in overtime. The Zamboni was kind of parked back behind those doors. Olaf Kjenstad, was one of our players. He was number 61.

"He took the puck from inside our own blue line and went coast-to-coast and scored the game-winning goal. And it was in the goal where the Zamboni is parked right behind the glass. So, you could see the Zamboni parked there and just the natural call came out: 'He shoots, he scores and you can bring that Zamboni out and circle it all around the ice.'

"So it happened very organically, very naturally there. So I kept doing it and then I kept doing it when I got to Springfield, Massachusetts. I even had one Owner at the time tell me, 'I'm not sure I really like that.' But I kept doing it. And then people started bringing signs to the rink that said, 'bring out the Zamboni,' and I kept doing it. And I've done it in St. Louis since Day One."

MESSAGE TO BLUES FANS

As is a common theme amongst members of the sports media, it is a well known fact that without the fans our jobs would either A) not exist or B) they'd have a lot less meaning. So, each of the broadcasters in this book took a couple of minutes to address you, the fans, directly.

KERBER: "Well, that's simple. I mean, Brett Hull said it best when he said, 'we don't have a game without the fans' and that's 100% true. My message to Blues fans is, I love being afforded the privilege of bringing them, their team and the sport that they love and with the history of those who came before us in the booth and the standard that we expect to carry on because of them. We hope we do it at a high level for a really long time. They are the ones that invite us into their cars, into their homes, by tuning in, to listening to us. And that is a privilege and something that we should never take for granted."

DARREN PANG
TV: COLOR ANALYST

First Season on Blues TV: 2009-10
Seasons on Blues TV (including 2020-21): 12

Birthday: February 17, 1964 Hometown: Meaford, ON

College/University: N/A

BIOGRAPHY

Making it to the National Hockey League as a player is one of the hardest things to do in professional sports. But sticking in the league might be even harder. Whether it's a lack of roster spots or a bout with the injury bug, there's plenty of reasons why players don't manage to stay in the NHL for very long. And while Darren Pang had the skill/talent necessary to ascend to the best hockey league in the world, his bad injury luck prevented him from staying for very long.

So, at a fairly early age, Pang knew he needed a second career and it just so happened that when he was growing up, he had a fondness for broadcasting. It was a way to stay in the game he so loved, so he went for it. Now, let's get Pang's recollection of how this story unfolded.

PANG: "There was no question that, broadcasting, even at an early age, for me, I was such a big fan of Danny Gallivan. The words that he used, the way he described the action. Most of the Hockey Night in Canada games on Saturday nights were Maple Leafs games. But in Ottawa, we got the Montreal Canadiens games as much as we did the Toronto games.

"I can still imitate Danny Gallivan, some of the things that he said and the nuances. Just the way he described the game, he was my favorite. The next favorite that I had, I mean, it's funny because now I'm his son's partner, but it's Dan Kelly. He did so many games and so many big games, including the '87 Canada Cup. I was a big fan of listening to Dan Kelly, who was also from Ottawa. So, maybe that's what attracted me to Dan. Even as I got older and played in the NHL, Dan Kelly did two-seasons of my career before he passed away.

"(When) I was playing Junior Hockey in Ottawa with the 67's. They always had a cable show there. I was often a guest on the cable show and I believe, looking back at it, I probably would have been a better student in school if I had known that broadcasting could have been a career for me. When I turned pro, I played in cities like Milwaukee, Saginaw, Halifax and Indianapolis.

"As many people know who played in the minors, you're asked to do a lot more in the community than you would be when you're in the NHL; whether it's speaking at a local church or going to a youth hockey group. I often ended up on radio shows and in Saginaw, for two-years, I co-hosted a morning show from eight to nine in the morning on a radio station before I went to practice. I guess, about that point, I was starting to really pay attention to radio, to TV and to broadcasting. I wasn't sure if I was going to be a Hockey Analyst, but I did like the radio aspect of it."

Acknowledging his affection for broadcasting was the first step, but in order to put those early experiences into action as a full-on second career, Pang first needed a reason to no longer be an NHL player. And in the 1989 playoffs, he got his reason.

PANG: "I actually tore my ACL during the playoffs against Calgary in 1989. I had surgery in September, so it knocked me out of that '89-'90 season. Although I did come back in March, went to the minors and finished my career with Indianapolis before retiring. But while I was injured and rehabbing my ACL with the Blackhawks, a Producer named Lisa Seltzer, who was the Producer and Director for the Chicago Blackhawks at the time, asked the Blackhawks GM Bob Pulford if I could do some college hockey while I was rehabbing my knee. So I was hired by SportsChannel in Chicago and I did games as an analyst on TV. So that was a great step in the right direction for me to segue from being a player to starting a new career.

"When I retired from the Blackhawks and I did those college games, I continued doing that, but I also started at the ground floor. The Blackhawks asked me to do a hotline that they had for their fans. It was updated and hosted by me three-times a day. I updated it. I had a recorder, walked into the locker room and I put stories together. I'd also edit them. It was called 'Hawk Talk with Darren Pang.' So I did that and then I also did a radio pre-game, between periods and post-game show for every Blackhawks game on WBBM NewsRadio 78, with a fellow named Brian Davis.

"I continued to do that for four-years, but in 1993, in August, I was asked to go to Bristol, Connecticut, to audition for this new network called ESPN2. The Deuce was looking for players who had just retired and had some stories to tell. I ended up getting the job with ESPN and ESPN2, in 1993. So, I stayed with them for 13-years before they lost the rights to the NHL. It was an unbelievable network to start your career with. They were just so professional and they taught me so much about broadcasting, interviewing and every aspect of a broadcast. It was a special time of my life when I was starting there with ESPN. And besides that, we had the rights to the All-Star Games. We did the Stanley Cup Final a couple of years. We shared them with Fox. I was able to do the Olympics in Nagano in '98 or CBS. I did the 2002 Olympics for NBC in Salt Lake. And I did the 2010 Olympics in Vancouver with CTV in Canada.

"So, along the way, I was able to branch out and do a number of different events that were pretty special to me. And when I got the word that I was basically a free agent after ESPN lost the rights, I had a number of calls with Outdoor Network. I guess I just felt like after working for ESPN for so long that I wanted a bit of a change.

"I got a phone call from Mike Barnett, who was the General Manager of the Arizona Coyotes at the time. I got a phone call that (Wayne) Gretzky was going to be coaching. Cliff Fletcher was also there. So they put me on a phone call and asked if I want to come out and be the Analyst for the Coyotes. That was a real change in my life working for a team full-time. I worked for them for four-years, had a wonderful time, some of the most fun I've ever had in my life. Unfortunately, it came to a halt when they went into bankruptcy.

"When that happened, John Davidson was the President of the St. Louis Blues. He called me a couple of times and just asked if I'd be interested in going to St. Louis. At the time, I didn't think it was the right place for me because I never played for St. Louis. I had a great deal of respect for Bernie Federko, who was in the existing role. But as I talked to John Davidson more and more and I talked to Bernie about it, I talked to friends like Kelly Chase and they described it as a great place to go.

The fans wouldn't be bothered by the fact that I was a former Chicago Blackhawk.

"John Davidson said something pretty funny to me actually, he said, 'why are you worried about that?' And I said, 'well, it's the Hawks and the Blues. They don't like each other. It was a big rivalry.' And he said, 'don't kid yourself. You weren't that good anyway.' I always laugh when I think about it. I was kind of like, 'wait a second here.' But his point was, I'd been a broadcaster for 25-years. I'd worked national games. Just give it a chance, a bit of a leap of faith on both parts and see if they like you, see if you like it. If you don't, then that's okay, but I have a feeling it's going to work.

"So, it's been just an incredible ride to be a part of the St. Louis Blues and to have the fans take me in as one of their own; have the alumni take me in as one of their own. It says an awful lot about the marketplace and the people there in St. Louis, because it's just been an incredible ride, with a great network, at Fox Sports Midwest. An unbelievable partner in John Kelly and our production crew is first rate all the way. It's working regional, but we try to run it like a national show and I think that's what people appreciate about our show with Fox sports Midwest."

FAVORITE PLAYER(S) GROWING UP

PANG: "Growing up in Ottawa, at that time, we did not have an NHL team. So most Ontario kids either liked the Toronto Maple Leafs or the Montreal Canadiens. Montreal was only an hour-and-40-minutes away. The Montreal Canadiens were my favorite team growing up.

"I was totally inspired by Yvan Cournoyer, Guy Lafleur and Steve Shutt. Ken Dryden was one of my favorite goalies. I think I was attracted to the fact that when I was playing hockey just outside of Ottawa, we always had winning teams and it seemed like we'd always go to tournaments. We were always competitive. If we weren't winning, we were right there. And I think that's what attracted me to the Montreal Canadiens, because they won all the time. I liked cheering for winners. So I cheered for Montreal."

HOCKEY AFTER DARK -- TALES AWAY FROM THE RINK

Being as well traveled as somebody like Darren Pang, it's hard to narrow down your favorite experiences to a single one. And that just means you've had a lot of wonderful experiences throughout your career, which is always a positive thing. So, Pang chose a few different experiences of his to share with all of you.

PANG: "When I was with the Arizona Coyotes, Todd Walsh was the sideline reporter. We did the opening to one of our shows on Broadway Street in Nashville, when Nashville had just come into the league. It was a fun place. He had all kinds of connections and we did our open in the Ryman Auditorium. That was one of the most special opens for a game that I've ever seen. I mean, Johnny Cash and Neil Young and all these great musicians had played there at the Ryman.

"With the St. Louis Blues, the year that I got there, we went to Stockholm, Sweden to open up the season against Detroit. That was a great way to get to meet and know all of these guys who have now been friends (of mine) for 11-years. To go on those boat rides through the canals of Stockholm and get to know one another and end up at Pubs and have some laughs along the way.

"As a broadcaster, John Kelly and I, about two-years ago, on November the 11th, we opened a show on Remembrance Day. We did it right in the World War One museum, which was brand new, in downtown St. Louis. That was incredibly special. My grandfather fought in World War I. My father was also in service in Canada and same with John Kelly's family. So that was a very special time to pay tribute to our veterans and open up our show on that particular night."

PANG'S FAVORITE BLUES GAMES HE'S CALLED

For somebody as emotionally invested as Darren Pang, it should come as no surprise that two of his favorite games that he's been on the call for, have come against two heated opponents, in the midst of tense playoff battles. Some of that is probably the former player in him shining through. But some of it is also his unbridled joy for the game and the game's big moments.

PANG: "We've had some great first round match-ups before the national networks took over. There was a period of time where I thought the Blues could win two Stanley Cups in about a four-year period. They didn't, because they faced off against LA -- LA won The Cup -- and they faced off against Chicago and Chicago won The Cup.

"But there was a game in particular and John Kelly just had a heck of a call. I think we were down by two men, short-handed, in overtime against LA at home. Alexander Steen stole the puck from Jonathan Quick and scored short-handed in overtime to win it. That was an incredibly special team. You could start to feel the confidence of the team, of the core players and of the city in big games. Because when I first got there, I really found that the fan base always went to the bad games.

"They always went to something that went wrong previously and it kind of bothered me, because I was going in there with a fresh set of eyes and thinking this team's going to win. And yet, when something went bad, I think the fan base just naturally went back to something else that went bad years before that. I think that goal was such an incredible moment to get over a hump. That would be one goal that I would remember like it's yesterday.

"Another one would be Game Seven against Chicago. The series was incredible. There was a lot of stuff going back and forth. There was some bad blood, obviously. It's the Blackhawks and the Blues. And in the past, the Blackhawks had gotten the best of the Blues.

"With about four-minutes to go on home ice, Troy Brouwer scored on the doorstep and it was just such an exhilarating, emotional call. It was a moment, a true moment where the Blues, in 2016, were knocking on the door. They knocked off the champs of the year before and there was hostility, but they didn't back down and then they scored one of the biggest goals in Blues history. John Kelly and I were on the call for that."

SIGNATURE PHRASE

It's rare in Hockey to find a Color Analyst who actually has a special saying, or sayings, that fans equate with them. That's usually something reserved for Play-by-Play announcers. However, Darren pang is the exception, as he's been encouraged, right from the beginning, to use his enthusiastic sayings to enhance his broadcasts.

PANG: "I'll go back to John Davidson. When I retired in 1990 and began the commitment of trying to be an Analyst, I read an article in Sports Illustrated and I cut it out and put it on my fridge. It was everything that John Davidson did to prepare for a game. J.D. had 'Oh Baby!' He would say that a lot. At the beginning of my career, it happened in a game at ESPN.

"Steve Levy and I were doing the game at the Meadowlands in New Jersey. A young player got recalled by New Jersey and I spoke to him in the morning. He just had this colorful attitude and he was sharper than a tack. A little guy with good hands.

"His name was Steve Sullivan. I was kind of talking about him all game long, but he wasn't doing anything and then he got the puck. We were right in that basket overlooking the ice. It was a great location.

"He got the puck, faked to his right, put the puck between Janne Niinimaa's legs, went to his left, went around another defenseman, faked the goalie -- I think it was (Ron) Hextall -- went forehand, backhand, under the bar and in. And before Steve Levy could say 'he shoots, he scores,' I said, 'Holy Jumpin! what a play!' I was so excited because I'd been selling the player all game long and at that moment, he didn't let me down. It was really a bad play for a Color Commentator, because I cut the legs right out of my Play-by-Play guy. But it was genuine excitement. I remember Steve Levy after the game saying, 'I don't know where that came from, but you've got to save that for special moments, because that was unbelievable.'"

That's not Pang's only special saying though. He also has one that's derived from a children's card game.

PANG: "'The nine of hearts' is another one that I use quite often. It's based on the card game Euchre. It's a Canadian game and you have partners.

“If your partner calls 'Trump or Clubs' and you have the nine of hearts, you can't help them. It's become a saying of mine. You know, if you try to date a girl in High School and she turned you down, I'd say to my buddies, 'nah, I got the nine of hearts.'

“So then, as it turns out, I'm doing these games and one game, somebody made this great move. And I just kind of blurted out, 'He just gave him the nine of hearts. Oh my goodness. He just gave him the nine of hearts.'”

MESSAGE TO BLUES FANS

As is a common theme amongst members of the sports media, it is a well known fact that without the fans our jobs would either A) not exist or B) they'd have a lot less meaning. So, each of the broadcasters in this book took a couple of minutes to address you, the fans, directly.

PANG: “Thank you. They didn't give me the nine of hearts. They welcomed me with open arms. They gave me an opportunity to prove myself. Not playing for St. Louis, I think they tested my loyalty and wondered where it would be. And then they found out where it was. So, there was no question that when you go into a city and you become part of the community and they want your trust. So, that's what I would say, I would say, ‘Thanks.’”

TAMPA BAY LIGHTNING

DAVID MISHKIN
RADIO: PLAY-BY-PLAY

First Season on Lightning Radio: 2002-03
Seasons on Lightning Radio (including 2020-21): 18

Birthday: September 13, 1969 Hometown: New York, NY

College/University: Yale University

BIOGRAPHY

The art, or rather game, of being a sports broadcaster, is one of chance, luck, preparation and skill. You need the right opportunity to open at the right time and to have the right connections and the right ability to get one of those coveted gigs. They don't just grow on trees you know. There's a finite number of teams and a finite number of broadcasting spots. So you better strike when the iron is hot, otherwise, you'll be left out in the cold.

Tampa Bay's David Mishkin is one example of a broadcaster who was able to take full advantage of his talents and connections in order to climb the ladder to get to where he is today.

MISHKIN: "Growing up, I was a big sports fan and followed all the sports. I was born in New York and I kind of came into sports cognizance when I was still living in New York. But when I was nine, my family moved to suburban Boston. So I was growing up in two pretty sports crazy towns and those markets had teams in all the sports, baseball, football, basketball and hockey, as well as other sports.

"So, when I got into broadcasting, I mean, I was a sports fan and I'm still a sports fan. But, I got into broadcasting when I was an undergraduate and joined our college radio station as an extracurricular activity and wanted to do sports because it was an opportunity there.

"It was kind of like when I saw that there was an opportunity to talk about sports and for the college students to do Play-by-Play, it was almost like the light-bulb went on that this was something I wanted to try. And once I tried it, I decided that this was something I wanted to pursue when I was done with college. But I was a sophomore at that point. So, even though I knew pretty early in my college trajectory that this was something I wanted to pursue, I had a couple of more years to gain experience and I gravitated toward hockey.

"I mean, particularly my junior and senior years, I did a lot of different sports. I did the football games. I did Men's and Women's basketball. I did the hockey. We did some baseball. So I got exposed to a variety of different sports, but I gravitated toward hockey, in part, because I was really the only one who wanted to do the games during my junior and senior years. And I seemed to have a knack right off the bat for seeing a player and being able to kind of regurgitate that quickly; which is the biggest challenge in hockey, keeping up with the play.

"So, from the get-go, I found that I could keep up with the play. Now I had a long way to go in terms of sounding seasoned and gaining experience in terms of making the broadcast sound smooth and fluid, but the most important building block, I think for hockey Play-by-Play, especially on radio, is making sure that you can identify the players quickly, so you don't fall behind.

"Then, the third part of it was, once I had decided that this was something I wanted to pursue, I kind of figured that there might be a little less competition for hockey than some of the other sports. In fact, I didn't even know how to go about pursuing an opportunity in basketball or football, because it seemed like there wasn't really an extensive minor league system for those sports that people were either doing it and had been doing it at the major league level for an in-depth amount of time where they kind of came up by doing college games; college basketball and college football. But it was clear that you didn't just apply to a

University as opposed to a minor league baseball team or a minor league hockey team where you could apply to a team. And so, I kind of put my eggs in the hockey basket and worked in hockey those last two-years that I was an undergrad, gaining as much experience as I could and was able to put together a demo tape that landed me a job in the East Coast Hockey League. So I ended up being lucky.

"I mean, I was one-week removed from graduating and I packed up my car and drove to Johnstown, Pennsylvania to start my pro broadcasting career.

"(Going back to) when I first got started in college there was not a lot of opportunity to use other broadcasters as a sounding board, with notable exceptions of the upperclassmen. So, when I joined the college radio station as a sophomore, we had a bunch of seniors who were in the sports department and they encouraged me to go to games and call games into a recorder, which I did. And then I would listen back to those games, but they would too. They'd give me some general feedback.

"But I was the one who had to kind of decide how I wanted to call a game and if we're going to use hockey as an example, because I did a lot of hockey as I was saying during my college years. I made two specific decisions about how I wanted to call games and it was based probably more on what I would want to hear if I were a listener."

Of course, those decisions were influenced by Mishkin's favoritism towards the broadcasters he himself grew up listening to as a fan of the sports teams up in Boston.

MISHKIN: "Johnny Most is at the top of the list. I don't know that I sound like Johnny Most, I mean, he had a gravelly voice. I loved listening to him on the radio for the Celtics and the reason that I loved listening to him was that he didn't leave any doubt as to where his allegiance was. He was the Celtics announcer and he wanted them to do well and let you know it.

"I just loved the way that he enhanced the experience of following the games, whether I was listening on the radio or in those days, it was a lot easier to match the radio call with what was on the television screen; like if they were getting to The Final, let's say the NBA Finals, you could sync up the radio call much more easily than it is nowadays, because I don't think that the television delay was as pronounced.

"But I liked all the Boston announcers and for different reasons. I want to say that I mostly followed the Bruins on television with Fred Cusick, who was definitely pro Bruins. I think Johnny Most was probably a little more fired up about things that went the Celtics way, or didn't go the Celtics' way then Fred Cusick. But Fred Cusick would get very animated when the Bruins would score. And I mean, my broadcast style, one of the things that I made a decision about when I first started doing it in college was, because I liked team announcers who didn't have a problem showing emotion, maybe that's the wrong way of putting it.

"They gave themselves permission to show emotion and I liked that. That's the way I wanted to call games. And a lot of that was formed from these hometown announcers who I grew up listening to, whether it was Johnny Most or Fred Cusick. For the Red Sox, I did listen a lot on the radio to Ken Coleman and Joe Castiglione. They did the games for a lot of my childhood on the radio.

"So, I gave myself permission to be excited if I felt excited and that was not so much the X's and O's, but it was more the flavor of the broadcast. The other decision was very much X's and O's, which was, I wanted to be as descriptive as possible, which in hockey is a bit challenging because the play moves so quickly. So you can make a choice about how descriptive you were going to be and there's no right or wrong answer to this. But when I made up my mind, I wanted to stay on the puck as much as I could and find a way to describe, in simple terms that you can get out quickly, because the puck is going to be moving, as to where it is.

"Every time a play happens and by play, I mean a player touches the puck or passes the puck or there's a battle for the puck. The three questions that I wanted to answer were: who has the puck? Where is that player and what is he doing? And that kind of formed how I describe what I was seeing. You can't describe everything. The game is too quick for that. But I, from a very early point in my broadcasting career, made the decision that I was going to try and be as descriptive as I could in a way that was digestible for the listener. I wasn't giving too much information that it became impossible to follow along. And at the risk of repeating myself, there's no right or wrong way to do it. That's a choice.

"I mean, there are plenty of broadcasters who are less descriptive in terms of where the puck is at all times and they still are calling a really descriptive game. And some people might listen to me and say, 'well, I don't need to know that the puck is going D-to-D. I'd rather hear some anecdote. If what is happening on the ice is not critical to a play happening that may lead to a scoring chance or a goal or something noteworthy, then talk about something else rather than some guy passing it back and forth with his defense partner.' I chose to stay on the puck and describe the pass, back and forth, from one partner to the next. And so, those two broad decisions about how I wanted to do it, informed how I did it. And then it was a matter of getting reps and getting experience. Like I said, I got two seasons worth basically of doing Yale Hockey as a junior and a senior. And that was strong enough, or the demo that I came out with was strong enough, to get me that first job."

From making his decision about style to getting the requisite experience, Mishkin was on the way to becoming a professional broadcaster. Now he just needed to get some additional seasoning to smooth things out. And there's no better place to get that seasoning than from your fellow broadcasters who are working their way up the same ladder you are.

MISHKIN: "Once I got into the hockey broadcasting circle, which is often the most difficult step to take, then you start meeting other broadcasters. One guy who I remember giving me great feedback was Joe Beninati, who's now the Capitals TV Play-by-Play broadcaster. But when I was in Johnstown, my first year, we had a loose affiliation with the Bruins interestingly and their top affiliate, 'cause Johnstown was in the ECHL, which is like two steps below the NHL; their top affiliate was in Providence at the time. And Joe was the broadcaster in Providence. So we had an affiliation agreement. I think that's how we originally got to know each other and he encouraged me or maybe I even asked him if I could send him a demo and he listened to it. He took the time to give me some feedback.

"We developed a friendship and that friendship has lasted to this very day. But the interesting thing is that, fast forward a few years later, I was in Hershey, which was my second stop. And then, within two-weeks of me taking the job with Hershey, Joe got the job with the Capitals, he was leaving Providence and he recommended me for the job. The Providence team called me and I had already just arrived in Hershey. I said, 'thanks, I really appreciate it. But I literally just took this job.' And it worked out. I mean, it all worked out and they ended up going in a different direction obviously. It wasn't that hire, but their next hire was Dave Goucher, another good friend of mine, who ended up becoming the Radio voice of the Boston Bruins. And now he's in Vegas. Dave and I had gotten to know each other in the ECHL, 'cause I was in Johnstown and he was in Wheeling, which was a close rival. So we would see each other a lot.

"And, again, it was a direct route for me. I mean, again, some other broadcasters may have jumped around to more teams and in the Minor Leagues. Sometimes you end up on a team that has to move or can't sustain its financial stability. Unfortunately, a broadcaster may have to find another team, through no fault of their own. But so, my final year at Johnstown, we affiliated again, the ECHL is kind of a loose affiliation.

"It's not quite like the AHL to the NHL. I mean the NHL roster, like the full roster, beyond the players who are actually playing on the NHL team. Their full roster usually consists of players who may not have turned pro yet. So they're still playing amateur hockey, or players in the top minor league. And there's usually only a handful of their signed players who need to find another place to play.
And that would be the ECHL.

"Often it's the goalie, maybe because a team can only have two goalies at a time, there's only one net. So, if you have a couple of highly regarded goalie prospects who aren't ready for the NHL, you might have one play in the AHL on one play in the ECHL; so they both get ice time. But that's why the affiliations are looser. So, my last year in Johnstown, we affiliated with Hershey, which was with the Flyers at the time; that was '93-'94. So, through the affiliation agreement, Hershey was two, three-hours down the road from Johnstown, I got to know the management there. A couple of players went up too and that's the other thing that can happen. If the AHL team loses players to recall, they may have to pluck some players from the ECHL to fill out their roster, even if those players are not necessarily under contract to the parent team.

"So that happened a couple of times. And what happened was, Dan Kamal, who had been the Hershey Bears broadcaster for 12-years, left and went to Atlanta to join the Atlanta Knights in the IHL at the time. The IHL was kind of a rival league to the AHL, but it was comparable. It was a top Minor League. And I think that Dan saw that

Atlanta might be in line to get an NHL team, which eventually Atlanta did. And he ended up becoming the Radio voice of the Thrashers when they ended up getting an NHL team.

"I think it may have been an opportunity. Like he was just ready for a change and trying something new. So, he left and Hershey was looking for a broadcaster. And as is often the case, it's the demo, but it's also knowing a little bit about the candidate. And I think the fact that I had met, under different circumstances, both the General Manager and the Assistant General Manager in Hershey at the time, helped me. They were able to call my General Manager in Johnstown, with whom they had a working relationship, to learn a little bit about me off-air; what are my work habits? How do I fit in, in a team environment -- stuff that is not necessarily readily available when you're listening to a demo. And so that's how I got the job.

"(So) I was in Hershey from 1994 until 2002; that's eight-years. I spent 11 total years in the minors; three in Johnstown and eight in Hershey. And so the two men who were in management in Hershey when I was hired in 1994, the General Manager was Jay Feaster and the Assistant General Manager was Doug Yingst. In 1998, Jay Feaster left to become the Assistant General Manager of the Lightning. He had an opportunity to work for Jacques Demers, who was the GM at the time. So Jay relocated to Tampa and by the time 2002 rolled around, he was now the General Manager. I'd been in the league (AHL) for a while at this point and had gotten to know a lot of different people in the hockey world.

"One of those people was Bob Hartley, who was our coach in Hershey when we won the Calder Cup in 1997. He had since moved on to become Head Coach of the Avalanche at that time. And in 2001, the Avalanche won the Stanley Cup with him as Head Coach. So, like everything, there's an element of who you know. But who you know is not like some closed door, dark room nefarious thing. I think the who you know part is more about knowing somebody so that you can pass along information to a colleague who is in a hiring position so that they feel confident the person they are bringing in is the right person.

"So, Bob and I had a really good relationship, still do and the job opened with the Lightning. John Ahlers, who was the Radio Play-by-Play broadcaster with the Lightning, had an opportunity to go to

Anaheim to do TV, which he did and he's still there. So, the job opened up. Jay got me on the phone and said, 'I think John Ahlers is leaving, get your stuff ready to get it down here.' At that point, the General Manager at the NHL level is not making the hire, but he certainly can exert some influence, which he did.

"And again, he hired me in Hershey. So, if there's a job opening and he thinks highly of me he's going to say, 'I strongly think that you should give this person a listen' to our Director of Broadcasting at the time. And then, on top of that, Bob Hartley called the President of the Lightning, because the broadcaster didn't go into the hockey ops side, it went into the business side. So the President of the team was kind of the person at the top of the food chain for the business side.

"So, he got a call from Bob Hartley, who just won the Stanley Cup and was singing my praises; that has an impact. So yes, the demo has to be good and you have to impress the person listening to your demo. But if you can get that extra oomph from somebody vouching for you and somebody who's in a prominent position already within the league, it does make a difference. Part of it is luck. Part of it is the stars aligning. But part of it is you putting yourself in a position so that you can walk through that door when the stars align or at least when it opens up a little bit. You put yourself in a position through the work that you've done day in and day out."

FAVORITE PLAYER(S)/TEAM(S) GROWING UP

MISHKIN: "I played a little bit of hockey; played a year or two maybe when I was 11 or 12 and then got away from it. I probably did play more baseball and basketball. I was never particularly gifted in terms of being an athlete. I mean, I was okay. I could hold my own. But I knew that wasn't really in the cards for me to keep pursuing it.

"My interests kind of went elsewhere in terms of participating in sports. So, I don't know that I really emulated myself after (any players). The Rangers, I don't really remember rooting for a specific player. I remember the run to The Final in '79. I remember interestingly, my broadcast partner, Phil Esposito was a big part of that team.

"I remember the Maloneys and John Davidson from those teams. But I was probably a little young to be honest with you. Prior to that, even though I remember liking them, '76, '77, '78, they really weren't good. I mean, they just weren't. That '79 team kind of came out of the blue. They were better in the early-70's when I wasn't really aware of what was going on in terms of hockey.

"With the Bruins, I liked Rick Middleton. I liked Barry Pederson. He was there. They ended up trading Pederson for Cam Neely, which turned out to be a pretty good trade for the Bruins because Pederson's years in Vancouver weren't as good as they were when he was with Boston. And then Neely was the opposite. His best years came when he was playing for the Bruins. And Ray Bourque was obviously an elite player. So, I mean, those were probably the guys that I remember most from that era."

HOCKEY AFTER DARK -- TALES AWAY FROM THE RINK

When you're on the road as often as sports broadcasters are, you tend to develop bonds with your fellow broadcasters that maybe you wouldn't necessarily do if you were always at home. There's a phrase for this and it's called your work family. Now, sometimes that work family is more work than family and other times that work family is more family than work. And those situations are when you know you've really got a fantastic relationship going. For David Mishkin, he was able to meet a fellow broadcaster who not only became more family than work, but he also got to find a fun way to explore the various cities he travels to with the Lightning.

MISHKIN: "One of my closest friends is our television Pre-game/Intermission Host named Paul Kennedy, who has been a broadcaster since the '70s. He's the Godfather to my kids. I mean, we have a very, very close relationship and it's interesting. We kind of knew each other. My first year 2002-03, we had a different Intermission Host.

"Paul had been the Intermission Host and Pre-game Host in the first-year of the Lightning, which was a decade earlier. And then he ended up doing some other stuff. But by the time 2003-04 arrived, they were looking for a new Pre-game/Intermission Host; Fox Sports, which is our local regional broadcast partner. They decided to have Paul come back and do it.

"So we met that first-year and that was the year the Lightning won the Stanley Cup for the first time; in 2004. And we became friends. But our friendship really solidified. So, we had the lockout year in 2004-05 and it was during that time I really got into running. I'd always kind of run for exercise. Like if I felt I needed to exercise. But I became much more committed to it. I was doing it basically every day.

"When the 2005-06 season started, if I was home, I'd run outside, but on the road, I'd just go into the hotel gym. And I didn't know that Paul was also a very dedicated runner. We were in Anaheim, I was going to the gym and I ran into him in the lobby and he said, 'where are you going?' And I said, 'I'm going to the gym.' He's like, 'no, no, no, you're going to come outside with me.'

"So we ran together and because he's been doing it for decades, not only working as a broadcaster, but running the cities, he knew a variety of different routes around every city that we went to. So, like clockwork, we would run when we'd get to a city. The next day, usually in the morning, we'd meet up, we'd go for a run together and it's an incredible way to see the city that you're in.

"I had a tour guide kind of. You spend 45-minutes to an hour with someone. I don't even know how many times a year we would do it; 60 times a year, year after year after year after year. I mean, you're talking about stuff other than just hockey, although that was some of it. So you become really, really close."

MISHKIN'S FAVORITE LIGHTNING GAME HE'S CALLED

The 2019-20 NHL season will forever be remembered as the season that COVID-19 cut short. The League, like the rest of the world, was thrown into chaos and it took several months before hockey was able to resume, at which point, a new playoff format was constructed, with the goal of crowning a Stanley Cup champion.

The Lightning got through the Round-Robin Round as well as each of the three traditional rounds before finally clinching their first Stanley Cup championship since 2004. There were plenty of memorable games and moments during the team's run to The Cup; including a five-overtime thriller against Columbus. And Radio man David Mishkin called it all, as he has for close to two-decades. However, when it comes to games that top his list, you have to go back to Tampa's 2004 Cup run to find the answer.

MISHKIN: "We had a lot (of memorable games) just in this last playoff run and it's probably too soon for me to fully digest and appreciate what just happened. But I almost feel like it would be doing a disservice if I didn't mention some of the games that literally just happened in the last two-months; including that five-overtime game. That was the longest game I've ever called. My previous long had been a triple-overtime game.

"But going back beyond this year that just finished, probably the most memorable broadcast for me was Game Six of the '04 Stanley Cup Final, which was in Calgary. The Lightning were trailing that series three-games-to-two and Marty St. Louis scored in double-overtime to extend the series and get it to a seventh game; which the Lightning would then win back home two nights later. So that's probably the one that's at the top of the list.

"The entire region in Calgary and outskirts, it was a Sea of Red. I mean, I know how it feels, whether you're up three-two or down three-two, but they were hoping that that was going to be their Stanley Cup game. Talking about a hostile environment, the Lightning went in and were able to win that game in dramatic fashion.

"So that's probably the one that I would pick, but I'm going to reserve judgment on some of the games that were just played during this last Stanley Cup run."

SIGNATURE PHRASE

When you think of how your favorite announcers call a game there are many thoughts that cross your mind. One is their style, how energetic are they? How descriptive are they? Another is how their voice comes across. Are they monotone? Are they overly excitable? These are the things fans think about and so do the broadcasters, who have to find a way to not only tell the story of the game, but to do so in a way that entices fans to tune in.

So, sometimes broadcasters come along who, even though they don't have their own vocabulary, a la Doc Emrick or Mike Lange, they do just enough to distinguish themselves from the rest and it's all in their diction. One such broadcaster like this is David Mishkin.

MISHKIN: "I think most people say 'score' with me really loudly. I didn't make a decision that this is what I wanted to say. It wasn't like a catchphrase, but I think, going back to that early decision I made to say it, if you're excited get excited. So, it's not so much the fact that I'm saying 'score.' A lot of broadcasters say it, but how it sounds and probably how excited I can get is probably what most people equate with me if you were to ask.

"If you were to ask Lightning fans about me, that would probably be one of the first things that they would say. However, the funny thing is that, even if a game has say four-goals, that four-goal calls in the span of like a two-and-a-half hour broadcast. So it's really a very small percentage of the actual work that goes into calling a game. But that's the stuff that's more memorable because those are the plays that spell the difference between winning and losing."

MESSAGE TO LIGHTNING FANS

As is a common theme amongst members of the sports media, it is a well known fact that without the fans our jobs would either A) not exist or B) they'd have a lot less meaning. So, each of the broadcasters in this book took a couple of minutes to address you, the fans, directly.

MISHKIN: "I feel incredibly lucky and privileged to be able to do something and have that thing be something that I love to do; which doesn't always happen. The fact I've been well-received here, it means a lot. It really has meant that I've had an opportunity to call games in one market for coming up on two decades now. And if the fans hadn't received me well, that would not have been the case. So I am very thankful for the reception that I've gotten and thankful for having had the opportunity to do something that I love to do."

TORONTO MAPLE LEAFS

GORD MILLER
TV (TSN 4): PLAY-BY-PLAY

First Season on Maple Leafs TV (TSN 4): 2013-14
Seasons on Maple TV (TSN 4) (including 2020-21): 7

Birthday: June 21, 1965 Hometown: Edmonton, AB

College/University: N/A

BIOGRAPHY

Have you ever wondered what your life would be like if not for one specific event that took place when you were growing up? Come on, raise your hands, we've all done it.

Well, for Gord Miller, even though he had a love of sports and broadcasting, who's to say whether he embarks on his decades-long career or not, if not for a little divine intervention on the part of Mother Nature?

MILLER: "I lived in Edmonton and was going to High School in the early 1980s. The Oilers had just started and to be honest, I got into broadcasting because I don't like the rain. Our school had a high-end track and field set up and we had to work there when other schools had their track meets. I was raking a long jump pit in the rain and the announcer didn't show up. The announcer booth was covered, so I went and did that instead."

Perhaps it was fate giving Miller the nudge he needed to start down his career path.

MILLER: "I'd do the announcements in my High School. And then, a guy came up and he said, 'there's a high school basketball tournament, 'would you like to do (it)?' I said, 'Sure.' And I wound up being the PA announcer for the University of Alberta, Golden Bears basketball and hockey. The Edmonton Trappers were a Triple-A team. I did their PA announcing and in 1983, in the summer, CBC hired me to help out on the weekends doing highlights for them.

"That was '83 and in '84 TSN started. Two of our guys left to go to TSN. They replaced one right away, a couple people auditioned for the other job while I was filling-in. I was only 19 then. And eventually they hired me in 1986 full-time after I filled-in for almost two-years.

"I did enjoy doing the PA announcing for my High School and I did love sports. But I didn't know you could make a living doing it. I remember watching Vin Scully calling the 1982 NFC Championship game and thinking, 'wow, what a great job. I wonder what he does during the day?' And someone said, 'no, that's his job.' 'Really? You can do that full-time?'

"At the time, when I started working in Edmonton, I mean, the Oilers were one of the best teams in the NHL. There was a lot going on and it was a great introduction to it. The CBC network used me a lot for reports on the Oilers and everything else. TSN first offered me a job in 1988. I turned it down. And then, in 2000 they offered me a job and I took it."

It's a job he's held in one form or another to this very day.

Of course, you need to go back to his days as a kid and as a teenager to find the origins of his love for hockey; beyond just the Oilers being a winning team.

MILLER: "All the kids in the neighborhood played; so I played. Now, those days, you only saw the Vancouver Canucks once in a while (on TV). I mean, you didn't have hockey on TV all the time. But, the one thing was John Davidson's wife's family is from my area in Southern Alberta and he was a big deal. John was a big deal back then. He was a big Junior star in Calgary. When he came back in the summer, that was a big deal.

"I played hockey until I was 16. The Oilers entered the NHL in '79, but before that they were in the World Hockey Association. (Wayne) Gretzky came in '78, I think. So, I was always interested in hockey. I loved it. The Oilers, in the early '80s kind of exploded onto the scene. In '81, they upset Montreal. In '83 they went to The Final. '84, they won The Cup for the first time and I was just starting out then. It was just an amazing time to be around them."

John Davidson of course, later became a Hall of Fame Broadcaster and eventually, a highly respected President with several different NHL teams. So, while JD was an influence on Miller, so too were some of the biggest broadcasters of the time.

MILLER: "There were three I listened to growing up. Danny Gallivan, Dan Kelly and Bob Cole, were who I really admired and liked.

"They called all the big moments. Dan Kelly's call of Bobby Orr's goal, I still remember. Bob Cole was calling the big games. Danny Gallivan, Montreal was such a great team in the '70s, so I heard Danny Gallivan a lot. They were the voice of the big moments. That's why you were kind of drawn to them."

Miller carried those moments with him throughout his career and was eventually able to get to know, meet and learn from those broadcasters in a one-on-one setting.

"When I started out, the late Don Wittman was terrific to me. Don did a lot of games in Edmonton and was very supportive of me and encouraging. Bob Cole was great to me early on in my career. I was lucky enough to be around him a lot. And I was lucky to meet Danny Gallivan. I became friends with Bob Cole and even had dinner with Dan Kelly when traveling to Philadelphia.

"It was incredible. Those guys were so helpful to me and I've always tried to be that way with young broadcasters, because those guys were that way with me."

PLAYER(S) MILLER GREW UP WITH

MILLER: "Ken Daneyko actually broke my collarbone in a game. There were a lot of players in our area, like Ken Daneyko and there was a goaltender named Darrell May. Lyndon Byers was a guy in the neighborhood. Gord Donnelly. Kelly Hrudey was a little older. There were a lot of good players around there."

HOCKEY AFTER DARK -- TALES AWAY FROM THE RINK

Sometimes a story is more about remembering a specific interaction than about an entire lengthy set of events. But just because it's not lengthy doesn't mean it doesn't hold the same weight to the person who experienced it.

For Gord Miller, there have been two interactions in his career -- away from the broadcast booth -- that stand out to him.

MILLER: "I think about the late Johnny Bower and what a gentleman he was and just running into Johnny at an event. It was a dinner in his honor in Mississauga, Ontario, that I was emceeing. He pulled me aside and said, 'I really like watching you on TV.' He said, 'you talk about the goalies a lot.' Johnny was always teased about that.

"So I think about that, because when you do a legacy team like that, there's a long line of history and those guys were around a lot. And to know that Johnny Bower was watching and enjoyed my work, meant a lot to me.

"(There was also) a national game I did. Prime Minister (Stephen) Harper, I ran into him at a game and he said, 'Oh yeah, I saw you doing a game the other day.' When you realize he's watching, you don't realize the numbers, but you realize that someone like that's watching; that's pretty cool."

MILLER TALKS DEALING WITH NHL'S LONGEST GAMES

In today's day and age, everybody wants things faster and faster. People are no longer content to wait for information or to take a long time to get somewhere. It's all about instant gratification and the advancement in technology has fueled this.

Yet, even as the world speeds up and some sports leagues make the mistake of trying to do the same -- yes, I'm looking at you MLB and Commissioner Rob Manfred -- there is still a time and place for some never-ending, edge of your seat, marathon-style sporting events.

The National Hockey League, during the regular-season, has implemented new rules over the last couple decades to attempt to prevent games and the schedule from becoming even more grueling than it already is. Take three-on-three overtime and the shootout as examples. Both were implemented to prevent games from dragging on and on.

But come playoff time, those restrictions go out the window and that's when hockey fans can be on high alert for something special. Overtime playoff hockey is one of the most exciting and dramatic sports events a fan can witness. And without the limits of the regular-season, it is straight five-on-five for 20-minutes; or more, depending on the situation.

There is no limit to the number of overtime periods a game may need to determine a winner in the NHL's playoffs. That is when things can get wacky. And Gord Miller knows this all too well.

MILLER: "Well, I just did the five-overtime game between Tampa and Columbus. I've done some long overtime games. I mean, I did the five-overtime game between Dallas and Anaheim in '03. I've done some really long overtime games. I would say those are the ones that stand out.

"You never know how long the game is going to be. I mean, it could end at any moment. So, you're just staying in that moment and not really thinking about whether it's going to go three, four, or five-overtimes. I've had experience with them.

"You're going to hit a cluster where it's the 10th longest game, the ninth-longest game, moving up that list. I mean, in terms of doing a long game like that, at things like the Olympics and the World Championship in the World Junior, I do multiple games in a day. So I'm used to calling six, seven periods in a day. That doesn't bother me. I'm used to it. That doesn't bother me at all. I'm quite used to that.

"The great thing about my job is you go to the rink and you don't know what's going to come next. You have no idea what's going to be next.

"(My Color Analyst) Brian Boucher played in the Keith Primeau game. So, (during the Columbus-Tampa game) I was just joking with him and talking to him. But I think, secretly, he wanted their game to remain the longest in modern history. He was happy the Flyers win still stood. And of course, we called the Keith Primeau game. But, he's the guy who made 57-saves in that game. So, just joking with Brian Boucher about it. The difference between calling a game like that and broadcasting it is quite something. But I mean, it is interesting that he had sort of the experience of both."

MOST FAMOUS CALLS

When you've had as long of a career as Gord Miller, you're bound to have made a few calls that are just a cut above the rest. And it's those calls that regardless of how much time goes by, will always be remembered by hockey fans.

The first of which was Miller's World Junior call on a Jordan Eberle goal that has since managed to take on a life of its own.

MILLER: "Can you believe it?!"

According to Miller, that one, "gets played a lot up here (in Canada)."

The other is one that essentially announced the arrival of Sidney Crosby as a superstar in the NHL.

MILLER: "Crosby scored against Montreal in his rookie-year, early in the year; scored in a shootout. I'll always remember that. 'Welcome to The Crosby Show Canada.'"

MESSAGE TO MAPLE LEAFS FANS

As is a common theme amongst members of the sports media, it is a well known fact that without the fans our jobs would either A) not exist or B) they'd have a lot less meaning. So, each of the broadcasters in this book took a couple of minutes to address you, the fans, directly.

MILLER: "I think what I appreciate from (the Maple Leafs fans) is the passion they feel for their team and the roots their team has in the community. And I think the message I would give them is it's a long term love affair and it can be painful. And that's part of the joy of it, right? The pain is part of the joy of it. And that's part of being a sports fan -- the highs and the lows. And that's why we love it. It's unpredictable. I appreciate their passion for their team and for the game."

VANCOUVER CANUCKS

BRENDAN BATCHELOR
RADIO: PLAY-BY-PLAY

First Season on Canucks Radio: 2017-18
Seasons on Canucks Radio (including 2020-21): 4

Birthday: February 16, 1989 Hometown: Coquitlam, BC

College/University: British Columbia Institute of Technology

BIOGRAPHY

Every generation of sports fans has its broadcasters who are the defining soundtrack for their respective teams. It doesn't matter what sport or team it is, because this is always and will always be the case. The Vancouver Canucks fan base has been exceptionally blessed over the years from a broadcast perspective.

It doesn't matter whether you're talking about TV or Radio, because names like: Jim Robson, Jim Hughson and John Shorthouse transcend the mediums they have called Canucks games on. Now, another name is working hard to be included in that list and that is current Canucks radio man, Brendan Batchelor. So Vancouver fans, let's learn about the man who is one of, if not thee, youngest Play-by-Play broadcasters in the entire National Hockey League.

BATCHELOR: "Like many other Canadian kids, I loved hockey for as long as I can remember. I was playing street hockey in my driveway from the age of three or four. I was playing organized ice hockey from the age of four. As a kid growing up, I had a table hockey set. I did the Play-by-Play on my street hockey games. I did the Play-by-Play playing the NHL video game. And at that point it was all just something that I sort of thought was make-believe and playing like kids do; imagining that you're broadcasting the game.

"Then, when I got into High School and was a little older and started really thinking about what I would want my career to be, I thought, 'Hey, it would be pretty cool to get paid to talk about hockey.' So, that's when I sort of decided that Play-by-Play was something that I would really pursue."

Of course, Bachelor would not have had those thoughts if his dad hadn't first introduced him to the game of hockey.

BATCHELOR: "My dad, he was someone who, his parents were British and they had ended up in Canada at the end of the war (World War II). (They did come over during the war as my Grandfather was a Royal Air Force Fighter Pilot and he came to Canada to train the Canadian pilots. Then my dad was born after the war when they settled down roots here).

"They kind of lived in a rural area and so he didn't get to play organized hockey growing up. Obviously, back in the '50s, when he was a kid, organized hockey wasn't as developed as it was when I was growing up. So he never played organized hockey growing up, but he always loved the sport and ended up playing as an adult and had a love for the game. I believe he always said that he wanted to make sure his kids could play hockey if they wanted to. So he introduced me to the sport and I just fell in love with it from there."

So his dad was the one who introduced him to the sport, now let's now find out which broadcasters inflamed his passion for being a Play-by-Play announcer.

BATCHELOR: "Jim Robson obviously was one who, he retired while I was still a kid, but I remember listening to him and really admiring the way he called the game, even as a little kid. Bob Cole was a big presence on Canadian TV growing up. He would always be calling the games nationally on Hockey Night in Canada. So he was someone I listened to a lot.

"Chris Cuthbert, who's now at SportsNet, was an excellent Play-by-Play guy. Then, locally in Vancouver, Jim Hughson, who now has gone on to be the lead voice for Hockey Night in Canada and John Shorthouse are two other very strong Canucks Play-by-Play guys who really were big influences for me growing up as a fan of the team and following them closely.

"To have three excellent broadcasters who called games for the Canucks while I was growing up, in Robson, Hughson and Shorthouse, I think probably played a big role in my desire to want to call games.

"When you're trying to hone your craft, you'll listen to broadcasters who you think do a good job. You're not trying to copy them or steal things from them, but you can take elements from any broadcaster you listen to and apply them to your own call to try and make yourself better.

"So, when I was a kid, I didn't think about it too much. And then, when I was really pursuing it as a career, I think I've always sort of had my own style, although people would tell you that it's pretty evident that I've been influenced by some of the Vancouver Play-by-Play guys and a guy like John Shorthouse in particular. But that was never something that was really conscious for me. It was just sort of something that happened."

Now that we know about Batchelor's influences, let's delve into his journey from dreaming kid to Canucks radio man.

BATCHELOR: "The last couple of years of High School, I was trying to think about what I wanted to do for a career and covering sports in some capacity I thought would be an ideal career choice). That was something that jumped to the front of my mind. And that really sort of informed my choice of where I wanted to go to school.

"I actually went for one-year to Ryerson University, which is in Toronto, for their journalism degree. But that was more print journalism based, or at least that was my experience. It became pretty clear to me that I wanted to pursue Play-by-Play and pursue broadcasting.

"So, after one-year of Ryerson, I dropped out and was accepted into the British Columbia Institute of Technology. Their broadcast journalism program as it was called at the time, was widely recognized as one of the best in Western Canada, if not the best. Most of the guys who had the job or the jobs that I wanted had gone to BCIT. So, it was something I was thinking about even before I went to college; that I was looking at a guy like John Shorthouse and saying, 'I want to do that. He went to BCIT so I should probably go there too.'

"I didn't do a lot of Play-by-Play in College, actually. That program was more based towards teaching you how to become a newscaster. But those are all skills that you can then take and apply to sports. So, not just myself, but a number of my classmates went through that program and went on to become Sportscasters in some capacity or another.

"While I was attending BCIT, the Burnaby Express as they were called, who played in the BC Hockey League, allowed the BCIT campus radio station to broadcast some of their games. So I got to do a handful of those games while I was going to school. But anybody who was in the program who wanted to do sports put their name on that list. So there was a long list of people who wanted to call games.

"I maybe called three or four games of Play-by-Play during college and it was all hockey. I didn't have experience doing any other sports at that point. Then, after I graduated, I was working at what was then known as TEAM 1040 AM Radio. It was the lone all sports radio station in Vancouver at the time, but I was doing production work and doing the hourly sports update casts and doing a bit of reporting covering the BC Lions, the local CFL team. I was sort of biding my time while getting experienced in the industry and waiting for an opportunity to do Play-by-Play. I graduated from BCIT in 2010 and then I got my first Play-by-Play job for the Surrey Eagles of the BCHL in 2012-13.

"They're a Junior A hockey (team and league). It's essentially a feeder league for College Hockey where there's lots of players in that league who go on to get scholarships and play College Hockey in The States. I only did the Play-by-Play there for one-year, but the team was really good. They won the British Columbia Provincial Championship and went all the way to the National Championship Semi-Finals. So I got a lot of experience calling important playoff games that year.

"Then, that following off-season, the Vancouver Giants who play in the Western Hockey League, which is the top level of Junior Hockey in Canada; I knew they were looking for a Play-by-Play broadcaster. So I applied and I got that job, in part because I was working at TEAM 1040 AM Radio and the Vancouver Giants games were broadcast on TEAM 1040 AM Radio.

"So, people at the radio station knew me and that helped me get the job with the hockey team. That first year I just did the Play-by-Play. And then the following season, I was also hired full-time with the Giants to be the Director of Media Relations, as well as the Play-by-Play. I did that for three more seasons. So four-seasons in all with the Vancouver Giants; starting in 2013-14 and ending in '16-'17. Then, in the summer of 2017, the radio rights for the Canucks games changed stations. Rogers, who is the parent company of SportsNet and the SportsNet radio stations in Canada, acquired the rights.

"They were building a brand new sports radio station to compete with the station that I had previously worked at. And they acquired the Canucks rights as a result. So I applied at that point and was hired to do games for the Canucks."

So, Batchelor had quite the ladder-climbing journey. Once he got to the NHL though, he still needed to get comfortable in his own shoes -- just like any young broadcaster -- and he received terrific guidance from several broadcasters.

BATCHELOR: "Well, I would have to mention John Shorthouse, first of all, because he does the games on TV for the Canucks and I do the games on radio. So, we spend a ton of time together on the road and travel together and all that stuff. John's been a great mentor for me, giving advice and sort of showing me the ropes I guess, early on in my first season a bit. Jim Robson as well, actually, he's retired now obviously. I believe he's in his 80's. He's been someone who I've been able to chat with and he's been a tremendous resource for advice. Jim Hughson as well, he used to call Canucks games and now he's with Hockey Night in Canada, has been great.

"Another person who comes to mind for me is John Wiedeman, who calls the games for the Chicago Blackhawks on radio. He and I have had some really good conversations and he's been very kind to me. For the most part, you talk to broadcasters around the league and they're all really good guys. You all sort of immediately hit it off because you have something in common, which is your passion for the sport and your passion for Play-by-Play.

"A guy like Alex Faust, who does the LA Kings games, he's similar in age to me. So we're in some ways going through very similar experiences and it's a team in the same division, so we see each other a lot. He's a guy who I'll always stop and have a chat with. Even guys who I don't see as often, like Brendan Burke, who's a guy I always look forward to seeing and chatting with in the press box the two times a year we see the Islanders. I could probably list 10 more people who deserve to be included in that list, but those are the names who come to mind first."

With all the excellent sources of advice that Batchelor cultivated, he was and is well suited to run with his role of Canucks radio Play-by-Play man. And in case you're wondering who gave him the single best piece of advice, that would be Jim Robson, who explained to Batchelor about the importance of always making sure to mention how much time is on the clock and what the score is.

Since radio is a strictly audio medium, listeners can't see what's going on or any graphics on a screen, therefore it's the broadcasters responsibility to keep the listening audience well informed; not just of the time and score, but also of where the puck is.

BATCHELOR: "The most critical information you have to give a listener is where the puck is on the ice. I talk to broadcast students and I'll say it to them regularly. I could say, 'Brock Boeser passes to Quinn Hughes and he scores' and that would be accurate. But if you're listening on the radio, you have no idea what's happened. Whereas if I say 'Brock Boeser has the puck in the left circle, passes it back to the point, Hughes with a slap-shot scores and he beats the goaltender high glove side.' Then, suddenly you have a picture of that play in your mind. And that's, to me, especially in radio, crucially important to being an effective Play-by-Play broadcaster.

"It's not just describing what happened, but providing a degree of detail that isn't too much, because you don't want to essentially be an essay about what happened and not be able to keep up with the play, but you've got to be concise. You've got to be accurate and you have to paint a picture. And that really is something that I focus on before every single broadcast I do."

FAVORITE PLAYER(S) GROWING UP

BATCHELOR: "Well, I think like anyone else who grew up in the early-to-mid-90's, I loved Wayne Gretzky. And so I was a big fan of his as a player. But, growing up in the Vancouver area, in the equivalent of a Vancouver suburb, I was a Canucks fan from a very young age. Of course, the Canucks went to the Stanley Cup Final and lost to the Rangers in 1994. I was all-in following that team and Pavel Bure was my favorite player. He was the one guy who I tried to emulate, whether it was the way I played or just watching him play. He was always my guy, my favorite player, for sure."

HOCKEY AFTER DARK -- TALES AWAY FROM THE RINK

There's no worse feeling as a human being than feeling helpless. When there's nothing you can do but wait, it can be excruciating. And believe it or not, sports broadcasters will occasionally go through the same exact thing. Only, when they do so, it's often magnified. For Canucks radio man Brendan Batchelor, his helpless moment came on air; which is Trouble with a capital "T."

BATCHELOR: "One memorable period for me for the wrong reasons, which kind of is on the air and off the air is that I was losing my voice for a stretch of about a week-and-a-half during one season. I'd have to look back at the schedule to remember when it was exactly, but it was coming right out of the Christmas break. It probably would have been Christmas 2018 into 2019. Just on Boxing Day, I sort of had a little tickle in my throat and we had to broadcast a game and start a long road trip on the 27th.

"By the time we got to the broadcast on the 27th, my voice was sounding pretty gravelly. That was something where it was a busy road trip. So, you're calling a lot of games and not a lot of time. For the most part, I felt fine. Like I wasn't sick or feeling poorly. It's just my voice was not there, for whatever reason. You're on the road, so it's not like they can have someone come fill in for you, so you just sort of have to battle through it.

"My Color Analyst, Corey Hirsch, was really great about understanding that it meant he had to talk more on the broadcast, because I was struggling. I can remember being on the road for New Year's and all the other broadcasters were planning to go out and celebrate New Year's. And I was like, 'Oh, I just got to stay in my hotel room and hammer back tea and lozenges and lie in bed and try and make sure that I can get my voice back because that's something for broadcasters, that's the one thing you can't lose.

"I could have an awful flu and feel like garbage, but if I have my voice I can still broadcast the game and I'll deal with feeling like garbage. But when your voice isn't for you, you feel so helpless as a broadcaster. So that was one road trip that I really had to battle through. And Corey was really great about helping me out through that and we made it through. Just one of those things that people probably wouldn't think about, but that can be a broadcaster's worst nightmare that can happen."

BATCHELOR'S FAVORITE CANUCKS GAME HE'S CALLED

No matter how many or how few years you've been in a broadcast booth, you're bound to have a couple of moments that will stand the test of time in your memory bank as ones you'll never forget. Brendan Batchelor has been doing games on Canucks radio for less than a handful of years and during that time, the Canucks haven't been among the NHL's elite teams; although they are young, exciting and improving rapidly.

However, during Batchelor's brief tenure, he's already managed to rack up a trio of moments that will stay with him forever.

BATCHELOR: "I think Elias Pettersson's first game in the NHL against the Calgary Flames will always be memorable because he just sort of announced himself as an elite young player in the league in his very first game. I can remember how loud Rogers Arena was that night. For him to have such a great performance against the Calgary Flames in his first game.

"Also, certainly it was very different this year, calling the playoffs off a monitor remotely, but being able to call a series-clinching, overtime winning goal for the Canucks with Chris Tanev scoring in overtime for them to eliminate Minnesota in the play-in round is something that I'll always remember.
It'll always sort of be my first playoff overtime call. Although again, we weren't there. So, the emotion around it was very different calling it from the studio in Vancouver, as opposed to having a full arena exploding with a playoff overtime winner.

"And then, of course, Daniel and Henrik Sedin's last game, because those are guys who, when they broke into the league or when they were drafted by the Canucks, I was 10-years-old. So I grew up as a fan of theirs. I can remember waiting outside after Canuck practices to get their autograph when I was a kid. And then here I was, doing the Play-by-Play of their last home game, was the one that really stands out, because they combined for the overtime winner for the Canucks to beat the Coyotes in overtime.

"I can just remember the emotion around that game because the Canucks were out of the playoffs. It didn't really mean anything in the grand scheme of things, yet tickets were hard to come by in Vancouver for that game. And the building was absolutely packed. Just the roar of the crowd when those two guys combined to score that overtime winner.

"I can remember my producer, who is a little bit younger than me, he's in the booth with us every single game. He grew up as a fan of the Sedins too and when they scored that goal, he was sitting right next to me in the booth and he immediately erupted in tears just because of the emotion of their careers in Vancouver ending that way. So that's a game that really stands out to me as well."

SIGNATURE PHRASE

For many fans, when they think of their favorite broadcasters, they tend to think of one of two things. They either think of a memorable call from a favorite game. Or they think about a simple phrase the broadcaster often uses when the situation calls for it.

However, in Vancouver and around the world, Canucks fans who tune in on the radio are treated to a little something different. Instead of a catchphrase or saying, they are treated to an inclusive message from their broadcaster Brendan Batchelor. It's one of the most unique things I've ever heard a broadcaster do and I'll let Batchelor explain the rest.

BATCHELOR: "Traditionally in Vancouver, Jim Robson, was the Voice of the Canucks for many years and every game he would welcome, shut-ins, people in hospitals, the blind, people in prisons and he would sort of mention them every game as saying, 'we're welcoming all of these people who are tuning in this way.' And I know that meant a lot to a lot of people, to be included.

"So, when I got the Canucks job, I always really admired that he did that and I thought it was very commendable and it was clear that it meant a lot to the people who he would mention; people who are going through a difficult time, whether they're in hospital or going through something and they have to only tune into the game on the radio.

"I thought, 'is there something I can do that's similar? I'm not going to steal his tradition that he always did, but is there a way that I could include people and bring them in to make them feel like a part of the broadcast?' And the thing that came to mind for me was, it's the Vancouver Canucks and certainly we're on the air in Vancouver. Lots of people listen in Vancouver, but our broadcasts go out across the province of British Columbia, on a number of stations along our network. And then, in today's day and age, people can listen on the internet from all around the world. So, what I do every game and have done since I got the job is I will say, 'thanks for listening to our broadcast tonight, whether you're in Coquitlam, Cranbrook or wherever you're tuning in.'

"I always mention two towns or cities in British Columbia and I change which cities I mention every game. So, I might say, 'whether you're listening in Vancouver or Whistler,' one game and I might say, 'whether you're listening in Kelowna or Victoria,' the next game. But I specifically, when I got the job, wrote out a spreadsheet with 82 different combinations of cities so that I would have a unique couple of cities to mention for every game of the regular-season and so, that people around the province of British Columbia would feel included; where if you're in a city far away from Vancouver, way up North, like Fort St. John and you're listening to the game and you hear the broadcaster say, 'Hey, thanks for listening.'

"If you're in Fort St. John and you have a connection there where you're like, 'Hey, I'm in Fort St. John. This is someone who hasn't forgotten about people who are listening all around the province.' So that was sort of my first thought when I decided to do that. And then what I would add to it is, I would say, 'Hey, thanks for listening wherever you are.' I would mention the two cities and I would say, 'Hey, send us a tweet and let us know where you're listening from.' Just because in today's day and age with social media, that's a great way to engage fans and listeners.

"It's sort of grown into something pretty special where, we'll routinely have people tweet us saying, 'Hey, I'm listening in Australia' or 'I'm in England' or 'I'm in China' or 'I'm up early in the morning' or 'for me, it's the middle of the afternoon' or whatever. They'll send us photos of where they're listening to the game from.

"So, it really has sort of grown into something that for me is quite rewarding and pretty special to realize that it's very easy. It's the Vancouver Canucks. I live in the Vancouver area. We're very focused on the coverage we provide locally, but it really makes you think about the fact that there are people all over the world who are fans of this team and tune into the broadcast on a lot of nights.

"For many people who live outside the country and maybe the games aren't as easily accessible for them as they are in Canada, in the United States, it's their main way to stay in touch with the hockey team they love. So that to me is something that initially I just thought, 'Hey, let's be inclusive. Let's talk about other people in the province and other cities in the province and not just be very Vancouver based.' And now it's grown into something where you realize that the broadcast really has a reach that in the age of the internet and of social media, goes all the way around the world. And we have a way to connect with those people who are listening on the other side of the world too. So that's something that's pretty special."

MESSAGE TO CANUCKS FANS

As is a common theme amongst members of the sports media, it is a well known fact that without the fans our jobs would either A) not exist or B) they'd have a lot less meaning. So, each of the broadcasters in this book took a couple of minutes to address you, the fans, directly.

BATCHELOR: "Thank you to everyone who tunes into our broadcasts and is a fan of the Vancouver Canucks. As someone who grew up as a Canucks fan, I have an understanding of the passion people have for this team. And it's something I think about every game when I put on the headset to broadcast the game. It's a unique privilege that I have, to be able to broadcast these games and to be able to connect with so many fans and to be able to be the voice of some of the big moments for the hockey club and hopefully some very big moments in the years to come with the young core group they have right now. So, without the fans, I wouldn't have a job. I wouldn't be able to live my dream.

"I just really appreciate everyone who follows this team and has a passion for this team, because I'm someone who, as a kid growing up, I had a passion for this team. It's something pretty special. It has been a big part of my life and continues to be a big part of my life now that I'm broadcasting the game. I hope we're doing a good job in conveying the emotions of the fan base and the passion the fans have for the hockey club. And as I said before, hopefully there'll be some big moments and memorable games and maybe even a Stanley Cup sometime here in the next few years to bring everyone together."

VEGAS GOLDEN KNIGHTS

DAN D'UVA
RADIO: PLAY-BY-PLAY

First Season on Golden Knights Radio: 2017-18
Seasons on Golden Knights Radio (including 2020-21): 4

Birthday: February 20, 1985 Born in: Nutley, NJ

College/University: Syracuse University and Fordham University

BIOGRAPHY

As a sports fan growing up "not 10-minutes from Brendan Byrne Arena " in New Jersey, Dan D'Uva had a number or professional sports team to root for. And while the Jets and Mets provided more heartbreak than anything else, the Devils lavished him with three Stanley Cup championships during an eight-year span from 1995-2003.

It wasn't just the players on the ice who D'Uva loved. He also tuned into the Devils radio and television broadcasts every chance he got. Whether it was the team of Mike Miller and Randy Velischek on radio or Doc Emrick and Chico Resch on television, D'Uva didn't care, he loved them all. And that's the foundation for his career as a broadcaster.

When he was 14-years-old, the Devils were embarking on their second Stanley Cup championship (1999-2000 season) and D'Uva would go to games with a microcassette tape recorder, sit in the upper deck of the arena and practice his Play-by-Play skills. After all, he wanted to call his High School's hockey games and he needed to get as much practice in as possible.

What D'Uva would do is, he and his buddy Guy Benson would position themselves between the upper and lower decks inside the Devils arena. They'd be perfectly placed between the two broadcast locations and whenever one broadcast was in a commercial break, they'd go over to that broadcast booth area and wait around to try and meet the likes of Doc Emrick and Mike Miller. So, they got to know the Devils broadcasters and over time developed relationships with them, to the point where D'Uva would take the microcassette tapes he made of himself and he'd show them to Miller and Emrick in order to get their feedback on what he was doing right and wrong.

That feedback proved to be invaluable as he used their advice to further hone his skills and when he eventually graduated from College, he ended up as the broadcaster for the Trenton Devils, who functioned as New Jersey's ECHL affiliate.

And after a successful run working for the franchise that so enamored him as a youth, D'Uva moved up to the AHL with the Syracuse Crunch (who are affiliated with the Tampa Bay Lightning). D'Uva spent five-years with the Crunch before then getting his NHL break and joining the Vegas Golden Knights in 2017. And a whole lot happened during that journey from High School to the NHL.

Bringing things back to that 1999-2000 hockey season, a young Dan D'Uva and his friend Guy Benson were hoping to call their High School's hockey games and boy did they get more than they could have ever dreamed.

D'UVA: "It so happened that the Ridgewood Maroons Varsity Hockey team had an incredible, magical run in the New Jersey State playoffs that year. Ridgewood had only had a Varsity Hockey program for a few years. It was not a long storied program that had been around a long time. They'd only had a team for a few years, but they reached the State Semi-Finals.

"They were in the Final Four in the state of New Jersey and because the program was new and had yet to experience great success, we, as the broadcasters, were welcomed into the fold with open arms. So when there was a team bonding trip to go paintballing, we, as the broadcasters, were included in that. When the team would go on long bus rides from Ridgewood down to Red Bank, we were 14, 15-years-old. We didn't have Driver's Licenses.

"So we would travel on the team bus. They really made sure that we were part of that group. So we felt like a part of that team. The players, the coaches, the parents of the players, even the bus driver were part of that team. And like I said, they had this incredible season and went on to win enough playoff games. It was such a special experience that particular hockey season."

With experiences like that before he even got to College, D'Uva was well positioned to become a highly successful sports Play-by-Play announcer. But he also likes to credit those who influenced him, because without their influence, he might not have chosen to go down that path. And the list of those he liked to listen to -- and study -- is an impressive one. The likes of Doc Emrick, Marv Albert, Kenny Albert, Sam Rosen, Jiggs, McDonald, Howie Rose, Mike Miller and Gary Thorne, were the ones who D'Uva would listen to any and every chance he got, with Doc and Marv being particularly high priorities to listen to.

Their collective influences stuck with D'Uva as he graduated from High School and went off to College to continue to hone his craft. First it was off to Syracuse and then to Fordham. And along the way, he also became involved with the Cape Cod Baseball League, which holds a special place in his heart, even to this day. In fact, D'Uva was a pretty decent Varsity Baseball player himself, so even though he's been working in hockey, baseball still remains part of his life too.

In the summer of 2003, after graduating High School and before shipping off to College, D'Uva and his pal Benson successfully pitched their idea to the Chatham A's of the Cape Cod League. At the time, there were no broadcasts of the Cape Cod League, plus D'Uva and Benson wanted to continue to call games together even though they were going to different Colleges. So, with the green light from the A's, they were able to keep their dynamic duo intact and that led to something much larger.

To this day, D'Uva is involved with the Cape Cod League as he hires the student broadcasters who currently call games throughout the league. And he coaches them as well. It's his way of passing on the lessons he learned from the likes of Doc Emrick, Mike Miller and others. It hasn't mattered whether he was in Trenton, Syracuse or now in Vegas, but every summer, D'Uva continues to come back to the league for a few weeks to coach up the new crop of broadcasters. And that, as much as his own broadcasting career, is what defines him.

FAVORITE PLAYER(S) GROWING UP

D'UVA: "I wore number four for Scott Stevens. The only problem was, I am not nearly as big as Scott Stevens. So my career as a defenseman was not going to go very far. I played defense and wore number four, largely because of Scott Stevens. I always loved Marty Brodeur, but I was never a goalie. I think maybe I dressed as a goalie for one or two games for my roller hockey team in High School. I was most enamored with Scott Stevens, his tough, gritty, leadership qualities. He just seemed to be the epitome of what a hockey player should be and I had so much respect for him. I think I also went as Scott Stevens for Halloween one year and put paint on my face to make it look like I'd been in a fight."

HOCKEY AFTER DARK -- TALES AWAY FROM THE RINK

When you're a professional sports broadcaster, beyond really knowing your sport and your team, you also need to know two things. One, you need to know how to appreciate the opportunity you have. Two, you need to know how to travel and have fun.

It's safe to say, Dan D'Uva certainly appreciates the position he's in with the Golden Knights and he most certainly knows how to have some responsible fun. That being said, I'm going to let him take over the story from here in regards to some of his favorite experiences that have taken place outside the broadcast booth.

D'UVA: "Here's the backstory. It's the launch of the franchise. There was the shooting that Sunday night, October first. The team went on the road (to start the season). They beat Dallas. They beat Arizona.

Now they've come back home and they've changed the entire structure and mood of the opening ceremony.

"But it's still the launch of the franchise. And they did it just right. That whole day and that game will always be memorable. And thank goodness they won. They won 5-2. They were winning 4-0 in the middle of the first period. So they coasted to a win.

"Now, there's this promenade outside of T-Mobile Arena that looks down upon the Plaza and this large promenade balcony area was reserved by the team for the players, coaches, family members, a number of players had their parents visiting and whatnot. Then you had the coaches and Bill Foley, the Owner was there of course and a number of the executives. And of course, the broadcasters.

"We were still getting to know each other. You're meeting players and their parents. Everybody was brand new. So you were still getting to know everybody. Folks had, for the most part, trickled out and the crowd was dwindling. And Dave Goucher and I were still there exchanging stories, because, of all the people there, he and I have the most similar background in terms of working up the hockey Play-by-Play ladder; from College to the minors and then to the NHL. Again, we had not known each other. I certainly knew of Dave. I admired Dave a ton. He was one of the guys I really enjoyed listening to. I will always remember Dave and I trading hockey broadcasting stories.

"We were among the last handful of people at this post-game event. We were just sitting outside T-Mobile Arena, looking around, almost in disbelief of the scene we were witnessing and the events that had transpired in the previous week. Here we were, you almost had to pinch yourself. Like, is this really going on? I remember Dave telling me about his very first NHL broadcast, because I had just done my first NHL broadcast. He was telling me about how he'd interviewed Pat Burns and how nervous he was. I just remember thinking how neat it is to have someone to share this experience with.

"In other words, when you're broadcasting minor league hockey, you're the only broadcaster. You don't have a Color Commentator. There's not another Play-by-Play guy who works for the team. In the minors, you're the only broadcaster. So, now, all of a sudden here I have, not only someone who I was working with as professional colleagues, but I think Dave Goucher is one of the best broadcasters in the sport.

And here we are, I'm going to get to spend time with this guy. He was so down to earth.

"We started telling each other Bruce Springsteen stories, cause we're both huge Bruce Springsteen fans. So, I think that post-game conversation, fueled by several glasses of red wine, which we mutually enjoy, will always stick with me. And that'll lead me to one other story with Dave Goucher.

"We were playing the Devils in 2018. We were playing the Devils on a Sunday. We flew from Vegas to New Jersey on Saturday afternoon. Dave has a friend who can get us tickets -- we had to pay for them -- but he could get us tickets, at face value, to see (Bruce) Springsteen on Broadway and we landed in New Jersey later than originally planned.

"We kind of figured we'd catch a train or whatever, but it ended up being so close (time wise). So, we got an Uber from the hotel in Short Hills (New Jersey), all the way to Broadway. There was so much traffic. We got out of the Uber and we walked the last few blocks to the Walter Kerr Theater. We got there, if the show was supposed to be curtaining up at eight, we got there at 7:52.

"We got the tickets, we went upstairs and we knew the show was going to start right on time. There wasn't going to be any delay. There was no warm-up show. And the woman who was serving drinks was starting to pack up the drinks, the wine and everything. And I said, 'sorry, mam, I'm so sorry. Is there any chance we can get two glasses of red wine?' And she put her arms up, looked around and to no one in particular exclaimed, 'these are my last customers!'

"She took the bottle of red wine and filled up two plastic Springsteen cups, 'glug, glug, glug.' I think they were $25 each. I was all too happy to pay for it, because I handed one glass to Dave. We quickly got to our seats and as we were sitting down, the lights went down and Springsteen came out and it was an amazing show.

"Then, at the end of the show, everyone's standing to give a standing ovation. Springsteen bows to the crowd. Then he turns to his right and bows toward one of the boxes. And we see (former) President Barack Obama waving to Bruce and being hustled out the side door by the Secret Service. 'Like, Oh my goodness, we got to see the same show as the President.' It was a great show. And we went after the show, across the street and had a pint or two at the Irish Pub there. Then we walked down through Times Square, had a couple slices of pizza and then got back in an Uber to Short Hills, New Jersey and rested up in time for the Devils game the next day."

D'UVA'S FAVORITE GOLDEN KNIGHTS GAME HE CALLED

Nobody in their wildest dreams could have predicted the type of season the Vegas Golden Knights ended up having their first year in the NHL (2017-18). The Golden Knights shattered expectations and records with the most successful inaugural season an Expansion Team ever had. And that included going all the way to the Stanley Cup Final.

While the Knights only won one game against the Capitals in The Final -- they won Game One 6-4 in Vegas -- it was still an unbelievable season for the new Vegas franchise.

Prior to their Game One victory, in which Tomas Nosek had two-goals -- including the game-winner -- Dan D'Uva was able to bring a little extra attention to the franchise as he unofficially played host/tour guide for Mike "Doc" Emrick. D'Uva and Emrick go way back and it was a joy for D'Uva to be able to share this experience with "Doc" ahead of them both calling that night's game -- Emrick on television and D'Uva on radio.

D'UVA: "It was neat for a few reasons. I'll start with going into the Stanley Cup Final. First of all, it's just amazing that they're in the Stanley Cup Final. And Mike 'Doc' Emrick, had not been to a Golden Knights game the whole season, either in Vegas or at another venue. So he was coming to Vegas just to broadcast The Cup Final. But he wanted to not only prepare for the games by doing the normal media ops, he also wanted to see the team practice.

"He wanted to see the team practice facility, which was not going to be available for the regular media. So, I knew when he was coming in and I said, 'well, Doc, I could pick you up and we'll have breakfast and we'll go and I'll drive you out to the practice rink.' He said, 'great.' So I did. I picked him up at his hotel. We drove back. I kind of showed him around a little bit. We had breakfast at a coffee shop that I go to almost every game day when we're at home.

"So we went over there and had coffee and a breakfast sandwich. I remember as we sat down, they put us at a table kind of near the entrance. And Doc said to me, 'would you prefer to sit with your back to the door?' And I thought, 'why would he ask me that?' And then I realized he was concerned that people would recognize me and might bother me. And I'm thinking, 'no, that's okay, Doc, why don't you sit with your back to the door?' People are gonna recognize him a lot more than they're going to recognize me. But very thoughtful of him, as usual.

"He was wearing his Bowling Green polo shirt. He knew he couldn't favor the Golden Knights or the Capitals, but he knew that both General Managers, Brian MacLellan for the Caps and George McPhee for the Golden Knights, were both Bowling Green alumni and had been teammates there. So he was wearing his white Bowling Green polo shirt to breakfast.

"Then, we went over to the practice facility and I kind of sent a text message to our PR person to let him know, 'just so you know, I'm bringing Mike Emrick over.' And I think he kind of passed the word around to George McPhee and to Bill Foley. This was a Sunday, there was going to be a team practice, but nobody would have been in the office. It was sort of a quiet time at the facility.

"So I think when I gave them that heads up, a couple of people, including George and Bill Foley, made it a point of being there to say hello to Doc. George and Doc know each other, but Bill Foley had never met Mike Emrick before. So I was there to introduce Mike Emrick to Bill Foley, which was a pretty neat moment. And they went over and watched practice together.

"Then I drove Doc back to the hotel and there was the regular media availability that afternoon at T-Mobile Arena. So that was a pretty neat set up to the start of the Stanley Cup Final, because now, all of a sudden, eyeballs are on the Golden Knights in a way that they had not been all season; even with the incredible regular-season and playoff run, there's something different about the Stanley Cup Final."

MESSAGE TO GOLDEN KNIGHTS FANS

As is a common theme amongst members of the sports media, it is a well known fact that without the fans our jobs would either A) not exist or B) they'd have a lot less meaning. So, each of the broadcasters in this book took a couple of minutes to address you, the fans, directly.

D'UVA: "What comes to mind for me is the relationship that I attempt to develop with the listener. And I would hope that the listener appreciates the relationship that I'm attempting to build every minute I'm on the air. I mentioned Marty Glickman so often because he had so many great philosophies about sports broadcasting. And among the most notable, in my mind, 'is consider the listener, put the listener first.' And when Marty says, 'consider the listener,' it's singular, not plural. That we as broadcasters, think about that one person on the other end of the radio and we're connecting with you. Well, there might be hundreds, thousands, maybe millions of people tuned in.

"Right now, It's just me and you. And I try very hard to cultivate that sense, that relationship with the listener -- singular. And when I meet people who listen to the broadcast, they speak to me as if they know me. And that is a tremendous compliment. They might not realize that they're complimenting me, but when they speak with me in a way that is so familiar that they've had so many conversations with me before, that it would be normal to speak with me that way, when in fact I've never met that person. I take that as a huge compliment, because it means that my desire to build a relationship with you, the listener, to create that space through the airwaves is progressing. We're getting somewhere.

"I think that some fans like announcers who have clever catchphrases, who have a homer sound, they get really excited when the home team does something good, but they sound like they're in a funeral home when the other team does something good. Don't get me wrong, I want the team I'm covering to do well. After all, I am employed by them.

"But at the same time, what's most important to me is that you can trust me. When Marty Glickman says, 'consider the listener,' he adds, 'with accuracy, fairness, and objectivity.' And I remember talking to Mike Emrick about this, being a team's announcer and Doc had done the Flyers and had also filled in for some Rangers broadcasts. Now, here, he was the voice of the Devils. How could he be the broadcaster he needed to be while not demonstrating any sort of undue subjectivity? He didn't want to be a homer and at the same time, didn't want to pretend like he was not the Devils broadcaster, right? And the advice that Lou Lamoriello offered Mike Emrick, which Mike Emrick has offered to me is, 'simply be real.' That might be over simplistic, but it made all the sense in the world to me.

"In other words, I need you the listener to trust what I'm saying and that the information I'm going to provide to you is not through rose colored glasses. I'm not sugarcoating things. I'm going to give you the information as accurately as I can. Are there moments when I might offer a little bit of an opinion? Maybe. But I try to limit that as much as I can, because everybody has an opinion. So, it's real. I don't pretend to not have opinions. I just try to limit when I share them.

"I might present a story in a particular way that might indicate my feeling about something, but I don't want to make a decision for you. I don't want to draw a conclusion for you. I want to help you toward a conclusion, toward an opinion. In other words, think of a little kid who's throwing a temper tantrum and a mom or dad says to the kid, 'stop that. Don't do that. Do this instead.'

"Well, that only sets the kid off even more, right? People don't want to be told what to do or what to think. People want to feel as though they've made their own decisions and drawn their own conclusions. And that is what I'm trying to do as a broadcaster in developing that relationship, developing that trust and helping you to make your own conclusions. And that was one of the challenges with Vegas that I think people ask me a lot about, how much do you need to educate the fans in Vegas? They've never had an NHL team before. And I thought, well, that's true, but they've had minor league hockey there. Oh and by the way, this is 2017. It's not 1927.

"We have the internet, we have YouTube, we have broadcast cable television. If somebody is not sure about something, they can Google it in three seconds or they can learn the game the way I did, by watching and listening. Mike Emrick didn't sit me down and give me Hockey 101.

"No, I learned from watching the games, listening to the games, playing the game. Sure, I had coaches and whatever who helped me learn the game. No doubt about it. But I learned the game by watching and listening and picking it up as I observed. And I want to do the same thing for the fans of Vegas and for any fan, because I don't want to dumb it down for you.

"I'm not going to talk down to you and put you in a place where you feel like you don't know as much as I do. That's not fair to you. That's condescending. And again, if I'm trying to develop a relationship with you, I don't want to be condescending. Who would want to be friends with someone who's condescending? That's no good. And at the same time, I also don't want to assume that, you know everything that I know, because that's condescending too. That could be taken the wrong way.

"So, I try to be as real as I can be. When there's an icing, I might not recite the rules for icing but I might paint the picture to show you where the puck is going. And the player doesn't get to the invisible line created by the face-off dots. So, the linesman blows his whistle. It's another icing against the Golden Knights. Context clues, right? This is all a long way of saying, I care very much about the relationship that I build with the listener. And I hope that the passion a fan has for the team, they recognize is the same passion that I put into the broadcast for him or her."

DAVE GOUCHER
TV: PLAY-BY-PLAY

First Season on Golden Knights TV: 2017-18
Seasons on Golden Knights TV (including 2020-21): 4

Birthday: July 23, 1969 Hometown: Pawtucket, RI

College/University: Boston University

BIOGRAPHY

Growing up in New England, Dave Goucher was surrounded by sports, with baseball and hockey being his favorites. He played both, but eventually one had to win out over the other. And the winner by technical knockout was hockey. Goucher started playing hockey at the age of five and he loved it from the second he first set his skates on the ice.

It's actually a rather interesting story of how that happened.

GOUCHER: "A girl who lived across the street from me, her boyfriend at the time, was an Assistant Coach for a Squirt level hockey team. So you're talking about five, six and seven-year-old kids. He asked my parents, 'what do you think about Dave playing hockey?' And that was kind of the impetus for it. I think my parents, like a lot of parents, as their kids start to get a little bit older, were looking for activities and once I started, I couldn't get enough of it."

I guess hockey fans should try and track down that Assistant Coach and say "thank you," because who knows if Goucher would have ended up gracing the hockey world with his broadcasting skills if not for that initial push to play the frozen sport we all love.

While you all set about finding that Assistant Coach, I'll get back to telling Goucher's story of how he ended up as the Golden Knights' Play-by-Play voice.

Along with playing the sport of hockey, Goucher and his family would go to the occasional Bruins game to cheer on their team. But even when he wasn't there in person, Goucher would always make sure to tune in to the broadcasts of the Bruins' games. Whether it was listening to Bob Wilson on radio or Fred Cusick on television, Goucher would be listening intently to what was going on in the game.

Wilson's voice especially stuck with Goucher as he loved listening to the baritone, ebb and flow of Wilson's Play-by-Play style. And that appropriately measured style was especially important to Goucher.

Eventually, Goucher ended up pursuing a career in broadcasting when he came to the realization that his hockey playing skills weren't going to distinguish him enough to make it as a player. He did play through High School and a year of prep school, but he realized that while he was a good player, there are tons of good players all over the place and that he just wasn't going to be able to take that particular path any further.

It was going to be a stretch in Goucher's own words, to walk on to the Boston University hockey team. B.U. had a great communications program though and the idea of broadcasting, which had been in the back of his mind for awhile, was now going to come to the forefront.

In fact, that idea had been percolating for years as Goucher would "announce" the games played in the street in front of his house. That started around the age of seven or eight, so the idea of broadcasting certainly had plenty of time to marinate.

So, since he wasn't going to be playing for Boston University -- he was the last JV cut his Sophomore year -- and he still wanted to remain part of the sport, he decided to get involved with the student radio station. Goucher started calling games during his Junior year and as he put it, "nobody listened and nobody cared. Which was probably a good thing. They weren't missing much because I wasn't very good."

As a young broadcaster he had room to grow, which he did. In addition to calling B.U. hockey games, he also did some of their football and baseball games. By the time he graduated in 1993, Goucher estimated he had called roughly 45 hockey games, which was enough for him to make a demo tape.

Goucher then took the tape and sent it to the teams in the ECHL, AHL and IHL.

As luck would have it, an ECHL team in Wheeling, West Virginia, who had a split affiliation with the Montreal Canadiens and the

Edmonton Oilers, called up Goucher and said they liked his tape. So, he drove 12-hours in his car down to Wheeling to meet with the team's General Manager, as well as some other people and after a little over a day down in West Virginia, he drove back to Rhode Island waiting to hear what would come next.

Roughly three-weeks after the interview, he received the call that the team was hiring him, to his own stunned disbelief and late in the summer of 1993, he packed up his stuff and moved down to Wheeling to begin his broadcasting career.

GOUCHER: "Wheeling was close to Pittsburgh and the Penguins had won the Stanley Cup in '91 and '92. So, now it's '93 and there was a very rich hockey environment in Wheeling because of its proximity to Pittsburgh and the success the Penguins had. I was there from '93 to '95, so I did two-seasons and the team was a big fish in a small pond. Our building held 5,400 people. We averaged 5,000 fans a night. We did all of our games on FM Radio and we did a dozen games on television on the local NBC affiliate. So it was a great experience for me.

"My first year, they lost in the Semi-Finals. The second year they had the best record in the regular-season and got upset in the first-round of the playoffs. So, I did those two seasons and then the Providence Bruins in the American Hockey League, Boston's farm team, were looking for an announcer. That was the summer of '95. Again, I threw my hat in the ring and was fortunate enough to land the job. So, I did two-years in the ECHL and then made the jump to the AHL.

"I was there for five-years, from 1995 to 2000. My fourth year, the team won the Calder Cup. Peter Laviolette was the Head Coach and Bill Armstrong was the Assistant Coach. They took over a team that finished dead last in the AHL in 1997-98 and turned it around and won the Calder Cup the following season. So they literally went from worst in the league to winning the championship in a year. So, that was a great experience to be around that group.

"Then, the next year, 1999-2000, we lost in the Conference Final in seven-games and that ended up being my last season, because the Boston Bruins were looking for an announcer. At that point in my life, the only job I really ever wanted was the Bruins radio job. They were conducting the search and there were probably 60 people who were in the running. Then they narrowed it down to 10 to five, to three and finally to one. And fortunately enough for me, I was that person. So, at that point, that was the dream job for me. And I was lucky to do that for 17-years."

After 17-years in his dream role, Goucher began to feel like he had maxed out what he wanted to do, to a certain extent. He wasn't actively looking to leave. But when the Vegas television job came about, it was "too good an opportunity to pass up." He wanted something unique and wasn't going to leave Boston for any old job. But Vegas was't any old job. He was making the move from radio to television -- in which he'd had a drop of experience over the course of his career -- and he was going to be the first ever voice of a professional team in Las Vegas. So, from a growth perspective, it was exactly the type of gig that he wanted.

It wasn't quite as simple as just applying and landing the job though. There were over 200 people who were interested in the role and who wouldn't be? Lucky for Goucher, an old Bruins connection was in charge of putting together the entire communications team in Vegas. Eric Tosi had been the Media Relations Manager for the Bruins and had known Goucher for over 10-years.

It started out as just a casual conversation, but things quickly began to fall into place and eventually it worked out where Goucher was brought over to the team with Shane Hnidy to form the first ever Golden Knights television broadcast team.

FAVORITE PLAYER(S) GROWING UP

GOUCHER: "If you go back to the early-80s, Ray Bouorque would be high on the list. Rick Middleton, Barry Pederson, they were kind of the core guys on those teams. Terry O'Reilly. They would all be on the list."

HOCKEY AFTER DARK -- TALES AWAY FROM THE RINK

In the National Hockey League, you are not on an island as a broadcaster. You are part of a team or crew. There are many moving pieces and parts. There are relationships that are built. In the Minor Leagues it's just you, so it's a very different feel.

Dave Goucher knows the difference very well and it's that special bond he's developed with his fellow Golden Knights broadcasters that means so much to him.

GOUCHER: "One of the biggest things for Myself, Shane (Hnidy), Dan (D'Uva) and Gary (Lawless), is the bond we've all formed as a group. We have a media bus that we have on the road. We fly to a city, we land and we hop on our own media bus, we're not on the team bus. So the back of that bus is just a real special spot. We have music going, we're singing, we're telling jokes, we're talking hockey.

"So, I think that's the biggest thing, is just the comradery among the four of us. I think a funny story would be, we were in Nashville this year and I love music. I try to play the guitar. Shane had a friend who was a musician in Nashville and he convinced the guy to get me up on stage. He, I and another guitarist, we played 'Let Her Cry' by Hootie and the Blowfish. So I played guitar and sang it. That was a pretty nerve wracking experience to say the least.

"There were probably 30 people in the bar, but it looked like 3,000 when you're sitting on that small stage. The other thing that probably comes to mind is when the team won the Western Conference in 2018. We came back to Vegas from Winnipeg and kind of our whole group went to the Cosmo on the strip and had a little celebration. Shane and I, especially, we're very close. Our families are very close.

"We spend a lot of time together. I tell people, the reason that it works on television, in my opinion for us, is because of all the time we spend together when we're not on television. That chemistry, it's hard to find. You can't fake it. I think either you have it or you don't."

GOUCHER'S FAVORITE GOLDEN KNIGHTS GAME CALLED

There have been and will continue to be many things written and said about the tremendous first season the Vegas Golden Knights had in 2017-18. The instant success the team had was astounding and early in the regular-season there were many skeptics who repeatedly dismissed it as a fluke. No team could be this good right out of the gate as an Expansion Franchise. That was a common criticism levied against the Golden Knights. People kept waiting for them to come back down to Earth.

Well, that never happened and arguably still hasn't even four-years into the Golden Knights' existence. But when Tampa Bay came to town for the first time in December 2017, that was the turning point of when a lot of people started to believe this team really was as good as it seemed.

You see, the Lightning came into Vegas on December 19, 2017, touting the best record in the NHL and were just dominating their opponents. If ever there was a team that was going to cut Vegas down to size, it was the Lightning. People were sure Tampa was going to win.

Um...about that…

Things started off well for Tampa, as the visitors led 2-0 after 20-minutes of play. But Vegas tied the game with two in the second second period and then took the lead on a Erik Haula power-play goal early in the third period. The Lightning came back to tie the game at 3-3 on a Victor Hedman goal with just under four-minutes remaining in regulation. Overtime looked likely, even with Vegas on the power-play as time wound down.

GOUCHER: "Tampa Bay came into Vegas in December with the best record in the league, led the league in every category and Shea Theodore scored with 2.3 seconds left, on the power-play, to win the game. I thought the roof was going to come off T-Mobile, it was just so loud. The building exploded."

You read that right. Vegas' Shea Theodore scored with 2.3 seconds left on the clock to win the game for the home team 4-3. And while two points in the standings are always nice, the win gave a new sense of credibility to the young franchise as many people started to truly believe they were for real.

MESSAGE TO GOLDEN KNIGHTS FANS

As is a common theme amongst members of the sports media, it is a well known fact that without the fans our jobs would either A) not exist or B) they'd have a lot less meaning. So, each of the broadcasters in this book took a couple of minutes to address you, the fans, directly.

GOUCHER: "It's been incredibly humbling to see how much they love the game and they love this team. When I picked up and moved everything, my whole life out here. My wife and I came out here three-years ago, we didn't know what to expect. And it's been beyond belief. It's exceeded every possible expectation, from how welcoming people have been, how beautiful this area of the country is and how fantastic our quality of life is. The climate is unbelievable. The ease with which you can get around is great and just how much they love this team and they love the sport.

"So, that for me is incredibly gratifying, especially coming from a market where, you've four major league teams, you've got really good college sports. And teams in that city have been around forever. The Bruins are an Original 6 team. They've all had great success over the years. So, to leave that city, in that market and come to a city where they never had a major league team and to see it grow into all that it's become in three short years is incredible."

SHANE HNIDY
TV: COLOR ANALYST

First Season on Golden Knights TV: 2017-18
Seasons on Golden Knights TV (including 2020-21): 4

Birthday: November 8, 1975 Hometown: Neepawa, Manitoba

College/University: N/A

BIOGRAPHY

Shane Hnidy grew up in a small town in which he estimated there were about 3,500 people. So, in order to create enough sports teams, everybody needed to play. Not that he minded. He loved sports. Sports was his life. He played baseball, football, basketball, volleyball, golf, tennis and of course, hockey; which was the most prominent.

He started out learning how to power skate and then by the ages of four, five, six, he started to play the game. Hnidy and his friends would play road hockey in minus 30-degrees celsius in the winter time and they'd use the snowbanks on the sides of the road as boards.

By the time he was 14, Hnidy stopped playing other sports, with the exception of golf and focused solely on hockey. Hockey was the sport he excelled at and when he was a Junior in High School, he moved away from home to play Junior Hockey for the Swift Current Broncos in the WHL.

He was traded during the following season to the Prince Albert Raiders. That was the 1992-93 season. Then, in 1994, he was drafted in the seventh-round by the Buffalo Sabres. Of course, shortly after the draft, the NHL went through a lockout, so his first pro camp was wiped away.

HNIDY: "Then the next year, unfortunately I didn't agree then. I took the long road, played out my full Junior time till I was 20-years-old. I thought about going to a Canadian University. Then, at that time I got a call to go play in the East Coast Hockey League in Baton Rouge with the Kingfish. Funny story, the Head Coach of that team was Pierre McGuire.

"I had a blast. I was there a couple of months and then I was called up to the Saint John Flames of the American Hockey League, who were affiliated with Calgary. I finished the season (1996-97) there. Then I signed a year in the IHL with the Grand Rapids Griffins and played one-year in the IHL and then I signed my first pro contract with the Detroit Red Wings.

"They were basically a Hall of Fame team. So I spent two-years in their minor league system. Detroit only called up two guys during that time, which, nowadays, is unheard of. But back then, that was the Scotty Bowman way. If they needed someone, they signed a wily old vet. Then they traded my rights to the Ottawa Senators and I made the Senators in 2000 and started my NHL career.

"I played for a bunch of teams and finished with the Bruins in 2011. I was with them for their Cup win. Strange story. The season before I was with Minnesota. I played previously with Boston. I did a year in between with the Wild. And then I went to Arizona's camp and tore my rotator cuff in camp without a contract.

"I went back to Manitoba, Winnipeg where my family was without a contract, without a future. I was kind of feeling sorry for myself and my family gave me a big kick in the rear and said, 'why don't you try and work your way back? You could get a late contract.' I did some aggressive rehab, cause it's a five to six month rehab. In January Boston called and said, they were looking for depth, 'let us know how you feel in a month.' I went out and they signed me and I did that Cup run.

"But in the meantime, I was able to, for the first time, kind of think of what I was going to be. I looked at my options. I did some radio shows and talked about hockey and really enjoyed it. So, I went on to win The Cup with the Bruins and that summer, being in Winnipeg where our home was, the Jets were coming back and I got a call, actually the day I had the Stanley Cup driving from Winnipeg in the limo with my family to Neepawa, Manitoba for the celebration.

"I got a call from TSN Radio 1290, which was starting up and with the return of the Jets, they were looking for an Analyst. I said, 'well, I'm very interested. Right now I'm kind of busy. I'll get back to you in a few days.'"

After a few days, Hnidy decided he was all in on a career as a broadcaster and things quickly fell into place for him to debut on radio with the newly returned Winnipeg Jets.

HNIDY: "I broke in right away in 2011-12, the first season the Winnipeg Jets returned. I became an Analyst on radio. So I spent two-years on the radio. I think it was during Year Two that someone couldn't make it to the game and I was thrown between the glass to do TV for the first time. Doing radio is certainly the best way, especially for a former player, to step in. It's the best way to learn, to talk and to have the Analyst learn the ins and outs, the timing of when to jump in and how to describe a play. When I did the TV game, it was seamless for whatever reason. I remember going home that night and saying, 'now I know what I want to do. I want to analyze games on TV.'"

While doing games for the Jets, Hnidy was able to learn on the fly how to be an Analyst and he credits several broadcasters in helping him learn the nuances of the trade. Among them are Brian Munz, Rick Ralph and especially Dennis Beyak.

From there, Hnidy continued to hone his skills and when the opportunity to join the Vegas Golden Knights came about in 2017, he was excited about the possibility of joining a new franchise and helping build hockey in the non-traditional market that was Las Vegas. Like many people, he threw his hat in the ring and when the name was pulled out of the hat, it read Shane Hnidy, so Hnidy joined the new franchise and hasn't looked back.

FAVORITE PLAYER(S) GROWING UP

HNIDY: "In the '80s, I was an Oilers fan. Wayne Gretzky, when he came in, kind of the age I was at, that was the team. They were exciting. And I think it was because my brother was older and he was an Islanders fan. So I think I kind of picked the Oilers just so we could go back and forth. I also liked Cam Neely of the Bruins and I also liked Marty McSorley, because he was a forward who moved to defense. And I did that my junior year. He played a tough game. I liked the guys who played more of a hard nose game."

HOCKEY AFTER DARK -- A PICTURE SAYS IT ALL

The first-year of existence for the Vegas Golden Knights was really something to behold. It started with as dark a moment as there can be, a mass shooting in the city of Las Vegas. But through the darkness came light as the new franchise was able to help heal the city and galvanize its new fan base by putting together a season for the history books.

In many ways, taking on the task of healing the city helped to also bring the new team together much quicker than normal and that went for the broadcast team as well. Everybody, players, coaches, management and broadcasters. They all came from various places across the hockey world to be part of this new franchise. They were a bunch of moving parts, but by the time the Western Conference Final ended in triumph over Winnipeg, they were one well oiled machine. And a family too.

HNIDY: “We're a close knit group. One thing that stands out was when they (the Knights) won the Western Conference championship the first year in Winnipeg. The picture we took together captured the moment. It was such an unexpected season with how it came together.

“It started with tragedy in October, then this team comes along and turns themselves into the golden misfits and what they did for the city. To be a part of that, for this magical run that they're now going to the Stanley Cup Final. So I remember that we won in Winnipeg and I remember we flew back and we all went, called our significant others and we all met for a drink.

“The special feeling of kind of looking back and saying, 'can you believe it?' We came together as a brand new organization and they just won the Western Conference Final in Year One as an expansion team. That was a special moment as we all sat down and shared a beverage down on the strip.”

That special moment was captured forever in a picture that says far more than 1,000 words.

HNIDY'S FAVORITE GOLDEN KNIGHTS GAME HE CALLED

Winning is the greatest feeling in sports. And not only is it the greatest feeling, but it also is the best answer to any question. There were plenty of questions about the Vegas Golden Knights in their inaugural season. One of which was, "this team can't possibly be for real? Can it?" So many people expected the wheels to fall off at any second. It was just too incredible to think an expansion team could be that successful right away.

Well, winning answered that question by saying, "yes, an expansion team could be that good right away." And it was on a special road trip that many around the team, including the broadcasters, really began to believe that this was all for real.

HNIDY: "It was the dad's trip, Year One, when they beat Nashville and Dallas back-to-back. And at that time, we were thinking, 'when's the bottom going to come out? When's the magic carpet gonna disappear from under this team? Because this is unbelievable.' Then they beat those two teams and I remember we were talking, we said, 'this isn't a fluke, this team's for real.' Gerard Gallant was the Head Coach at the time and he said, that's exactly the moment when he knew that this team was for real. He always believed in them, but everybody else was waiting, thinking, 'it's got to end at some time, right?'"

By the time their season came to an end in the Stanley Cup Final, people around the league realized their folly and understood the Golden Knights were indeed for real. So, again, winning is the only answer you need.

MESSAGE TO GOLDEN KNIGHTS FANS

As is a common theme amongst members of the sports media, it is a well known fact that without the fans our jobs would either A) not exist or B) they'd have a lot less meaning. So, each of the broadcasters in this book took a couple of minutes to address you, the fans, directly.

HNIDY: "Thank you. Just their passion for the sport. My message would be thank you for your love of the team, of the organization, for your love even, beyond that, of the sport. They have embraced the sport of hockey, which you can tell from our conversation has been my life.

"I always joke, I'm glad I was able to get into broadcasting, because I'm not qualified in much else outside of the game. The fans here have embraced the Golden Knights and have embraced the sport of hockey. They've embraced us as part of the organization. It's just been absolutely a fantastic three-years. To be part of it and to see not only them bringing the incredible energy, that building's electric, whether it's a Monday or Wednesday, you would think it's Friday.

"They bring the energy and if it's not there, it's in various places. The people here love the Golden Knights and now the growth of hockey. And just the way they've seen the kids and the numbers of the learn to skate programs, the numbers of the junior Golden Knights, to the numbers all around in minor hockey have just grown massively to the point where now we've got an American Hockey League team coming. They've built more ice sheets. So it just shows that hockey does work in the desert. So, thank you."

WASHINGTON CAPITALS

JOHN WALTON
RADIO: PLAY-BY-PLAY

First Season on Capitals Radio: 2011-12
Seasons on Capitals Radio (including 2020-21): 10

Birthday: April 2, 1973 Hometown: Minneapolis, MN

College/University: Miami University (Oxford, OH)

BIOGRAPHY

There's an old saying. When you do what you love, you'll never work a day in your life. And for many sports broadcasters, this rings especially true as they get to attend every game for free while being paid to be the voice of that team. What could be better?

Well, maybe being a player could be better, but let's be honest, most people aren't athletically inclined or talented enough to be one of the best players in the world in their preferred sport. It's just a fact. So, taking playing off the table, broadcasting is the next best thing and it's a wonderful experience to have the pleasure of doing. And just like for players, it often takes quite a while before the broadcasters can reach the top league; in this case, the NHL.

John Walton's story follows this path to a "T" and he's enjoyed every single second of it.

WALTON: "My dad took me to my first game when I was seven. We went to old Williams Arena on the campus of the University of Minnesota and from that, I watched the North Stars growing up and I just never looked back. I was a big fan of Bob Kurtz and Tom Reid, when they were doing North Stars games on Channel Nine back in the day. And now I get to call those guys colleagues, which is really fun for me. I don't think they like it so much (chuckles), but that's where it started for me. And I never looked back.

"(In regards to other broadcasters) I was always a fan of Mike Emrick and thrilled with my NBC work to be able to be alongside him from time to time and around various buildings. Washington gets a lot of games on National TV, so I get to see him quite a bit. He was a big influence on me.

"(So too was) Ken Wilson, of the St. Louis Blues on KMOX (Radio). My family moved to Ohio right before (I went to) High School. So, the North Stars were a little tougher for me to follow then and I kind of followed the Blues there for a while, just because I could, because I could listen to the games on KMOX. So, Ken Wilson was definitely a favorite of mine too.

"He was very energetic in his delivery and I'll sneak an 'Oh Baby' in every now and then. It's kind of an homage to him. It's not emulating, but I mean, you're influenced by, at the very least. I think we all are to a certain extent, by those who we enjoy in the business.

"I think it was when I was a freshman in college at Miami and started doing student radio that I really thought that maybe I could make a run at it. I found that it came to me pretty naturally. And just after two-years of student radio, I started doing it for the campus FM station for real. As far as the college stuff was concerned. And then that morphed eventually into work in the American Hockey League in Cincinnati.

"I began my hockey play-by-play career at Miami University in Oxford, Ohio, where I was the Voice of the Redskins from 1994-96, and also announced football and basketball at WRBI-FM 103.9 in Batesville, Indiana during that time. And in addition to sports, I was also a disc jockey at 97 X, WOXY-FM in Oxford, a station recognized by Rolling Stone Magazine four times in the 1990's as one of the magazine's '15 Best Radio Stations.'

"In addition to hockey, I also served as the Public Address Announcer for the Cincinnati Reds from 1996-2002 at Riverfront Stadium/Cinergy Field. And during my time in Cincinnati, I was also the first Play-by-Play voice of the AHL's Cincinnati Mighty Ducks from 1997-2000; as well as a sports anchor/helicopter traffic reporter for WLW-AM 700 in Cincinnati.

"I think, in Cincinnati, the biggest thing was that you get used to what this is going to look like. I mean, an 80-game season was a lot different than 32 in college and the rigors of the travel and all of that stuff. So I think that was probably the biggest thing there."

Eventually, all of that experience led Walton to joining the Hershey Bears in the AHL as the team's Play-by-Play broadcaster for nine-seasons; during which, the Bears experienced three Calder Cup championship seasons -- 2006, 2009 and 2010.

WALTON: "I still say Hershey, outside of the National Hockey League, is the best place to call a game. You're in front of 10,000 people every night and it's a state-of-the-art-building. The team has been around for more than 80-years. It was a real blessing really to be able to be part of that community for almost 10-years. That teaches you how to be in the NHL, because they certainly expect a very high standard from you as far as the broadcast is concerned. And I think that they did me a pretty big favor in helping me become a better broadcaster and getting you ready for the NHL.

"(Eventually) I interviewed for (the Capitals Radio job) and a couple other people came in as finalists as well. But, thankfully The Bears were very good under the Washington flag and went to The Final, four times in five-years, winning three times. And my games were broadcast in Washington during that time too.

"So, they kind of knew what they were getting. They kind of got to know what I was all about. I was fortunate enough that when they needed somebody that they thought of me. I was actually in the car when I got the call. It was the best feeling, I think, professionally, outside of being part of a Stanley Cup winner.

"I think that day might even have been better because that was a long road to get there after (spending the) better part of 15-years trying to get yourself there. And then you finally get the call and you know you're going."

FAVORITE PLAYER(S) GROWING UP

WALTON: "I would say Gilles Meloche, Craig Hartsburg, Dino Ciccarelli, Don Beaupre and Dennis Maruk. Funny enough, there were so many trades between Washington and Minnesota. There's almost as much similarity between those players of that era between the Capitals and North Stars as there are between the Stars and Dallas. So, I've gotten to know Dennis Maruk personally. I've gotten to know Don Beaupre too; good friends with his son Connor. So it's kind of fun for me to bring it full circle to be able to watch those guys growing up and then getting to know them later in life for having worked in this job."

HOCKEY AFTER DARK -- TALES AWAY FROM THE RINK

Camaraderie, it's of the utmost importance for a sports broadcasting crew. That's no surprise. These broadcasters often spend more time with each other than they do their own families. It's all part of the job. So, it helps when you're able to get away from the rink and go do something fun; you know, besides being part of a NHL game.

WALTON: "The Radio guys and the TV guys, we hang together on the road. So we do a lot of cool stuff. This past year we went on a tour in Napa when we had an off-day in San Jose that Joe Beninati set up, which was just phenomenal. We did a Seaplane excursion and did it as an intermission on television in Vancouver, which was pretty funny because a couple of our guys aren't that thrilled about heights or motion of small aircraft.

"In Edmonton, when the Nationals were in the World Series, the unofficial mascot of The Nationals had become Baby Shark. So, we dressed up Joe B. in a shark costume and paraded him around Edmonton and sent the video back home. That was pretty good.

"He only insisted that he could wear his very expensive tie with the suit, which probably only made it funnier for the viewers at home. It's important, you're on the road a lot and you're around them (your fellow broadcasters) more than your family, so it's good to have a good group and we certainly do. A lot of times, we'll even put it on video and then tweet it out and the fans usually get a pretty big kick out of that."

WALTON'S FAVORITE SINGULAR CAPITALS MOMENT

Sports games are often filled to the brim with individual singular moments. Some stand out more than others, while some are quickly forgotten. Meanwhile, the most iconic of those moments go on to live forever in the hearts and minds of everybody connected with that particular instance of time.

For John Walton, there can be only one choice as to his favorite Capitals moment and it's one the franchise waited 44-years for. I'm of course talking about Washington's first-ever Stanley Cup championship, when the Capitals came from behind in Game Five to beat the Vegas Golden Knights and send the District of Columbia into a state of sheer ecstasy.

WALTON: "You're thinking that, after 44-years, a lot of people had waited a long time and had a lot of heartbreak in between. So, being kind of on the edge of that was a pretty good feeling in and of itself. And I think you just had the feeling that before it was all over that they just weren't going to be denied that night, which was an odd feeling for anybody involved with the Capitals after what had been a not so great stretch; even in my time there. But that day was pretty magical.

"And even down after two periods, you just had the feeling when you were in the building that night, that they were going to find a way. (Devante) Smith-Pelly tied it. (Lars) Eller gave them the lead.

"I remember looking up at the last TV time-out and they had the live shot NBC was coming back with, which was outside our building and Chinatown and DC and the streets were filled. It was pretty emotional to see all of that unfolding back home. And then a few minutes later, it was over and a few minutes after that we were on the ice and I even got to throw it over my head when I was down there. So that's certainly a night I'll never forget.

"It was really down to the last face-off cause it was just a one-goal game and the face-off was still in the zone. So I think all the way up to the very end you were calling the game because it still was in doubt. It wasn't like they were jumping up and down, because it was truly over. They had to win one more face-off and Lars Eller thankfully was able to do that.

"So I think it's like any other game really, except for the fact that so much was on the line. You call it to the best of your ability. You know more people are listening than ever before and they're depending on you to deliver the moment. And I think that's what you strive for and that's what we all strive for.

"We kept it for about 15-minutes and then we turned it over. Our Studio Host was on site. So, we turned it over to him. I don't even remember the exchange of how that all went down, to be honest with you. But I know we got in the elevator and we couldn't wait to get down there. And thankfully we were able to be part of that celebration, which was, it was just unreal. To be able to be part of something like that, you hope it's more than once in a lifetime. But everybody should get to do it once and I'm glad that we had that chance."

WALTON'S FAVORITE CAPITALS GAME HE'S CALLED

So much has gone wrong for the Capitals in their franchise's history. Too often, especially over the past two decades, the team was supremely talented, but just could not get over the hump from being a great team to being a champion. And more often than not, there was one particular team standing in their way; the Pittsburgh Penguins.

At minimum they've been Conference rivals. But ever since the NHL's last round of league-wide realignment, they've been much more than mere Conference rivals. They've been Division rivals. And that means they face each other more than they face most of the league, which can lead to some white hot moments between the two clubs.

For years, Washington would be the superior regular-season team, but when the lights were brightest in the playoffs, it was Pittsburgh who was the superior club.

Well, that all changed during the 2017-18 Stanley Cup Playoffs as the Capitals finally slayed the Penguins and it was all thanks to Evgeny Kuznetsov's Eastern Conference Semifinals, Game 6, overtime game-winning, series-clinching goal.

WALTON: "It was the biggest goal in franchise history, even bigger than the Lars Eller goal in Game Five (of the Stanley Cup Final), because the Caps, they still would have had more life if they lost Game Five. They still had two more chances to win. Obviously winning The Cup that night will be the one that everyone remembers. But the goal itself, Pittsburgh had, even in recent times, had beaten them in '16 and '17.

"In '16, everybody thought the Caps were going to win it and they didn't. A Presidents' Trophy season ending with Pittsburgh beating them. The Penguins had their number. So, you felt like if the Caps were ever going to win the Stanley Cup, they were going to have to go through Pittsburgh. And doing it in Pittsburgh and doing it in the dramatic fashion that they did. I think that set the tone for the rest of the series. It was just an incredible moment and one this franchise badly needed. I think that was something that they had to have and had that feeling to be able to go into the next series against Tampa and ultimately against Vegas."

SIGNATURE PHRASE

Sports fans absolutely love it when their team's broadcaster says something memorable. It might come out of the blue. Or it might be at the end of a long arduous journey. Either way, fans will always latch on to a call, or saying that they feel is worth remembering and using again.

In that sense, the creation of a signature call is two-fold. One, the broadcaster has to say something that adequately fits the moment they're trying to describe. And two, the fans have to like it to the extent where it takes on a life of its own.

Now, it doesn't always have to be fans who give that extra life to a call. It could be a colleague, or somebody else who hears it and thinks it's worth using again. And for John Walton, it was the Head Coach of the Hershey Bears, when he was doing the team's Play-by-Play, who thought Walton's "*Good morning, Good afternoon, Good night (team just defeated by his team)*" was worth using again and again.

WALTON: "I started to do it in Hershey actually. I wasn't even going to bring it with me, except that, because of all the games that had been broadcast in Washington, that I had done up there, it was the first question I got from Tarik El-Bashir, who at the time, was a beat writer for the Washington Post. And once he asked, I said (to myself), 'well, maybe it is a bigger deal than I thought it was. If the Washington Post is asking me about it, maybe I should keep it.' And ultimately I decided to. The rest, as they say, is history.

"Really the only thing that it was, it was a big game with Wilkes-Barre / Scranton, Pittsburgh's affiliate, where we needed a win and we'd been in their building, rallied in the third and won it. And it just kinda came out one night. The next night we won in similar fashion and I decided to use it again. Then I forgot about it the third time and then my Head Coach at the time said, 'Hey, that's a pretty good line. Maybe you should stick with it.' It kind of just stuck after that. It was right about the time we were switching over to Washington affiliation anyway. And it just kind of followed me through that time, which is kind of fun."

And now Capitals fans get to hear after every Washington win.

MESSAGE TO CAPITALS FANS

As is a common theme amongst members of the sports media, it is a well known fact that without the fans our jobs would either A) not exist or B) they'd have a lot less meaning. So, each of the broadcasters in this book took a couple of minutes to address you, the fans, directly.

WALTON: "I pride myself in giving an energetic call for the home team, combined with providing an unbiased view of the game itself. Trust is the most important factor between broadcaster and fan. To believe us when things are going well, we need to tell you when things are not. We strive to have fun on the air to make the call as entertaining as possible for the listener. That's the goal every single night."

WINNIPEG JETS

BRIAN MUNZ
RADIO / TV: PLAY-BY-PLAY / COLOR ANALYST

First Season on Jets Radio / TV : 2011-12
Seasons on Jets Radio / TV: 9

Birthday: April 23, 1975 Hometown: Humboldt, Saskatchewan

College/University: Western Academy

BIOGRAPHY

Sometimes you just know that you don't have what it takes to see certain dreams through. And it's not your fault. Many children around the world dream of one day being professional athletes with millions of adoring fans. Unfortunately, less than one-percent are talented enough to make those dreams come true.

Again, it's not anybody's fault. It's just an extremely difficult dream to achieve and there's nothing wrong with chasing that dream.

For Brian Munz, he knew this was a dream he wouldn't be able to see through to completion, so instead, he found another way to be involved with the sport he so loved. And that led to a dream he could see through.

MUNZ: "I didn't have any relatives or anything who played the game (of hockey). It was just something that me and my buddies would always do after school. I went to elementary school in Regina and we had a lake at the end of our street and literally it was every day after school, you'd race home, put your skates on and then you'd put the skate guards on.

"Fortunately enough for me, the lake was three houses down from the end of my street. So, you would walk out of the house on your guards and then jump on the lake and play hockey until you were told to come home for supper. And jeez, that's what I remember doing all through elementary school until we moved to Humboldt where I still call home today and my parents live.

"Then, being in a small town of around 5,000 people, the local hockey rink, the Elgar Petersen Arena it's called, was the gathering place where everybody went. That's where you continued to love the game. And obviously the Broncos were the big story in town and you ended up going to High School with some of those guys, who became your friends for life.

"I knew that I would never have the opportunity to play, so I took to the next best thing. At those games in the Saskatchewan Junior Hockey League, when the Broncos were playing, I kind of befriended the local radio broadcaster (Neil Shewchuk) and he was nice enough to take me up to the booth.

"That's really when I fell in love with the idea that this is what I wanted to do and I was lucky enough to be able to do it, not only being able to call games for my hometown team, but then I went to Prince Albert in the Western Hockey League, followed by the American League and then obviously the NHL. So, much like for players, coaches, trainers, management and officials, it's the same road for broadcasters where you start in Junior and try to climb your way up.

"After 90-seconds of skating on the ice with those guys in school, I knew I wasn't going to be able to go anywhere in terms of playing the game. So, I quickly turned my attention to the other side. But they will attest to it as much as me, I loved getting out there and I knew how bad I was. But I just loved being out on the ice and playing. And again, I knew I had absolutely no future in playing the game. So, I gave up on that dream and very, very fast.

"From a broadcast standpoint, Peter Loubardias, who's currently the Color Analyst on Calgary Flames radio, was the voice of the Pats in Regina. In Regina, he took me up to the booth a few times and I got to see what it was like. The radio station did a Junior Pats broadcaster (contest).

"So I won the honor in a draw to do that one night. And after doing that, I was hooked. I got to spend some time pregame with him and see what went into the broadcast and all that kind of stuff. That really locked it in for me. Pete and I laugh about it now, because we see each other on a pretty regular basis when the Jets and Flames play.

"He knows how much he's meant to me in my career. And then, you just look at the Canadian broadcasters and I get it now, young guys asking me, who are calling Junior hockey now, for the same advice. So, I think it's important to give back to the young guys for the guys who did it for myself."

"Just having a chance to listen to the games on the radio and watch on TV. I thought that'd be a pretty cool job and set my focus on that when I was in High School and just kind of went on from there and went in and registered at the Western Academy of Broadcasting in Saskatoon. It was a shorter course at that point where you do six months in the school and then you do an apprenticeship after that.

"I reached out to radio stations in Saskatchewan and luckily enough CJNB in North Battleford was the one that accepted me. So I did my practicum there. And then when that came to an end, I literally sent every small radio station in British Columbia, Alberta, Saskatchewan and Manitoba a demo tape and Duncan BC, out of the blue, on Vancouver Island gave me a call one day and said they liked what I had and wanted to know if I was willing to move to Vancouver Island and the rest is history for my start. So that's how I got into it."

Once Munz made it to the NHL (and yes, he made several stops along the way from Duncan BC to TSN) he continued to try and soak up as much knowledge as he could in an effort to further his own abilities and he's never been afraid to pay it forward either.

MUNZ: "At the NHL level, Ralph Strangis, who was the voice of the Dallas Stars, was a guy who I just randomly reached out to and he's been terrific ever since. Pete Weber was the same way with the Nashville Predators. Chris Cuthbert from TSN, who now works for Sportsnet. Chris, for me, is the gold standard in Canada.

"I really like how Chris calls the game and even when we're around each other now, I just kind of watch how he interacts with people and how he prepares for his games. And then, the home runs for me, since living in Winnipeg, the five-years that I called the Moose games, the American League team, at CJOB radio, Bob Irving was the Sports Director. He's been the voice of the Blue Bombers in the CFL for, I think it's been four decades now.

"Getting a chance to learn from him. And then, Dennis Beyak, is obviously a guy who I spend every day with in the winter and is one of the most respected broadcasters, not only in Canada, but in the US as well with his work for TSN. He came into Winnipeg to do the television and I got the radio gig and we didn't know each other. We have a ton of mutual friends from Saskatchewan. So I've been really fortunate to have a lot of really good people who have answered the phone when I have asked a question and I guess now I try and do that for the young broadcasters who are coming up themselves."

FAVORITE PLAYER(S) GROWING UP

MUNZ: "The Western Hockey League was what I looked at. Being a young elementary school kid in Regina, it was the path for the stars. Mike Sillinger was the big star then. He was my guy. I laugh about it now because I've gotten to know Mike as we've both grown older and then we kind of chuckle about it. He was my hero. When I was in Grade Four, Five, Six, Seven kind of thing, that was his Junior years with The Pats.

"I think whatever local town you're in, I think that's the team you always end up cheering for and that's kind of the way it was for me.

"NHL-wise, to be honest with you, just being on the Prairies at that point, you always saw a lot of Edmonton. You saw a lot of Los Angeles because of the Gretzky trade. So I would say that I probably followed those two teams the most, but again, for me, my NHL was the Western Hockey League.

"I grew up a fan of the (Regina) Pats and also, just for whatever reason it was, I vividly remember being in Regina and Mike Modano would come in with the Prince Albert Raiders. He was the other guy who I kind of really gravitated to. And then, down the road, being the voice of the Raiders, I got to know Mike and we built a bit of a friendship here over the last number of years that I've been in the NHL. It's kind of cool, I've gotten to know my two childhood idols in both Sillinger and Modano.

"(But in terms of other players in the WHL) they were with the Pats. It was Mike Sillinger. It was Frank Kovacs. It was Jamie Heward. Trent Kachur was a defenseman who lived just around the corner from me. That's where he billeted with a family. I thought that was the coolest thing in the world. Junior hockey players just lived around the corner and they'd come out on the lake and they'd skate with us. So, I remember Trent was there, Mike Dyck was there, Brad Miller spent some time in the Buffalo Sabres organization. Guys like that.

"At that point, they were only 16- to 20-years-old themselves, but they were kind of your rock stars.

"And then, when I got into Grade Nine, you're closer to the same age as those guys in Humboldt and then you're going to High School with them and they become your friends.

"I went to high school in Humboldt with Brendan Witt, who obviously went on to a great career in the NHL. Regan Mueller was a star player as well. He went on to Swift Current and Seattle, in the Western Hockey League. Those would be kind of the two big guys my age. Brad Lauer was a Humboldt guy and Jared Bednar as well, who now coaches in Colorado (with the Avalanche).

"So, those were kind of the guys when I got to High School who were not only my friends, but guys you rooted for, because you wanted to see them do well. And all of those guys made a name for themselves for hockey players in Saskatchewan, for sure."

EXTRA HOCKEY -- MUNZ'S FAVORITE JETS HIGHLIGHTS

In Canada, Hockey is not just a sport. It's a religion, a way of life if you will. Things we take for granted in the U.S., in regards to hockey, are treated as massive events north of the border. And Brian Munz has accumulated a trio of these types of events during his career calling Jets games.

MUNZ: “Well, I think the obvious highlight was Game One against Montreal. Just the excitement, the buzz of the National Hockey League being back in Winnipeg. The anticipation for that game and just how the whole thing played out.

“Unfortunately, the Jets lost, but I talk about how good of a person Dennis (Beyak) is. It was his game to call on the radio, and he let me do Play-by-Play for the second period. So he did the first period and third. He didn't have to do it.

“I vividly remember we were going into the first intermission and the Jets hadn't scored a goal yet. It was kind of like, 'okay, am I actually going to get to call the Jets first goal,' because Carey Price kept them off the board in the opening period. Low and behold, I didn't. Nik Antropov scored early in the third period.

“So, Dennis got to call the Antropov goal. That is still very famous in Winnipeg. But it was something special for him to allow me to call that second period. It's obviously a memory for me that'll stand out forever.

“Continuing with the Jets, obviously as the years have gone on, the team has gotten better and better. Game Seven, a couple of years ago against Nashville in the Western Conference Final. They lost Game Six in Winnipeg and there were a couple of days before that game was played inside Bridgestone Arena. I don't think anybody outside of the people who were on that plane gave the Jets a chance to win that game. And they went in and won.

“To be down in the room after the game and around the team and then flying back to Winnipeg after the game when you just got the group together, it still gives me chills just thinking about how exciting that was for the organization; for all of us around the team. I can't imagine what it would be like to be a player in that regard. And then, when we got home, just the excitement of the city, to have the Jets get into the Western Conference Final, into the Final Four was pretty amazing.

“And then, last year, the Jets and Flames played the Tim Hortons Heritage Classic at Mosaic Stadium in Regina, home of the Saskatchewan Roughriders. And being a Saskatchewan guy, being a diehard Rider fan, having an NHL game in the city I was born in was great.”.

"To have that game outdoors on the Prairie against the Calgary Flames. I guess it kind of comes full circle. Pete (Loubardias) was there with the Flames on the other side of it. So, to have a guy that you looked up to and then be in that city and all, it was pretty special."

It's more than just events that Munz holds dear, as he has also established quite the rapport with the de facto face of the NHL, Sidney Crosby.

MUNZ: "Just living in the NHL is a dream. You get to see how well all of these players are treated. But there's one player who has never disappointed me off-ice. The Jets were in the Southeast division for the first couple of years they were in the NHL.

"So, based on the fact that we played in Eastern Conference, we saw a lot of Sidney Crosby. And I have had a chance now to meet and talk to Sid probably close to 20 times. I don't know what the exact number is. But to just watch how he deals with people and to understand that he's the face of the National Hockey League and how he handles his day. You go into the room to do the morning media scrums and get your broadcast ready and he's never in a hurry to leave. He understands his role.

"I've told people so many times that I've had so many great one-on-one visits with Sid and I think he knows who I am from my job, but we had no connection prior to that. Every time he sees me, he stops, he waits. He has a conversation. So I would honestly say that every meeting with him is a highlight because of what a great person he is.

"Jared Bednar and I host the Conexus Credit Union Humboldt Broncos Memorial Golf Tournament which honours the 29 people who were on the bus in 2018 now every summer. And again, it kind of brings us back to Sid where we got a jersey from him the first year and then the second year, right away, it was, 'how'd the golf tournament go? Do you need anything else? Don't be afraid to ask.'

"So just the pro that he is, is something that really stands out for me. I would say he's been the highlight each and every time."

MUNZ'S FAVORITE JETS GAME HE'S CALLED

Hockey by its nature is supposed to be a low-scoring game. Yes, over the years there have been some supremely talented players and teams who made high-scoring games seem normal. And yes, there have been cycles throughout the NHL's history where high-scoring affairs can be expected versus other times when they're rarer than a goalie scoring against the opposing team.

But regardless of whether or not high-scoring games are commonplace or not, they almost always bring an extra level of excitement to those in attendance and to those listening or watching at home. And for Brian Munz, he had the opportunity to call a Jets game in which the final score seemed more appropriate for baseball than for hockey.

MUNZ: "The Jets played in Philadelphia on October 27, 2011, and it was a 9-8 final score. Shane Hnidy and I were calling that game on radio and obviously 17-goals was a crazy night. The mixing board in the booth blew up. It started smoking after about the 12th or 13th goal. It was crazy."

Crazy indeed!

All nine of Winnipeg's goals were scored by different players. Tell me the last time you can recall a team scoring that many times and not having a single player record multiple goals. Go ahead, I'll wait patiently by the phone.

The game was such a back-and-forth affair that the deciding goal wasn't scored until there was just 1:06 left in regulation time. For Munz and Hnidy, it must have been a relief when Andrew Ladd scored what ended up as the game-winning goal. An overtime period would surely have been too much for the radio equipment that had survived to that point in the game.

MESSAGE TO JETS FANS

As is a common theme amongst members of the sports media, it is a well known fact that without the fans our jobs would either A) not exist or B) they'd have a lot less meaning. So, each of the broadcasters in this book took a couple of minutes to address you, the fans, directly.

MUNZ: "Continue to enjoy the ride. This team's getting better and better. And if you remember back to what it was like coming out of Atlanta and the young players who were in the organization, have grown into the leaders on this team, there's not many left right now. But, you think of the young faces who have solidified themselves now as NHL superstars. And then the excitement of the number of young draft picks the Jets have now.

"I think the best is yet to come for this team. So many exciting moments we've lived out through nine-years. I'm really excited to see what the next decade really has for this club, because based on the talent they've been able to draft and develop, this team is a contender in the Western Conference and I think we'll compete and hopefully win a Stanley Cup one day for sure."

NBC

JOHN FORSLUND
TV: PLAY-BY-PLAY

First Season on NBC TV: 2010-11
Seasons on NBC TV (including 2020-21): 11

Birthday: February 14, 1962 Hometown: Springfield, MA

College/University: Springfield College (Undergrad) / Adelphi University (Master's)

BIOGRAPHY

Sometimes a childhood obsession can grow into a Hall of Fame-esque career. You obviously don't know it at the time, but life, fate, destiny, whatever you want to call it, has a way of guiding you in the right direction to fulfill your dreams.

John Forslund doesn't recall exactly why he sat down to watch a hockey game at the age of eight-years old. It could have something to do with the fact that he was just really into sports. Who knows what force acted on him at that moment. But one thing we do know is that he's gone on to have one of the top careers in the NHL as a Play-by-Play broadcaster.

He was the voice of the Hartford Whalers/Carolina Hurricanes franchise for over two-decades. He's been a go-to guy for NBC for over a decade and now, with the 2021-22 season several months away, he's slowly inching towards his next great adventure as the first ever Play-by-Play voice of the new Seattle Kraken; the NHL's 32nd and newest franchise.

But what exactly was that moment that put him on this path?

FORSLUND: "I remember, distinctly, where I was when Bobby Orr scored The Cup-winning goal in 1970, which gave the Bruins the Stanley Cup that year. I was eight-years-old and I was at my aunt's house and it was Mother's Day.

"I remember watching the game by myself and I remember at the time, being infatuated with not only the game, but I think even more so, the cadence of the play call, which was on CBS that afternoon, it was the great Dan Kelly who did the game. So I started to kind of get the bug for it.

"I think I was like any other kid. I mean, I played a variety of sports. I got to hockey probably too late in my development. As an athlete, I played a lot of baseball, a lot of basketball, a little bit of football. But my dad and I had a connection with hockey. There was a Minor League team in Springfield, Massachusetts, where I grew up. He took me to games coinciding in and around that time. I think when I was about 10, I started to get the bug to go to games with him on a regular basis. And then what I started to do was just announcing games off the television.

"My parents, I believe it was 1972, they bought me a tape recorder for Christmas. I started doing the games as a hobby. My dad actually did color with me and I did that all the way through my teens and took it very seriously. My mom was pretty intelligent about this because she knew that I needed to read more as a student. I didn't like to read. I was bored, like a lot of kids, with reading.

"So she said, 'why don't you start reading books about something you love?' And so I kinda went into hockey. Again, I loved all the sports. They came seasonal for us in those years. When it was winter time, it was football. It was hockey, basketball and so on. But I started reading about the history of hockey. So all of that kind of came together.

"I went through High School. I had a conversation with my Guidance Counselor. She asked me what I'd like to do with my life and I told her I wanted to be a Play-by-Play broadcaster in the National

Hockey League. Honest to God that's what I told her. And she said, 'wow, I really don't know how to steer you in that direction.'

"Remember this was probably around 1977-78 and if you recall, ESPN was founded in 1979. So we hadn't even got into the cable age yet. There wasn't a lot of opportunity. She kinda wanted me to be a little bit more safe with a career choice. So I went to education. I was going to coach High School baseball and teach at a High School. And that's what I went to school for. And then at Springfield College, I took one elective in broadcast journalism. I had some great advice from the teacher of the course, who was a News Director.

"As I voiced over the '81 Super Bowl as part of my final exam, he told me, 'if you ever get an opportunity to do this professionally, go for it, because you have an ability and maybe a talent that you can't really teach in the classroom.'

"I kept it in the back of my mind. I went to graduate school for athletic management or as they called it at the time athletic administration, which has now become Sports Management. I had an internship in the American Hockey League with the Springfield team. The Owner of the team asked me if I had any broadcast experience. I told him, 'yeah I've got experience.' But I never had to tell him who or how. He just gave me a chance to get on the air and help their Play-by-Play guy, who was in his first year, as his Color guy on radio in addition to my administrative duties.

"One thing led to another, they hired me the next season. I became their Play-by-Play voice. When I say I did this a lot growing up as a hobby, it was a fascination and an obsession with me.
So I did a lot of this stuff in terms of experience and kind of crafted my own way of doing things. A lot of my friends in High School and in College, said, 'you ought to be a sportscaster someday.' I would impersonate others. I'd do my own thing.

"So anyway, one thing led to another. I was very lucky, but I worked hard at it. And then that was the beginning of a seven-year career in the American Hockey League as a broadcaster and a PR man, which led me to the NHL."

Forslund's career in the AHL and NHL had a couple of twists and turns along the way, but before we dive into that, it's important to note who his broadcasting inspirations were as he picked up tips early in his life from watching/listening to these individuals; which in turn helped him to develop his own style of calling games.

As with any kid growing up in the 1970s, Dan Kelly was a biggie for Forslund. So too were Fred Cusick on Bruins television and Bob Wilson on Bruins radio. In fact, if you fast forward to the mid-90's, Cusick actually recommended Forslund to be his replacement when the former was retiring. And while Forslund did audition for the job, he eventually chose to stay with the Whalers/Hurricanes franchise and moved to North Carolina.

A couple of other broadcast inspirations for Forslund were Bob Cole and Pat Summerall. Forslund got to know and meet Cole while he was working for the Springfield Indians in the American Hockey League. And it was Summerall's style of calling games that really resonated with him as Summerall had a way of calling games by using few words and letting the moments breathe. Both of which are a unique and powerful way of conveying what is going on in the games.

Of course, those weren't the only inspirations for Forslund, as he journeyed through the early parts of his career, he also got to draw wisdom from the likes of Jiggs McDonald, Mike "Doc" Emrick and others. So, basically, you have a who's who of broadcasters who had an impact on Forslund's career and he's thankful for each and every one of them.

Now, let's get back to Forslund's journey.

FORSLUND: "From '84 to '91, I was in Springfield and in '91, I was offered an opportunity to go to Hartford as Chuck Kaiton's Color man and as a Hockey Information Director. So in other words, they wanted to bring on a PR guy who had experience, to work strictly with the Hockey Operations Department.

"They wanted to segregate it from business and they wanted to take the current PR Director of the Whalers and make him the business PR guy and give me this job, which I accepted. And I thought that's what I was walking into after the Indians won their second straight Calder Cup. The first one in '90 with the Islanders, the second one in '91 with Hartford. So the Hartford people were familiar with my work and they wanted to bring me on board. They were also bringing in Jimmy Roberts, our coach at Springfield, as the new Head Coach of the Whalers.

"So we were going there together. But what happened was, the PR guy, who'd been there for a few years and did a really good job, for whatever reason, didn't like this move at all. He wanted to continue on in a more conventional PR job where you do it all. He went to the Pittsburgh Penguins and actually quit the Whalers, which opened up the PR job. And the owner of the team offered me the job.

"I was 29. I had to make a tough decision. I had to forgo broadcasting for a little while, even though I didn't want to do it, but the job paid me an unbelievable salary at the time, plus full benefits. We were starting a young family. My wife and I got married in '86. She was working full-time, but we wanted to start having kids and I needed, for lack of a better phrase, a real job and I was failing at some of my efforts to get Play-by-Play gigs in the NHL.

"So I was at a crossroads. It was either how long can I make what I was making in the American League and just give up and do something else or can I continue on, kind of in what I'm doing, but not really. So what I did is I took the Whaler job and I continued as a broadcaster with SportsChannel with the American Hockey League Game of The Week. So I did one game per week on television and then, in '94, ownership changed in Hartford. Peter Karmanos, Jim Rutherford and their group came in.

"They asked me to stay on as their PR guy. I told them I wasn't interested and I really wanted to get into broadcasting. I was going for the Islanders TV job at the time as there was a falling out with Jiggs (McDonald). It looked like Jiggs was leaving or being forced out. Anyway, I was going to try and go for that. And they said, 'well, just see us through.' And that was in '94, the first lockout. So we didn't have hockey in the fall. And we had a 48-game schedule.

"The original plan that season was to have SportsChannel do 60 games of the 82 and 22 games would be on over the air television on an ABC affiliate, which was Channel Eight in New Haven. I would do those games and Emile Francis was my Color guy.

"But what ended up happening was, it went from 82 to 48-games because of the lockout. So the TV schedule then became 47-games SportsChannel, one-game Channel Eight and that was my game. It was in Madison Square Garden against the Rangers. So that was the first game I ever did Play-by-Play in the National Hockey League on television.

"That off-season, there was a contract squabble or disagreement between the team and SportsChannel. The team wanted to hire its own broadcasters and Jim Rutherford remembered what my goal was and he thought that there was a chance he might lose me. So he offered me the job and made a decision. To this day, it was a bad thing at the time, but it was great for me.

"Then in '95-'96, I became the full-time TV Play-by-Play announcer and Daryl Reaugh, now in Dallas, was my first Color guy. And then, in '97 we moved to Raleigh. And in 2010-11, Sam Flood from NBC called me and asked me to do some games for them. So I started doing that in January of 2011."

FAVORITE PLAYER(S) GROWING UP

FORSLUND: "Bobby Orr was my favorite player bar none. Second favorite was Phil Esposito. I can tell a story of when Phil was traded to the Rangers. We were playing street hockey at the time and my dad came home from work. So we cleared the streets, got the nets out of the way. My dad rolled down the window and he said, 'the Bruins traded Espo.'

"I didn't know for whom or for what, I didn't even ask him which team. Then he moved along and went home and I was going home shortly for dinner. I threw my stick and my stick went flying, boomerang fashion, across a yard, right into a window of a neighbor's house. It broke the window. I ended up paying for that out of chores and allowance money. And I was grounded for a couple of days."

HOCKEY AFTER DARK -- TALES AWAY FROM THE RINK

When you've been around the game of hockey as long as John Forslund has, you're bound to have seen it all. That may be a tired phrase, but it usually holds up. And in Forslund's case, you better believe he's seen everything. He was the voice of the Whalers/Hurricanes franchise for over two-decades and of all the things he's witnessed, the following story takes the cake.

FORSLUND: "It was right at the beginning. I think it's one of the best stories. It's in the '97-'98 season. I was the TV announcer, but it was pre-season, so no television. I was helping out Chuck Kaiton on the radio side; doing color for him.

"The game was against the Detroit Red Wings, Stanley Cup champions and Scottie Bowman coming in and all this stuff. It was a Friday night and it was the night they were going to debut the mascot, this figure named Stormy. An Anthropomorphic ice hog. Basically it's a pig suit. But what they decided to do was to have this big promotion, tell the fans they are gonna debut the mascot in a way you've never seen before.

"So, what ended up happening was we were on the air in the Pre-game show, all the lights were out in the arena, Greensboro Coliseum. It's a cavernous building. 22,000 seats. Very few people were at the game, obviously. And right before the face-off and the anthems, here comes the Zamboni on the ice with a spotlight.

"In one corner of the arena, they have the oldest Pig Caller in the state of North Carolina. He was in his 90's, I believe. They had him situated where the gates open and he's got both feet out on the ice; just one step out on the ice. He's doing a pig call. 'Suey. Suey.'

"The Public Address Announcer says, 'ladies and gentlemen, a momentous occasion for that Carolina Hurricanes, the first ever team mascot will be unveiled tonight. He'll come out of the Zamboni now.' What happened was, they were going to lift the lid off the Zamboni and the mascot was inside the Zamboni. But somebody had the bright idea to stuff it with dry ice.

"So there's smoke coming out of the Zamboni. Well, this thing is at center ice and the guy's still yelling 'suey, suey.' Anyway, there's nothing happening. There's this long delay, which was probably for 30-seconds. It felt like 10-minutes. The Zamboni driver then looks over at the PR guy and cuts his throat. Like, 'cut the cord on this program.'

"Anyway, the guy nearly passed out, was almost asphyxiated by the dry ice in the Zamboni; the mascot. So the Zamboni turned around and sped off the ice. They took the guy and luckily he was fine. He continued to be the mascot. He just wanted the job. Nobody sued anybody. But they almost killed Stormy that night.

"Believe it or not, as the Zamboni left the ice surface, this Pig Caller was still screaming 'suey, suey.' He's still screaming and the crowd is laughing.

"Ken Kal, the voice of the Red Wings, looks up at us. He was just below us in his location. He's like, 'The guy's dead.' And Chuck's going on with the pre-game show. He's paying no attention to the ceremony. I'm laughing hysterically, really not something we should have been laughing at, but we didn't know exactly what was going on.

"At the time, I thought they forgot to put him in there. We didn't find out till we saw them scurrying about that there was actually somebody inside the Zamboni. Then the ambulance came and they took him away. And that is a true story. And that's one of the funniest, scariest things I've ever seen. It's not the same person anymore but that's how Stormy debuted as the Carolina Hurricanes' mascot in September 1997."

FORSLUND'S FAVORITE GAMES HE'S CALLED

Having been the voice of the Whalers/Hurricanes franchise for over two-decades and having done games for NBC for a decade, John Forslund has had many opportunities to call memorable games. In fact, there's probably too many to count. To narrow down a list of thousands to just a handful is likely close to impossible, but we gave it a try and Forslund has a few games he'd like to share his memories of with you, the fans.

Let's start with his Hurricanes game and then we'll get to his national NBC games.

With Carolina during the 2019-20 season, sadly it wound up being his last with the team, Forslund was on the call for what went down as arguably the most memorable game of the entire NHL season. Which game am I referencing? The David Ayres game of course.

Let me bring you quickly up to speed. Each NHL arena is mandated to have an emergency goalie on hand in case both goaltenders on a single game are knocked from the game due to injury. Should that undesirable situation unfold, the emergency goalie will enter the game.

Well, on the night of February 22, 2020, the Hurricanes were in Toronto to take on the Maple Leafs when James Reimer and then Petr Mrazek were both felled by injuries. Enter Ayres, a 42-year-old who had served as a practice goalie for the Toronto Marlies of the AHL and had also driven the Zamboni from time to time.

This was the worst possible situation for Carolina, except for the fact they had a lead. Although, the look on Head Coach Rod Brind'Amour's face would tell you he expected that lead to disappear quickly.

As it turns out, there was no need to worry as Ayres came in and kept the Maple Leafs in check while authoring one of the game's most improbable stories. Carolina held on to win the game and even Forslund and his broadcast crew were able to emerge from the game unscathed.

FORSLUND: "This past season, the David Ayers game, the spare goalie against Toronto.That is so unique, so historic and it also worked out very well for the Hurricanes and the fans. When you put all of that together and the fact that, on the fly, we were learning about this guy; we were googling him and getting information and we had zero information. We had zero support. You're not prepared for this. This is something that comes out of left field.

"The beauty of doing what we do is that it's like a reality show. You can prepare for hours to do a game, but there's no script. You absolutely have no idea what's going to happen when the pucks drop. So, the David Ayres game, I would say, in all my time with the Hurricanes, was the most unusual, in a way as exciting as a playoff game and professionally challenging and rewarding to see how we did the game.

"We didn't botch anything. It worked out great. We even got his name correct. There's no pronunciation guide for an emergency goalie. There's a safety net and confidence when you get something right. When you're on the air live and you don't know, you're never confident. No one knew if we're saying his name (right). It could have been pronounced a different way. But it all came together. It all worked and I would say that one there sticks out."

That's Forslund's Carolina game, now let's get to his picks for NBC.

FORSLUND: "Every game we did in the bubble was remarkable. Every game we did in the bubble and I did 44, from a production standpoint, because production was done on-site and remote in Stamford. And what we did, competitive games and the historic nature of the return to play, will always be a highlight in my career.

"The other singular game for me that stands out is the 2017, 100th anniversary, Centennial Classic, outdoor game, which is the only outdoor game I've done. Toronto vs Detroit on January 1, 2017, at BMO Field in Toronto and the game went to overtime.

"Austin Matthews won it for the Maple Leafs. There was a reviewed goal in the last two seconds of regulation where Detroit tied the game, but Pierre McGuire, Brian Boucher, Jeremy Roenick, Kathryn Tappen and I did the game. That to me is a highlight, because we were in Toronto (for the) hundredth anniversary. The hundredth anniversary team was introduced before the game. A beautiful day with unbelievable conditions. That's the only outdoor game I've ever been to, let alone announced."

SIGNATURE PHRASE

When you think about signature calls or catch phrases for sports broadcasters, there's usually a great deal of emphasis put on them by the announcer. The point is to grab the fans' attention and excite them. It's all about the entertainment value and what's more entertaining than saying something fans can imitate, put on t-shirts and chant alongside the broadcaster.

With all that being said, there are times when a catch phrase or signature call has a much deeper meaning to it and for John Forslund, who's known for having a whole dictionary worth of sayings, his primary call of "Hey, Hey, what do you say?" is one such call with a deeper meaning.

FORSLUND: "I have a few of them, but the one that supersedes them all is, 'Hey, Hey, what do you say?' The backstory on that is, my dad was a youth baseball coach growing up. He used to say that on the field. He used to say that to people you would meet, 'Hey, Hey, what do you say' was kind of his thing.

"So, when I first started being paid, when my internship turned into a full-time job in 1985, the first paycheck I got was on January 12th, 1985. I did the game that night, he came to the game with my mom. I was still living at home. I was lucky enough to work and live in the same hometown. Anyway, I came home after going out after the game with my fiancé, who's now my wife. I came home and that night, my dad tragically passed away in his sleep.

"I wanted to show him my paycheck because it was my first paycheck with a team logo on it. I couldn't believe I was getting paid for what I did. He died at a young age, was taken from us and all this. Then, the next couple of years, as I was traveling around the American League on buses, I was pretty shaken up and depressed by this.

"I figured I wanted to honor him somehow. And I thought that when a goal was scored that night, I would utilize the phrase, 'Hey, Hey, what do you say?' And I did. And then I figured, either that season or the season after, I would use it on goals that determine the game. So from 1987, to the present, when I do a local game and I feel the game is in the bag and it can happen in the second period, very rarely. But I have done it. Third period, obviously. Overtime, no question. The game's over, that's the stamp on the call. It always had been with the Whalers; first with the Indians and with the Whalers. Then I brought it to Carolina.

"I don't use it on national television because it shows bias towards one team. Maybe someday it'll be accepted. Early in my career, there was ridicule. Some media critics thought it was a trite thing to say. I didn't care. Some fans from other markets, they're partisan. They don't like it. I get it. It's personal. It's just me and my father. So it's for my dad and I still use it."

MESSAGE TO NBC FANS

As is a common theme amongst members of the sports media, it is a well known fact that without the fans our jobs would either A) not

exist or B) they'd have a lot less meaning. So, each of the broadcasters in this book took a couple of minutes to address you, the fans, directly.

FORSLUND: "I'm very lucky, because I feel in my profession I have the utmost in common with the fans. And that is our love of the game. I love hockey with all my heart and soul. I love my job with the hurricanes, with all my heart and soul. I think I dumped all of that into my time with the hurricanes. It's unfortunate that it kind of went down the road that it did. It was not my choice. I've told various people; reporters, since it happened, that it's something I'll never get over -- the fact that this relationship with the hurricanes and the fan base was brought to a halt.

"And really, the fan base is the one that bothers me the most, not necessarily my job, but the fact that my connection with what has been a very passionate fan base here, at times, it's been ridiculed, at times it's had attrition because of the lack of success of the team.

"But, by and large, I think we've done a really good job here of building the brand of the hurricanes since inception. And I'm proud of that. And I want to thank the fans for giving me the energy to do what I did for a number of years. With that being said, I'm not stepping aside anytime soon. And whether it be on national games where I'm serving two fan bases, I hope they understand that my energy is there for them.

"My energy and my preparation is there to do the best possible job I can do game in and game out. And if I do end up with another team, they're going to get John Forslund full on and I will just repeat whatever I did with Springfield, Hartford and most recently, for 23-years, with Carolina. But, I look forward to it, because I think I'm lucky. I'm still young enough and vibrant enough, thank God and healthy enough to keep doing this. And I want to. And I hope there are better days ahead."

PIERRE MCGUIRE
TV: INSIDE THE GLASS ANALYST

First Season on NBC TV: 2005-06
Seasons on NBC TV (including 2020-21): 16

Birthday: August 8, 1961 Hometown: Englewood, NJ

College/University: Hobart College

BIOGRAPHY

There are just some people in this world who are born to be part of hockey. I don't know the answer as to how this happens, but it does and that is the perfect way to describe Pierre McGuire. He was born to be in hockey. He played it. He coached it. He worked in management. And he's done TV and radio. Am I missing anything? Short of being an Owner I'm fairly certain he's checked all the boxes.

MCGUIRE: "I always wanted to be involved in sports since I was a little boy. The first game I ever went to was at The Old Madison Square Garden. My grandfather took me to a Montreal Canadiens vs New York Rangers game. I would say I was probably five or six-years-old. So in the mid-60s. I'll never forget walking into the arena. I'll never forget the sounds. I'll never forget the smells. I'll never forget the lighting, never forget the smoke in the building.

"There's so much that I remember, but right from the start, when I was a little boy, I was always fascinated by sports. I always wanted to be in it. I never ever had any thoughts about being on TV or on the radio or any of that. I always wanted to be involved, whether it was as a player or as a coach or something like that. I never thought that I'd ever work on television."

McGuire may have never thought his passion for hockey would lead to television work, however, it's easy to find out where his passion comes from.

MCGUIRE: "When you grew up in Montreal you saw the Montreal Canadiens and you saw them winning almost every year. You saw the great players they had back in the late-60s, early-70s and all through the '70s. That was right in my wheelhouse from when I was growing up. So it's hard not to want to be part of something when you see just how great an organization is, how great their players are, how much success they had and the energy around the organization. That was a big thing for me.

"I always really respected the Canadiens and the way they did their business and the brand they had. It was a treat to be able to go to a game in Montreal. I remember as a kid, it was just so hard to get tickets. And I remember being able to go with my brothers from time to time and man just sitting in The Forum and being able to be there. It was just an amazing thing. It was an unbelievable thing."

But it wasn't just his love for the Montreal Canadiens that grew McGuire's passion for sports. It was also his family.

MCGUIRE: "My parents always encouraged us to be involved in a lot of extracurricular activities, whether it was being in sports or learning how to play a musical instrument. Our parents were amazingly supportive. My brothers and I and my sister were really fortunate in the house where we grew up. Sports were really encouraged. They did everything they could to get us involved in different leagues. I was really grateful as a young person growing up in the house that I grew up in to have the support of my family.

"My parents let me go to a really good High School in New Jersey called Bergen Catholic High School to play sports (football and hockey) my junior and senior year. They trusted me to do that. I was a young kid and they let me go do that. And I'm forever grateful, because it was probably two of the best years I ever had in my life. I just loved my teammates. I loved the school, loved everything about it. So I was really grateful to have the support of my family that I had. I was very fortunate, again, my experiences as a youth really helped enhance my life tremendously and I'm forever grateful to those."

Shortly after finishing his High School career, McGuire started taking the appropriate next steps in his journey to employment in the hockey world.

MCGUIRE: "I played College Hockey for four-years. I played professional hockey over in Europe. I signed with the New Jersey Devils, but I chose not to go to the Minor Leagues when I was sent there by New

Jersey. That's the day I got released; when I didn't want to go down to the American League or even the IHL back then.

"I got into coaching and I started coaching college; and I coached in college for six-years. Then I got hired in the National Hockey League by the Pittsburgh Penguins and was part of their management team and coaching staff for 1991 and 1992 when we won the Stanley Cup.

"In 1997-98, I was coaching St. Louis' farm team down in Baton Rouge, Louisiana and a friend of mine called me up and he said, 'Hey, this radio station in Montreal wants to talk to you.' So I said, 'give them my number.' Ted Blackman was the Station Manager of CJAD Radio in Montreal and they were the rights holders of the Montreal Canadiens.

"He called me up and he said, 'listen, we have some of your interviews from when you were coaching in Hartford and Ottawa. We really think you would be excellent as a Radio Analyst for the Montreal Canadiens. Would you come in and take a test to do it?' I said, 'well, I'll be in Montreal when the season's over.'

"So, I went up and visited my mother and father and I went and did a test. At the end of it, they offered me a job and they said we want to change the radio dynamic of the Montreal Canadiens.' And they wanted to hire me as their Color Analyst.

"I did that for two-years and then I got hired by the national carrier of the NHL in Canada; TSN. I went to move to Toronto and I got on TV in Toronto and in 2004, NBC approached me and said, 'we'd love to have you work for us if you think you could broadcast the games from between the benches.' And I said, 'I know I can. (But) I don't think the league will allow you.' And they said, 'leave that to us.'

"Then we had the lockout, obviously, in 2005 and then I started working for NBC in '05-'06. It's been a wild ride, but my opportunity came because Ted Blackman, who's no longer alive, approached me about coming to work for the Montreal Canadiens. And I'm really glad that I did."

FAVORITE PLAYER(S) GROWING UP

MCGUIRE: “Jean Beliveau was one of my favorites. Larry Robinson was one of my favorites. I had so much respect for Yvan Cournoyer. It was pretty amazing to be there. It was such a good team. They always had a steady array of good players coming in. I always cheered for the organization. The players they had were exceptional and it was just a treat to be able to grow up watching them.”

MCGUIRE’S FAVORITE NBC GAME HE’S CALLED

Being in a fairly different role from 90% of the other broadcasters, Pierre McGuire has had many opportunities to experience the game of hockey at a level and vantage point that most can only dream of. As NBC’s Inside The Glass Analyst, McGuire has heard and seen things during games that either don’t show up in the game record footage or that need to be re-examined after the fact. So, with so many different experiences, it’s hard for him to pick just one game that stood out.

Instead, he’s picked snippets of several games for you to take a closer look at. Enjoy your time looking through his eyes in Inside The Glass.

MCGUIRE: “The biggest thing was in 2010. I'll never forget the Patrick Kane goal in Philadelphia to clinch The Cup for the Hawks. Their first Stanley Cup since 1961. I'll never forget, everybody thought the puck wasn't in, but Kane knew the puck was in. So I'll never forget that.

“I couldn't tell one way or the other. But what I did know and I pushed my talk back to the truck because I saw Kane celebrating. I said, 'I think this thing is over. That guy knows he scored.' You could tell he knew right away. So it's kind of an interesting piece of video. If you ever watch it, you see the play and you just see his reaction and he just comes skating down the center of the ice away from the net where he just scored. It was really surreal. That's my takeaway from that.

“I'll (also) never forget the Bruins winning their Game Seven in Vancouver in 2011. Just the emotion in the building in Vancouver and the way the Bruins won. That was one of the more emotional Game Seven's I've been around. So I thought that was spectacular.

"What I remember the most is a player who I used to coach. We had gotten together the night before, Mark Recchi who's now in the Hockey Hall of Fame. We got together for a glass of wine at our hotel and we were just talking about his career and how special it had been. He'd won The Cup in '91 in Pittsburgh. He'd won The Cup in '06 in Carolina. And this looked like it was going to be his Swan song, his last game, whether they won it or not in Game Seven in Vancouver.

"As soon as the outcome was pretty much sealed, I looked over at the bench and I just saw Recchi. One of my most cherished pictures is an interview I did with him after the game on the ice and his arms around me and you can just see he's swelling with pride.

"(Then) I (also) remember the '07 Stanley Cup of Anaheim because the Ducks actually let me stand on their bench to broadcast the games. Brian Burke, their General Manager, allowed that to happen because there was no inside the glass position. I think that's the first time that ever happened in sports, where you actually had an analyst on a team's bench calling the game. That was because of Brian Burke and his awareness of the importance of the media.

"There were no issues at all with the players. In fact, there's a funny story during the course of the game. We started that earlier in the playoffs, so it wasn't like it just happened in The Final. I did a lot of Anaheim games that year. So I was on their bench a lot. So they kind of just got used to it to be honest. But there's a funny moment. I want to say it was in the Colorado-Anaheim series, where I said, 'that was an egregious turnover.' And one of the players turned around and he said, 'what does that mean?' I had to explain what egregious means.

"It was pretty funny. The whole bench kind of got a snicker out of that one. But the players were great. The trainers were great. The coaching staff led by Randy Carlyle was phenomenal. Again, I can't give Brian Burke enough credit for that. I think that really helped solidify Inside the Glass; that Stanley Cup run by Anaheim in 2007, really allowed the position to grow and Brian deserves a lot of credit for that. So do the Ducks.

"There are the Olympics too. The 2010 Olympics with Canada and the U.S. And Canada won in overtime when (Sidney) Crosby scored the Golden Goal. I'll never forget that. That was a spectacular moment.

“I just wanted a great Gold Medal game. I really did. What blew me away in that one was you could hear Crosby screaming. And if you ever listen to the tape, you hear him going 'Iggy. Iggy. Iggy.' He says it three times. And again, Jarome Iginla found him wide open in front of Ryan Miller and I was right on the shooting line. So I saw that puck go in. And right then, you just don't say anything as a broadcaster, you let the emotion of the event take over, let the pictures tell the story. And that's what we did. (Chris Cuthbert and I did that game.)”

MESSAGE TO NBC FANS

As is a common theme amongst members of the sports media, it is a well known fact that without the fans our jobs would either A) not exist or B) they’d have a lot less meaning. So, each of the broadcasters in this book took a couple of minutes to address you, the fans, directly.

MCGUIRE: “Thank you so much for your passion and your energy concerning the game. Without the fans we wouldn't have anything to do with the game. There'd be no broadcast. There'd be no games. There'd be no players on the ice. Our fans are amazingly loyal. In my opinion, they're the best fans in all of sports and I'm just grateful for every day; them taking interest in our game and watching the product on television or listening to the product on the radio.

“It's an amazing sport to be part of and I can tell you, everybody who works in my profession, every single day, approaches it like it's a Game Seven. They approach every game as if it's a Game Seven. Nobody's taking shortcuts in our business. We do it, a lot of people do it, because we really care about the fans and want to give back to the game.”

NHL NETWORK

JAMISON COYLE
TV: HOST

First Season on NHL Network TV: 2014-15
Seasons on NHL Network TV (including 2020-21): 7

Birthday: April 14, 1984 Hometown: Nashua, NH

College/University: Syracuse University

BIOGRAPHY

Becoming a Sports TV Host is not the usual path one takes to in the sports broadcasting industry. Usually, an aspiring broadcaster wants to do Play-by-Play, or, in the event they're a former athlete, they want to do Color Commentary. Hosting is not what many people strive for. Then again, nobody said Jamison Coyle was "most people."

That's not to say Hosting was always in Coyle's sights. However, even he'll admit that doing Play-by-Play just wasn't for him. Sure, he could do it in a pinch if needed. But Hosting was where he found his niche and he's quickly risen to the top of his profession.

But first, let's quickly check in on a young Jamison Coyle to find out a little about his upbringing.

COYLE: "I grew up playing and my parents didn't have any background in hockey or anything like that. They just saw a learn to skate type program and signed me up for it. The way my mom kind of tells the story is, I went, I did the first skills practice and I spent probably 98% of the time, just like a baby deer on ice; the entire time I could barely stand up.

"So after that first hour practice, skate session, I came home and my mom was like, 'Oh, he's never going to want to do that again.' She asked if I liked it and I said, 'I loved it.' I loved being on the ice and it was just such a cool thing to me. Growing up in New Hampshire, it was cold enough. In our yard I built a rink. I just loved the sport. I loved everything about it. I grew up playing all the way through High School and it's still a huge part of my life."

During his childhood and early teen years playing sports, Coyle also loved to watch/listen to his favorite teams on television and radio. In those days, the Bruins and Red Sox consumed him and were highly important, so it's only natural that those team's broadcasters left a mark on a young Coyle.

COYLE: "Growing up, the voices of my childhood were Derek Sanderson and Fred Cusick for TV38 in Boston. You'd get a fuzzy feeling when you heard those voices because you knew the Bruins were on. It was let's gather around the TV and watch the Bruins tonight. On the Red Sox side of things, it was Sean McDonough and then transitioned into Don Orsillo. For me, it was about the regional broadcast. Those were the teams I was watching and those were the broadcasters who I heard on a daily basis."

During his time in High School Coyle realized he wasn't talented enough to one day become a pro athlete, although he feels he likely could have played Division III in College. So, since he still wanted to stick around the game of hockey, he decided to pursue a career in broadcasting, especially once he realized it was a profession he could actually shoot for.

So, Coyle set off for Syracuse University's famed broadcasting program and along the way, he developed plenty of skills as a News Reporter. Just don't ask him to cover the weather as that one-time try flopped. However, once Coyle got situated in the realm of sportscasting, he quickly took to Hosting and hasn't looked back.

COYLE: "My first job out of school was in Dalton, Georgia, a really small town just South of Chattanooga. I was a News Reporter for three-months there. And then, after that, a sports position opened up at the same station in Dalton, Georgia. I took that and I've kind of been in sports ever since.

"So I went from Dalton, Georgia, to Terre Haute, Indiana and then from Terre Haute, Indiana to Wichita, Kansas. And then, from Wichita, Kansas to Boston. That was my big break to get to a regional sports network (NESN). That was a dream come true. Then, when I found out 'Oh, wow, I can do hockey full-time,' a job at the NHL Network came open and I landed it luckily."

During his journey, Coyle also met some very important people.

COYLE: "I met my wife in Indiana. Some of my best friends, still to this day and people who were in my wedding, come from my stop in small town, Kansas. So, looking back, it was a long journey to get to where I wanted to be, but also in the same realm, it wasn't.

"I graduated in 2006 and then I was in Georgia. Then from 2007-2010, I was in Indiana and then from 2010 to 2014, I was in Boston. Then, 2014-15, I moved to the New York City area, for the NHL network. And that's where I've been since."

You may find yourself asking how Coyle so quickly landed at the NHL Network, well it's actually a funny story.

COYLE: "While working at NESN, I kind of had my eye on the NHL Network and this was while they were still based in Toronto.

"I had an Agent at the time and I made it pretty clear 'Hey, this is really what and where I want to target.' So we were having conversations with the folks in Toronto and they were fully staffed and I was perfectly fine at NESN at the time. But then I came to find out, MLB Network made a bid for the broadcast rights or the partnership with the NHL and the NHL Network.

"So, lo and behold, we find out that the NHL Network is going down to Secaucus, New Jersey and it's going to be under the same roof as MLB Network. My agent tells me that and I'm like, 'Oh my God, dream job. I grew up playing hockey and baseball. Two of the four big sports are going to be in one building. That's incredible. Let's really pursue that.'.

"Luckily for me, he had clients working at MLB Network, so he had the connections. The folks who would be running the NHL Network were already in the building on the baseball side of things. So, he got me an audition and everything happened so quickly. I remember this was all happening in the summer, around August.

"The NHL season was going to fire up the first week of October. So it happens in August and they fly me down for the audition. It was probably the most nervous I've ever been, but I was prepared. I think I auditioned pretty well. I got an audition with E.J. Hradek, who, he's a true pro and now he's a good friend of mine and we actually share an office together, but he was phenomenal to work with. We had instant chemistry.

"I think I did a great job in my audition. The funny thing about the audition was, everything was happening so quickly with MLB Network kind of taking over and running the operations for the National Hockey League Network, that when I did my audition and we're doing a hockey game, the scores you put up at the end, well it had hits, runs and errors because they still had baseball things going.

"They hadn't built hockey yet and they weren't even ready to do hockey type stuff. All of that stuff was in the works and they were trying to be built in the two months that they had until launch. So it was very interesting. But like I said, I was lucky enough to get a call. They said they liked me and how soon could I get down there?

"So, in a span of about three-weeks, my life just flipped. We sold our house. We moved to New Jersey. We had a one-year-old kid and away we went. It was an absolute whirlwind those first couple of weeks; just new job, new city, new network.

"I mean, it was mind blowing and my head was spinning, but it was incredible how we kind of got that thing off the ground and running. In the seven-years I've been here, we've kind of taken steps every year to get better and put on a better product for the fans. I'm very proud of where we started and I'm even prouder of where we're at today."

FAVORITE TEAM(S) GROWING UP

COYLE: "When you're born and raised in New England, you're born and raised to root for the Bruins. So the Bruins were the team I rooted for growing up and the team that I still kind of pull for now. Black and gold all the way. But it's interesting, my grandfather spoke French and he lived in New Hampshire as well. So, when we went over there, I had to watch Canadiens games in French with him. He watched Montreal.

"I rooted for the Bruins and then I also kind of liked Toronto, just the color scheme and everything growing up. I was probably the only kid in New Hampshire rolling around with the Toronto Maple Leafs starter jacket, back when those were kind of popular in the day. So my allegiances growing up were kind of the Leafs and the Bruins, but more so the B's. Then I learned the history of the teams and learned that you can't really root for both at the same time."

HOCKEY AFTER DARK -- TALES AWAY FROM THE RINK

When you're not affiliated with any one team in the league it's important to remain neutral when breaking down the events of a game. Sure, you can show excitement over something special taking place, but it's usually best to keep things calm, cool and collected.

That went out the window during and immediately after Game Seven of the Western Conference First-Round series between the Sharks and Golden Knights in 2019. The NHL Network Analysts who were charged with recapping the wildness of that game were left utterly speechless and could not contain themselves over the epic collapse that had transpired on the ice.

COYLE: "The one that really jumps out to me was a couple of years ago. I think it was the first-round, Vegas and San Jose. We're about to come on after the four-goal comeback in Game Seven for our Post-Game show and it was myself, Kevin Weekes and Ken Daneyko. At that point, our makeup was done and we were just watching as fans. To see that game unfold in the way that it did.

"Weekes has been there. Daneyko has been there. So, to watch those guys just kind of lose their minds over what we were seeing, it was so fun. It's something I'll never forget. And then we had to come on right after that game.

"I remember the first thing was, we usually give a quick reaction and then we get right into the highlights. And I remember being like, 'all right, Dano, what did we just see?' It was supposed to be like 15 to 20-seconds, but he went into detail of everything we saw in those last five-minutes of regulation. The four power-play goals. And then, at the end of it, he goes, 'I know I just spoke for about eight-minutes but I'm at a loss for words.'

"It's still like one of the funniest things I've ever heard, because he just kept going and going, he couldn't help himself, because it was the most incredible thing we've ever seen. It was just so fun."

That's just one example of the fun that the broadcasters for the NHL Network can have. Another is when they get to travel.

COYLE: "We were on site for the 2017 Stanley Cup Final. I love all the people I work with and we're always in and out of the studio. We have great chemistry. We go out for dinners and stuff. But to see the scene that we saw in Nashville. I'll defer to the Analysts, the pros who have been there and seen almost everything there is to see in sports. And they'd never seen anything like what we saw in Nashville for that Final run; just the camaraderie and the spirit of that city. The people on Broadway and downtown.

"For me, being a huge country music fan and being there at the same time of Game Six of the Stanley Cup Final, as a country music festival is going on, it was just so surreal. It's such a cool atmosphere that I don't think has been recreated since. Vegas was bananas because it's Vegas. But for me, with all the country fans in and around Bridgestone Arena, that was not only one of the best business trips I've ever been on but just one of the coolest things I've ever been a part of, because the magic in that city was something else. It was incredible. The set-up there is perfect."

MESSAGE TO NHL NETWORK FANS

As is a common theme amongst members of the sports media, it is a well known fact that without the fans our jobs would either A) not

exist or B) they'd have a lot less meaning. So, each of the broadcasters in this book took a couple of minutes to address you, the fans, directly.

COYLE: "I would say thank you for challenging us. We don't take the knowledge of our fan base for granted at all. The fans who tune into the NHL Network are passionate hockey fans. We don't get the casual fan. We have very intelligent, highly passionate, very vocal (fans). And I'll say that in a very nice way. That's what we love about the sport of hockey. I feel like it's different, right? It's almost like a cult. And we have a chip on our shoulder because we're not the most popular sport out there, but I will put us up there with the most passionate sport and the most passionate people.

"I can not go to work and wing it or half-ass it. I have to be on my toes, be prepared and be as good as I can be on every single night because I think our fans deserve that. And if I don't do that, trust me, they will let me know. I love the fact that our fans are so intelligent and passionate and they hold us accountable each and every night. So, I thank them for making us and personally me better at my job."

E.J. HRADEK
TV: ANALYST/HOST

First Season on NHL Network TV: 2011-12
Seasons on NHL Network TV (including 2020-21): 10

Birthday: July 29, 1960 Hometown: White Plains, NY

College/University: Pace University

BIOGRAPHY

There are certain times in a person's life when they have to make hard decisions regarding where they are, where they're going, where they want to go and what they're going to do when they get there. None of it is easy and it can cause many sleepless nights. But as long as you have a passion for something you're doing, it can make those decisions easier.

E.J. Hradek didn't have any particular connection to hockey. He didn't have any family who played it or worked in the sport. He wasn't a particularly adept player where he was going to one day make it to the NHL as a player. But he knew he loved hockey. Why? Even he can't really articulate that. But he can articulate just how much he loved sports in general and how he knew early in life that the sports industry was where he wanted to end up.

So, now, let's take a journey with Hradek, back through all of his decisions and let's take a moment to appreciate how his career came to be. As always, I'll let him narrate the tale.

HRADEK: "I don't know if there was any rhyme or reason to why I kind of fell in love with hockey. I didn't have anybody in my house who was a hockey fan. I was just a big sports fan going back to when I was a small boy and I really enjoyed all the sports. But for some reason, I really kind of took to hockey. I can remember being a young kid wearing a team jacket for a youth hockey team that had the crossed flags of the U.S. and Canada.

"That's one of those memories that sticks with me. I didn't get to really play ice hockey until I was in my mid-teens, but I played a lot of street hockey and things of that nature. Like I said, I was just a pretty big sports fan as a kid and that was just an offshoot of it. It was just in my blood, I guess.

"The sports landscape was obviously much different and it was one where it was the four major sports. Today, College sports are much more important on the horizon and there's soccer and European soccer and auto racing. All these sports were going on then as well, but in the U.S. at that time, it was pretty much the four majors: baseball, football, basketball and hockey.

"We played a lot of street hockey. We played a lot of Wiffle Ball. We played a lot of touch football. We played a lot of basketball. Street hockey was just one of those things where I just kind of gravitated towards it. I can remember having a Montreal Canadiens jersey when I was very young that was a Christmas gift. When the Islanders came into existence in the early-70s I ended up being an Islanders fan at that time."

Along with loving sports, Hradek also had a strong sense of appreciation for the broadcasters of the day.

HRADEK: "The gold standard in the U.S. at the time was Dan Kelly, who did the St Louis Blues games and then he would appear on national broadcasts when they wouldn't be on. CBS actually had a hockey package in the late-60s, early-70s. They'd have Sunday afternoon games and Dan Kelly would do those games. His voice is kind of emblazoned in my memory; the way he would call games with a flourish and his sound. He just had a great voice, a great style and a real passion for the game from the standpoint of a young person listening."

That fondness for sports and broadcasting fueled Hradek's early forays into the sports industry.

HRADEK: "I can remember in the early-70s, I was a big Green Bay Packers fan. I've been a big Green Packers fan for most of my life and I can remember having a tape recorder that I got as a birthday or Christmas gift and sitting in front of the TV and trying to broadcast the Packers-Redskins playoff game in 1972.

"That was the first time that I did that for sure. As I got older, I just was looking to be in sports. I was a print journalist for a good while. When I was starting in College, I got a job as a part-time Sports Writer or a Freelance Sports Writer for the local paper, covering High School games and some other various sporting events in the community.

"I worked for a place called Sports Ticker, which later kind of ended up as part of the ESPN family. It was a data entry tracking thing. That's when we'd be in an office. It was a bunch of us. A lot of the guys ended up going on to work in other parts of the business. I mean, John Giannone, for example, who's the Rangers Sideline Reporter on their TV broadcasts, he was somebody who worked at Sports Ticker. There were a number of guys like that who went on to other things.

"I've been very fortunate. I always knew I wanted to be in sports. I always laugh now that if I wasn't doing what I do, I'd have to go out and get a real job and it's way too late for that.

"I graduated from Pace in '85. I started in '79-'80. Then I was out of school for about a year and then I came back into school and finished out. When I came back, I was working a full-time job at PepsiCo. So I was working in Westchester County in New York as a full-time Mail Clerk there five-days a week and then going to school at night and then playing on the club hockey team, which meant practicing at 10, 10:30, 11 o'clock at that time. So when I look back on that part of my life, I do wonder how bad I managed to get through it, but I did.

"That was the time that I really kind of turned myself around. I think I matured and understood exactly what I needed to do to try to get where I wanted to go. There were still a lot of things I really was uncertain of at that time. I didn't have that person in my family who could guide me or give me that right, kind of sage advice to push me in the right direction. So I was always kind of feeling my way along. When I got out of school, I continued to work at PepsiCo for a short period of time and then I got the opportunity to go over to the Sports Ticker, which was in Scarsdale, New York. That was probably around '85-'86.

"We answered phones. It was kind of a data entry set up where we had a computer system where people would call in from the various games all over North America and Canada, with updates of the games. We would pick up the phone and take those calls. Then we would put that information into a kind of a data entry set up.

"We would write previews and recaps and things like that. Sometimes we'd write some stories for the wire service.

"I think my most memorable circumstance when I was there was a couple years into it. The (Wayne) Gretzky trade happened in August of '88. I was there at night and the story started to come in about that and I had to decide whether the story merited us putting it out on our wire. After making a few calls and figuring out that the story did have legs, I sent it out over the wire and then the next day it ended up happening.

"Then after that, I ended up getting a job for the New York Post, which was huge for me at the time. The path was you would come in there as a Clerk, an Agate Clerk. Your job, basically at that point, was to input all kinds of the small information that goes into newspapers, really small type information and they would run that every day.

"There were a lot of commands that had to be put into place to have that going to print appropriately. Stuff like horse racing results and standings. Real low man on the totem pole kind of work. But at the time I got the job, I was ecstatic, because I thought being at the New York Post in like '88-'89, 'wow, this is a great opportunity.' And the odd part of it was that after nine-months, I quit, because I just found out that there were too many people trying to climb up the same ladder. There was a lot of infighting and it was unappealing.

"At 28 or 29, I figured I needed to make something happen sooner and not realizing that there's a lot of life to be led. So I had that job for about nine-months and met some interesting people there. I can remember Peter Vecsey, who was the big basketball guy at the time and went on to do some basketball television work as an Insider/Analyst, counseling me when I told him that I was leaving. He was like, 'well life is like basketball. You gotta get under the basket and block out and wait for the rebounds.'

"I was like, 'yeah, but this doesn't seem like it's gonna happen for me here.' So I ended up getting another job as an Editor for a sports monthly. At the time, there were monthly magazines that would come out at different times of the year. Some of them were annual and they would come out once a year and it was a group of magazines.

"So I did that for a year or two and then that led me to a job working for Beckett Hockey Monthly, which was a magazine. Beckett Publications was more of a collectibles group. The baseball card industry kind of boomed in the early-90s and this gentleman, James Beckett, was at the forefront of pricing cards. They had what we would call a price guide and that was the centerpiece of their magazine.

"They were in Dallas, Texas, where their offices were and they were having a hard time finding someone to come down and edit their magazine.

"You had to know something about collectibles, but they wanted someone who really understood hockey to come in and be the Editor. So they brought me down there and after a couple of interviews, they ended up offering me the job, which I accepted. I moved to Texas and I moved down to Dallas.

"I did that job for three or four-years and in the interim the Minnesota North Stars moved to Dallas to become the Dallas Stars. That gave me an opportunity to have a team right in my backyard and only a handful of people in town really understood hockey. It gave me a great opportunity to do a lot of different things. I ended up working with the radio station down there. Sports radio had just started really down in Dallas.

"I ended up doing a one-hour weekly radio show with a couple of other guys and running tape. So that kind of pushed me more into the broadcast end of my career. That was kind of the first beginning of that and that was probably around '94. I got to Dallas in like '90 and I was there through 1996. But I was at Beckett between '90 and '94. Then I was doing that radio show and doing some other various hockey freelancing for the other two-years.

"Then I decided in '96, I just wasn't sure where things were going at that side of my career. I decided to come back to the New York area and when I was leaving I talked to people like the Stars' General manager Bob Gainey, the Assistant GM, Doug Armstrong and the Player Personnel people like Craig Button and Les Jackson.

"So all these people I got to have relationships with and when I came back to New York, I had a meeting with Les Jackson and I said, 'I'm going back. I could go to games and serve as kind of a Scout for you guys,' because there's Rangers, Islanders, Devils right in the New York area. There's also the Flyers, Capitals and Bruins on the fringes. There's minor league teams all over that area.

"So I threw it out as kind of an idea. Just give me this opportunity, we'll see how it goes. You don't have to pay me. Just pay for whatever my incidentals are, whether it be trains or gas or whatever it took me to get to a place. But I would provide the reports and you guys could decide over a period of a couple of months, if what I was providing was worthwhile. And I could decide over that same time if I enjoyed doing it. So I went back to New York and I started doing some of that scouting work and it really worked out. Les Jackson was impressed with what I was able to provide and I was really enjoying looking at the sport from another perspective and meeting these older Scouts. Some of them were former players.

"I remember Garnet 'Ace' Bailey was a wonderful, wonderful guy and was really open and inviting. But there were a bunch of them. And I learned a lot. I sat next to these guys and they kind of took me under their wing a little bit. I listened and learned a totally different perspective about the game. It really helped me move forward. So I did that for a couple of years, I would say between '96 and '99, Jesus. Then, a guy who I had worked with in Dallas was going to be a Senior Editor at ESPN magazine, which was launching at that time, in '98-'99.

"He brought me in for an interview and offered me a job as the Associate Editor dealing mainly with hockey."

Hradek took the job after much soul-searching and in a funny twist, the Dallas Stars went on to win the Stanley Cup the following Spring. Oh well. If he'd stayed with the Stars he'd have a championship ring. But there's no doubt he made the right decision.

Once at ESPN, Hradek slowly began to build a name for himself and eventually that led to him proposing some TV and radio spots for himself to his superiors. And much like Les Jackson with the Stars, they gave him a chance. However, the journey with ESPN came to a halt a few years after the network and the NHL parted ways. Hradek initially made it through the split, but the writing was on the wall.

His bosses at ESPN thought highly of him, with good reason, but with hockey no longer a main piece of the ESPN puzzle, the returns were diminishing. So, when Hradek got the chance, he began to dip his toes in the waters known as the NHL Network. For a while he did freelance work for the NHL Network while also keeping his ESPN job. But eventually the time came to make a choice and when the NHL Network offered him a full-time gig in 2011, he took it and has been a prominent part of the network's broadcasts ever since.

FAVORITE PLAYER(S) GROWING UP

HRADEK: "Gordie Howe was probably the first player where I was like, 'Oh, he's like Mr. Hockey.' He was playing for the Detroit Red Wings when I was little. He was one. Mickey Redmond, who has since become a broadcaster for the Red Wings for many, many years now, but he was a 50-goal scorer with the Red Wings. He had a big shot. I remember trying to emulate that when playing street hockey. And then, when I got to be on the ice, I can remember, even though I was just learning and trying to hold onto the boards and figure it out. I was thinking about Yvan Cournoyer with the Canadiens, 'the Road Runner' and how fast he was. So those are some of the ones who come to mind for me."

HOCKEY AFTER DARK -- TALES AWAY FROM THE RINK

When you work in media you have the unique situation where you're usually competing with all the other media outlets for coverage, but you're also establishing a relationship with the other reporters. It can be a lonely experience going to cover an event and not having travel companions or people to go for a meal with.

So, what normally happens is, the various reporters who are covering that event or game, they'll usually find some time to get together for a meal, for a drink, to take in a ballgame, etc. Sometimes you get to do that with reporters from the same outlet you're from and other times you do that with competing reporters. Either way, it usually ends up being a pretty good time.

E.J. Hradek has been on all sides of this type of relationship throughout the course of his career and it is those away from the rink memories that will always stand the test of time.

HRADEK: "I've had the good fortune of working with a lot of great people and people who I've really enjoyed working with, going back to Don La Greca, who I've had a really good working relationship with. We're still friends to this day. He was someone who, in the early days of the radio show, would go to the Stanley Cup Final. I'd be going for ESPN, but I would do things for the radio show as well. So, I was lucky with that. Bill Pidto and Deb Placey are people I worked with as well. They're both real pros, really good friends and great people and enjoyed that.

"That leads me to Steve Mears, who came in (to NHL Network), I guess right around 2012. Steve was obviously younger than me. He had been the Islanders' radio guy. He had kind of worked his way up radio Play-by-Play and worked his way up from the ECHL and got that opportunity. The Islanders were kind of a little bit of a star-crossed franchise for many years there and they decided to go to a different approach and then Steve was let go; really nothing he did wrong.

"The Islanders were just doing something different. So, he kind of was looking for that next opportunity. I think he was working in Pittsburgh and they (NHL Network) hired him to be the Co-Host with me, where he'd be the Host and I'd be the Analyst on NHL Live at that point in time. It's since changed to NHL Now.

"But Steve and I worked together for, I guess, five or six-years and became good friends. So, when we would travel for the Stanley Cup Final, that would be the opportunity to go places. There was one-year when San Jose and Pittsburgh were in The Final and we went to see a Giants-Dodgers game in San Francisco. That was awesome. We had ended up getting really good seats and being down the first baseline, like two or three rows off the field. So that was something we always liked to do.

"Later, he still would work The Final for NHL International, broadcasting for them. So we would have a chance to travel during The Cup Finals even after he left the NHL Network to take his current job as the Play-by-Play voice of the Penguins. I think it was a Cardinals-Cubs game we went to together. And again, we lucked out. I think one of the Cardinals' broadcasters ended up getting us really good seats right down by the dugout. We went to see U2 in Pittsburgh one-year during one of The Finals. So that was great. Again, when you're traveling, you're having dinners together, you're looking for things to do.

"I know earlier in my career, when I was still at ESPN and I was more on the print side, Barry Melrose and Steve Levy had been covering the Stanley Cup Final for years and years and years. That was always a big assignment for them and to their credit, I owe them both a debt. They kind of took me under their wing a little bit. They would have dinners, do things and they would include me, which they really didn't have to. So we became friends and I feel like I'm still friends with those guys to this day."

HRADEK'S FAVORITE NHL NETWORK GAME HE'S CALLED

When you work for a network whose purpose is to break down the highlights of games rather than broadcast games in their entirety, it can be difficult for the Analysts and Hosts to choose just a single game or a handful of games that would stand out to them. After all, they're not seeing the whole game. They're seeing snippets, or highlights, because they have to jump from game-to-game at the drop of a hat.

However, the NHL Network, over the years, has managed to gain some very valuable inventory in the form of non-NHL hockey games. And it is that inventory that sets the network apart from some of its competitors.

One such property the NHL Network carries and produces on its own is the annual World Junior Championships and it was during one of those tournaments that E.J. Hradek got to do more than just be an Analyst or a Host.

HRADEK: "During the work stoppage in the 2012-13 season, we didn't play until January. So, Steve Mears was just coming to the NHL network at that time and part of his deal was that he would be able to pursue Play-by-Play opportunities when they arose. And he would do Play-by-Play of different events that the NHL did or the NHL Network had some kind of play in.

"So, the World Junior Championships, the NHL Network has had them on its network for the last 10 or 11-years. Steve called those games for the five or six-years that he was at the NHL Network and the first year, because we were in a stoppage and because I was under contract, they asked me to do the Color. Those games that year were played in Russia, in Sochi I guess, where they eventually would have the Olympics; somewhere in that area of Russia.

"But Steve and I were flown to Denver to call the games off of a monitor at the big Comcast facility in Denver. And when I say it was a big facility, I can't even describe it to you. It was like Fort Knox. It was like a couple of city blocks big. And it was a place where all kinds of Comcast Network stuff would come in and out of there; the signals would come in and out of Denver. It was a monstrous facility that was in Denver. We were calling these games and the local time in Denver would be on at 3:00 AM, 4:00 AM. Steve and I would go into this big cavernous studio and I think Stu Mitchell was the Producer who was with us.

"Joe Whelan, who had been a long time Rangers Producer and now is doing the Columbus Blue Jackets broadcasts, he was with us and provided a lot of experience and a lot of help for us, which was really valuable, because Steve had done a lot of games, but he had not done something like this off a monitor for television. I had not. The funny thing about the World Juniors is, I was one of the first people to really, in the United States, really cover them, from a national media standpoint when I was at ESPN. I had my scouting background. I knew the value of that tournament.

"It was kind of a snapshot of the future star players who would be coming into the league. And I was able to convince ESPN to let me go cover it. They sent me to Winnipeg in 1998-99 for two-weeks. I stayed up there for the entire tournament. I was probably the only American National Reporter on that one. And then I went to Moscow one-year. I went to Finland. The first U.S. Gold Medal in that tournament was 2004, with the Zach Parise team. Ryan Suter and a bunch of guys like Ryan Kesler (on that team) ended up going out to the NHL and playing very well there. But they were part of that first U.S. Gold Medal team. I may have been the only American Reporter in Finland covering that.

"So I had a real history with that tournament. And then in 2012-13, I got to be the Color Analyst for the American games. And the Americans went on to win the Gold Medal. It was something that a lot of people watched and I can remember Wayne Gretzky texting me. That experience doing that World Juniors was terrific and it was unusual to be calling games off a monitor in Denver with a really good staff of people who were up into the early morning hours calling these games and doing these live broadcasts on the NHL Network in the U.S..

"So the fact that we did a Gold Medal game and they won the Gold Medal, it was (terrific). Seth Jones was on that team, as were all kinds of really good high-end players who have gone on to have terrific careers in the National Hockey League. So I would say that was for sure the thing that stood out and it was just so unusual and such a different circumstance. I think, in the end, we were also doing a really good job broadcasting it. A lot of that goes to Steve doing the Play-by-Play and to guys like Joe Whelan, who produced the games and Stu Mitchell, who was someone who was out there helping us as well. Those guys deserve a lot of the credit and that was a great experience for me."

MESSAGE TO NHL NETWORK FANS

As is a common theme amongst members of the sports media, it is a well known fact that without the fans our jobs would either A) not exist or B) they'd have a lot less meaning. So, each of the broadcasters in this book took a couple of minutes to address you, the fans, directly.

HRADEK: "First and foremost would be, thanks. Thank you very, very much for watching and paying attention and following the things I've done in my career. That'd be the first thing. I mean, without people watching and being interested, I mean, we're off doing something else, right? So, that's the first thing, a huge thank you.

"Hockey, it's a big family. It's a little bit of a, I guess some would say a niche in the United States. But it's a big niche and there's a lot of people who love this game and it's a growing number of people. So, I'm just really thrilled to be a part of that family. And I know when things happen within that hockey community, people do have a tendency to kind of take care of one another. I think that's a really nice aspect of it as well.

"It's a great, great game and it's the ultimate team game. Guys are on the ice for 40, 50 seconds, really, with the rare exception at a time. With the advanced statistics now and all kinds of things that go on with the game. The leading player in the game this past year, per 60 minutes, to have the puck on his stick was Thomas Chabot of the Ottawa Senators at 2:43. I mean, think about that. It's a 60 minute game and the guy who has had the puck on his stick the most per 60 minutes, it's just 2:43. It's such a team game and there's so many different roles.

"Players have to play the game for a team to be successful. Lou Lamoriello has had the analogy to an orchestra over the years and he's told his players that. And he's told us in the media that. It's so true. The drummers have to drum and the violin players have to play the violin and the horn section has to do their job. And in our game, in hockey, everyone has to do a particular job and they're all important.

"So, for the fans out there who love hockey, hopefully they appreciate that. Doing things, like being a great tennis player, being a great boxer or different individual sports, or even some sports like in baseball, a great hitter or a great pitcher. I mean, all these little elements have to come together in hockey and it's so unique. And so, I think the group of people who watch this game and are drawn to it, are drawn to that at its core. It's such a team game and you need help from everybody to be successful. So, again, a big thanks to everybody for watching over the years and I think everybody who is a part of this group of people who love hockey, it's a tight knit group, for sure."

SPORTSNET

JOHN BARTLETT
TV: PLAY-BY-PLAY

First Season on SportsNet/HNIC TV: 2014-15
Seasons on SportsNet/HNIC TV (including 2020-21): 7

Birthday: November 28, 1978 Hometown: Newmarket, ON

College/University: Centennial College Toronto

BIOGRAPHY

Have you ever wondered how different your life would be if not for one accidental event? Go ahead, give it some thought, I'm sure there's at least one instance in your life that if it was changed, your whole world would be different.

Well, John Bartlett is pretty happy with how his life turned out, but if it wasn't for one certain event, who knows if his career would have gone the way it has? What is the event that possibly changed the course of his life? How about I let him tell you the whole tale.

BARTLETT: "Like most young Canadian kids, I grew up playing hockey and loved it from a young age. I had fun being a goalie. So you always sort of saw the game a little differently in that way, I suppose. But, the interesting part for me is how hockey playing and the broadcasting side sort of crossed over with each other. I had the unique fortune, I guess you could say, of calling hockey while I was still playing in my teenage years.

"The first hockey game I ever called was simply sort of an opportunity that happened out of the blue. I was the PA Announcer for the local Junior team in town, which is where I got to know Ron MacLean, because he was reffing in the same league and would come to town sometimes. So that's how far back Ron and I actually go, before we worked together too.

"So, I was the PA Announcer for the Newmarket 87 Hurricanes team in town. One day, the local Rogers Cable TV station was doing a Triple-A hockey game in Newmarket and they had brought me in just to do the music for the building that night. I didn't even have to announce I was just doing the music that night. I had just come from playing a game myself, earlier.

"I had just come out of the shower after playing. I had a ball cap and I thought I was hiding up in the press box all night, so it didn't matter. So, I go to the rink, I go up there and I'm all set to do my stuff that night.

"The people who were supposed to show up to do the Play-by-Play for the local television station that night, for whatever reason, didn't show up and they weren't there. So they came down to me and asked me, 'Hey, if you find somebody else to do the music for us here, do you think you could slide down and do the Play-by-Play for us?'

"They knew I was a PA Announcer and I said, 'sure, okay, I'll give it a shot.' So I slid over into the booth and I was 15 at the time. There I am in a shirt and tie with a ball cap on, I wasn't expecting anyone to see me all night and on I go. I jumped on and called my first ever hockey game and had a blast with it. I kind of knew that was going to be something I'd want to pursue from that moment. And that came in October of 1995.

"So I started working on that and then, much like a player, I just progressed my career the same way. I started from there doing Junior Hockey games, Junior A Hockey games and that led me to the OHL. Then that led me into the American Hockey League, which then led me to the NHL. So my path is really very similar to what a player would go through."

So, now that we know about his accidental first Play-by-Play experience, let's dive into how he followed that up.

BARTLETT: "I did minor hockey, so that led to doing some Junior C Hockey on Sunday nights with the Bradford Bulls. Then I went to the Junior A loop and started doing games for the Newmarket 87's and Hurricanes. They changed their name midway through. That was the team I was also the PA Announcer for. So I had started doing games there and then it led to an opportunity where I started doing some work in the Ontario Hockey League.

"I had an opportunity to go to Barrie and work with the Barrie Colts. I ended up spending five-seasons with the Barrie Colts and that opportunity led me to the American Hockey League with the Toronto Marlies.

"I got hired by the Marlies for their first season when they moved from St. John's Newfoundland. So, I did six-seasons in the American Hockey League in Toronto and then the opportunity came up to go to Montreal to start on radio on the Canadiens' broadcasts. So, I moved out to Montreal and did three-seasons on radio before the TV opportunity came up with SportsNet.

"So, then I shifted over to television. I did four more seasons on TV in Montreal before SportsNet wanted to bring me back to Toronto for more national games, more Hockey Night in Canada and to do some of the Toronto Maple Leafs games. And I guess that kind of brings us up to where I am now.

"It meant a lot (to be asked to come do Hockey Night in Canada broadcasts) because, Hockey Night in Canada was always the standard that you aspired to. Every time you do a Hockey Night in Canada game, it's always a little different and it should be different. Everything about Saturday night, especially in Canada, has a different feel to it.

"I think the thing about Saturday night is, especially when you look at the history of it, you look at all the people who have worked there and the big names who have been part of the legacy of the show. That's the biggest key. When you do a Hockey Night in Canada game, you're not just doing a game, you should also be honoring the legacy of everyone who's been there before you.

"So, I think you carry that with you. I know I do. It's a responsibility. I find myself extremely fortunate to be able to sort of sit in the same chair as Danny Gallivan, Bob Cole and Dick Irvin Jr.

"There's no school on Sunday. You get to stay up late and watch the game. It's not like a midweek game where you've got school the next day and the kids have to be in bed. Parents would usually let the kids stay up and watch their team on Saturday night. Every youngster sits in front of the TV to see their team and cheer on their favorite player.

"They don't care what the standings are necessarily that night. They just want to watch their team and cheer them on, on Hockey Night in Canada. So, I always think that there's a little bit of a different feeling you have on a Saturday as well, when it comes to how families are taking in the game.

"Anytime you get to do a Hockey Night in Canada game, I think it's an honor and a privilege and it's something that's very special and means a lot to a lot of people. You're sort of carrying on that legacy of what those before you have brought and that's the standard you have to set for yourself to live up to every game."

FAVORITE PLAYER(S) GROWING UP

BARTLETT: "Growing up being a goalie, you always looked to all the goalies in the league and at that time, Patrick Roy was probably one of the top or the top goalie in the league; especially with what he did during the '93 Cup run. But growing up, all my family had come from Montreal, so I grew up a Canadiens fan. Patrick was someone who a lot of kids looked up too. I mean, look at how much he influenced so many goalies of that time and era with his style. Guy Carbonneau was another player who I always enjoyed watching and had a lot of respect for."

BARTLETT'S FAVORITE HNIC GAMES HE'S CALLED

Whether it's your first ever broadcast for a storied program or an emotional playoff series where the fans are so loud the building quite literally shakes, there are always many different games for you to fondly remember during the course of your career.

John Bartlett has been doing Hockey Night in Canada games for close to a decade now and while he's experienced many different games, in many different venues, there are two that standout to him and for differing reasons.

BARTLETT: "Well, certainly my first Hockey Night in Canada game; that one's always special and always will be special. It was in Ottawa. I still have the puck from it somewhere. It was in January of 2015, Ottawa played Carolina and the Hurricanes won 6-3. To be honest with you, I really just remember the excitement and that feeling, when the game started and we had that first throw to break and you realize you're throwing to break and saying 'Hockey Night in Canada.' That's probably when it really hits you that you're saying it. You're not just pretending to say it, you're actually saying it on the real show."

That's one, now let's hear number two.

BARTLETT: "There was one playoff series I did with the New York Islanders, last year where they returned to The Coliseum against Pittsburgh, where they swept Pittsburgh. Those first two games in The Old Barn were something else. There was emotion with the fans. Not excitement. I mean, beyond excitement. There was personal emotion for the fanbase to be back in there and you felt it. I remember, I think it was in Game Two, the building was so loud that at one point, I actually felt my chair shaking a little up in the box. That was something fun to be a part of."

SIGNATURE PHRASE

How many times, as a fan, have you swore at your television, at your radio, at your computer, your tablet, your phone or some other device that you're watching a game on? How many times have you swore while in the stands watching a game live? Chances are you've done this more times than you can count. But while you can do that without consequence -- usually -- there are those who can't do that because they would lose their jobs. And yes, I am talking about the broadcasters. They have feelings just like you, the fans, but they aren't allowed to express themselves in the same way.

Oh sure, every now and again you hear about a viral moment in which a broadcaster forgot about the rules and said something on air that they shouldn't have. They are human after all and humans make mistakes.

However, John Bartlett has found a way around this sticky situation. His phrase of "Oh my stars" is used in place of those words that he can't utter on air.

BARTLETT: "The one fans would know that I do use is 'oh my stars!' That's saved for something that's a really big play. It might be a play where, if you're a fan in the stands, you might say something that you can't say on air. So it gives you that moment. When I started using that on radio, if you heard that, you knew it was a really big moment in the game and something you'd probably want to catch on the highlight reel later."

MESSAGE TO SPORTSNET FANS

As is a common theme amongst members of the sports media, it is a well known fact that without the fans our jobs would either A) not exist or B) they'd have a lot less meaning. So, each of the broadcasters in this book took a couple of minutes to address you, the fans, directly.

BARTLETT: "Thank you. Thank you for allowing us into your homes and being part of your lives for so many years and for so many generations. And I hope that we can continue to carry on the legacy for generations to come. As times change, the game changes and so does the broadcast, but the spirit of Hockey Night in Canada hopefully will and should always live on."

RON MACLEAN
TV: HOCKEY NIGHT IN CANADA HOST

First Season on Hockey Night in Canada: 1986-87
Seasons on Hockey Night in Canada (including 2020-21): 35

Birthday: April 12, 1960 Hometown: Zweierucek, Germany

College/University: N/A

BIOGRAPHY

When it comes to legendary careers in Hockey Television, there are many names who come to mind. Most of those names are generally Play-by-Play announcers, with a couple Color Commentators mixed in. But, you shouldn't overlook the Hosts. And when it comes to Hosts, the bar is set by longtime Hockey Night in Canada Host, Ron MacLean.

MacLean wasn't the first Host for the legendary program, nor would he say he's the best to ever do it. But there's no denying that since he took over the primary Hosting role some 35-years ago, there's been no better television Host anywhere in the NHL than Ron MacLean.

But did you know, this career path wasn't what LacLean initially had in mind for himself? It's funny, because, as he would put it, "it was all happenstance." Don't get me wrong, he always loved hockey, but the idea of being a Host for Hockey Night in Canada never really crossed his mind.

So, let's find out how this "happenstance career" got going and there;s no better place to start than his childhood. Take it away Ron and yes, that's me throwing the show over to you.

MACLEAN: "It's kind of a wild story. In 1964, my dad was stationed in Whitehorse, Yukon territory. Whitehorse, Yukon would be like going to Alaska as an American. Whitehorse, I think it's at 60 degrees North Latitude. So my Father was based in Yukon, in Whitehorse and that's in the Arctic, or close to the Arctic. So, long winters and we didn't have live television.

"So, I'm a boy and I'm four-years-old in '64. We don't have live television if you can believe it. The satellites hadn't gone up in orbit yet. So we would get all our TV on videotape, including Hockey Night in Canada. The games were sent on two-inch videotape to the North and I would watch the game.

"At four, five, six-years-old, you didn't realize that the outcome had been decided 24 to 48-hours earlier. There was no such thing as Twitter back then. So I would watch the hockey games and my parents knew and would get a great kick out of watching me watch my Leafs, because they knew the score and I didn't. So that's kind of how it started for me; it was taped hockey games.

"Of course, the benefit of being in the North was there was a really long outdoor Winter season. So I skated and played hockey religiously as a boy up there and fell in love with the game; more that way than I did through the NHL or the broadcasts. I actually fell in love with the playing of the sport. But the two coincided.

"It wasn't long before I built my life around Hockey Night in Canada. I would set up shop in my bedroom where I had a black and white TV, which was the lucky TV. If I watched the Leafs in color, on our main television, out in the front room, they'd lose.

"If I watched them in black and white, they'd win. So it wasn't long before I was holed up in my bedroom always watching on a tiny little television, a 12-inch screen, in black and white. But I would get my snacks ready. I was a big fan of sunflower seeds and red nibs licorice. Everything had to be set up and I had to be in front of the TV for the very beginning of the broadcast. I wanted to hear the Hosts, whether it was Ward Cornell, way back in the day, or Dave Hodge. I wanted to hear everything that was said about the game. It's so funny, I was indirectly training for the life I ended up leading."

That is funny. A job he never had any intention of pursuing, he was being trained for at a young age. Of course, as MacLean alluded to, he also played the game quite a bit as a youngster, which certainly helped o grow his overall knowledge of the sport.

MACLEAN: "I started playing first. My parents were not sports ans. They were sort of arts, literature and political science junkies. Our ome was filled with music and news; no sports. But my next door ighbor, Dwight, came by the house and invited me to go to another neighbor's home, where they had a backyard rink. And that's how it all started.

"Once I started getting the bug for actually playing the game. Those two families introduced me to Saturday Night Hockey, which honestly, if I'm not mistaken, they actually ran the videotape of the previous week's Saturday up there. So again, we weren't getting live transmission until 1968, when the annex satellite went in the sky and CBC was finally live in the North. I was eight-years-old then."

Even though his parents weren't the prototypical sports fans, it turned out his Mother actually had quite the connection to the game of hockey and that connection helped shape MacLean's early fandom.

MACLEAN: "My mother, although she was into music and the news, her family history, her first cousin is Al MacNeil, who coached the Montreal Canadiens to the Stanley Cup in 1971. So she had a little bit of a connection to the game. The Sydney Millionaires and Glace Bay Miners were teams in Cape Breton, Nova Scotia, where she was raised. She knew of them but she didn't really take the bait. She was kind of detached from that whole storyline. But as soon as I started to love hockey, then she explained to me my history with Al MacNeil and the Montreal Canadiens. And being a boy who wanted to have a rival, I went the other way. She was Habs. So I had to be Leafs just for the fun of it."

Now that we know about MacLean's upbringing, let's start to get this broadcast going and find out if that inadvertent training had paid off. Or, better yet, let's find out how much of that inadvertent training stuck with him and whose influence it was.

MACLEAN: "The heavy influences were the Alberta broadcasters: Al McCann; Ernie Afaganis and John Wells. They were all the Sports Hosts based in Alberta. Ed Whalen, with whom I worked, was a Host of Stampede Wrestling and the Flames broadcasts. So they were local broadcasters who each brought a different style. I think Al McCann was the one who I tried to emulate. He was just a DJ. I had no aim to get into this, even though I loved it, devoutly. Everything was happenstance. I didn't apply to a radio station.

"As far as Hockey Night in Canada is concerned, I had the greatest respect for their hosts: Ward Cornell; Dave Hodge; Brian McFarlane and Dick Irvin Jr. As for the Play-by-Play, it goes without saying Danny Gallivan and Foster Hewitt were, to me, the Gods of The

Gondola. But I really enjoyed Dan Kelly. He called Mario Lemieux's Canada Cup-winning goal in 1987, which was an epically great call. I remember his call of Red Berenson's six-goals in a game. I can remember him calling Red Berenson's sixth goal of the game against the Philadelphia Flyers, going around Ed Van Impe. Personally, I think that's the finest call of a goal in history.

"That's the one that sparked (something) in me. For the first time, I kind of went away from being a fan to being an admirer of the person's work. It struck me that as great as Berenson's goal was, that the man who provided the call had generated a feeling in me that now, for the first time, linked me to the notion that I might want to pursue that job."

Now that we have our foundation, let's begin to ramp up the story and find out how MacLean got to where he is today.

MACLEAN: "I got a call out of the blue to go to work as a part-timer because a friend in High School was sick. So I replaced him on a button pushing shift for nine hours, real simple stuff. And one thing led to another. I always looked at the guys like Al McCann and Bruce Bowie as achievable. They were just sort of the nice guys who weren't too flamboyant. They were thoughtful. They were good storytellers, good interviewers. I felt like that was something that I could possibly do.

"The initial path was to be a Disc Jockey. I was spinning records and again, you're always inadvertently training for your career. The joy of DJing as it applies to hosting TV, is that every song has a music bed. It could be four-seconds before the vocals begin. It could be 22-seconds and the DJ talks over the music and then butts out the minute the singer starts singing.

"We call that hitting the post or hitting the fade. If you can tell that little story in four-seconds on that particular song or in 22-seconds as the case may be and finish your thought at the 22-second mark, that's fantastic. So you do it over and over again and you watch it several times.

"If you talk over the singer that's considered a real no-no on the radio. So I was learning how to mentally edit on the fly, how to think of 22-seconds or 42 seconds. It was great training for TV where everything's done on counts.

"A lot of times you're being counted off the air, counted to commercials. So it was one of the greatest benefits of a nine-year career in radio, starting in '76 and ending in '84. I thought I would do that. I thought I would be a full-time DJ announcer. I wasn't great. I thought I would do a hybrid show of music and interviews, which was more along the lines of things that ran on public service radio.

"Anyway, there was a (divine) intervention, John Shannon was a producer at Hockey Night in Canada, based in Calgary at the time. He out of the clear blue, phoned me up in the Spring of 1984 and he said, 'Ron, TSN, the sports network is starting their operation and they're hiring a lot of the commentators out of Alberta. They're taking Jim Van Horne and John Wells and Peter Watts. So there's lots of job openings, including the Flames broadcasts, the midweek telecasts. The Flames on Two and Seven need a new Host cause Jim Van Horne is going to TSN in Toronto. I'd like you to apply.' And that's how it happened.

"It was like a complete thunderbolt. The reason John thought I could do that job was because I was the Weatherman in Red Deer. When you were the noon-to-four Radio DJ at CKRD in Red Deer, whoever did the noon-to-four radio shift automatically was assigned as the Weather Presenter on the six o'clock evening television news. They had a TV station.

"So I was the weather person in Red Deer, Alberta. It's a little town and at the time it was about 40,000 people. It was a big thing. It was an agriculture based community, so the weather person was actually kind of a star because they gave the relative humidity, which was important. Anyway, I did that and when our equipment would malfunction during the news or the farm news or the sports, none of which I did, I just did the weather. But when the equipment would break down, as it invariably did in a small town market, they would ask me to fill the time to make up for the clips that didn't run.

"I would have to do maybe a 10-minute weather cast and I didn't have 10-minutes to talk about the weather. So I would forecast sports events instead. And that's what John Shannon tapped into and thought, 'Hmm, this kid seems to know sports and can dance a little, tap dance. So I'm going to give him a shot at auditioning for this Flames on Two and Seven position that's been vacated by Jim Van Horne.' I went down and nine of us all auditioned, separate times of course, but same day. We went one after the other. And I got the gig. God knows what John saw in me because I was a deer in headlights; just terrified and stiff. But somehow he had faith and the rest is history.

"It was funny because he called me around April or May and then I didn't hear back from him. He went off to his home in the interior of British Columbia, a real hot, sunny vacation spot. He kind of shut down for a couple of months and then he phoned me back in late August and the audition was at the start of September. It all happened, bang, bang. I got married on September 1st and on September 7th, I started in Calgary. It was just completely crazy and a leap of faith. I ended up going to Calgary and that started my Flames telecasts.

"The color guy was John Davidson. So I traveled for those two-years. I did 60 games, all of them with John Davidson. He was freshly retired. The first night I worked was Halloween night in Landover, Maryland, which was where the rink was. I was pretty pleased with how it went. I was by no means gonna win an Oscar, but I got through it, for all my fears. It seemed to be smooth and went well enough that I was quite happy getting on the team bus.

"We were traveling to the airport to fly to Detroit for a game the next day. I got on the team bus, quite pleased with myself. Then, John Davidson was sitting beside me. He said, 'look, Ron, you did a great job tonight and everything's great. But when you get on the team bus and the team has lost the game, you can't be happy-go-lucky. You have to kind of feign disappointment and consternation. They don't want you to be joking. There's no room for levity after a loss.' So that was my first lesson in what it's like in the bigs."

We're almost there. In order to go from doing Flames games to getting to be part of Hockey Night in Canada, MacLean needed one more thing to happen.

MACLEAN: "Intervention. And again, I give John Shannon credit. So what happened is, Dave Hodge, who was the preeminent Host, had accepted a job at CKNW radio in Vancouver, a 25-year contract. A ig, big contract. He was going to sustain his Hockey Night in Canada ork. But the one outlier there was, now that he was going to go to ancouver to do the radio and Hockey Night, he had asked the Canadian oadcasting corporation, 'anytime the Canucks have a Saturday night me game, I would prefer to host in Vancouver.' So that meant they needed somebody for about 10 Saturday nights at Toronto Maple Leafs games.

"So John Shannon picked up the phone, phoned me and he said, 'Ronnie, phone, Don Wallace, the Executive Producer of Hockey Night in Canada, tell him you'd be interested in doing those 10 Saturday nights that Dave's working in Vancouver' and that's how it happened.

"So I go to do that, basically a part-time gig. They also needed me to do the Wednesday Night Toronto Maple Leafs shows. Dave had moved to Vancouver, so he'd no longer work the midweek broadcasts, which were called on CHCH. So that means I'll go down to Toronto to do 10 Saturday nights and roughly 30 Wednesday night Toronto Maple Leafs broadcasts; 40-games a year. I went down and then in March of that year, Dave had his famous falling out with the CBC or the failure to complete a telecast of Philadelphia-Montreal. Dave kind of walked away and that's where I kind of inherited a more significant role anchoring Hockey Night.

"My first broadcast was October 10, 1986 and that was Buffalo Sabres at Toronto Maple Leafs. In those years, the show started at eight o'clock Eastern and it ran until 11 o'clock Eastern. Now we do a double-header every Saturday with a prime time game at seven Eastern and a West coast prime time game at 10:00 PM Eastern or 7:00 PM Pacific time. I think the double-header format started in 1994, but for the first few years we were on at eight o'clock Eastern.

"Grapes (Don Cherry) and I worked together for the first time on that October 10th broadcast. So, even though Dave Hodge was anchoring, he was anchoring in Vancouver and he threw to me to do the Coach's Corner. So that was the first time we worked together. One of the pieces of advice I was given before I commenced my Hockey Night in Canada career was 'Ron, your eyes tend to wander all over the place and they flit up and down the guests. Could you try and stop that.'

"So I was really paying attention, trying to focus my vision and my eyes on Don's and not having them wander all over the place. My eyes got watery, trying to do that. A tear actually rolled down my left cheek, which was not visible to the viewer at home because the camera was situated to my right. But anyway, it was a traumatic start and Don kind of bailed me out by talking the entire six-minutes, which as we would find out he would do anyway, forevermore. But it was kind of a crazy start."

FAVORITE PLAYER(S) GROWING UP

MACLEAN: "The story that I kind of really was smitten with was the story of Jacques Plante. Once I got into hockey, I got into it in the ways that you did back then; collecting hockey cards and getting my hands on The Hockey News and every other format that I could enjoy the game I would get.

"I had heard this story of Plante and when Plante came back, obviously he returned with the St. Louis Blues. But he did come to Toronto, in 1970-71. So I was just 10, 11-years-old. And his story was a great source.

"When I was a boy, I played a little bit of goaltending and I played out. I played both positions because I was just really fascinated with the Plante story, to the extent that I thought maybe I'll try goaltending. But I couldn't stand the pressure. When I would lose games as a goalie, it just ate me up. When I would lose games playing center or defense, no big deal, it was the goalie's fault.

"By the time I reached Pee-Wee, I decided to just play out. But Plante was one great influence, because of the whole fascination I had with 'wow, he wore a mask, really? And wow, he signaled to his defensemen icing. That's interesting.' When he came back, he was just amazing. In Toronto in '71, he had a 1.89 goals-against-average as a 42-year-old. He was just exceptional."

As a quick aside, while MacLean never got to meet Plante, he did meet his former goalie partner, Glenn Hall and it was an interview with Hall that really made MacLean feel like he belonged in the world of hockey broadcasting.

MACLEAN: "My first playoff broadcast with Hockey Night in 'anada was in the '86-'87 season. That year I did a Toronto at St. Louis layoff game. And for me, that was kind of the Cat's Meow. I thought, 'ow, how exciting and how lucky.' But if I really think about it, the oment where I felt, I've kind of made it and I hate to use that term, but the moment I felt legitimately a part of this tradition and this iconic thing hockey and the NHL, was the All-Star Game in St. Louis.

"So my first playoff game was in St. Louis in '87 and then the All-Star game was held in the spring of '88 in St. Louis. And I interviewed Glen Hall, the legendary goaltender. I never did meet Jacques Plante, but Glenn I met many times. I worked as a Flames Host for two-seasons, '84 and '85 and he was the Goalie Consultant/Coach in Calgary. So I got to hang around Glenn Hall and for me, somehow, that was kind of divinity. That was the moment that I felt I had really kind of broken through. When Glenn and I had a really nice chat at the All-Star Game in St. Louis, I felt legitimized."

HOCKEY AFTER DARK -- TALES AWAY FROM THE RINK

Hockey Night in Canada is unlike any other production in the entire National Hockey League. It is as iconic as hockey programming gets. But when the cameras stop filming and the microphones are turned off, the broadcasters who comprise the Hockey Night programs are just like any others. They enjoy each other's time and will collect many stories over the course of their travels. Yet, sometimes, the most valuable experience they can have is simply getting to know and develop respect for each other. And that's something Ron MacLean treasures deeply.

MACLEAN: "Bob Cole and Harry Neale were the dynamic duo when I was there at the beginning. They worked for a lot of years together. And Bob was impeccable in his commitment to pronunciations, details and facts. Everything had to be right. He was extremely rigid about that. And it was a great lesson. He was a comfort in the way we worked together, but he was so professional.

"I just remember when we would get in the car to take a taxi anywhere, to the game, from the hotel, etc. Bob had to sit in the passenger seat next to the driver. Sometimes I was the driver. If we were in certain cities I would rent a car. I would drive, Bob would be to my right and then Don Cherry and Harry Neale would be in the back seat. But Bob had to be the Co-Pilot. He didn't do the driving himself, but he was always the Co-Pilot, cause he has his pilot's license.

"I remember a dinner in Cambridge. We were in Boston doing the Bruins and we stayed at the Charles Hotel in Cambridge. Chris Cuthbert was just a young, aspiring broadcaster and he came to dinner. He was actually flying through on his way to do updates at a game in Washington. Washington was playing either New Jersey or Pittsburgh. So, Chris joined us for dinner and he was quiet like I was. We were both young at the time. This is still back in the '80s. And it was always nice to sit with Bob Cole at dinner and hear his stories. And Chris, of course, was looking at Bob with an eye to, 'what does it take to be that guy? To be that top Play-by-Play guy in the business?' And it turns out Bob Cole is a Pilot, he has his pilot's license and he's won national curling championships. He's won rowing championships. I mean, the guy had a story that was the most interesting man in the world story.

"I think Chris and I both felt a little defeated that night, that we'll never make it; with a guy with this many gifts. But Bob was a joy. I just think of those many times we took trains when we would go from Toronto to Detroit, just to listen to the stories. I was just extremely blessed to hang out with three guys who had seen and done it all.

"We had a kind of a ritual back in the day after the broadcast. We would go for a drink with the whole crew in the lobby bar or hotel bar. And then he and I would finish the night. Don was usually first to bed, then Harry and then I would go knock on Bob's door. He and I would sit and talk till some ungodly hour about business or life. He was an incredible mentor to me. He taught me early on that new brooms must sweep. He was always cognizant of a new major sponsor or a new corporate takeover and how to be prepared. However good this may be, it may not last. But he lasted and pleasantly so."

MACLEAN'S FAVORITE HNIC BROADCASTS

When you talk about Hockey Night in Canada, you talk about a nulti-generation broadcast that has become as much a part of Canadian ore as anything. Canada and Hockey Night in Canada just go hand in and. They were made for each other. The broadcasters who are selected to work for the program are considered to be like royalty by many of the program's fans.

Ron MacLean has been hosting Hockey Night in Canada for many, many years. And during that time, he's had an innumerable amount of opportunities to cover events and experience things that ordinary hockey fans can only dream about. With that in mind, let's find out which broadcast of Hockey Night in Canada stands out to MacLean as his favorite. (HINT: It's not what you may be thinking).

MACLEAN: "The All-Star broadcast in '88 in St. Louis. That night Mario Lemieux had three-goals and three-assists in a 6-5 overtime win. It was (Wayne) Gretzky versus Lemieux. I got to interview Glenn Hall. Just everything about that night I will never forget. I've always had a love of the All-Star Game, which is a game that we all complain about. It's not competitive or they're just throwing in their hats. But it's not like that when you're around it. The respect you see, especially from the younger players who come and have the chance to suit up in the dressing room with Gretzky or Mario, that, to me, is something that I've always loved.

"The Stanley Cup is magical. To put it on the line for nine-weeks, it's the toughest trophy in sports to win. Covering that is also the crème de la crème. The first one I ever did was in St. Louis in '87. So I think of that. And I think of the '94 Cup Final. It was the Rangers and Vancouver Canucks. That was just an amazing playoffs and the scene in New York, when they lost Game Five, with all the police on horseback and the clump, clump, clump and empty streets of a blown opportunity. That one really stands out. I was lucky, in my first seven-years at Hockey Night, we had five Cups in Canada. We had the Oilers win in '87, '88 and '90. The Calgary Flames in '89 and the Montreal Canadiens in '93.

"So there were tremendous street parties and scenes around the country and energy around The Cup coming to Canada. And we haven't won it since, which is just unbelievable. We had another good seven-year window from 2004, when Calgary made The Final and lost to Tampa. Edmonton got there in '06. Ottawa got there in '07. Vancouver in '11. But nobody won it. So I think the energy of a Stanley Cup for us with a Canadian club, obviously, you feel the flags flying on cars and in apartment windows. That energy is hard to top. But I still go back to the '88 All-Stars. That's the night I thought, 'wow, what a privilege.'"

MESSAGE TO SPORTSNET FANS

As is a common theme amongst members of the sports media, it is a well known fact that without the fans our jobs would either A) not exist or B) they'd have a lot less meaning. So, each of the broadcasters in this book took a couple of minutes to address you, the fans, directly.

MACLEAN: "The lesson you learn from watching an athlete in the cross hairs is so applicable to your personal life. We just went through the most incredible Stanley Cup playoffs, with no fans in the buildings and it hearkens to Jordan's 'champions are made when nobody's watching.' My message is, you're not what you're perceived to be. We all use, he's a bum or he's overpaid or whatever we say; none of that's the truth. The players just proved that by playing in empty houses with every ounce of their being and that applies to you. You as a person can learn from that example that, 'you're not what you're perceived to be. You are what you are.' And what you are requires a lot of hard work.

"As a fan, it's nice that you go and share with others and it's an appreciation of that fact. There's nowhere, not a hospital, not a school, not a church, where as many people come together and root for somebody to do well. So, it's a very nice thing and as I said, the lesson that you're learning is that, 'you're not what you're perceived to be.' You actually had to have been something that you yourself decided upon."

ACKNOWLEDGEMENTS

For those who think that writing a book is easy, it's not. And you need more than just yourself to finish such a project. Therefore, it's important to thank those who have helped you along the way. So, I would like to acknowledge the following people for their roles in this project.

Rick Ball, John Bartlett, Brendan Batchelor, Josh Bogorad, Andy Brickley, Jamison Coyle, Ken Daniels, Willy Daunic, Dan Dunleavy, Dan D'Uva, John Forslund, Jim Fox, Josh Getzoff, Steven Goldstein, Dave Goucher, Bob Heethuis, Shane Hnidy, E.J. Hradek, Jim Jackson, Chris Kerber, Don La Greca, Matt Loughlin, Ron MacLean, Matt McConnell, Bob McElligott, Conor McGahey, Pierre McGuire, Steve Mears, Jack Michaels, Gord Miller, David Mishkin, Randy Moller, Brian Munz, Jason Myrtetus, Tyson Nash, Nick Nickson, Darren Pang, Greg Picker, Daryl Reaugh, Tom Reid, Francisco X. Rivera, Dan Robertson, Dan Rusanowsky, Tim Saunders, Judd Sirott, Nicolas St-Pierre, Tripp Tracy, John Walton, Pete Weber, John Wiedeman, Dan Wood and Paul Woods all took time out of their busy schedules to be interviewed for this book and told their stories with the same enthusiasm they share with the fans while doing their jobs.

My parents -- Mandi and Seth -- sister -- Tara -- grandparents -- Morton, Stanley, Yvonne and Zella -- uncles -- Andrew, Lenny, Scott and Glenn -- and aunts -- Yvonne, Anita and Brooke -- all of whom provided support throughout the book writing process.

My friends -- Samantha Bruno, Deanna Chillemi, Brittany Ciraolo, Taylor Chiaia, Lauren DeCordova, Liana DeNaro, Jessica DiMari, Gabriela Fleschner, Julia Greene, Leanna Gryak, Meredith Halpert, Stef Hicks, Maria Koutros, Christina Luddeni, Sarah Naomi Montag, Zoë Puccia, Arianna Rappy, Michele Rosati, Amanda Sorrentino, Jessica Sorrentino, Brianna Torkel, Victoria Wehr, Maggie Wince, Jared Bell, Trevor Blenman, Andrew Bodnar, Skylar Bonné, Walt Bonné, Jimmy Brandow, Danny Randell, Bobby Denver, Robert DeVita, Brandon Dittmar, Jared Fertig, Landon Goldfarb, Daniel Greene Shawn Kontorov, Chris Kopchinski, Peter Koutros, Michael Manna, Matt Mattone, Logan Miller, Matt Moers, Mike O'Brien, Dan O'Shea, Reid Packer, Chris Pellegrino, Max Rappy, Harris Rosado, Jason Russo

Aaron Shepard, Daniel Sokolovsky, Anthony Spadaro, William Storz, Mike Taverna, Douglas Vitulli, Joey Wilner and Eddie Zinser -- all of whom provided assistance and support throughout the book process as well.

A special thank you to Elana Yavetz for designing the cover.

And to my fellow media members/colleagues/etc. who have helped to guide and influence my career -- Kenny Albert, Pete Albietz, Michael Ali, Mark Alken, Marty Appel, Christian Arnold, Steve Baker, Howard Baldwin, Gerhard J. Baumer, Jessica Berman, Neil Best, Jeff Beukeboom, Dennis Beyak, Martin Biron, Justin Birnbaum, Ron Blomberg, Josh Bogorad, Amanda Borges, Greg Bouris, Ryan Braithwaite, Larry Brooks, Frank Brown, Brendan Burke, Pat Calabria, Matt Calamia, Pete Caldera, Steve Cangialosi, Rick Carpiniello, Marc Champagne, Scott Charles, Michelle Checchi, Hawley Chester III, Ryan Chiu, Bobby Ciafardini, Hayley Cohen, Russ Cohen, Brian Compton, Eric Compton, Colin Cosell, Rich Coutinho, Charlie Cucchiara, Jack Curry, Ken Daneyko, John Davidson, Jeff Day, John Dellapina, Bob de Poto, Weston DeWitt, Anthony DiComo, Rachel Schwartz Dixon, Roland Dratch, Ron Duguay, Chris Ebert, Clint T. Edwards, Mike "Doc" Emrick, Katie Epifane McCarthy, Annie Fariello, John Fayolle, Jeff Filippi, Matt Fineman, Sean D. Fiorello, Stan Fischler, Sean J. Folger, Peter Fosso, John Franco, Grant Fuhr, Shanna Fuld, Jim Gallagher, John Giannone, Rod Gilbert, Butch Goring, Adam Graves, Andrew Gross, Alan Hahn, Randy Hahn, Anders Hedberg, Larry Hirsch, Shannon Hogan, Nick Holmer, Eric Hornick, Kelly Hrudey, Jason Jackson, Rick Jeanneret, E.J. Johnston, Mike Johnston, Marc Kaplan, Howie Karpin, Kelly Keogh, Kevin Kernan, Chris King, Allan Kreda, Eddie Lack, Tom Laidlaw, Jon Lane, Paul Lauten, Jon Ledecky, Dave Maloney, Mike Mancuso, Joel Mandelbaum, Andrew Marchand, Dan Marrazza, Corey Masisak, Jim Matheson, Elyse Matsumoto, Patrick McCormack, Brianne McLaughlin, Lance Medow, Kevin Meininger, Barry Meisel, Bob Melnick, Sal Messina, Joe Micheletti, Neil Miller, Bobby Mills, Mike Morreale, Lucky Ngamwajasat, Brandon Noble, Bobby Nystrom, Michael Obernauer, Arda Ocal, Pat O'Keefe, Veronica Paone, Craig Patrick, Glenn Petraitis, Phil Pritchard, Deb Placey, Brad Polk, Glenn "Chico" Resch, Mike Richter, Lenn Robbins, Howie Rose, Dan Rosen, am Rosen, Mark Rosenman, Larry Roth, Chris Ryan, Christopher Ryan,

Bryce Salvador, Samuel Sandler, Leo Scaglione Jr., Dan Schoenberg, Sarah Servetnick, Ashley Scharge, Neil Smith, Arthur Staple, Dave Starman, Regan R. Staudt, Derek Stepan, Colin Stephenson, John Sterling, Jim Sullivan, Brent Sutter, Rob Taub, Rich Torrey, Al Trautwig, Leslie Treff, Mike Vaccaro, Jimmy Valdes, David Valentin, Steve Valiquette, Paul Vincent, Colleen Wagoner, Mollie Walker, Ryan Watson, Kevin Weekes, Ed Westfall, Craig Wolff, Cory Wright, Steve Zipay, Victoria K. Zocco and Alyse Zwick.

SOURCES

****NOTE: All interviews were conducted either in-person, over the phone or via email in order to obtain the necessary quotes and information.*

****NOTE: All statistics, dates, locations, etc. were gathered via box scores from NHL.com or Hockey-Reference.com.*

ABOUT THE AUTHOR

Matthew Blittner, born and raised in Brooklyn, New York, has been covering the New York Islanders, New Jersey Devils and New York Rangers for multiple publications since the beginning of the 2016-17 NHL season. Along the way, he has covered each of the teams' respective playoff runs over the past several seasons.

Among the publications Matthew Blittner has written for are: MSGNetworks.com, The Fischler Report, The Hockey News Magazine, NY Extra and NY Sports Day.

In addition to his responsibilities covering the NY/NJ hockey scene, Matthew obtained his Master's Degree in Sports Management from CUNY Brooklyn College in February of 2017 -- graduating with Summa Cum Laude honors.

Matthew's latest book, "Voices of The NHL," is the fourth in his career and gives a behind the scenes look at the lives of the broadcasters who are calling NHL games during the 2020-2021 season and have been with their respective teams or networks for years.

Visit him onTwitter @MatthewBlittner.

Made in United States
Orlando, FL
02 May 2022